THE COMIC ◆◆◆
in Theory & Practice

◆◆◆ EDITED BY

John J. Enck

Elizabeth T. Forter
LAWRENCE COLLEGE

Alvin Whitley
UNIVERSITY OF WISCONSIN

Prentice-Hall, Inc., Englewood Cliffs, New Jersey

ACKNOWLEDGEMENTS

BASIL BLACKWELL: for permission to reprint "A Voyage to the Country of the Houyhnhnms" from *Gulliver's Travels* by Jonathan Swift.

THE BRILL TRUST: for permission to reprint "Wit and Its Relation to the Unconscious" from *The Basic Writings of Sigmund Freud*, trans. and ed. by Dr. A. A. Brill, copyright © 1938 by Random House, Inc.

CURTIS BROWN LTD.: for "Notes on the Comic" by W. H. Auden, reprinted by permission of the author; and for "Showing Off" from *Personal Pleasures* by Rose Macaulay, by permission of Jean Babbington Macaulay and Victor Gollancz, Ltd.

THE CLARENDON PRESS: for permission to reprint "humour" from *A Dictionary of Modern Usage* by H. W. Fowler.

COWARD MCCANN, INC.: for permission to reprint "Some Remarks on Humor" in *A Subtreasury of American Humor* by E. B. and K. S. White, copyright © 1941, 1954 by E. B. and K. S. White.

THE JOHN DAY CO., INC.: for "Lemmings" by Donald A. Stauffer from *The War Poets*, Oscar Williams, ed., by permission of Ruth M. Stauffer.

DODD, MEAD & CO.: for permission to reprint "On Riding" from *Excuse It, Please!* by Cornelia Otis Skinner, copyright © 1929 by Cornelia Otis Skinner; and "My Financial Career" from *The Leacock Roundabout* by Stephen Leacock.

DOUBLEDAY & CO., INC.: for permission to reprint "Laughter" by Henri Bergson from *Comedy*, copyright © 1956 by Wylie Sypher; and "mehitabel dances with boreas" from *the lives and times of archy and mehitabel* by Don Marquis, copyright © 1950 by Doubleday & Co., Inc.

E. P. DUTTON & CO., INC. and WILLIAM HEINEMANN, INC.: for permission to reprint "Laughter" from *And Even Now* by Max Beerbohm, copyright © 1921 by E. P. Dutton & Co., Inc., renewal 1949 by Max Beerbohm.

FABER AND FABER: for permission to reprint "Macavity: the Mystery Cat" from *Old Possum's Book of Practical Cats* by T. S. Eliot.

HARCOURT, BRACE & CO.: for permission to reprint "Why I Live at the P. O." from *A Curtain of Green* by Eudora Welty, copyright © 1941 by Eudora Welty; and "Macavity: the Mystery Cat" from *Old Possum's Book of Practical Cats*, copyright © 1952 by T. S. Eliot.

HARPER & BROS.: for permission to reprint "A Wooden Darning Egg" from *The Carpentered Hen* by John Updike, copyright © 1956 by John Updike.

HENRY HOLT & CO., INC.: for permission to reprint "Departmental" from *A Further Range* by Robert Frost, copyright © 1936 by Robert Frost.

ALFRED A. KNOPF, INC.: for permission to reprint from *The Thread of Laughter* by Louis Kronenberger, copyright © 1952 by Louis Kronenberger.

LITTLE, BROWN & CO.: for permission to reprint "Dr. Arbuthnot's Academy" from *The Night the Old Nostalgia Burned Down* by Frank Sullivan, copyright © 1952 by Frank Sullivan; this piece originally appeared in the *New Yorker*.

PHAIDON PRESS LTD.: for permission to reprint "On the Essence of Laughter" from *The Mirror of Art* by Charles Baudelaire.

THE NEW YORKER: for permission to reprint "The Catbird Seat" by James Thurber; and for "A Reasonable Facsimile" by Jean Stafford, copyright © 1957 by the New Yorker Magazine, Inc., by permission of the Author.

THE PUBLIC TRUSTEE AND THE SOCIETY OF AUTHORS: for permission to reprint "Meredith on Comedy" from *Our Theatre in the Nineties* by Bernard Shaw.

RANDOM HOUSE, INC.: for permission to reprint "Under Which Lyre" from *Nones* by W. H. Auden, copyright © 1946 by W. H. Auden.

CHARLES SCRIBNER'S SONS: for permission to reprint from *Feeling and Form* by Susanne K. Langer, copyright © 1953 by Charles Scribner's Sons.

THE VIKING PRESS, INC.: for permission to reprint "You Were Perfectly Fine" from *The Portable Dorothy Parker*, copyright © 1929, 1944 by Dorothy Parker; "Laura" from *The Short Stories of Saki* by H. H. Munro, originally published by John Lane the Bodley Head, Inc.; and "The Frogs Asked for a King" from *The Fables of La Fontaine*, tr. Marianne Moore, copyright © 1954 by Marianne Moore

Preface

These theories and examples of the comic should provide adequate materials for exercises in controlled research on the freshman level. More advanced students may find this anthology a brief introduction to a subject which has no end.

Without revealing our own views, the first part of the book presents the comic in theory from Aristotle to contemporary critics in approximately chronological order. Similarly, the comic in practice does not collect our personal favorites but balances familiar pieces and neglected ones, cheerful reports and disillusioned fantasies. Such diversity should help the student to test, expand, and eventually know his own preferences and tastes.

In choosing examples, we reluctantly omitted scenes from plays and novels because only complete selections seemed artistically justifiable. ("A Voyage to the Country of the Houyhnhnms" forms a nearly independent unit.) The appended lists suggest further readings in longer works. With a single exception, all the narratives and poems were written originally in English. Anything requiring elaborate historical annotation was ruled out. In the theories we pruned away any passage too restricted to one time or place or philosophic system.

The texts are reprinted exactly from reliable, modern editions, although a few obvious corrections have been made and some superfluous notes and chapter headings silently dropped. The date in brackets following the title of each work is the year of first publication in a book, except, of course, for those by Aristotle and Chaucer and for the two pieces taken from magazines. A superior number in the text itself indicates the original pagination. We have added questions to form bases for class discussions and themes but have not presumed to answer them. Everyone laughs, and many have supposed they understood why and how and at what. With independent research and thought, students may find their merriment less innocent and more judicious.

J. J. E.

E. T. F.

A. W.

Madison, Wisconsin

Contents

vii

Part II

Essays, Narratives, & Verse

Contents

Part III
For Discussion & Themes

COVER *Front:*   "Clown Linon," photograph by Rolf Hegi; printed in *Du,* no. 216,
                 February, 1959. By permission of Conzett & Huber Druckerei und
                 Verlag, Zurich, Switzerland.

      Back: Marcello Moretti as Arlecchino in Carlo Goldoni's "The Servant of
                 Two Masters." American Premiere of the Piccolo Teatro di Milano,
                 presented by Jerry Hoffman at the City Center, 1960.

Part I

THEORY

Humour

◈◈◈   H. W. FOWLER

H. W. Fowler, s. v. "humour" [1926], in *A Dictionary of Modern English Usage* (Oxford, The Clarendon Press, 1937), rev. ed.

HUMOUR, *wit, satire, sarcasm, invective, irony, cynicism, the sardonic*. So much has been written upon the nature of some of these words, & upon the distinctions between pairs or trios among them (wit & humour, sarcasm & irony & satire), that it would be both presumptuous & unnecessary to attempt a further disquisition. But a sort of tabular statement may be of service against some popular misconceptions. No definition of the words is offered, but for each its motive or aim, its province, its method or means, & its proper audience, are specified. The constant confusion between sarcasm, satire, & irony, as well as that now less common between wit & humour, seems to justify this mechanical device of parallel classification; but it will be of use only to those who wish for help in determining which is the word that they really want. [240]

	MOTIVE or AIM	PROVINCE	METHOD or MEANS	AUDIENCE
humour	Discovery	Human nature	Observation	The sympathetic
wit	Throwing light	Words & ideas	Surprise	The intelligent
satire	Amendment	Morals & manners	Accentuation	The self-satisfied
sarcasm	Inflicting pain	Faults & foibles	Inversion	Victim & bystander
invective	Discredit	Misconduct	Direct statement	The public
irony	Exclusiveness	Statement of facts	Mystification	An inner circle
cynicism	Self-justification	Morals	Exposure of nakedness	The respectable
The sardonic	Self-relief	Adversity	Pessimism	Self [241]

4

Poetics

◆◆◆ ARISTOTLE

Aristotle, from "Poetics" [c. 335–323 B.C.], in *Aristotle on the Art of Fiction*, tr. L. J. Potts (Cambridge, Cambridge University Press, 1953).

THIS is the difference that marks tragedy out from comedy; comedy is inclined to imitate persons below the level of our world, tragedy persons above it. . . . [19]

But a temperamental difference of character caused poetry to break sharply into two. The more serious writers imitated illustrious doings, involving illustrious persons; the lighter-minded imitated those of low people, at first in the form of flytings, while the others were writing hymns and encomiums. . . . So it came about that some of the early poets wrote in heroic verse and others in iambics. And just as Homer was the great exemplar of high poetry, being the only poet who not only wrote nobly but also made the dramatic imitations, so too he was the first to adumbrate the outlines of comedy by making his drama not vituperative but ludicrous; in fact the relationship between the *Margites* and our comedies is analogous to that between the *Iliad* and *Odyssey* and our tragedies. But as soon as tragedy and comedy had become available, those whose natural temperaments [21] impelled them towards one or the other kind of poetry wrote comedies instead of lampoons, and tragedies instead of epics, because comedy and tragedy were grander and esteemed more highly. To examine whether or no the organic evolution of tragedy is now complete, and to settle that question both absolutely and in relation to the stage, does not belong to our present discussion.

Going back to the improvisations in which it at first consisted (and so did comedy—tragedy began with the leaders of the dithyramb, and comedy with the leaders of the phallic performances which still survive as customary practices in many of our cities), it grew up little by little as its organs were perceived and developed one after another. . . . [22]

Comedy is, as I have said, an imitation of lower types; though it does not include the full range of badness, nevertheless to be ridiculous is a kind of deformity. The causes of laughter are errors and deformities that do not pain or injure us; the comic mask, for instance, is deformed and distorted but not painfully so. We know something of the stages through which tragedy passed and the men to whom they were due, but there are no early records of comedy, because it was not highly valued. It was a long time before comic dramas were licensed by the magistrate; the earlier comedies were produced by amateurs. Comedy had already acquired certain outlines by the time of the earliest comic poets whose names are known. Who added masks or prologues or extra actors, and other such matters, we have no means of knowing. The fable-structure first came from Sicily (Epicharmus and Phormis); at Athens, Crătes was the first to drop the lampoon form and make unified stories, that is to say fables. . . . [23] To unify is to make a man of a certain description say or do the things that suit him, probably or necessarily, in the circumstances (this is the point of the descriptive proper names in poetry); what Alcibiades did or what happened to him is an agglomeration. In comedy this has now become clear. They first plot the fable on a base of probabilities, and then find imaginary names for the people—unlike the lampooners, whose work was an agglomeration of personalities. . . . [29] The next best plot, which is said by some people to be the best, is the tragedy with a double plot, like the *Odyssey,* ending in one way for the better people and in the opposite way for the worse. But it is the weakness of theatrical performances that gives priority to this kind; when poets write what the audience would like to happen, they are in leading strings. This is not the pleasure proper to tragedy, but rather to comedy, where the greatest enemies in the fable, say Orestes and Aegisthus, make friends and go off at the end, and nobody is killed by anybody. [34]

Author's Preface to
Joseph Andrews

◊◊◊ HENRY FIELDING

Henry Fielding, from "Author's Preface" [1742], in *Joseph Andrews* (New York, Rinehart & Co., Inc., 1948).

Now, a comic romance is a comic epic poem in prose; differing from comedy, as the serious epic from tragedy: its action being more extended and comprehensive; containing a much larger circle of incidents, and introducing a greater variety of characters. It differs from the serious romance in its fable and action, in this; that as in the one these are grave and solemn, so in the other they are light and ridiculous: it differs in its characters by introducing persons of inferior rank, and consequently, of inferior manners, whereas the grave romance sets the highest before us: lastly, in its sentiments and diction; by preserving the ludicrous instead of the sublime. In the diction, I think, burlesque itself may be sometimes admitted; of which many instances will occur in this work, as in the description of the battles, and some other places, not necessary to be pointed out to the classical reader, for whose entertainment those parodies or burlesque imitations are chiefly calculated.

But though we have sometimes admitted this in our diction, we have carefully excluded it from our sentiments and characters; for there it is never properly introduced, unless in writings of the burlesque kind, which this is not intended to be. Indeed, no two species of writing can differ more widely than the comic and the burlesque; for as the latter is ever the exhibition of what is monstrous and unnatural, and where our delight, if we examine it, arises from the surprising absurdity, as in appropriating the manners of the highest to the lowest, or *è converso;* [xviii] so in the former we should ever confine ourselves strictly to nature, from the just imitation of which will flow all the pleasure we can this way convey to a sensible reader. And perhaps there is one reason why a comic writer should of all others be the least excused for deviating from nature, since it may not be

7

always so easy for a serious poet to meet with the great and the admirable; but life everywhere furnishes an accurate observer with the
ridiculous.

I have hinted this little concerning burlesque, because I have often
heard that name given to performances which have been truly of the
comic kind, from the author's having sometimes admitted it in his
diction only; which, as it is the dress of poetry, doth, like the dress of
men, establish characters (the one of the whole poem, and the other
of the whole man), in vulgar opinion, beyond any of their greater
excellences: but surely, a certain drollery in stile, where characters
and sentiments are perfectly natural, no more constitutes the burlesque, than an empty pomp and dignity of words, where everything
else is mean and low, can entitle any performance to the appellation of
the true sublime. . . . [xix]

The only source of the true Ridiculous (as it appears to me) is
affectation. But though it arises from one spring only, when we consider the infinite streams into which this one branches, we shall presently cease to admire at the copious field it affords to an observer. Now,
affectation proceeds from one of these two causes, vanity or hypocrisy:
for as vanity puts us on affecting false characters, in order to purchase
applause; so hypocrisy sets us on an endeavour to avoid censure, by
concealing our vices under an appearance of their opposite virtues.
And though these two causes are often confounded (for there is some
difficulty in distinguishing them), yet, as they proceed from very
different motives, so they are as clearly distinct in their operations:
for indeed, the affectation which arises from vanity is nearer to truth
than the other, as it hath not that violent repugnancy of nature to
struggle with, which that of the hypocrite hath. It may be likewise
noted, that affectation doth not imply an absolute negation of those
qualities which are affected; and, therefore, though, when it proceeds
from hypocrisy, [xxi] it be nearly allied to deceit; yet when it comes
from vanity only, it partakes of the nature of ostentation: for instance,
the affectation of liberality in a vain man differs visibly from the same
affectation in the avaricious; for though the vain man is not what he
would appear, or hath not the virtue he affects, to the degree he would
be thought to have it; yet it sits less awkwardly on him than on the
avaricious man, who is the very reverse of what he would seem to be.

From the discovery of this affectation arises the Ridiculous, which
always strikes the reader with surprise and pleasure; and that in a

higher and stronger degree when the affectation arises from hypocrisy, than when from vanity; for to discover any one to be the exact reverse of what he affects, is more surprising, and consequently more ridiculous, than to find him a little deficient in the quality he desires the reputation of. I might observe that our Ben Jonson, who of all men understood the Ridiculous the best, hath chiefly used the hypocritical affectation.

Now, from affectation only, the misfortunes and calamities of life, or the imperfections of nature, may become the objects of ridicule. Surely he hath a very ill-framed mind who can look on ugliness, infirmity, or poverty, as ridiculous in themselves: nor do I believe any man living, who meets a dirty fellow riding through the streets in a cart, is struck with an idea of the Ridiculous from it; but if he should see the same figure descend from his coach and six, or bolt from his chair with his hat under his arm, he would then begin to laugh, and with justice. In the same manner, were we to enter a poor house and behold a wretched family shivering with cold and languishing with hunger, it would not incline us to laughter (at least we must have very diabolical natures if it would); but should we discover there a grate, instead of coals, adorned with flowers, empty plate or china dishes on the sideboard, or any other affectation of riches and finery, either on their persons or in their furniture, we might then indeed be excused for ridiculing so fantastical an appearance. Much less are natural imperfections the object of derision; but when ugliness aims at the applause of [xxii] beauty, or lameness endeavours to display agility, it is then that these unfortunate circumstances, which at first moved our compassion, tend only to raise our mirth.

The poet carries this very far:

> None are for being what they are in fault,
> But for not being what they would be thought.

Where if the metre would suffer the word Ridiculous to close the first line, the thought would be rather more proper. Great vices are the proper objects of our detestation, smaller faults, of our pity; but affectation appears to me the only true source of the Ridiculous. [xxiii]

The Difficulty of
Defining Comedy

◆◆◆ SAMUEL JOHNSON

Samuel Johnson, from "The Difficulty of Defining Comedy" [1751], in
The Rambler (London, Dodsley, Owen, 1794), 4 vols.

IT is one of the maxims of the civil law, that *definitions are hazardous*.
Things modified by human understandings, subject to varieties of
complication, and changeable as experience advances knowledge, or
accident influences caprice, are scarcely to be included in any standing
form of expression, because they are always suffering some alteration
of their state. Definition is indeed, not the province of man; every thing
is set above or below our faculties. The works and operations of nature
are too great in their extent, or too much diffused in their relations, and
the performances of art too inconstant and uncertain, to be reduced to
any determinate idea. It is impossible to impress upon our minds an
adequate and just representation of an object so great that we can
never take it into our view, or so mutable that it is always changing
under our eye, and has already lost its form while we are labouring
to conceive it.

   Definitions have been no less difficult or uncertain [III, 112] in criticisms than in law. Imagination, a licentious and vagrant faculty, un-
susceptible of limitations, and impatient of restraint, has always endeavoured to baffle the logician, to perplex the confines of distinction,
and burst the inclosures of regularity. There is, therefore, scarcely any
species of writing, of which we can tell what is its essence, and what
are its constituents; every new genius produces some innovation,
which, when invented and approved, subverts the rules which the
practice of foregoing authors had established.

   Comedy has been particularly unpropitious to definers, for
though, perhaps, they might properly have contented themselves, with
declaring it to be *such a dramatic representation of human life, as may
excite mirth,* they have embarrassed their definition with the means
by which the comic writers attain their end, without considering that

10

the various methods of exhilarating their audience, not being limited by nature, cannot be comprised in precept. Thus, some make comedy a representation of mean, and others of bad men; some think that its essence consists in the unimportance, others in the fictitiousness of the transaction. But any man's reflections will inform him, that every dramatic composition which raises mirth is comic; and that to raise mirth, it is by no means universally necessary, that the personages should be either mean or corrupt, nor always requisite, that the action should be trivial, nor ever that it should be fictitious.

If the two kinds of dramatic poetry had been defined only by their effects upon the mind, some absurdities might have been prevented, with which the compositions of our greatest poets are disgraced, who, for want of some settled ideas, and [III, 113] accurate distinctions, have unhappily confounded tragic with comic sentiments. They seem to have thought, that as the meanness of personages constituted comedy, their greatness was sufficient to form a tragedy; and that nothing was necessary, but that they should crowd the scene with monarchs, and generals, and guards, and make them talk, at certain intervals, of the downfal of kingdoms, and the rout of armies. They have not considered, that thoughts or incidents, in themselves ridiculous, grow still more grotesque by the solemnity of such characters; that reason and nature are uniform and inflexible; and that what is despicable and absurd, will not, by any association with splendid titles, become rational or great; that the most important affairs, by an intermixture of an unseasonable levity, may be made contemptible, and that the robes of royalty can give no dignity to nonsense or to folly.

"Comedy," says Horace, "sometimes raises her voice"; and tragedy may likewise, on proper occasions, abate her dignity; but as the comic personages can only depart from their familiarity of stile, when the more violent passions are put in motion, the heroes and queens of tragedy should never descend to trifle, but in the hours of ease, and intermissions of danger. [III, 114]

A Comparison between Laughing and Sentimental Comedy

◆◆◆ OLIVER GOLDSMITH

Oliver Goldsmith, from "A Comparison between Laughing and Sentimental Comedy" [1765], in *The Works of Oliver Goldsmith,* ed.
Peter Cunningham (London, John Murray, 1878), 4 vols.

THE THEATRE, like all other amusements, has its fashions and
its prejudices; and when satiated with its excellence, mankind begin
to mistake change for improvement. For some years tragedy was the
reigning entertainment; but of late it has entirely given way to comedy,
and our best efforts are now exerted in these lighter kinds of composition. The pompous train, the swelling phrase, and the unnatural
rant, are displaced for that natural portrait of human folly and frailty,
of which all are judges, because all have sat for the picture.

But, as in describing nature it is presented with a double face,
either of mirth or sadness, our modern writers find themselves at a
loss which chiefly to copy from; and it is now debated, whether the
exhibition of human distress is likely to afford the mind more entertainment than that of human absurdity?

Comedy is defined by Aristotle to be a picture of the frailties of
the lower part of mankind, to distinguish it from tragedy, which is an
exhibition of the misfortunes of the great. When comedy therefore
ascends to produce the characters of princes or generals upon the stage,
it is out of its walk, since low life and middle life are entirely its object.
The principal question therefore is, whether in describing low or
middle life, an exhibition of its follies be not preferable to a detail of
its calamities? Or, in other words, which deserves the preference—the
weeping sentimental comedy, so much in fashion at present, or the
laughing and even low comedy, which seems to have been last exhibited by Vanbrugh and Cibber?

If we apply to authorities, all the great masters in the dramatic art
have but one opinion. Their rule is, that as tragedy displays the
calamities of the great, so comedy should excite our laughter, by

ridiculously exhibiting the follies of the lower part of mankind. Boileau, [III, 342] one of the best modern critics, asserts, that comedy will not admit of tragic distress. . . .

Nor is this rule without the strongest foundation in nature, as the distresses of the mean by no means affect us so strongly as the calamities of the great. When tragedy exhibits to us some great man fallen from his height, and struggling with want and adversity, we feel his situation in the same manner as we suppose he himself must feel, and our pity is increased in proportion to the height from whence he fell. On the contrary, we do not so strongly sympathise with one born in humbler circumstances, and encountering accidental distress: so that while we melt for Belisarius, we scarce give halfpence to the beggar who accosts us in the street. The one has our pity; the other our contempt. Distress, therefore, is the proper object of tragedy, since the great excite our pity by their fall; but not equally so of comedy, since the actors employed in it are originally so mean, that they sink but little by their fall.

Since the first origin of the stage, tragedy and comedy have run in distinct channels, and never till of late encroached upon the provinces of each other. Terence, who seems to have made the nearest approaches, yet always judiciously stops short before he comes to the downright pathetic; and yet he is even reproached by Caesar for wanting the *vis comica*. All other comic writers of antiquity aim only at rendering folly or vice ridiculous, but never exalt their characters into buskined pomp, or make what Voltaire humorously calls "a tradesman's tragedy."

Yet notwithstanding this weight of authority, and the universal practice of former ages, a new species of dramatic composition has been introduced under the name of *sentimental comedy,* in which the virtues of private life are exhibited, rather than the vices exposed; and the distresses rather than the faults of mankind make our interest in the piece. These comedies have had of late great success, perhaps from their novelty, and also from their flattering every man in his favourite foible. In these plays almost all the characters are good, and exceedingly generous; they are lavish enough of their *tin* money on the stage; and though they want humour, have abundance of sentiment and feeling. If they happen to have faults or foibles, the spectator is taught not only to pardon, but to applaud them, in consideration of the goodness of their hearts; so that folly, instead of being ridiculed, is commended, and the comedy aims at touching our passions, without the power of being truly pathetic. In this manner we are likely to lose one great source of entertainment on the stage; for while the comic poet is invading the province of the tragic muse, he leaves her lovely sister quite neglected. Of this, however, he is no way solicitous, as he measures his fame by his profits.

But it will be said, that the theatre is formed to amuse mankind, and that it matters little, if this end be answered, by what means it is obtained. If mankind find delight in weeping at comedy, it would be cruel to abridge them in that or any other innocent pleasure. If those pieces are denied the name of comedies, yet call them by any other name, and if they are delightful, they are good. Their success, it will be said, is a mark of their merit, and it is only abridging our happiness to deny us an inlet to amusement.

These objections, however, are rather specious than solid. It is true, that amusement is a great object of the theatre; and it will be allowed, that these sentimental pieces do often amuse us; but the question is, whether the true comedy would not amuse us more? The question is, whether a character supported throughout a piece, with its ridicule still attending, would not give us more delight than this species of bastard tragedy, which only is applauded because it is new? . . . [III, 343]

The other objection is as ill-grounded; for though we should give these pieces another name, it will not mend their efficacy. It will continue a kind of mulish production, with all the defects of its opposite parents, and marked with sterility. If we are permitted to make comedy weep, we have an equal right to make tragedy laugh, and to set down in blank verse the jests and repartees of all the attendants in a funeral procession.

But there is one argument in favour of sentimental comedy which will keep it on the stage, in spite of all that can be said against it. It is of all others the most easily written. Those abilities that can hammer out a novel, are fully sufficient for the production of a sentimental comedy. It is only sufficient to raise the characters a little; to deck out the hero with a riband, or give the heroine a title; then to put an insipid dialogue, without character or humour, into their mouths, give them mighty good hearts, very fine clothes, furnish a new set of scenes, make a pathetic scene or two, with a sprinkling of tender melancholy conversation through the whole, and there is no doubt but all the ladies will cry, and all the gentlemen applaud.

Humour at present seems to be departing from the stage; and it will soon happen that our comic players will have nothing left for it, but a fine coat and a song. It depends upon the audience, whether they will actually drive those poor merry creatures from the stage, or sit at a play as gloomy as at the tabernacle. It is not easy to recover an art when once lost; and it will be but a just punishment, that when, by our being too fastidious, we have banished humour from the stage, we should ourselves be deprived of the art of laughing. [III, 344]

On Wit and Humour

William Hazlitt, from "On Wit and Humour" [1819], in *Lectures on the English Poets and the English Comic Writers,* ed. William Carew Hazlitt (London, George Bell & Sons, 1884).

MAN is the only animal that laughs and weeps; for he is the only animal that is struck with the difference between what things are, and what they ought to be. We weep at what thwarts or exceeds our desires in serious matters: we laugh at what only disappoints our expectations in trifles. We shed tears from sympathy with real and necessary distress; as we burst into laughter from want of sympathy with that which is unreasonable and unnecessary, the absurdity of which provokes our spleen or mirth, rather than any serious reflections on it.

To explain the nature of laughter and tears, is to account for the condition of human life; for it is in a manner compounded of these two! It is a tragedy or a comedy—sad or merry, as it happens. The crimes and misfortunes that are inseparable from it, shock and wound the mind when they once seize upon it, and when the pressure can no longer be borne, seek relief in tears: the follies and absurdities that men commit, or the odd accidents that befal them, afford us amusement from the very rejection of these false claims upon our sympathy [1] and end in laughter. If everything that went wrong, if every vanity or weakness in another gave us a sensible pang, it would be hard indeed: but as long as the disagreeableness of the consequences of a sudden disaster is kept out of sight by the immediate oddity of the circumstances, and the absurdity or unaccountableness of a foolish action is the most striking thing in it, the ludicrous prevails over the pathetic, and we receive pleasure instead of pain from the farce of life which is played before us, and which discomposes our gravity as often as it fails to move our anger or our pity!

Tears may be considered as the natural and involuntary resource of the mind overcome by some sudden and violent emotion, before it has had time to reconcile its feelings to the change of circumstances: while laughter may be defined to be the same sort of convulsive and

16

involuntary movement, occasioned by mere surprise or contrast (in the absence of any more serious emotion), before it has time to reconcile its belief to contradictory appearances. If we hold a mask before our face, and approach a child with this disguise on, it will at first, from the oddity and incongruity of the appearance, be inclined to laugh; if we go nearer to it, steadily, and without saying a word, it will begin to be alarmed, and be half inclined to cry: if we suddenly take off the mask, it will recover from its fears, and burst out a-laughing; but if, instead of presenting the old well-known countenance, we have concealed a satyr's head or some frightful caricature behind the first mask, the suddenness of the change will not in this case be a source of merriment to it, but will convert its surprise into an agony of consternation, and will make it scream out for help, even though it may be convinced that the whole is a trick at bottom.

The alternation of tears and laughter, in this little episode in common life, depends almost entirely on the greater or less degree of interest attached to the different [2] changes of appearance. The mere suddenness of the transition, the mere baulking our expectations, and turning them abruptly into another channel, seems to give additional liveliness and gaiety to the animal spirits; but the instant the change is not only sudden, but threatens serious consequences, or calls up the shape of danger, terror supersedes our disposition to mirth, and laughter gives place to tears. . . . [3]

To understand or define the ludicrous, we must first know what the serious is. Now the serious is the habitual stress which the mind lays upon the expectation of a given order of events, following one another with a certain regularity and weight of interest attached to them. When this stress is increased beyond its usual pitch of intensity, so as to overstrain the feelings by the violent opposition of good to bad, or of objects to our desires, it becomes the pathetic or tragical. The ludicrous, or comic, is the unexpected loosening or relaxing this stress below its usual pitch of intensity, by such an abrupt transposition of the order of our ideas, as taking the mind unawares, throws it off its guard, startles it into a lively sense of pleasure, and leaves no time nor inclination for painful reflections. [4]

The essence of the laughable then is the incongruous, the disconnecting one idea from another, or the jostling of one feeling against another. The first and most obvious cause of laughter is to be found in the simple succession of events, as in the sudden shifting of a dis-

guise, or some unlooked-for accident, without any absurdity of character or situation. The accidental contradiction between our expectations and the event can hardly be said, however, to amount to the
ludicrous: it is merely laughable. The ludicrous is where there is the
same contradiction between the object and our expectations, heightened by some deformity or inconvenience, that is, by its being contrary
to what is customary or desirable; as the ridiculous, which is the highest degree of the laughable, is that which is contrary not only to custom
but to sense and reason, or is a voluntary departure from what we
have a right to expect from those who are conscious of absurdity and
propriety in words, looks, and actions.

Of these different kinds or degrees of the laughable, the first is
the most shallow and short-lived; for the instant the immediate surprise of a thing's merely happening one way or another is over, there
is nothing to throw us back upon our former expectation, and renew
our wonder at the event a second time. The second sort, that is, the
ludicrous arising out of the improbable or distressing, is more deep and
lasting, either because the painful catastrophe excites a greater curiosity, or because the old impression, from its habitual hold on the imagination, still recurs mechanically, so that it is longer before we can
seriously make up our minds to the unaccountable deviation from it.
The third sort, or the ridiculous arising out of absurdity as well as
improbability, that is, where the defect or weakness is of a man's own
seeking, is the most refined of all, but not always so pleasant as the last,
because the same contempt and disapprobation [5] which sharpens
and subtilises our sense of the impropriety, adds a severity to it inconsistent with perfect ease and enjoyment. This last species is properly
the province of satire. The principle of contrast is, however, the same
in all the stages, in the simply laughable, the ludicrous, the ridiculous;
and the effect is only the more complete, the more durably and
pointedly this principle operates. . . . [6]

You cannot force people to laugh: you cannot give [7] a reason
why they should laugh: they must laugh of themselves, or not at all.
As we laugh from a spontaneous impulse, we laugh the more at any
restraint upon this impulse. We laugh at a thing merely because we
ought not. If we think we must not laugh, this perverse impediment
makes our temptation to laugh the greater; for by endeavouring to
keep the obnoxious image out of sight, it comes upon us more irresistibly and repeatedly; and the inclination to indulge our mirth, the

longer it is held back, collects its force, and breaks out the more violently in peals of laughter. In like manner, any thing we must not think of makes us laugh, by its coming upon us by stealth and unawares, and from the very efforts we make to exclude it. A secret, a loose word, a wanton jest, make people laugh. Aretine laughed himself to death at hearing a lascivious story. Wickedness is often made a substitute for wit. . . . The consciousness, however it may arise, that there is something that we ought to look grave at, is almost always a signal for laughing outright: we can hardly keep our countenance at a sermon, a funeral, or a wedding. . . .

Misunderstandings . . . , where one person means one thing, and another is aiming at something else, [8] are another great source of comic humour, on the same principle of ambiguity and contrast. . . . Again, unconsciousness in the person himself of what he is about, or of what others think of him, is also a great heightener of the sense of absurdity. It makes it come the fuller home upon us from his insensibility to it. His simplicity sets off the satire, and gives it a finer edge. It is a more extreme case still where the person is aware of being the object of ridicule, and yet seems perfectly reconciled to it as a matter of course. So wit is often the more forcible and pointed for being dry and serious, for it then seems as if the speaker himself had no intention in it, and we were the first to find it out. Irony, as a species of wit, owes its force to the same principle. In such cases it is the contrast between the appearance and the reality, the suspense of belief and the seeming incongruity, that gives point to the ridicule, and makes it enter the deeper when the first impression is overcome. Excessive impudence . . . or excessive modesty . . . or a mixture of the two . . . are equally amusing. Lying is a species of wit and humour. To lay anything to a person's charge from which he is perfectly free, shows spirit and invention; and the more incredible the effrontery, the greater is the joke.

There is nothing more powerfully humorous than what is called *keeping* in comic character, as we see it very [9] finely exemplified in Sancho Panza and Don Quixote. The proverbial phlegm and the romantic gravity of these two celebrated persons may be regarded as the height of this kind of excellence. The deep feeling of character strengthens the sense of the ludicrous. Keeping in comic character is consistency in absurdity; a determined and laudable attachment to the incongruous and singular. The regularity completes the contradiction; for the number of instances of deviation from the right line, branching out in all directions, shows the inveteracy of the original bias to any extravagance or folly, the natural improbability, as it were, increasing every time with the multiplication of chances for a return to common sense, and in the end mounting up to an incredible and unaccountably ridiculous height, when we find our expectations as invariably baffled. The most curious problem of all, is this truth of absurdity to itself. That reason and good sense should be consistent, is not wonderful: but that caprice, and whim, and fantastical prejudice, should be uniform and infallible in their results, is the surprising thing. But while this characteristic clue to absurdity helps on the ridicule, it also softens and harmonises its excesses; and the ludicrous is here blended with a certain beauty and decorum, from this very truth of habit and sentiment, or from the principle of similitude in dissimilitude. The devotion to nonsense, and enthusiasm about trifles, is highly affecting as a moral lesson: it is one of the striking weaknesses and greatest happinesses of our nature. That which excites so lively and lasting an interest in itself, even though it should not be wisdom, is not despicable in the sight of reason and humanity. We cannot suppress the smile on the lip; but the tear should also stand ready to start from the eye. . . . [10]

Humour is the describing the ludicrous as it is in itself; wit is the exposing it, by comparing or contrasting it with something else. Humour is, as it were, the growth of nature and accident; wit is the product of art and fancy. Humour, as it is shown in books, is an imitation of the natural or acquired absurdities of mankind, or of the ludicrous in accident, situation, and character: wit is the illustrating and heightening the sense of that absurdity by some sudden and unexpected likeness or opposition of one thing to another, which sets off the quality we laugh at or [15] despise in a still more contemptible or striking point of view. Wit . . . is the imagination or fancy inverted, and so applied to given objects, as to make the little look less, the mean more light and worthless; or to divert our admiration or wean our affections from that which is lofty and impressive, instead of producing a more intense admiration and exalted passion, as poetry does. . . . Wit hovers round the borders of the light and trifling, whether in matters of pleasure or pain; for as soon as it describes the serious seriously, it ceases to be wit, and passes into a different form. Wit is, in fact, the eloquence of indifference, or an ingenious and striking exposition of those evanescent and glancing impressions of objects which affect us more from surprise or contrast to the train of our ordinary and literal preconceptions, than from anything in the objects themselves exciting our necessary sympathy or lasting hatred. The favourite employment of wit is to add littleness to littleness, and heap contempt on insignificance by all the arts of petty and incessant warfare; or if it ever affects to aggrandise, and use the language of hyperbole, it is only to betray into derision by a fatal comparison, as in the mock-heroic; or if it treats of serious passion, it must do it so as to lower the tone of intense and high-wrought sentiment, by the introduction of burlesque and familiar circumstances. . . . [16]

And, indeed, this may be considered as the best defence of the contested maxim—That *ridicule is the test of truth;* viz., that it does not contain or attempt a formal proof of it, but owes its power of conviction to the bare suggestion of it, so that if the thing when once hinted is not clear in itself, the satire fails of its effect and falls to the ground. . . . A flippant jest is as good a test of truth as a solid bribe; and there are serious sophistries,

> "Soul-killing lies, and truths that work small good,"

as well as idle pleasantries. Of this we may be sure, that ridicule fastens on the vulnerable points of a cause, and finds out the weak sides of an argument; if those who resort to it sometimes rely too much on its success, those who are chiefly annoyed by it almost always are so with reason, and cannot be too much on their guard against deserving it. Before we can laugh at a thing, its absurdity [22] must at least be open and palpable to common apprehension. Ridicule is necessarily built on certain supposed facts, whether true or false, and on their inconsistency with certain acknowledged maxims, whether right or wrong. It is, therefore, a fair test, if not of philosophical or abstract truth, at least of what is truth according to public opinion and common sense; for it can only expose to instantaneous contempt that which is condemned by public opinion, and is hostile to the common sense of mankind. Or to put it differently, it is the test of the quantity of truth that there is in our favourite prejudices. [23]

On Simple and Sentimental Poetry

◆◆◆ FRIEDRICH SCHILLER

Friedrich Schiller, from "On Simple and Sentimental Poetry" [1795], in *Essays Aesthetical and Philosophical* (London, George Bell & Sons, 1884).

THE QUESTION has often been raised as to the comparative preference to be awarded to tragedy or comedy. If the question is confined merely to their respective themes, it is certain that tragedy has the advantage. But if our inquiry be directed to ascertain which has the more important personality, it is probable that a decision may be given in favour of comedy. In tragedy the theme in itself does great things; in comedy the object does nothing and the poet all. Now, as in the judgments of taste no account must be kept of the matter treated of, it follows naturally that the aesthetic value of these two kinds will be in an inverse ratio to the proper importance of their themes.

The tragic poet is supported by the theme, while the comic poet, on the contrary, has to keep up the aesthetic character of his theme by his own individual influence. The former may soar, which is not a very difficult matter, but the latter has to remain one and the same in tone; he has to be in the elevated region of art, where he must be at home, but where the tragic poet has to be projected and elevated by a bound. And this is precisely what distinguishes a soul of beauty from a sublime soul. A soul of beauty bears in itself by anticipation all great ideas; they flow without constraint and without difficulty from its very nature—an infinite nature, at least in potency, at whatever point of its career you seize it. A sublime soul can rise to all kinds of greatness, but by an effort; it can tear itself from all bondage, to all that limits and constrains it, but only by strength of will. Consequently the sublime soul is only free by broken efforts; the other with ease and always.

The noble task of comedy is to produce and keep up in us this freedom of mind, just as the end of tragedy is to re-establish in us this freedom of mind by aesthetic ways, when it has been violently suspended by passion. Consequently it is necessary that in tragedy the poet, as if he made an experiment, should *artificially* suspend our freedom [293] of mind, since tragedy shows its poetic virtue by re-establishing it; in comedy, on the other hand, care must be taken that things never reach this suspension of freedom.

It is for this reason that the tragic poet invariably treats his theme in a practical manner, and the comic poet in a theoretic manner, even when the former, as happened with Lessing in his 'Nathan,' should have the curious fancy to select a theoretical, and the latter should have that of choosing a practical subject. A piece is constituted a tragedy or comedy not by the sphere from which the theme is taken, but by the tribunal before which it is judged. A tragic poet ought never to indulge in tranquil reasoning, and ought always to gain the interest of the heart; but the comic poet ought to shun the pathetic and bring into play the understanding. The former displays his art by creating continual excitement, the latter by perpetually subduing his passion; and it is natural that the art in both cases should acquire magnitude and strength in proportion as the theme of one poet is abstract, and that of the other pathetic in character. Accordingly, if tragedy sets out from a more exalted place, it must be allowed, on the other hand, that comedy aims at a more important end; and if this end could be actually attained it would make all tragedy not only unnecessary, but impossible. The aim that comedy has in view is the same as that of the highest destiny of man, and this consists in liberating himself from the influence of violent passions, and taking a calm and lucid survey of all that surrounds him, and also of his own being, and of seeing everywhere occurrence rather than fate or hazard, and ultimately rather smiling at the absurdities than shedding tears and feeling anger at sight of the wickedness of man. [294]

On the Essence of Laughter

◆◆◆ CHARLES BAUDELAIRE

Charles Baudelaire, from "On the Essence of Laughter" [1855], in *The Mirror of Art,* tr. & ed. Jonathan Mayne (London, Phaidon Press Ltd., 1955).

BUT THERE is one case where the question is more complicated. It is the laughter of man—but a true and violent laughter—at the sight of an object which is neither a sign of weakness nor of disaster among his fellows. It is easy to guess that I am referring to the laughter caused by the grotesque. Fabulous creations, beings whose authority and *raison d'être* cannot be drawn from the code of common sense, often provoke in us an insane and excessive mirth, which expresses itself in interminable paroxysms and swoons. It is clear that a distinction must be made, and that here we have a higher degree of the phenomenon. From the artistic point of view, the comic is an imitation: the grotesque a creation. The comic is an imitation mixed with a certain creative faculty, that is to say with an artistic *ideality*. Now human pride, which always takes the upper hand and is the natural cause of laughter in the case of the comic, turns out to be the natural cause of laughter in the case of the grotesque too, for this is a creation mixed with a certain imitative faculty—imitative, that is, of elements pre-existing in nature. I mean that in this case laughter is still the expression of an idea of superiority—no longer now of man over man, but of man over nature. Do not retort that this idea is too subtle; that would be no sufficient reason for rejecting it. The difficulty is to find another plausible explanation. If this one seems far-fetched and just a little hard to accept, that is because the laughter caused by the grotesque has about it something profound, primitive and axiomatic, which is much closer to the innocent life and to absolute joy than is the laughter caused by the comic in man's behaviour. Setting aside the question of utility, there is the same difference between these two sorts of laughter as there is between the *implicated* school of writing and the school of art for art's sake. Thus the grotesque dominates the comic from a proportionate height. [144]

From now onwards I shall call the grotesque 'the absolute comic', in antithesis to the ordinary comic, which I shall call 'the significative comic'. The latter is a clearer language, and one easier for the man in the street to understand, and above all easier to analyse, its element being visibly *double*—art and the moral idea. But the absolute comic, which comes much closer to nature, emerges as a *unity* which calls for the intuition to grasp it. There is but one criterion of the grotesque, and that is laughter—immediate laughter. Whereas with the significative comic it is quite permissible to laugh a moment late—that is no argument against its validity; it all depends upon one's quickness of analysis.

I have called it 'the absolute comic.' Nevertheless we should be on our guard. From the point of view of the definitive absolute, all that remains is *joy*. The comic can only be absolute in relation to fallen humanity, and it is in this way that I am understanding it. . . .

Furthermore, within the absolute and significative types of [145] the comic we find species, sub-species and families. The division can take place on different grounds. First of all it can be established according to a pure philosophic law, as I was making a start to do: and then according to the law of artistic creation. The first is brought about by the primary separation of the absolute from the significative comic; the second is based upon the kind of special capacities possessed by each artist. And finally it is also possible to establish a classification of varieties of the comic with regard to climates and various national aptitudes. It should be observed that each term of each classification can be completed and given a *nuance* by the adjunction of a term from one of the others, just as the law of grammar teaches us to modify a noun by an adjective. Thus, any German or English artist is more or less naturally equipped for the absolute comic, and at the same time he is more or less of an idealizer. . . . [146]

Germany, sunk in her dreams, will afford us excellent specimens of the absolute comic. There all is weighty, profound and excessive. To find true comic savagery, however, you have to cross the Channel and visit the foggy realms of spleen. Happy, noisy, carefree Italy abounds in the innocent variety. It was at the very heart of Italy, at the hub of the southern carnival, in the midst of the turbulent Corso, that Theodore Hoffmann discerningly placed his eccentric drama, *The Princess Brambilla*. The Spaniards are very well endowed in this matter. They are quick to arrive at the cruel stage, and their most grotesque fantasies often contain a dark element.

It will be a long time before I forget the first English pantomime that I saw played. It was some years ago, at the *Théâtre des Variétés*. Doubtless only a few people will remember it, for very few seem to have taken to this kind of theatrical diversion, and those poor English mimes had a sad reception from us. The French public does not much like to be taken out of its element. Its taste is not very cosmopolitan, and changes of horizon upset [147] its vision. Speaking for myself, however, I was excessively struck by their way of understanding the comic. It was said—chiefly by the indulgent, in order to explain their lack of success—that these were vulgar, mediocre artists—understudies. But that was not the point. They were English; that was the important thing.

It seemed to me that the distinctive mark of this type of the comic was *violence*. I propose to prove it with a few samples from my memories.

First of all, Pierrot was not the figure to which the late-lamented Deburau had accustomed us—that figure pale as the moon, mysterious as silence, supple and mute as the serpent, long and straight as the gibbet—that artificial man activated by eccentric springs. The English Pierrot swept upon us like a hurricane, fell down like a sack of coals, and when he laughed his laughter made the auditorium quake; his laugh was like a joyful clap of thunder. He was a short, fat man, and to increase his imposingness he wore a be-ribboned costume which encompassed his jubilant person as birds are encompassed with their down and feathers, or angoras with their fur. Upon his floured face he had stuck, crudely and without transition or gradation, two enormous patches of pure red. A feigned prolongation of the lips, by means of two bands of carmine, brought it about that when he laughed his mouth seemed to run from ear to ear.

As for his moral nature, it was basically the same as that of the Pierrot whom we all know—heedlessness and indifference, and consequently the gratification of every kind of greedy and rapacious whim, now at the expense of Harlequin, now of Cassandre or Léandre. The only difference was that where Deburau would just have moistened the tip of his finger with his tongue, he stuck both fists and both feet into his mouth. [148]

And everything else in this singular piece was expressed in the same way, with passionate gusto; it was the dizzy height of hyperbole.

Pierrot walks past a woman who is scrubbing her doorstep; after rifling her pockets, he makes to stuff into his own her sponge, her mop, her bucket, water and all! As for the way in which he endeavoured to express his love to her, anyone who remembers observing the phanerogamous habits of the monkeys in their famous cage at the Jardin des Plantes can imagine it for himself. Perhaps I ought to add that the woman's role was taken by a very long, very thin man, whose outraged modesty emitted shrill screams. It was truly an intoxication of laughter —something both terrible and irresistible.

For some misdeed or other, Pierrot had in the end to be guillotined. Why the guillotine rather than the gallows, in the land of Albion?. . . [sic] * I do not know; presumably to lead up to what we were to see next. Anyway, there it was, the engine of death, there, set up on the French boards which were markedly surprised at this romantic novelty. After struggling and bellowing like an ox that scents the slaughter-house, at last Pierrot bowed to his fate. His head was severed from his neck—a great red and white head, which rolled noisily to rest in front of the prompter's box, showing the bleeding disk of the neck, the split vertebrae and all the details of a piece of butcher's meat just dressed for the counter. And then, all of a sudden, the decapitated trunk, moved by its irresistible obsession with theft, jumped to its feet, triumphantly 'lifted' its own head as though it was a ham or a bottle of wine, and, with far more circumspection than the great St. Denis, proceeded to stuff it into its pocket!

Set down in pen and ink, all this is pale and chilly. But how could the pen rival the pantomime? The pantomime is the refinement, the quintessence of comedy; it is the pure comic element, purged and concentrated. Therefore, with the English actors' special talent for hyperbole, all these monstrous buffooneries took on a strangely thrilling reality. . . . [149]

I should perhaps add that one of the most distinctive marks of the absolute comic is that it remains unaware of itself. This is evident not only in certain animals, like monkeys, in whose comicality gravity plays an essential part, nor only in certain antique sculptural caricatures of which I have already spoken, but even in those Chinese monstrosities which delight us so much and whose intentions are far

---

* An author's points of ellipsis are indicated by [sic]; all others represent our excisions.—Eds.

less comic than people generally think. A Chinese idol, although it be an object of veneration, looks very little different from a tumble-toy or a pot-bellied chimney-ornament.

And so, to be finished with all these subtleties and all these definitions, let me point out, once more and for the last time, that the dominant idea of superiority is found in the absolute, no less than in the significative comic, as I have already explained (at too great a length, perhaps) : further, that in order to enable a comic emanation, explosion, or, as it were, a chemical separation of the comic to come about, there must be two beings face to face with one another: again, that the special abode of the comic is in the laugher, the spectator: and finally, that an exception must nevertheless be made in connection with the 'law of ignorance' for those men who have made a business of developing [152] in themselves their feeling for the comic, and of dispensing it for the amusement of their fellows. This last phenomenon comes into the class of all artistic phenomena which indicate the existence of a permanent dualism in the human being—that is, the power of being oneself and someone else at one and the same time.

And so, to return to my primary definitions and to express myself more clearly, I would say that when Hoffmann gives birth to the absolute comic it is perfectly true that he knows what he is doing; but he also knows that the essence of this type of the comic is that it should appear to be unaware of itself and that it should produce in the spectator, or rather the reader, a joy in his own superiority and in the superiority of man over nature. Artists create the comic; after collecting and studying its elements, they know that such-and-such a being is comic, and that it is so only on condition of its being unaware of its nature, in the same way that, following an inverse law, an artist is only an artist on condition that he is a double man and that there is not one single phenomenon of his double nature of which he is ignorant. [153]

The Expression of the Emotions in Man and Animals

◆◆◆ CHARLES DARWIN

Charles Darwin, from *The Expression of the Emotions in Man and Animals* [1872], ed. Francis Darwin (London, John Murray, 1904).

I WILL BEGIN by giving the three Principles, which appear to me to account for most of the expressions and gestures involuntarily used by man and the lower animals, under the influence of various emotions and sensations. I arrived, however, at these three Principles only at the close of my observations. . . . Facts observed both with man and the lower animals will here be made use of; but the latter facts are preferable, as less likely to deceive us. . . . Every one will thus be able to judge for himself, how far my three principles throw light on the theory of the subject. It appears to me that so many expressions [27] are thus explained in a fairly satisfactory manner, that probably all will hereafter be found to come under the same or closely analogous heads. I need hardly premise that movements or changes in any part of the body,—as the wagging of a dog's tail, the drawing back of a horse's ears, the shrugging of a man's shoulders, or the dilatation of the capillary vessels of the skin,—may all equally well serve for expression. The three Principles are as follows.

I. *The principle of serviceable associated Habits.*—Certain complex actions are of direct or indirect service under certain states of the mind, in order to relieve or gratify certain sensations, desires, &c.; and whenever the same state of mind is induced, however feebly, there is a tendency through the force of habit and association for the same movements to be performed, though they may not then be of the least use. Some actions ordinarily associated through habit with certain states of the mind may be partially repressed through the will, and in such cases the muscles which are least under the separate control of the will are the most liable still to act, causing movements which we recognize as expressive. In certain other cases the checking of one habitual movement requires other slight movements; and these are likewise expressive.

II. *The principle of Antithesis.*—Certain states of the mind lead to certain habitual actions, which are of service, as under our first principle. Now when a directly opposite state of mind is induced, there is a strong and involuntary tendency to the performance of movements of a directly opposite nature, though these are of no use; and such movements are in some cases highly expressive. [28]

III. *The principle of actions due to the constitution of the Nervous System, independently from the first of the Will, and independently to a certain extent of Habit.*—When the sensorium is strongly excited, nerve-force is generated in excess, and is transmitted in certain definite directions, depending on the connection of the nerve-cells, and partly on habit: or the supply of nerve-force may, as it appears, be interrupted. Effects are thus produced which we recognize as expressive. This third principle may, for the sake of brevity, be called that of the direct action of the nervous system. . . . [29]

Joy, when intense, leads to various purposeless movements—to dancing about, clapping the hands, stamping, &c., and to loud laughter. Laughter seems primarily to be the expression of mere joy or happiness. We clearly see this in children at play, who are almost incessantly laughing. With young persons past childhood, when they are in high spirits, there is always much meaningless laughter. The laughter of the gods is described by Homer as "the exuberance of their celestial joy after their daily banquet." A man smiles—and smiling, as we shall see, graduates into laughter—at meeting an old friend in the street, as he does at any trifling pleasure, such as smelling a sweet perfume. . . . [203]

Idiots and imbecile persons likewise afford good evidence that laughter or smiling primarily expresses mere happiness or joy. Dr. Crichton Browne, to whom, as on so many other occasions, I am indebted for the results of his wide experience, informs me that with idiots laughter is the most prevalent and frequent of all the emotional expressions. Many idiots are morose, passionate, restless, in a painful state of mind, or utterly stolid, and these never laugh. Others frequently laugh in a quite senseless manner. Thus an idiot boy, incapable of speech, complained to Dr. Browne, by the aid of signs, that another boy in the asylum had given him a black eye; and this was accompanied by "explosions of laughter and with his face covered with the broadest smiles." There is another large class of idiots who are persistently joyous and benign, and who are constantly laughing or smiling. Their countenances often exhibit a stereotyped smile; their joyousness is increased, and they grin, chuckle, or giggle, whenever food is placed before them, or when they are caressed, are shown bright colours, or hear music. Some of them laugh more than usual when they walk about, or attempt any muscular exertion. The joyousness of most of these idiots cannot possibly be associated, as Dr. Browne remarks, with any distinct ideas: they simply feel pleasure, and express it by laughter or smiles. With imbeciles rather higher in the scale, personal vanity seems to be the [204] commonest cause of laughter, and next to this, pleasure arising from the approbation of their conduct.

With grown-up persons laughter is excited by causes considerably different from those which suffice during childhood; but this remark hardly applies to smiling. Laughter in this respect is analogous with weeping, which with adults is almost confined to mental distress, whilst with children it is excited by bodily pain or any suffering, as well as by fear or rage. Many curious discussions have been written on the causes of laughter with grown-up persons. The subject is extremely complex. Something incongruous or unaccountable, exciting surprise and some sense of superiority in the laugher, who must be in a happy frame of mind, seems to be the commonest cause. The circumstances must not be of a momentous nature: no poor man would laugh or smile on suddenly hearing that a large fortune had been bequeathed to him. . . . [205] An observation, bearing on this point, was made by a correspondent during the recent siege of Paris, namely, that the German soldiers, after strong excitement from exposure to extreme danger, were particularly apt to burst out into loud laughter at the smallest joke. So again when young children are just beginning to cry, an unexpected event will sometimes suddenly turn their crying into laughter, which apparently serves equally well to expend their superfluous nervous energy.

The imagination is sometimes said to be tickled by a ludicrous idea; and this so-called tickling of the mind is curiously analogous with that of the body. Every one knows how immoderately children laugh, and how their whole bodies are convulsed when they are tickled. The anthropoid apes . . . likewise utter a reiterated sound, corresponding with our laughter, when they are tickled, especially under the armpits. I touched with a bit of paper the sole of the foot of one of my infants, when only seven days old, and it was suddenly jerked away and the toes curled about, as in an older child. Such movements, as well as laughter from being tickled, are manifestly reflex actions; and this is likewise shown by the minute unstriped muscles, which serve to erect the separate hairs on the body, contracting near a tickled surface. Yet laughter from a ludicrous idea, though involuntary, cannot be called a strictly reflex action. In this case, and in that of laughter from being tickled, the mind must be in a [206] pleasurable condition; a young child, if tickled by a strange man, would scream from fear. The touch must be light, and an idea or event, to be ludicrous, must not be of grave import. . . . [S]omething unexpected—a novel or incongruous idea which breaks through an habitual train of thought—appears to be a strong element in the ludicrous.

The sound of laughter is produced by a deep inspiration followed by short, interrupted, spasmodic contractions of the chest, and especially of the diaphragm. Hence we hear of "laughter holding both his sides." From the shaking of the body, the head nods to and fro. The lower jaw often quivers up and down, as is likewise the case with some species of baboons, when they are much pleased. . . . [207]

A man in high spirits, though he may not actually smile, commonly exhibits some tendency to the retraction of the corners of his mouth. From the excitement of pleasure, the circulation becomes more rapid; the eyes are bright, and the colour of the face rises. The brain, being stimulated by the increased flow of blood, reacts on the mental powers; [218] lively ideas pass still more rapidly through the mind, and the affections are warmed. . . . According to Sir C. Bell, "In all the exhilarating emotions the eyebrows, eyelids, the nostrils, and the angles of the mouth are raised. In the depressing emotions it is the reverse." Under the influence of the latter the brow is heavy, the eyelids, cheeks, mouth, and whole head droop; the eyes are dull; the countenance pallid, and the respiration slow. In joy the face expands, in grief it lengthens. Whether the principle of antithesis has here come into play in producing these opposite expressions, in aid of the direct causes which have been specified and which are sufficiently plain, I will not pretend to say. . . . [219]

Laughter is frequently employed in a forced manner to conceal or mask some other state of mind, even anger. We often see persons laughing in order to conceal their shame or shyness. When a person purses up his mouth, as if to prevent the possibility of a smile, though there is nothing to excite one, or nothing to prevent its free indulgence, an affected, solemn, or pedantic expression is given; but of such hybrid expressions nothing more need here be said. In the case of derision, a real or pretended smile or laugh is often blended with the expression proper to contempt, and this may pass into angry contempt or scorn. In such cases the meaning of the laugh or smile is to show the offending person that he excites only amusement. [221]

An Essay on Comedy
and the Uses of the Comic Spirit

GEORGE MEREDITH

George Meredith, from *An Essay on Comedy and the Uses of the Comic Spirit* [1877] (New York, Charles Scribner's Sons, 1897).

THERE ARE plain reasons why the Comic poet is not a frequent apparition; and why the great Comic poet remains without a [1] fellow. A society of cultivated men and women is required, wherein ideas are current and the perceptions quick, that he may be supplied with matter and an audience. The semi-barbarism of merely giddy communities, and feverish emotional periods, repel him; and also a state of marked social inequality of the sexes; nor can he whose business is to address the mind be understood where there is not a moderate degree of intellectual activity.

Moreover, to touch and kindle the mind through laughter, demands more than sprightliness, a most subtle delicacy. That must be a natal gift in the Comic poet. The substance he deals with will show him a startling exhibition of the dyer's hand, if he is without it. People are ready to surrender themselves to witty thumps on the back, breast, and sides; all except the head: and it is there that he aims. He must be subtle to penetrate. A corresponding acuteness must exist to welcome him. The necessity for the two conditions [2] will explain how it is that we count him during centuries in the singular number.... [3]

There has been fun in Bagdad. But there never will be civilization where Comedy is not possible; and that comes of some degree of social equality of the sexes. I am not quoting the Arab to exhort and disturb the somnolent East; rather for cultivated women to recognize that the Comic Muse is one of their best friends. They are blind to their interests in swelling the ranks of sentimentalists. Let them look with their clearest vision abroad and at home. They will see that where they [54] have no social freedom, Comedy is absent: where they are household drudges, the form of Comedy is primitive: where they are tolerably independent, but uncultivated, exciting melodrama takes its

34

place and a sentimental version of them. Yet the Comic will out, as they would know if they listened to some of the private conversations of men whose minds are undirected by the Comic Muse: as the sentimental man, to his astonishment, would know likewise, if he in similar fashion could receive a lesson. But where women are on the road to an equal footing with men, in attainments and in liberty—in what they have won for themselves, and what has been granted them by a fair civilization—there, and only waiting to be transplanted from life to the stage, or the novel, or the poem, pure Comedy flourishes, and is, as it would help them to be, the sweetest of diversions, the wisest of delightful companions. . . . [55]

The Comic poet is in the narrow field, or enclosed square, of the society he depicts; and he addresses the still narrower enclosure of [79] men's intellects, with reference to the operation of the social world upon their characters. He is not concerned with beginnings or endings or surroundings, but with what you are now weaving. To understand his work and value it, you must have a sober liking of your kind, and a sober estimate of our civilized qualities. The aim and business of the Comic poet are misunderstood, his meaning is not seized nor his point of view taken, when he is accused of dishonouring our nature and being hostile to sentiment, tending to spitefulness and making an unfair use of laughter. Those who detect irony in Comedy do so because they choose to see it in life. Poverty, says the satirist, has nothing harder in itself than that it makes men ridiculous. But poverty is never ridiculous to Comic perception until it attempts to make its rags conceal its bareness in a forlorn attempt at decency, or foolishly to rival ostentation. Caleb Balderstone, in his endeavour to keep up the honour of a noble household in a state of beggary, is an exquisitely [80] comic character. In the case of "poor relatives," on the other hand, it is the rich, whom they perplex, that are really comic; and to laugh at the former, not seeing the comedy of the latter, is to betray dulness of vision. Humourist and Satirist frequently hunt together as Ironëists in pursuit of the grotesque, to the exclusion of the Comic. That was an affecting moment in the history of the Prince Regent, when the First Gentleman of Europe burst into tears at a sarcastic remark of Beau Brummell's on the cut of his coat. Humour, Satire, Irony, pounce on it altogether as their common prey. The Comic Spirit eyes but does not touch it. Put into action, it would be farcical. It is too gross for Comedy.

Incidents of a kind casting ridicule on our unfortunate nature, instead of our conventional life, provoke derisive laughter, which thwarts the Comic idea. But derision is foiled by the play of the intellect. Most of doubtful causes in contest are open to Comic interpretation, and any intellectual pleading of [81] a doubtful cause contains germs of an Idea of Comedy.

The laughter of satire is a blow in the back or the face. The laughter of Comedy is impersonal and of unrivalled politeness, nearer a smile; often no more than a smile. It laughs through the mind, for the mind directs it; and it might be called the humour of the mind.

One excellent test of the civilization of a country, as I have said, I take to be the flourishing of the Comic idea and Comedy; and the test of true Comedy is that it shall awaken thoughtful laughter.

If you believe that our civilization is founded in common-sense (and it is the first condition of sanity to believe it), you will, when contemplating men, discern a Spirit overhead; not more heavenly than the light flashed upward from glassy surfaces, but luminous and watchful; never shooting beyond them, nor lagging in the rear; so closely attached to them that it may be taken for a slavish reflex, until its features are studied. It has the sage's brows, [82] and the sunny malice of a faun lurks at the corners of the half-closed lips drawn in an idle wariness of half-tension. That slim feasting smile, shaped like the long-bow, was once a big round satyr's laugh, that flung up the brows like a fortress lifted by gunpowder. The laugh will come again, but it will be of the order of the smile, finely tempered, showing sunlight of the mind, mental richness rather than noisy enormity. Its common aspect is one of unsolicitous observation, as if surveying a full field and having leisure to dart on its chosen morsels, without any fluttering eagerness. Men's future upon earth does not attract it; their honesty and shapeliness in the present does; and whenever they wax out of proportion, overblown, affected, pretentious, bombastical, hypocritical, pedantic, fantastically delicate; whenever it sees them self-deceived or hoodwinked, given to run riot in idolatries, drifting into vanities, congregating in absurdities, planning short-sightedly, plotting dementedly; whenever they [83] are at variance with their professions, and violate the unwritten but perceptible laws binding them in consideration one to another; whenever they offend sound reason, fair justice; are false in humility or mined with conceit, individually, or in the bulk—the Spirit overhead will look humanely malign and cast an oblique light on them, followed by volleys of silvery laughter. That is the Comic Spirit.

Not to distinguish it is to be bull-blind to the spiritual, and to deny the existence of a mind of man where minds of men are in working conjunction.

You must, as I have said, believe that our state of society is founded in common-sense, otherwise you will not be struck by the contrasts the Comic Spirit perceives, or have it to look to for your consolation. You will, in fact, be standing in that peculiar oblique beam of light, yourself illuminated to the general eye as the very object of chase and doomed quarry of the thing obscure to you. But to feel its presence and to see it is your assurance that [84] many sane and solid minds are with you in what you are experiencing: and this of itself spares you the pain of satirical heat, and the bitter craving to strike heavy blows. You share the sublime of wrath, that would not have hurt the foolish, but merely demonstrate their foolishness. . . . A perception of the comic spirit gives high fellowship. You become a citizen of the selecter world, the highest we know of in connection with our old world, which is not supermundane. Look there for your unchallengeable upper class! You feel that you are one of this our civilized community, that you cannot escape from it, and would not if you could. Good hope sustains you; weariness does not overwhelm you; in isolation you see no charms for vanity; personal pride is greatly moderated. [85]

Meredith on Comedy

Bernard Shaw, from "Meredith on Comedy" [1932], in *Our Theatres in the Nineties* (London, Constable & Co., Ltd., 1932), 3 vols.

TWENTY YEARS AGO Mr George Meredith delivered a lecture at the London Institution on Comedy and the Uses of the Comic Spirit. It was afterwards published in the New Quarterly Magazine, and now reappears as a brown buckram book, obtainable at the inconsiderable price (considering the quality) of five shillings. It is an excellent, even superfine, essay, by perhaps the highest living English authority on its subject. And Mr Meredith is quite conscious of his eminence. Speaking of the masters of the comedic spirit (if I call it, as he does, the Comic Spirit, this darkened generation will suppose me to refer to the animal spirits of tomfools and merryandrews), he says, "Look there for your unchallengeable upper class." He should know; for he certainly belongs to it. At the first page I recognize the true connoisseur, and know that I have only to turn it to come to the great name of Molière, who has hardly been mentioned in London during the last twenty years by the dramatic critics, except as representing a quaint habit of the Comédie Française. That being so, why republish an essay on comedy now? Who cares for comedy today?—who knows what it is?—how many readers of Mr Meredith's perfectly straightforward and accurate account of the wisest and most exquisite of the arts will see anything in the book but a brilliant sally of table talk about old plays: to be enjoyed, without practical application, as one of the rockets in the grand [III, 83] firework display of contemporary *belles-lettres*?

However, since the thing is done, and the book out, I take leave to say that Mr Meredith knows more about plays than about playgoers. "The English public," he says, "have the basis of the comic in them: an esteem for common sense." This flattering illusion does not dupe Mr Meredith completely; for I notice that he adds "taking them generally." But if it were to be my last word on earth I must tell Mr Meredith to his face that whether you take them generally or particularly—whether in the lump, or sectionally as playgoers, churchgoers, voters, and what not—they are everywhere united and made strong by the bond of their common nonsense, their invincible determination to tell and be told lies about everything, and their power of dealing acquisitively and successfully with facts whilst keeping them, like disaffected slaves, rigidly in their proper place: that is, outside the moral consciousness. The Englishman is the most successful man in the world simply because he values success—meaning money and social precedence—more than anything else, especially more than fine art, his attitude towards which, culture-affectation apart, is one of half diffident, half contemptuous curiosity, and of course more than clear-headedness, spiritual insight, truth, justice, and so forth. It is precisely this unscrupulousness and singleness of purpose that constitutes the Englishman's preeminent "common sense"; and this sort of common sense, I submit to Mr Meredith, is not only not "the basis of the comic," but actually makes comedy impossible, because it would not seem like common sense at all if it were not self-satisfiedly unconscious of its moral and intellectual bluntness, whereas the function of comedy is to dispel such unconsciousness by turning the searchlight of the keenest moral and intellectual analysis right on to it. Now the Frenchman, the Irishman, the American, the ancient Greek, is disabled from this true British common sense by intellectual virtuosity, leading to a love of accurate and complete consciousness of things—of intellectual mastery of them. This produces a positive enjoyment of disillusion (the most dreaded and hated of calamities in England), and consequently a love of [III, 84] comedy (the fine art of disillusion) deep enough to make huge sacrifices of dearly idealized institutions to it. Thus, in France, Molière was allowed to destroy the Marquises. In England he could not have shaken even such titles as the accidental sheriff's knighthood of the late Sir Augustus Harris. And yet the Englishman thinks himself much more independent, level-headed, and genuinely republican than the Frenchman—not without good superficial reasons; for nations with the genius of comedy often carry all the snobbish ambitions and idealist enthusiasms of the Englishman to an extreme which the Englishman himself laughs at. But they sacrifice them to comedy, to which the Englishman sacrifices nothing; so that, in the upshot, aristocracies, thrones, and churches go by the board at the attack of comedy among our devotedly conventional, loyal, and fanatical next-door neighbors; whilst we, having absolutely no disinterested regard for such institutions, draw a few of their sharpest teeth, and then maintain them determinedly as part of the machinery of worldly success.

The Englishman prides himself on this anti-comedic common sense of his as at least eminently practical. As a matter of fact, it is just as often as not most pigheadedly unpractical. For example, electric telegraphy, telephony, and traction are invented, and establish themselves as necessities of civilized life. The unpractical foreigner recognizes the fact, and takes the obvious step of putting up poles in his streets to carry wires. This expedient never occurs to the Briton. He wastes leagues of wire and does unheard-of damage to property by tying his wires and posts to such chimney stacks as he can beguile householders into letting him have access to. Finally, when it comes to electric traction, and the housetops are out of the question, he suddenly comes out in the novel character of an amateur in urban picturesqueness, and declares that the necessary cable apparatus would spoil the appearance of our streets. The streets of Nuremberg, the heights of Fiesole, may not be perceptibly the worse for these contrivances; but the beauty of Tottenham Court Road is too sacred to be so profaned: to its loveliness the strained bus-horse and his offal are the only accessories endurable by the beauty-loving [III, 85] Cockney eye. This is your common-sense Englishman. His helplessness in the face of electricity is typical of his helplessness in the face of everything else that lies outside the set of habits he calls his opinions and capacities. In the theatre he is the same. It is not common sense to laugh at your own prejudices: it is common sense to feel insulted when anyone else laughs at them. Besides, the Englishman is a serious person: that is, he is firmly persuaded that his prejudices and stupidities are the vital material of civilization, and that it is only by holding on to their moral prestige with the stiffest resolution that the world is saved from flying back into savagery and gorilladom, which he always conceives, in spite of natural history, as a condition of lawlessness and promiscuity, instead of, as it actually is, the extremity, long since grown unbearable, of his own notions of law and order, morality, and conventional respectability. Thus he is a moralist, an ascetic, a Christian, a truth-teller and a plain dealer by profession and by conviction; and it is wholly against this conviction that, judged by his own canons, he finds himself in practice a great rogue, a liar, an unconscionable pirate, a grinder of the face of the poor, and a libertine. Mr Meredith points out daintily that the cure for this self-treasonable confusion and darkness is Comedy, whose spirit overhead will "look humanely malign and cast an oblique light on them, followed by volleys of silvery laughter." Yes, Mr Meredith; but suppose the patients have "common sense" enough not to want to be cured! Suppose they realize the immense commercial advantage of keeping their ideal life and their practical business life in two separate conscience-tight compartments, which nothing but "the Comic Spirit" can knock into one! Suppose, therefore, they dread the Comic Spirit more than anything else in the world, shrinking from its "illumination," and considering its "silvery laughter" in execrable taste! Surely in doing so they are only carrying out the common-sense view, in which an encouragement and enjoyment of comedy must appear as silly and suicidal and "unEnglish" as the conduct of the man who sets fire to his own house for the sake of seeing the flying sparks, the red glow in the sky, the fantastic [III, 86] shadows on the walls, the excitement of the crowd, the gleaming charge of the engines, and the dismay of the neighbors. No doubt the day will come when we shall deliberately burn a London street every day to keep our city up to date in health and handsomeness, with no more misgiving as to our common sense than we now have when sending our clothes to the laundry every week. When that day comes, perhaps comedy will be popular too; for, after all, the function of comedy, as Mr Meredith after twenty years' further consideration is perhaps by this time ripe to admit, is nothing less than the destruction of old-established morals. Unfortunately, today such iconoclasm can be tolerated by our playgoing citizens only as a counsel of despair and pessimism. They can find a dreadful joy in it when it is done seriously, or even grimly and terribly as they understand Ibsen to be doing it; but that it should be done with levity, with silvery laughter like the crackling of thorns under a pot, is too scandalously wicked, too cynical, too heartlessly shocking to be borne. Consequently our plays must either be exploitations of old-established morals or tragic challengings of the order of Nature. Reductions to absurdity, however logical; banterings, however kindly; irony, however delicate; merriment, however silvery, are out of the question in matters of morality, except among men with a natural appetite for comedy which must be satisfied at all costs and hazards: that is to say, *not* among the English playgoing public, which positively dislikes comedy.

No doubt it is patriotically indulgent of Mr Meredith to say that

"Our English school has not clearly imagined society," and that "of the mind hovering above congregated men and women it has imagined nothing." But is he quite sure that the audiences of our English school do not know too much about society and "congregated men and women" to encourage any exposures from "the vigilant Comic," with its "thoughtful laughter," its "oblique illumination," and the rest of it? May it not occur to the purchasers of half-guinea stalls that it is bad enough to have to put up with the pryings of Factory Inspectors, Public Analysts, County Council Inspectors, Chartered Accountants and the like, [III, 87] without admitting this Comic Spirit to look into still more delicate matters? Is it clear that the Comic Spirit would break into silvery laughter if it saw all that the nineteenth century has to shew it beneath the veneer? There is Ibsen, for instance: he is not lacking, one judges, in the Comic Spirit; yet his laughter does not sound very silvery, does it? No: if this were an age for comedies, Mr Meredith would have been asked for one before this. How would a comedy from him be relished, I wonder, by the people who wanted to have the revisers of the Authorized Version of the Bible prosecuted for blasphemy because they corrected as many of its mistranslations as they dared, and who reviled Froude for not suppressing Carlyle's diary and writing a fictitious biography of him, instead of letting out the truth? Comedy, indeed! I drop the subject with a hollow laugh. [III, 88]

Laughter

◆◆◆ HENRI BERGSON

Henri Bergson, from "Laughter" [1900], tr. Cloudesley Brereton and Fred Rothwell, in *Comedy* (New York, Doubleday & Co., Inc., 1956).

THE FIRST POINT to which attention should be called is that the comic does not exist outside the pale of what is strictly *human.* A landscape may be beautiful, charming and sublime, or insignificant and ugly; it will never be laughable. You may laugh at an animal, but only because you have detected in it some human attitude or expression. You may laugh at a hat, but what you are making fun of, in this case, is not the piece of felt or straw, but the shape that men have given it,—the human caprice whose mould it has assumed. It is strange that so important a fact, and such a simple one too, has not attracted to a greater degree the attention of philosophers. Several have defined man as "an animal which laughs." They might equally well have defined him as an animal which is laughed at; for if any other animal, or some lifeless object, produces the same effect, it is always because of some resemblance [62] to man, of the stamp he gives it or the use he puts it to.

Here I would point out, as a symptom equally worthy of notice, the *absence of feeling* which usually accompanies laughter. It seems as though the comic could not produce its disturbing effect unless it fell, so to say, on the surface of a soul that is thoroughly calm and unruffled. Indifference is its natural environment, for laughter has no greater foe than emotion. I do not mean that we could not laugh at a person who inspires us with pity, for instance, or even with affection, but in such a case we must, for the moment, put our affection out of court and impose silence upon our pity. In a society composed of pure intelligences there would probably be no more tears, though perhaps there would still be laughter; whereas highly emotional souls, in tune and unison with life, in whom every event would be sentimentally prolonged and re-echoed, would neither know nor understand laughter. Try, for a moment, to become interested in everything that is being said and done; act, in imagination, with those who act, and feel with those who feel; in a word, give your sympathy its widest expansion: as though at the touch of a fairy wand you will see the flimsiest of objects assume importance, and a gloomy hue spread over everything. Now step aside, look upon life as a disinterested spectator: many a drama will turn into a comedy. It is enough for us to stop our ears to the sound of music in a room, where dancing is going on, for the dancers at once to appear ridiculous. How many human actions would stand a similar test? Should we not see many of them suddenly pass from grave to gay, on isolating them from the accompanying music of sentiment? To produce the whole of its effect, then, the comic demands [63] something like a momentary anesthesia of the heart. Its appeal is to intelligence, pure and simple.

This intelligence, however, must always remain in touch with other intelligences. And here is the third fact to which attention should be drawn. You would hardly appreciate the comic if you felt yourself isolated from others. Laughter appears to stand in need of an echo. Listen to it carefully: it is not an articulate, clear, well-defined sound; it is something which would fain be prolonged by reverberating from one to another, something beginning with a crash, to continue in successive rumblings, like thunder in a mountain. Still, this reverberation cannot go on for ever. It can travel within as wide a circle as you please: the circle remains, none the less, a closed one. Our laughter is always the laughter of a group. . . . [64]

Now, the effect of absentmindedness may gather strength in its turn. There is a general law, the first example of which we have just encountered, and which we will formulate in the following terms: when a certain comic effect has its origin in a certain cause, the more natural we regard the cause to be, the more comic shall we find the effect. Even now we laugh at absentmindedness when presented to us as a simple fact. Still more laughable will be the absentmindedness we have seen springing up and growing before our very eyes, with whose origin we are acquainted and whose life-history we can reconstruct. To choose a definite example: suppose a man has taken to reading nothing but romances of love and chivalry. Attracted and fascinated by his heroes, his thoughts and intentions gradually turn more and more towards them, till one fine day we find him walking among us like a somnambulist. His actions are distractions. But then his distractions can be traced back to a definite, positive cause. They are no longer cases of *absence* of mind, pure and simple; they find their explanation in the *presence* of the [68] individual in quite definite, though imaginary, surroundings. Doubtless a fall is always a fall, but it is one thing to tumble into a well because you were looking anywhere but in front of you, it is quite another thing to fall into it because you were intent upon a star. It was certainly a star at which Don Quixote was gazing. How profound is the comic element in the over-romantic, Utopian bent of mind! And yet, if you reintroduce the idea of absentmindedness, which acts as a go-between you will see this profound comic element uniting with the most superficial type. Yes, indeed, these whimsical wild enthusiasts, these madmen who are yet so strangely reasonable, excite us to laughter by playing on the same chords within ourselves, by setting in motion the same inner mechanism, as does the victim of a practical joke or the passer-by who slips down in the street. They, too, are runners who fall and simple souls who are being hoaxed —runners after the ideal who stumble over realities, child-like dreamers for whom life delights to lie in wait. But, above all, they are past-masters in absentmindedness, with this superiority over their fellows that their absentmindedness is systematic and organised around one central idea, and that their mishaps are also quite coherent, thanks to the inexorable logic which reality applies to the correction of dreams, so that they kindle in those around them, by a series of cumulative effects, a hilarity capable of unlimited expansion. . . . [69]

It is unnecessary to carry this analysis any further. From the runner who falls to the simpleton who is hoaxed, from a state of being hoaxed to one of absentmindedness, from absentmindedness to wild enthusiasm, from wild enthusiasm to various distortions of character and will, we have followed the line of progress along which the comic becomes more and more deeply imbedded in the person, yet without ceasing, in its subtler manifestations, to recall to us [71] some trace of what we noticed in its grosser forms, an effect of automatism and of inelasticity. Now we can obtain a first glimpse—a distant one, it is true, and still hazy and confused—of the laughable side of human nature and of the ordinary function of laughter.

What life and society require of each of us is a constantly alert attention that discerns the outlines of the present situation, together with a certain elasticity of mind and body to enable us to adapt ourselves in consequence. *Tension* and *elasticity* are two forces, mutually complementary, which life brings into play. If these two forces are lacking in the body to any considerable extent, we have sickness and infirmity and accidents of every kind. If they are lacking in the mind, we find every degree of mental deficiency, every variety of insanity. Finally, if they are lacking in the character, we have cases of the gravest inadaptability to social life, which are the sources of misery and at times the causes of crime. Once these elements of inferiority that affect the serious side of existence are removed—and they tend to eliminate themselves in what has been called the struggle for life—the person can live, and that in common with other persons. But society asks for something more; it is not satisfied with simply living, it insists on living well. What it now has to dread is that each one of us, content with paying attention to what affects the essentials of life, will, so far as the rest is concerned, give way to the easy automatism of acquired habits. Another thing it must fear is that the members of whom it is made up, instead of aiming after an increasingly delicate adjustment of wills which will fit more and more perfectly into one another, will confine themselves to respecting simply the fundamental conditions of [72] this adjustment: a cut-and-dried agreement among the persons will not satisfy it, it insists on a constant striving after reciprocal adaptation. Society will therefore be suspicious of all *inelasticity* of character, of mind and even of body, because it is the possible sign of a slumbering activity as well as of an activity with separatist tendencies, that inclines to swerve from the common centre round which society gravitates: in short, because it is the sign of an eccentricity. And yet, society cannot intervene at this stage by material repression, since it is not affected in a material fashion. It is confronted with something that makes it uneasy, but only as a symptom—scarcely a threat, at the very most a gesture. A gesture, therefore, will be its reply. Laughter must be something of this kind, a sort of *social gesture*. By the fear which it inspires, it restrains eccentricity, keeps constantly awake and in mutual contact certain activities of a secondary order which might retire into their shell and go to sleep, and in short, softens down whatever the surface of the social body may retain of mechanical inelasticity. Laughter, then, does not belong to the province of esthetics alone, since unconsciously (and even immorally in many particular instances) it pursues a utilitarian aim of general improvement. And yet there is something esthetic about it, since the comic comes into being just when society and the individual, freed from the worry of self-preservation, begin to regard themselves as works of art. In a word, if a circle be drawn round those actions and dispositions—implied in individual or social life—to which their natural consequences bring their own penalties, there remains outside this sphere of emotion and struggle— and within a neutral zone in which man simply exposes himself to man's curiosity—a certain rigidity of [73] body, mind and character that society would still like to get rid of in order to obtain from its members the greatest possible degree of elasticity and sociability. This rigidity is the comic, and laughter is its corrective. . . . [74]

Now, certain deformities undoubtedly possess over others the sorry privilege of causing some persons to laugh; some hunchbacks, for instance, will excite laughter. Without at this point entering into useless details, we will simply ask the reader to think of a number of deformities, and then to divide them into two groups: on the one hand, those which nature has directed towards the ridiculous; and on the other, those which absolutely diverge from it. No doubt he will hit upon the following law: *A deformity that may become comic is a deformity that a normally built person could successfully imitate.*

Is it not, then, the case that the hunchback suggests the appearance of a person who holds himself badly? His back seems to have contracted an ugly stoop. By a kind of physical obstinacy, by *rigidity,* in a word, it persists in the habit it has contracted. Try to see with your eyes alone. Avoid reflection, and above all, do not reason. Abandon all your prepossessions; seek to recapture a fresh, direct and primitive impression. The vision you will reacquire will be one of this kind. You will have before you a man bent on cultivating a certain rigid attitude whose body, if one may use the expression, is one vast grin. . . . [75]

We shall now understand the comic element in caricature. However regular we may imagine a face to be, however harmonious its lines and supple its movements, their adjustment is never altogether perfect: there will always be discoverable the signs of some impending bias, the vague suggestion of a possible grimace, in short, some favourite distortion towards which nature seems to be particularly inclined. The art of the caricaturist consists in detecting this, at times, imperceptible tendency, and in rendering it visible to all eyes by magnifying it. He makes his models grimace, as they would do themselves if they went to the end of their tether. Beneath the skin-deep harmony of form, he divines the deep-seated recalcitrance of matter. He realises disproportions and deformations which must have existed in nature as mere inclinations, but which have not succeeded in coming to a head, being held in check by a higher force. His art, which has a touch of the diabolical, raises up the demon who had been overthrown by the angel. Certainly, it is an art that exaggerates, and yet the definition would be very far from complete were exaggeration alone alleged to be its aim and object, for there exist caricatures that are more lifelike than portraits, caricatures in which the exaggeration is scarcely noticeable, whilst, inversely, it is quite possible to exaggerate to excess without obtaining a real caricature. For exaggeration to be comic, it must not appear as an aim, but rather as a means that the artist is using in order to make manifest to our eyes the distortions which he sees in embryo. It is this process of distortion that is of [77] moment and interest. And that is precisely why we shall look for it even in those elements of the face that are incapable of movement, in the curve of a nose or the shape of an ear. For, in our eyes, form is always the outline of a movement. The caricaturist who alters the size of a nose, but respects its ground plan, lengthening it, for instance, in the very direction in which it was being lengthened by nature, is really making the nose indulge in a grin. Henceforth we shall always look upon the original as having determined to lengthen itself and start grinning. In this sense, one might say that Nature herself often meets with the successes of a caricaturist. In the movement through which she has slit that mouth, curtailed that chin and bulged out that cheek, she would appear to have succeeded in completing the intended grimace, thus outwitting the restraining supervision of a more reasonable force. In that case, the face we laugh at is, so to speak, its own caricature.

To sum up, whatever be the doctrine to which our reason assents, our imagination has a very clear-cut philosophy of its own: in every human form it sees the effort of a soul which is shaping matter, a soul which is infinitely supple and perpetually in motion, subject to no law of gravitation, for it is not the earth that attracts it. This soul imparts a portion of its winged lightness to the body it animates: the immateriality which thus passes into matter is what is called gracefulness. Matter, however, is obstinate and resists. It draws to itself the ever-alert activity of this higher principle, would fain convert it to its own inertia and cause it to revert to mere automatism. It would fain immobilise the intelligently varied movements of the body in stupidly contracted grooves, stereotype in permanent grimaces the [78] fleeting expressions of the face, in short imprint on the whole person such an attitude as to make it appear immersed and absorbed in the materiality of some mechanical occupation instead of ceaselessly renewing its vitality by keeping in touch with a living ideal. Where matter thus succeeds in dulling the outward life of the soul, in petrifying its movements and thwarting its gracefulness, it achieves, at the expense of a body, an effect that is comic. If, then, at this point we wish to define the comic by comparing it with its contrary, we should have to contrast it with gracefulness even more than with beauty. It partakes rather of the unsprightly than of the unsightly, of *rigidness* rather than of *ugliness.*

We will now pass from the comic element in *forms* to that in *gestures* and *movements.* Let us at once state the law which seems to govern all the phenomena of this kind. It may indeed be deduced without any difficulty from the considerations stated above.

The attitudes, gestures and movements of the human body are laughable in exact proportion as that body reminds us of a mere machine. . . . [79]

Something mechanical encrusted on the living will represent a cross at which we must halt, a central image from which the imagination branches off in different directions. What are these directions? There appear to be three main ones. We will follow [84] them one after the other, and then continue our onward course.

1. In the first place, this view of the mechanical and the living dovetailed into each other makes us incline towards the vaguer image of *some rigidity or other* applied to the mobility of life, in an awkward attempt to follow its lines and counterfeit its suppleness. Here we perceive how easy it is for a garment to become ridiculous. It might almost be said that every fashion is laughable in some respect. Only, when we are dealing with the fashion of the day, we are so accustomed to it that the garment seems, in our mind, to form one with the individual wearing it. We do not separate them in imagination. The idea no longer occurs to us to contrast the inert rigidity of the covering with the living suppleness of the object covered: consequently, the comic here remains in a latent condition. It will only succeed in emerging when the natural incompatibility is so deep-seated between the covering and the covered that even an immemorial association fails to cement this union: a case in point is our head and top hat. Suppose, however, some eccentric individual dresses himself in the fashion of former times our attention is immediately drawn to the clothes themselves; we absolutely distinguish them from the individual, we say that

the latter *is disguising himself,*—as though every article of clothing were not a disguise!—and the laughable aspect of fashion comes out of the shadow into the light.

Here we are beginning to catch a faint glimpse of the highly intricate difficulties raised by this problem of the comic. One of the reasons that must have given rise to many erroneous or unsatisfactory theories of laughter is that many things are comic [85] *de jure* without being comic *de facto,* the continuity of custom having deadened within them the comic quality. A sudden dissolution of continuity is needed, a break with fashion, for this quality to revive. Hence the impression that this dissolution of continuity is the parent of the comic, whereas all it does is to bring it to our notice. Hence, again, the explanation of laughter by *surprise, contrast,* etc., definitions which would equally apply to a host of cases in which we have no inclination whatever to laugh. The truth of the matter is far from being so simple. . . . [86]

Let us go on to society. As we are both in and of it, we cannot help treating it as a living being. Any image, then, suggestive of the notion of a society disguising itself, or of a social masquerade, so to speak, will be laughable. Now, such a notion is formed when we perceive anything inert or stereotyped, or simply ready-made, on the surface of living society. There we have rigidity over again, clashing with the inner suppleness of life. The ceremonial side of social life must, therefore, always include a latent comic element, which is only waiting for an opportunity to burst into full view. It might be said that ceremonies are to the social body what clothing is to the individual body: they owe their seriousness to the fact that they are identified, in our minds, with the serious object with which custom associates them, and when we isolate them in imagination, they forthwith lose their seriousness. For any ceremony, then, to become comic, it is enough that our attention be fixed on the ceremonial element in it, and that we neglect its matter, as philosophers say, and think only of its form. Every one knows how easily the comic spirit exercises its ingenuity on social actions of a stereotyped nature, from an ordinary prize-distribution to the solemn sitting of a court of justice. Any form or formula is a ready-made frame into which the comic element may be fitted. [89]

To sum up, then, we have one and the same effect, which assumes ever subtler forms as it passes from the idea of an artificial *mechanisation* of the human body, if such an expression is permissible, to that of any substitution whatsoever of the artificial for the natural. A less and less rigorous logic, that more and [91] more resembles the logic of dreamland, transfers the same relationship into higher and higher spheres, between increasingly immaterial terms, till in the end we find a mere administrative enactment occupying the same relation to a natural or moral law that a ready-made garment, for instance, does to the living body. We have now gone right to the end of the first of the three directions we had to follow. Let us turn to the second and see where it will lead us.

2. Our starting-point is again "something mechanical encrusted upon the living." Where did the comic come from in this case? It came from the fact that the living body became rigid, like a machine. Accordingly, it seemed to us that the living body ought to be the perfection of suppleness, the ever-alert activity of a principle always at work. But this activity would really belong to the soul rather than to the body. It would be the very flame of life, kindled within us by a higher principle and perceived through the body, as though through a glass. When we see only gracefulness and suppleness in the living body, it is because we disregard in it the elements of weight, of resistance, and, in a word, of matter; we forget its materiality and think only of its vitality, a vitality which we regard as derived from the very principle of intellectual and moral life. Let us suppose, however, that our attention is drawn to this material side of the body; that, so far from sharing in the lightness and subtlety of the principle with which it is animated, the body is no more in our eyes than a heavy and cumbersome vesture, a kind of irksome ballast which holds down to earth a soul eager to rise aloft. Then the body will become to the soul what, as we have just seen, the garment was to the body itself—inert matter dumped down [92] upon living energy. The impression of the comic will be produced as soon as we have a clear apprehension of this putting the one on the other. And we shall experience it most strongly when we are shown the soul *tantalised* by the needs of the body: on the one hand, the moral personality with its intelligently varied energy, and, on the other, the stupidly monotonous body, perpetually obstructing everything with its machine-like obstinacy. The more paltry and uniformly repeated these claims of the body, the more striking will be the result. But that is only a matter of degree, and the general law of these phenomena may be formulated as follows: *Any incident is comic that calls our attention to the physical in a person, when it is the moral side that is concerned.*

Why do we laugh at a public speaker who sneezes just at the most pathetic moment of his speech? Where lies the comic element in this sentence, taken from a funeral speech and quoted by a German philosopher: "He was virtuous and plump"? It lies in the fact that our attention is suddenly recalled from the soul to the body. Similar instances abound in daily life. . . . Now, we have a speaker whose most eloquent sentences are cut short by the twinges of a bad tooth; now, one of the characters who never begins to speak without stopping in the middle to complain of his shoes being too small, or his belt too tight, etc. *A person embarrassed by his body* is the image suggested to us in all these examples. . . . [93]

Consequently, there is a natural relationship, which we equally naturally recognise, between the two images we have been comparing with each other, the mind crystallising in certain grooves, and the body losing its elasticity through the influence of certain defects. Whether or not our attention be diverted from the matter to the manner, or from the moral to the physical, in both cases the same sort of impression is conveyed to our imagination; in both, then, the comic is of the same kind. Here, once more, it has been our aim to follow the natural trend of the movement of the imagination. This trend or direction, it may be remembered, was the second of those offered to us, starting from a central image. A third and final path remains unexplored, along which we will now proceed.

3. Let us then return, for the last time, to our central image—something mechanical encrusted on something living. Here, the living being under discussion was a human being, a person. A mechanical arrangement, on the other hand, is a thing. What, therefore, incited laughter, was the momentary transformation of a person into a thing, if one considers the image from this standpoint. Let us then pass from the exact idea of a machine to the vaguer one of a thing in general. We shall have a fresh series of laughable images which will be obtained by taking a blurred impression, so to speak, of the outlines of the former and will bring us to this new law: *We laugh every time a person gives us the impression of being a thing.*

We laugh at Sancho Panza tumbled into a bedquilt and tossed into the air like a football. We laugh [97] at Baron Munchausen turned into a cannon-ball and travelling through space. But certain tricks of circus clowns might afford a still more precise exemplification of the same law. True, we should have to eliminate the jokes, mere interpolations by the clown in his main theme, and keep in mind only the theme itself, that is to say, the divers attitudes, capers and movements which form the strictly "clownish" element in the clown's art. . . . [98] Let us, then, start with the games of a child, and follow the imperceptible process by which, as he grows himself, he makes his puppets grow, inspires them with life, and finally brings them to an ambiguous state in which, without ceasing to be puppets, they have yet become human beings. We thus obtain characters of a comedy type. And upon them we can test the truth of the law of which all our preceding analyses gave an inkling, a law in accordance with which we will define all broadly comic situations in general. *Any arrangement of acts and events is comic which gives us, in a single combination, the illusion of life and the distinct impression of a mechanical arrangement.*

1. *The Jack-in-the-box.*—As children we have all played with the little man who springs out of his box. You squeeze him flat, he jumps up again. Push him lower, and he shoots up still higher. Crush him down beneath the lid, and often he will send everything flying. It is hard to tell whether or not the toy itself is very ancient, but the kind of amusement it affords [105] belongs to all time. It is a struggle between two stubborn elements, one of which, being simply mechanical, generally ends by giving in to the other, which treats it as a plaything. A cat playing with a mouse, which from time to time she releases like a spring, only to pull it up short with a stroke of her paw, indulges in the same kind of amusement.

We will now pass on to the theatre, beginning with a Punch and Judy show. No sooner does the policeman put in an appearance on the stage than, naturally enough, he receives a blow which fells him. He springs to his feet, a second blow lays him flat. A repetition of the offence is followed by a repetition of the punishment. Up and down the constable flops and hops with the uniform rhythm of the bending and release of a spring, whilst the spectators laugh louder and louder.

Now, let us think of a spring that is rather of a moral type, an idea that is first expressed, then repressed, and then expressed again; a stream of words that bursts forth, is checked, and keeps on starting afresh. Once more we have the vision of one stubborn force, counteracted by another, equally pertinacious. This vision, however, will have discarded a portion of its materiality. No longer is it Punch and Judy that we are watching, but rather a real comedy. . . . [106]

Let us scrutinise more closely the image of the spring which is bent, released, and bent again. Let us disentangle its central element, and we shall hit upon one of the usual processes of classic comedy,— *repetition*.

Why is it there is something comic in the repetition of a word on the stage? No theory of the ludicrous seems to offer a satisfactory answer to this very simple question. Nor can an answer be found, so long as we look for the explanation of an amusing word or phrase in the phrase or word itself, apart from all it suggests to us. Nowhere will the usual method prove to be so inadequate as here. With the exception, however, of a few special instances to which we shall recur later, the repetition of a word is never laughable in itself. It makes us laugh only [107] because it symbolises a special play of moral elements, this play itself being the symbol of an altogether material diversion. It is the diversion of the cat with the mouse, the diversion of the child pushing back the Jack-in-the-box, time after time, to the bottom of his box—but in a refined and spiritualised form, transferred to the realm of feelings and ideas. Let us then state the law which we think defines the main comic varieties of word-repetition on the stage: *In a comic repetition of words we generally find two terms: a repressed feeling which goes off like a spring, and an idea that delights in repressing the feeling anew. . . .* [108]

2. *The Dancing-jack.*—There are innumerable comedies in which one of the characters thinks he is speaking and acting freely, and consequently, retains all the essentials of life, whereas, viewed from a certain standpoint, he appears as a mere toy in the hands of another, who is playing with him. The transition is easily made, from the dancing-jack which a child works with a string, to Géronte and Argante manipulated by Scapin. Listen to Scapin himself: "The *machine* is all there," and again: "Providence has brought them into my net," etc. Instinctively, and because one would rather be a cheat than be cheated, in imagination at all events, the spectator sides with the knaves; and for the rest of the time, like a child who has persuaded his playmate to lend him his doll, he takes hold of the strings himself and makes the marionette come and go on the stage as he pleases. But this latter condition is not indispensable; we can remain outside the pale of what is taking place if only we retain the distinct impression of a mechanical arrangement. This is what happens whenever one of the characters vacillates between two contrary opinions, each in turn appealing to him, as when Panurge asks Tom, Dick and Harry

whether or not he ought to get married. Note that, in such a case, a comic author is always careful to *personify* the two opposing decisions. For, if there is no spectator, there must at all events be actors to hold the strings.

All that is serious in life comes from our freedom. The feelings we have matured, the passions we have brooded over, the actions we have weighed, decided upon and carried through, in short, all that comes from us and is our very own, these are the things that give life its ofttimes dramatic and [111] generally grave aspect. What, then, is requisite to transform all this into a comedy? Merely to fancy that our seeming freedom conceals the strings of a dancing-jack, and that we are, as the poet says,

> . . . [sic] humble marionettes
> The wires of which are pulled by Fate.

So there is not a real, a serious, or even a dramatic scene that fancy cannot render comic by simply calling forth this image. Nor is there a game for which a wider field lies open.

3. *The Snow-ball.*—The farther we proceed in this investigation into the methods of comedy, the more clearly we see the part played by childhood's memories. These memories refer, perhaps, less to any special game than to the mechanical device of which that game is a particular instance. The same general device, moreover, may be met with in widely different games, just as the same operatic air is found in many different arrangements and variations. What is here of importance and is retained in the mind, what passes by imperceptible stages from the games of a child to those of a man, is the mental diagram, the skeleton outline of the combination, or, if you like, the abstract formula of which these games are particular illustrations. Take, for instance, the rolling snow-ball, which increases in size as it moves along. We might just as well think of toy soldiers standing behind one another. Push the first and it tumbles down on the second, this latter knocks down the third, and the state of things goes from bad to worse until they all lie prone on the floor. . . . [112]

And again the same arrangement occurs in certain scenes of Don Quixote; for instance, in the inn scene, where, by an extraordinary concatenation of circumstances, the mule-driver strikes Sancho, who belabours Maritornes, upon whom the innkeeper falls, etc. Finally, let us pass to the light comedy of to-day. Need we call to mind all the forms in which this same combination appears? There is one that is employed rather frequently. For instance a certain thing, say a letter, happens to be of supreme importance to a certain person and must be recovered at all costs. This thing, which always vanishes just when you think you have caught it, pervades the entire play, "rolling up" increasingly serious and unexpected incidents as it proceeds. All this is far more like a child's game than appears at first blush. Once more the effect produced is that of the snow-ball.

It is the characteristic of a mechanical combination to be generally *reversible*. A child is delighted when he sees the ball in a game of ninepins knocking down everything in its way and spreading havoc in all directions; he laughs louder than ever when the ball returns to its starting-point after twists and turns and waverings of every kind. In other words, the mechanism just described is laughable even when rectilinear, it is much more so on becoming circular and when every effort the player makes, by a fatal interaction of cause and effect, merely results in bringing it back to the same spot. Now, a considerable number of light comedies revolve round this idea. . . . [114]

Life presents itself to us as evolution in time and complexity in space. Regarded in time, it is the continuous evolution of a being ever growing older; it never goes backwards and never repeats itself. Considered in space, it exhibits certain coexisting elements so closely interdependent, so exclusively made for one another, that not one of them could, at the same time, belong to two different organisms: each living being is a closed system of phenomena, incapable of interfering with other systems. A continual change of aspect, the irreversibility of the order of phenomena, the perfect individuality of a perfectly self-contained series: such, then, are the outward characteristics—whether real or apparent is of little moment—which distinguish the living from the merely mechanical. Let us take the counterpart of each of these: we shall obtain three processes which might be called *repetition, inversion,* and *reciprocal interference of series*. Now, it is easy to see that these are also the methods of light comedy, and that no others are possible.

As a matter of fact, we could discover them, as ingredients of varying importance, in the composition of all the scenes we have just been considering, and, *a fortiori,* in the children's games, the mechanism of which they reproduce. The requisite analysis would, however, delay us too long, and it is more profitable to study them in their purity by taking fresh examples. Nothing could be easier, for it is in [118] their pure state that they are found, both in classic comedy and in contemporary plays.

1. *Repetition.*—Our present problem no longer deals, like the preceding one, with a word or a sentence repeated by an individual, but rather with a situation, that is, a combination of circumstances, which recurs several times in its original form and thus contrasts with the changing stream of life. Everyday experience supplies us with this type of the comic, though only in a rudimentary state. Thus, you meet a friend in the street whom you have not seen for an age; there is nothing comic in the situation. If, however, you meet him again the same day, and then a third and a fourth time, you may laugh at the "coincidence." Now, picture to yourself a series of imaginary events which affords a tolerably fair illusion of life, and within this ever-moving series imagine one and the same scene reproduced either by the same characters or by different ones: again you will have a coincidence, though a far more extraordinary one. Such are the repetitions produced on the stage. They are the more laughable in proportion as the scene repeated is more complex and more naturally introduced—two conditions which seem mutually exclusive, and which the play-writer must be clever enough to reconcile. . . . [119]

2. *Inversion.*—This second method has so much analogy with the first that we will merely define it without insisting on illustrations. Picture to yourself certain characters in a certain situation: if you reverse the situation and invert the *rôles,* you obtain a comic scene. The double rescue scene in *Le Voyage de M. Perrichon* belongs to this class. There is no necessity, however, for both the identical scenes to be played before us. We may be shown only one, provided the other is really in our minds. Thus, we laugh at the prisoner at the bar lecturing the magistrate; at a child presuming to teach its parents; in a word, at everything that comes under the heading of "topsyturvy-dom." . . . [121]

3. We have dwelt at considerable length on repetition and inversion; we now come to the *reciprocal interference of series.* This is a comic effect, the precise formula of which is very difficult to disentangle, by reason of the extraordinary variety of forms in which it appears on the stage. Perhaps it might be defined as follows: *A situation is invariably comic when it belongs simultaneously to two alto-*

gether independent series of events and is capable of being interpreted in two entirely different meanings at the same time. . . .[123]

We will not carry any further this analysis of the methods of light comedy. Whether we find reciprocal interference of series, inversion, or repetition, we see that the objective is always the same—to obtain what we have called a *mechanisation* of life. You take a set of actions and relations and repeat it as it is, or turn it upside down, or transfer it bodily to another set with which it partially coincides—all these being processes that consist in looking upon life as a repeating mechanism, with reversible action and interchangeable parts. Actual life is comedy just so far as it produces, in a natural fashion, actions of the same kind; consequently, just so far as it forgets itself, for were it always on the alert, it would be ever-changing continuity, irreversible progress, undivided unity. And so the ludicrous in events may be defined as absentmindedness in things, just as the ludicrous in an individual character always results from some fundamental absentmindedness in [126] the person, as we have already intimated and shall prove later on. This absentmindedness in events, however, is exceptional. Its results are slight. At any rate it is incurable, so that it is useless to laugh at it. Therefore the idea would never have occurred to any one of exaggerating absentmindedness, of converting it into a system, and creating an art for it, if laughter were not always a pleasure, and mankind did not pounce upon the slightest excuse for indulging in it. This is the real explanation of light comedy, which holds the same relation to actual life as does a jointed dancing-doll to a man walking,—being, as it is, an artificial exaggeration of a natural rigidity in things. The thread that binds it to actual life is a very fragile one. It is scarcely more than a game which, like all games, depends on a previously accepted convention. Comedy in character strikes far deeper roots into life. With that kind of comedy we shall deal more particularly in the final portion of our investigation. But we must first analyse a certain type of the comic, in many respects similar to that of light comedy: the comic in words.

There may be something artificial in making a special category for the comic in words, since most of the varieties of the comic that we have examined so far were produced through the medium of language. We must make a distinction, however, between the comic *expressed* and the comic *created* by language. The former could, if necessary, be translated from one language into another, though at

the cost of losing the greater portion of its significance when introduced into a fresh society different in manners, in literature, and above
all in association of ideas. But it is generally impossible to translate [127]
the latter. It owes its entire being to the structure of the sentence or
to the choice of the words. It does not set forth, by means of language,
special cases of absentmindedness in man or in events. It lays stress on
lapses of attention in language itself. In this case, it is language itself
that becomes comic.

Comic sayings, however, are not a matter of spontaneous generation; if we laugh at them, we are equally entitled to laugh at their
author. This latter condition, however, is not indispensable, since the
saying or expression has a comic virtue of its own. This is proved by
the fact that we find it very difficult, in the majority of these cases, to
say whom we are laughing at, although at times we have a dim, vague
feeling that there is some one in the background.

Moreover, the person implicated is not always the speaker. Here
it seems as though we should draw an important distinction between
the *witty* (*spirituel*) and the *comic*. A word is said to be comic when
it makes us laugh at the person who utters it, and witty when it makes
us laugh either at a third party or at ourselves. But in most cases we
can hardly make up our minds whether the word is comic or witty.
All that we can say is that it is laughable. . . . [128]

1. Inadvertently to say or do what we have no intention of saying
or doing, as a result of inelasticity or momentum, is, as we are aware,
one of the main sources of the comic. Thus, absentmindedness is
essentially laughable, and so we laugh at anything rigid, ready-made,
mechanical in gesture, attitude and even facial expression. Do we find
this kind of rigidity in language also? No doubt we do, since language
contains ready-made formulas and stereotyped phrases. The man who
always expressed himself in such terms would invariably be comic.
But if an isolated phrase is to be comic in itself, when once separated
from the person who utters it, it must be something more than ready-
made, it must bear within itself some sign which tells us, beyond the
possibility of doubt, that it was uttered automatically. This can only
happen when the phrase embodies some evident absurdity, either a
palpable error or a contradiction in terms. Hence the following general rule: *A comic meaning is invariably obtained when an absurd
idea is fitted into a well-established phrase-form.* . . . [133]

2. "We laugh if our attention is diverted to the physical in a

person when it is the moral that is in question," is a law we laid down in the first part of this work. Let us apply it to language. Most words might be said to have a *physical* and a *moral* meaning, according as they are interpreted literally or figuratively. Every word, indeed, begins by denoting a concrete object or a material action; but by degrees the meaning of the word is refined into an abstract relation or a pure idea. If then the above law holds good here, it should be stated as follows: "*A comic effect is obtained whenever we pretend to take literally an expression which was used figuratively*"; or, "*Once our attention is fixed on the material aspect of a metaphor the idea expressed becomes comic.*" . . . [135]

We said that repetition is the favourite method of classic comedy. It consists in so arranging events that a scene is reproduced either between the same characters under fresh circumstances or between fresh characters under the same circumstances. Thus we have, repeated by lackeys in less dignified language, a scene already played by their masters. Now, imagine ideas expressed in suitable style and thus placed in the setting of their natural environment. If you think of some arrangement whereby [139] they are transferred to fresh surroundings, while maintaining their mutual relations, or, in other words, if you can induce them to express themselves in an altogether different style and to transpose themselves into another key—you will have language itself playing a comedy—language itself made comic. There will be no need, moreover, actually to set before us both expressions of the same ideas, the transposed expression and the natural one. For we are acquainted with the natural one—the one which we should have chosen instinctively. So it will be enough if the effort of comic invention bears on the other, and on the other alone. No sooner is the second set before us than we spontaneously supply the first. Hence the following general rule: *A comic effect is always obtainable by transposing the natural expression of an idea into another key.*

The means of transposition are so many and varied, language affords so rich a continuity of themes and the comic is here capable of passing through so great a number of stages, from the most insipid buffoonery up to the loftiest forms of humour and irony, that we shall forego the attempt to make out a complete list. Having stated the rule, we will simply, here and there, verify its main applications.

In the first place, we may distinguish two keys at the extreme ends of the scale, the solemn and the familiar. The most obvious effects are obtained by merely transposing the one into the other, which thus provides us with two opposite currents of comic fancy.

Transpose the solemn into the familiar and the result is parody. The effect of parody, thus defined, extends to instances in which the idea expressed in familiar terms is one that, if only in deference to [140] custom, ought to be pitched in another key. . . . [141]

To sum up, whether a character is good or bad is of little moment; granted he is unsociable, he is capable of becoming comic. We now see that the seriousness of the case is of no importance either: whether serious or trifling, it is still capable of making us laugh, provided that care be taken not to arouse our emotions. Unsociability in the performer and [154] insensibility in the spectator—such, in a word, are the two essential conditions. There is a third, implicit in the other two, which so far it has been the aim of our analysis to bring out.

This third condition is automatism. We have pointed it out from the outset of this work, continually drawing attention to the following point: what is essentially laughable is what is done automatically. In a vice, even in a virtue, the comic is that element by which the person unwittingly betrays himself—the involuntary gesture or the unconscious remark. . . . [155]

And so we come back, by a roundabout way, to the double conclusion we reached in the course of our investigations. On the one hand, a person is never ridiculous except through some mental attribute resembling absentmindedness, through something that lives upon him without forming part of his organism, after the fashion of a parasite; that is the reason this state of mind is observable from without and capable of being corrected. But, on the other hand, just because laughter aims at correcting, it is expedient that the correction should reach as great a number of persons as possible. This is the reason comic observation instinctively proceeds to what is general. It chooses such peculiarities as admit of being reproduced, and consequently are not indissolubly bound up with the individuality of a single person,—a possibly common sort of uncommonness, so to say, —peculiarities that are held in common. By transferring them to the stage, it creates works which doubtless belong to art in that their only visible aim is to please, but which will be found to contrast with other works of art by reason of their generality, and also of their scarcely confessed or scarcely conscious intention to correct and instruct. So we were probably right in saying that comedy lies midway between art and life. It is not disinterested as genuine art is. By organising laughter, comedy accepts social life as a natural environment; it even obeys an impulse [170] of social life. And in this respect it turns its back upon art, which is a breaking away from society and a return to pure nature. . . . [171] *Comic absurdity is of the same nature as that of dreams.* [180]

The behaviour of the intellect in a dream is exactly what we have just been describing. The mind, enamoured of itself, now seeks in the outer world nothing more than a pretext for realising its imaginations. A confused murmur of sounds still reaches the ear, colours enter the field of vision, the senses are not completely shut in. But the dreamer, instead of appealing to the whole of his recollections for the interpretation of what his senses perceive, makes use of what he perceives to give substance to the particular recollection he favours: thus, according to the mood of the dreamer and the idea that fills his imagination at the time, a gust of wind blowing down the chimney becomes the howl of a wild beast or a tuneful melody. Such is the ordinary mechanism of illusion in dreams.

Now, if comic illusion is similar to dream illusion, if the logic of the comic is the logic of dreams, we may expect to discover in the logic of the laughable all the peculiarities of dream logic. Here, again, we shall find an illustration of the law with which we are well acquainted: given one form of the laughable, other forms that are lacking in the same comic essence become laughable from their outward resemblance to the first. Indeed, it is not difficult to see that any *play of ideas* may afford us amusement if only it bring back to mind, more or less distinctly, the play of dreamland.

We shall first call attention to a certain general relaxation of the rules of reasoning. The reasonings at which we laugh are those we know to be false, but which we might accept as true were we to hear them in a dream. They counterfeit true reasoning just sufficiently to deceive a mind dropping off to sleep. There is still an element of logic in them, if you will, but it is a logic lacking in tension and, for that [181] very reason, affording us relief from intellectual effort. Many "witticisms" are reasonings of this kind, considerably abridged reasonings, of which we are given only the beginning and the end. Such play upon ideas evolves in the direction of a play upon words in proportion as the relations set up between the ideas become more superficial: gradually we come to take no account of the meaning of the words we hear, but only of their sound. It might be instructive to compare with dreams certain comic scenes in which one of the characters systematically repeats in a nonsensical fashion what another character whispers in his ear. . . . [182]

When the comic character automatically follows up his idea, he ultimately thinks, speaks and acts as though he were dreaming. Now, a dream is a relaxation. To remain in touch with things and men, to see nothing but what is existent and think nothing but what is consistent, demands a continuous effort of intellectual tension. This effort is common sense. And to remain sensible is, indeed, to remain at work. But to detach oneself from things and yet continue to perceive images, to break away from logic and yet continue to string together ideas, is to indulge in play or, if you prefer, in *dolce far niente.* So, comic absurdity gives us from the outset the impression [186] of playing with ideas. Our first impulse is to join in the game. That relieves us from the strain of thinking.

Now, the same might be said of the other forms of the laughable. Deep-rooted in the comic, there is always a tendency, we said, to take the line of least resistance, generally that of habit. The comic character no longer tries to be ceaselessly adapting and readapting himself to the society of which he is a member. He slackens in the attention that is due to life. He more or less resembles the absentminded. Maybe his will is here even more concerned than his intellect, and there is not so much a want of attention as a lack of tension: still, in some way or another, he is *absent,* away from his work, taking it easy. He abandons social convention, as indeed—in the case we have just been considering —he abandoned logic. Here, too, our first impulse is to accept the invitation to take it easy. For a short time, at all events, we join in the game. And that relieves us from the strain of living.

But we rest only for a short time. The sympathy that is capable of entering into the impression of the comic is a very fleeting one. It also comes from a lapse in attention. Thus, a stern father may at times forget himself and join in some prank his child is playing, only to check himself at once in order to correct it. . . . [187]

Here, as elsewhere, nature has utilised evil with a view to good. It is more especially the good that has engaged our attention throughout this work. We have seen that the more society improves, the more plastic is the adaptability it obtains from its members; while the greater the tendency towards increasing stability below, the more does it force to the surface the disturbing elements inseparable from so vast a bulk; and thus laughter performs a useful function by emphasising the form of these significant undulations.

Such is also the truceless warfare of the waves on the surface of the sea, whilst profound peace reigns in the depths below. The billows clash and collide with each other, as they strive to find their level. A fringe of snow-white foam, feathery and frolicsome, follows their changing outlines. From time to time, the receding wave leaves behind a remnant of foam on the sandy beach. The child, who plays hard by, picks up a handful, and, the next moment, is astonished to find that nothing remains in his grasp but a few drops of water, water that is far more brackish, far more bitter, than that of the wave which brought it. Laughter comes into being in the self-same fashion. [189] It indicates a slight revolt on the surface of social life. It instantly adopts the changing forms of the disturbance. It, also, is a froth with a saline base. Like froth, it sparkles. It is gaiety itself. But the philosopher who gathers a handful to taste may find that the substance is scanty, and the after-taste bitter. [190]

Laughter

Max Beerbohm, from "Laughter," in *And Even Now* (New York, E. P. Dutton & Co., Inc., 1921).

M. BERGSON, in his well-known essay on this theme, says ... [sic] well, he says many things; but none of these, though I have just read them, do I clearly remember, nor am I sure that in the act of reading I understood any of them. That is the worst of these fashionable philosophers—or rather, the worst of me. Somehow I never manage to read them till they are just going out of fashion, and even then I don't seem able to cope with them. About twelve years ago, when every one suddenly talked to me about Pragmatism and William James, I found myself moved by a dull but irresistible impulse to try Schopenhauer, of whom, years before that, I had heard that he was the easiest reading in the world, and the most exciting and amusing. I wrestled with Schopenhauer for a day or so, in vain. Time passed; M. Bergson appeared 'and for his hour was lord of the ascendant'; I tardily tackled William James. I bore in mind, as I approached him, the testimonials that had been lavished on him by all my friends. Alas, I was insensible to [303] his thrillingness. His gaiety did not make me gay. His crystal clarity confused me dreadfully. I could make nothing of William James. And now, in the fullness of time, I have been floored by M. Bergson.

It distresses me, this failure to keep pace with the leaders of thought as they pass into oblivion. It makes me wonder whether I am, after all, an absolute fool. Yet surely I am not that. Tell me of a man or a woman, a place or an event, real or fictitious: surely you will find me a fairly intelligent listener. Any such narrative will present to me some image, and will stir me to not altogether fatuous thoughts. Come to me in some grievous difficulty: I will talk to you like a father, even like a lawyer. I'll be hanged if I haven't a certain mellow wisdom. But if you are by way of weaving theories as to the nature of things in general, and if you want to try those theories on some one who will luminously confirm them or powerfully rend them, I must, with a hang-dog air, warn you that I am not your man. I suffer from a strong suspicion that things in general cannot be accounted for through any formula or set of formulae, and that any one philosophy, howsoever new, is no better than another. That is in itself a sort of philosophy, and I suspect it accordingly; but it has for me the merit of being the only one I can make head or tail of. If you try to expound any other philosophic system to me, you will find not merely [304] that I can detect no flaw in it (except the one great flaw just suggested), but also that I haven't, after a minute or two, the vaguest notion of what you are driving at. 'Very well,' you say, 'instead of trying to explain all things all at once, I will explain some little, simple, single thing.' It was for sake of such shorn lambs as myself, doubtless, that M. Bergson sat down and wrote about—Laughter. But I have profited by his kindness no more than if he had been treating of the Cosmos. I cannot tread even a limited space of air. I have a gross satisfaction in the crude fact of being on hard ground again, and I utter a coarse peal of —Laughter.

At least, I say I do so. In point of fact, I have merely smiled. Twenty years ago, ten years ago, I should have laughed, and have professed to you that I had merely smiled. A very young man is not content to be very young, nor even a young man to be young: he wants to share the dignity of his elders. There is no dignity in laughter, there is much of it in smiles. Laughter is but a joyous surrender, smiles give token of mature criticism. It may be that in the early ages of this world there was far more laughter than is to be heard now, and that aeons hence laughter will be obsolete, and smiles universal—every one, always, mildly, slightly, smiling. But it is less useful to speculate as to mankind's past and future than to observe [305] men. And you will have observed with me in the club-room that young men at most times look solemn, whereas old men or men of middle age mostly smile; and also that those young men do often laugh loud and long among themselves, while we others—the gayest and best of us in the most favourable circumstances—seldom achieve more than our habitual act of smiling. Does the sound of that laughter jar on us? Do we liken it to the crackling of thorns under a pot? Let us do so. There is no cheerier sound. But let us not assume it to be the laughter of fools because we sit quiet. It is absurd to disapprove of what one envies, or to wish a good thing were no more because it has passed out of our possession.

But (it seems that I must begin every paragraph by questioning the sincerity of what I have just said) *has* the gift of laughter been withdrawn from me? I protest that I do still, at the age of forty-seven, laugh often and loud and long. But not, I believe, so long and loud and often as in my less smiling youth. And I am proud, nowadays, of laughing, and grateful to any one who makes me laugh. That is a bad sign. I no longer take laughter as a matter of course. I realise, even after reading M. Bergson on it, how good a thing it is. I am qualified to praise it.

As to what is most precious among the accessories to the world we live in, different men hold different [306] opinions. There are people whom the sea depresses, whom mountains exhilarate. Personally, I want the sea always—some not populous edge of it for choice; and with it sunshine, and wine, and a little music. My friend on the mountain yonder is of tougher fibre and sterner outlook, disapproves of the sea's laxity and instability, has no ear for music and no palate for the grape, and regards the sun as a rather enervating institution, like central heating in a house. What he likes is a grey day and the wind in his face; crags at a great altitude; and a flask of whisky. Yet I think that even he, if we were trying to determine from what inner sources mankind derives the greatest pleasure in life, would agree with me that only the emotion of love takes higher rank than the emotion of laughter. Both these emotions are partly mental, partly physical. It is said that the mental symptoms of love are wholly physical in origin. They are not the less ethereal for that. The physical sensations of laughter, on the other hand, are reached by a process whose starting-point is in the mind. They are not the less 'gloriously of our clay.' There is laughter that goes so far as to lose all touch with its motive, and to exist only, grossly, in itself. This is laughter at its best. A man to whom such laughter has often been granted may happen to die in a work-house. No matter. I will not admit that he has failed in [307] life. Another man, who has never laughed thus, may be buried in Westminster Abbey, leaving more than a million pounds overhead. What then? I regard him as a failure.

Nor does it seem to me to matter one jot how such laughter is achieved. Humour may rollick on high planes of fantasy or in depths of silliness. To many people it appeals only from those depths. If it appeal to them irresistibly, they are more enviable than those who are sensitive only to the finer kind of joke and not so sensitive as to be mastered and dissolved by it. Laughter is a thing to be rated according to its own intensity.

Many years ago I wrote an essay in which I poured scorn on the fun purveyed by the music halls, and on the great public for which that fun was quite good enough. I take that callow scorn back. I fancy that the fun itself was better than it seemed to me, and might not have displeased me if it had been wafted to me in private, in presence of a few friends. A public crowd, because of a lack of broad impersonal humanity in me, rather insulates than absorbs me. Amidst the guffaws of a thousand strangers I become unnaturally grave. If these people were the entertainment, and I the audience, I should be sympathetic enough. But to be one of them is a position that drives me spiritually aloof. Also, there is to me something rather dreary in the notion of going anywhere [308] for the specific purpose of being amused. I prefer that laughter shall take me unawares. Only so can it master and dissolve me. And in this respect, at any rate, I am not peculiar. In music halls and such places, you may hear loud laughter, but—not see silent laughter, not see strong men weak, helpless, suffering, gradually convalescent, dangerously relapsing. Laughter at its greatest and best is not there.

To such laughter nothing is more propitious than an occasion that demands gravity. To have good reason for not laughing is one of the surest aids. Laughter rejoices in bonds. If music halls were schoolrooms for us, and the comedians were our schoolmasters, how much less talent would be needed for giving us how much more joy! Even in private and accidental intercourse, few are the men whose humour can reduce us, be we never so susceptible, to paroxysms of mirth. I will wager that nine tenths of the world's best laughter is laughter *at*, not *with*. And it is the people set in authority over us that touch most surely our sense of the ridiculous. Freedom is a good thing, but we lose through it golden moments. The schoolmaster to his pupils, the monarch to his courtiers, the editor to his staff—how priceless they are! Reverence is a good thing, and part of its value is that the more we revere a man, the more sharply are we struck by anything in him (and there is [309] always much) that is incongruous with his greatness. And herein lies one of the reasons why as we grow older we laugh less. The men we esteemed so great are gathered to their fathers. Some of our coevals may, for aught we know, be very great, but good heavens! we can't esteem *them* so. . . . [310]

Wit and Its Relation to the Unconscious

◆◆◆ SIGMUND FREUD

Sigmund Freud, from *Wit and Its Relation to the Unconscious* [1905], in
The Basic Writings of Sigmund Freud, tr. A. A. Brill (New York,
Random House, Inc., 1938).

ROUGHLY SPEAKING, one can distinguish three general stages
in the formation of the dream: first, the transference of the conscious
day remnants into the unconscious, a transference in which the conditions of the sleeping state [749] must co-operate; secondly, the actual
dream-work in the unconscious; and thirdly, the regression of the
elaborated dream material to the region of perception, whereby the
dream becomes conscious.

The forces participating in the dream-formation may be recognized as the following: the wish to sleep; the sum of cathexis which
still clings to the day remnants after the depression brought about by
the state of sleep; the psychic energy of the unconscious wish forming
the dream; and the opposing force of the *"censorship,"* which exercises
its authority in our waking state, and is not entirely abolished during
sleep. The task of dream-formation is, above all, to overcome the inhibition of the censorship, and it is just this task that is fulfilled by
the displacement of the psychic energy within the material of the
dream-thoughts.

Now we recall what caused us to think of the dream while investigating wit. We found that the character and activity of wit were
bound up in certain forms of expression and technical means, among
which the various forms of condensation, displacement, and indirect
representation were the most conspicuous. But the processes which
led to the same results—condensation, displacement, and indirect expression—we learned to know as peculiarities of dream-work. Does
not this analogy almost force us to the conclusion that wit-work and
dream-work must be identical at least in one essential point? I believe
that the dream-work lies revealed before us in its most important

characters, but in wit we find obscured just that portion of the psychic processes which we may compare with the dream-work, namely, the process of wit-formation in the first person. Shall we not yield to the temptation to construct this process according to the analogy of dream-formation? Some of the characteristics of dreams are so foreign to wit, that that part of the dream-work corresponding to them cannot be carried over to the wit-formation. The regression of the stream of thought to perception is certainly lacking as far as wit is concerned. However, the other two stages of dream-formation, the sinking of a foreconscious thought into the unconscious, and the unconscious elaboration, would give us exactly the result which we might observe in wit if we assumed this process in wit-formation. Let us decide to assume that this is the proceeding of wit-formation in the case of the first person. *A foreconscious thought is left for a moment to unconscious elaboration and the results are forthwith grasped by the conscious perception. . . .* [750]

We have approached the problems of the comic in an unusual manner. It appeared to us that wit, which is usually regarded as a sub-species of the comic, offered enough peculiarities to warrant our taking it directly under consideration, and thus it came about that we avoided discussing its relation to the more comprehensive category of the comic as long as it was possible to do so, yet we did not proceed without picking up on the way some hints that might be valuable for studying the comic. We found it easy to ascertain that the comic differs from wit in its social behavior. The comic is content with only two persons, one who finds the comical, and one in whom it is found. The third person to whom the comical may be imparted reinforces the comic process, but adds nothing new to it. In wit, however, this third person is indispensable for the completion of the pleasure-bearing process, while the second person may be omitted, especially when it is not a question of aggressive wit with a tendency. Wit is made, while the comical is found; it is found first of all in persons, and only later by transference may be seen also in objects, situations, and the like. We know, too, in the case of wit that it is not a strange person's, but one's own mental processes that contain the sources for the production of pleasure. In addition, we have heard that wit occasionally reopens inaccessible sources of the comic, and that the comic often serves wit as a façade to replace the fore-pleasure usually produced by the above described technique. All of this does not really point to a very simple relationship between wit and the comic. On the other hand, the problems of the comic have shown themselves to be so complicated, and have until now so successfully defied all attempts made by the philosophers to solve them, that we have not been able to justify the expectation of mastering it by a sudden stroke, so to speak, even if we approach it along the paths of wit. Incidentally we came provided with an instrument for investigating wit that had not yet been made use of by others; namely, the knowledge of dream-work. We have no similar advantage at our disposal for comprehending [762] the comic, and we may therefore expect that we shall learn nothing about the nature of the comic other than that which we have already become aware of in wit; in so far as wit belongs to the comic and retains certain features of the same, unchanged or modified in its own nature. . . . [763]

The comical appears primarily as an unintentional discovery in the social relations of human beings. It is found in persons—that is, in their movements, shapes, actions, and characteristic traits. In the beginning it is found probably only in their physical peculiarities and later on in their mental qualities, especially in the expression of the latter. Even animals and inanimate objects become comical as the result of a widely used method of personification. However, the comical can be considered apart from the person in whom it is found, if the conditions under which a person becomes comical can be discerned. Thus arises the comical situation, and this knowledge enables us to make a person comical at will by putting him into situations in which the conditions necessary for the comic are bound up with his actions. The discovery that it is in our power to make another person comical opens the way to unsuspected gains in comic pleasure, and forms the foundation of a highly developed technique. It is also possible to make one's self just as comical as others. The means which serve to make a person comical are transference into comic situations, imitations, disguise, unmasking, caricature, parody, travesty, and the like. It is quite evident that these techniques may enter into the service of hostile or aggressive tendencies. A person may be made comical in order to render him contemptible or in order to deprive him of his claims to dignity and authority. But even if such a purpose were regularly at the bottom of all attempts to make a person comical this need not necessarily be the meaning of the spontaneous comic.

As a result of this superficial survey of the manifestations of the comic we can readily see that the comic originates from widespread

sources, and that conditions so specialized as those found in the naïve cannot be expected in the case of the comic. In order to get a clue to the conditions [768] that are applicable to the comic the selection of the first example is most important. We will examine first the comic movement because we remember that the most primitive stage performance, the pantomime, uses this means to make us laugh. The answer to the question, "Why do we laugh at the actions of the clowns?", would be that their actions appear to us immoderate and inappropriate; that is, we really laugh over the excessive expenditure of energy. Let us look for the same condition outside of the manufactured comic, that is, under circumstances where it may unintentionally be found. The child's motions do not appear to us comical, even if he jumps and fidgets, but it is comical to see a little boy or girl follow with the tongue the movement of his pen-holder when he is trying to master the art of writing; we see in these additional motions a superfluous expenditure of energy which under similar conditions we save. In the same way we find it comical to see unnecessary motions or even marked exaggeration of expressive motions in adults. Among the genuinely comic cases we might mention the motions made by the bowler after he has released the ball while he is following its course as though he were still able to control it. All grimaces which exaggerate the normal expression of the emotions are comical, even if they are involuntary, as in the case of persons suffering from St. Vitus' dance (chorea). The impassioned movements of a modern orchestra leader will appear comical to every unmusical person, who cannot understand why they are necessary. Indeed, the comic element found in bodily shapes and physiognomy is a branch of the comic of motion, in that they are conceived as if they were the result of motion that has been carried too far or motion that is purposeless. Wide exposed eyes, a crook-shaped nose bent towards the mouth, handle-like ears, a hunch back, and all similar physical defects probably produce a comical impression only in so far as the movements that would be necessary to produce these features are imagined, whereby the nose and other parts of the body are pictured as more movable than they actually are. It is certainly comical if some one can "wiggle his ears," and it would undoubtedly be a great deal more comical if he could raise and lower his nose. A large part of the comical impression that animals make upon us is due to the fact that we perceive in them movements which we cannot imitate.
. . . [769]

Human beings are not satisfied to enjoy the comic as they encounter it in life, but they aim to produce it intentionally. Thus, we discover more of the nature of the comic by studying the methods employed in producing the comic. Above all one can produce comical elements in one's personality for the amusement of others, by making one's self appear awkward or stupid. One then produces the comic exactly as if one were really so, by complying with the condition of comparison which leads to the difference of expenditure; but one does not make himself laughable or contemptible through this; indeed, under certain circumstances one can even secure admiration. The feeling of superiority does not come into existence in the other when he knows that the actor is only shamming, and this furnishes us a good new proof that the comic is independent in principle of the feeling of superiority.

To make some one else comical, the method most commonly employed is to transfer him into situations wherein he becomes comical regardless of his personal qualities, as a result of human dependence upon external circumstances, especially social factors; in other words, some one resorts to the comical situation. This transferring into a comic situation may be real as in practical jokes, such as placing the foot in front of one so that he falls like a clumsy person, or making some one appear stupid by utilizing his credulity to make him believe some nonsense, etc., or it can be feigned by means of speech or play. It is a good aid in aggression, in the service of which, production of the comic is wont to place itself, in order that the comic pleasure may be independent of the reality of the comic situation; thus every person is really defenseless against being made comical.

But there are still other means of making one comical which deserve special attention and which in part also show new sources of comic pleasure. *Imitation,* for example, belongs here; it accords the hearer an extraordinary amount of pleasure and makes its subject comical, even if it still keeps away from the exaggeration of caricature. It is much easier to fathom the comic effect of caricature than that of simple imitation. Caricature, parody and travesty like their practical counterpart unmasking, are directed against persons and objects who command authority and respect and who are exalted in some sense. These are procedures which [776] tend to degrade. In the transferred psychic sense, the exalted is equivalent to something great and I want to make the statement, or more accurately to repeat the statement, that psychic greatness like somatic greatness is exhibited by means of an increased expenditure. It needs little observation to ascertain that when I speak of the exalted I give a different innervation to my voice, I change my facial expression, and attempt to bring my entire bearing as it were into complete accord with the dignity of that which I present. I impose upon myself a dignified restriction, not much different than if I were coming into the presence of an illustrious personage, monarch, or prince of science. I can scarcely err when I assume that this added innervation of conceptual mimicry corresponds to an increased expenditure. The third case of such an added expenditure I readily find when I indulge in abstract trains of thought instead of in the concrete and plastic ideas. If I can now imagine that the mentioned processes for degrading the illustrious are quite ordinary, that during their activity I need not be on my guard and in whose ideal presence I may, to use a military formula, put myself "at ease," all that saves me the added expenditure of dignified restriction. Moreover, the comparison of this manner of presentation instigated by empathy with the manner of presentation to which I have been hitherto accustomed, which seeks to present itself at the same time, again produces a difference in expenditure which can be discharged through laughter.

As is known, caricature brings about the degradation by rendering prominent one feature, comic in itself, from the entire picture of the exalted object, a feature which would be overlooked if viewed with the entire picture. Only by isolating this feature can the comic effect be obtained which spreads in our memory over the whole picture. This has, however, this condition; the presence of the exalted element must not force us into a disposition of reverence. Where such a comical feature is really lacking, caricature then unhesitatingly creates it by exaggerating one that is not comical in itself. It is again characteristic of the origin of comic pleasure that the effect of the caricature is not essentially impaired through such a falsifying of reality. . . . [777]

Two observations obtrude themselves upon the observer who reviews even only superficially the origin of comic pleasure from the difference of expenditure; first, that there are cases in which the comic appears regularly and as if necessarily; and, in contrast to these cases, others in which this depends on the conditions of the case and on the viewpoint of the observer. But secondly, that unusually large differences very often triumph over unfavorable conditions, so that the comic feeling originates in spite of it. In reference to the first point one may set up two classes, the inevitable comic and the accidental comic, although one will have to be prepared from the beginning to find exceptions in the first class to the inevitableness of the comic. It would be tempting to follow the conditions which are essential to each class.

What is important in the second class are the conditions, of which one may be designated as the "isolation" of the comic case. A closer analysis reveals something like the following relations:

a) The favorable condition for the origin of comic pleasure is brought about by a general happy disposition in which "one is in the mood for laughing." In happy toxic states almost everything seems comic, which probably results from a comparison with the expenditure in normal conditions. For wit, the comic, and all similar methods of gaining pleasure from the psychic activities, are nothing but ways to regain this happy state—euphoria—from one single point, when it does not exist as a general disposition of the psyche.

b) A similar favorable condition is produced by the expectation of the comic or by putting one's self in the right mood for comic pleasure. Hence when the intention to make things comical exists and when this feeling is shared by others, the differences required are so slight that they probably would have been overlooked had they been experienced in unpremeditated occurrences. He who decides to attend a comic lecture or a farce at the theater is indebted to this intention for laughing over things which in his everyday life would hardly produce in him a comic effect. He finally laughs at the recollection of having laughed, at the expectation of laughing, and at the appearance of the one who is to present the comic, even before the latter makes the attempt to make him laugh. It is for this reason that people later admit that they are ashamed of that which made them laugh at the theater.

c) Unfavorable conditions for the comic result from the kind of psychic activity which may occupy the individual at the moment. Imaginative or mental activity tending towards serious aims disturbs the [790] discharging capacity of the cathexis which the activity needs for its own displacements, so that only unexpected and great differences of expenditure can break through to form comic pleasure. All manner of mental processes far enough removed from the obvious to cause a suspension of ideational mimicry are unfavorable to the comic; in abstract contemplation there is hardly any room left for the comic, except when this form of thinking is suddenly interrupted.

d) The occasion for releasing comic pleasure vanishes when the attention is directly fixed on the comparison which is capable of giving rise to the comic. Under such circumstances the comic force is lost from that which is otherwise sure to produce a comic effect. A movement or a mental activity cannot become comical to him whose interest is fixed at the time of comparing this movement with a standard which distinctly presents itself to him. Thus the examiner does not see the comical in the nonsense produced by the student in his ignorance; he is simply annoyed by it, whereas the offender's classmates who are more interested in his chances of passing the examination than in what he knows, laugh heartily over the same nonsense. The teacher of dancing or gymnastics seldom has any eyes for the comic movements of his pupils, and the preacher entirely loses sight of humanity's defects of character, which the writer of comedy brings out with so much effect. The comic process cannot stand examination by the attention, it must be able to proceed absolutely unnoticed in a manner similar to wit. But for good reasons, it would contradict the nomenclature of "conscious processes" which I have used in *The Interpretation of Dreams,* if one wished to call it of necessity *unconscious.* It rather belongs to the *foreconscious,* and one may use the fitting name "automatic" for all those processes which are enacted in the foreconscious, and dispense with the attention cathexis which is connected with consciousness. The process of comparison of the expenditures must remain automatic if it is to produce comic pleasure.

e) It is exceedingly disturbing to the comic if the case from which it originates gives rise at the same time to a marked release of affect. The discharge of the affective difference is then as a rule excluded. Affects, disposition, and the attitude of the individual in occasional cases make it clear that the comic comes or goes with the viewpoint of the individual person; that only in exceptional cases is there an absolute comic. The dependence or relativity of the comic is therefore much greater than that of wit, which never happens but is regularly made, and at its production one may already give attention to the conditions under which it finds acceptance. But affective development is the most intensive of the conditions which disturb the comic, the significance of which is well known. [1] It is, therefore, said that the comic feeling comes most in tolerably indifferent [791] cases which

---

[1] "You may well laugh, that no longer concerns you."

evince no strong feelings or interests. Nevertheless, it is just in cases with affective release that one may witness the production of a particularly strong expenditure-difference in the automatism of discharge. When Colonel Butler answers Octavio's admonitions with "bitter laughter," exclaiming:

"Thanks from the house of Austria!"

his bitterness has thus not prevented the laughter which results from the recollection of the disappointment which he believes he has experienced; and on the other hand, the magnitude of this disappointment could not have been more impressively depicted by the poet than by showing it capable of effecting laughter in the midst of the storm of unchained affects. It is my belief that this explanation may be applicable in all cases in which laughing occurs on other than pleasurable occasions, and in conjunction with exceedingly painful or tense affects.

f) If we also mention that the development of the comic pleasure can be promoted by means of any other pleasurable addition to the case which acts like a sort of contact-effect (after the manner of the fore-pleasure principle in the tendency-wit), then we have discussed surely not all the conditions of comic pleasure, yet enough of them to serve our purpose. We then see that for these conditions, as well as for the inconstancy and dependence of the comic effect, no other assumption so easily lends itself as this one which traces the comic pleasure from the discharge of a difference, which under many conditions can be diverted to a different use than discharge.

It still remains to give a thorough consideration of the comic of the sexual and the obscene, but we shall only skim over it with a few observations. Here, too, we shall take the act of exposing one's body as the starting-point. An accidental exposure produces a comical effect on us, because we compare the ease with which we attained the enjoyment of this view with the great expenditure otherwise necessary for the attainment of this object. The case thus comes nearer to the naïve-comic, but it is simpler than the latter. In every case of exhibitionism in which we are made spectators—or, in the case of the smutty joke hearers—we play the part of the third person, and the person exposed is made comical. We have heard that it is the purpose of wit to replace obscenity and in this manner to reopen a source of comic pleasure that has been lost. On the contrary, spying out an exposure, forms no example of the comic for the one spying, because the effort he exerts thereby abrogates the condition of comic pleasure; the only thing remaining is the sexual pleasure in what is seen. If the peeper relates to another what he has seen, the person looked at again becomes comical, because the viewpoint that predominates is that the expenditure was omitted which would have been necessary for [792] the concealment of the private parts. At all events, the sphere of the sexual or obscene offers the richest opportunities for gaining comic pleasure beside the pleasurable sexual stimulation, as it exposes the person's dependence on his physical needs (degradation) or it can uncover behind the spiritual love the physical demands of the same (unmasking).... [793]

One reaches some solution of humoristic displacement if one considers it in the light of a defense process. The defense processes are the psychic correlates of the flight reflex and follow the task of guarding against the origin of pain from inner sources. In fulfilling this task they serve the psychic occurrence as an automatic adjustment, which, to be sure, finally proves harmful and, therefore, must be subjected to the control of the conscious thinking. A definite form of this defense, the failure of repression, I have demonstrated as the effective mechanism in the origin of the psychoneuroses. Humor can now be conceived as the loftiest of these defense [801] functions. It disdains to withdraw from conscious attention the ideas which are connected with the painful affect, as repression does, and it, thus, overcomes the defense automatism. It brings this about by finding the means to withdraw the energy from the ready held pain release, and through discharge changes the same into pleasure. It is even credible that it is again the connection with the infantile that puts at humor's disposal the means for this function. Only in childhood did we experience intensively painful affects over which today as grown-ups we would laugh, just as a humorist laughs over his present painful affects. The elevation of his ego, which is evidenced by the humoristic displacement—the translation of which would nevertheless read: I am too big to have these causes affect me painfully—he could find in the comparison of his present ego with his infantile ego. This conception is to some extent confirmed by the role which falls to the infantile in the neurotic processes of repression.

On the whole, humor is closer to the comic than wit. Like the former its psychic localization is in the foreconscious, whereas wit, as we had to assume, is formed as a compromise between the unconscious and the foreconscious. On the other hand, humor has no share in the peculiar nature in which wit and the comic meet, a peculiarity which perhaps we have not hitherto emphasized strongly enough. It is a condition for the origin of the comic that we be induced to apply—either *simultaneously or in rapid succession*—to the same thought function two different modes of ideas, between which the "comparison" then takes place and the comic difference results. Such differences originate between the expenditure of the stranger and one's own, between the usual expenditure and the emergency expenditure, between an anticipated expenditure and one which has already occurred. [1]

The difference between two forms of conception resulting simultaneously, which work with different expenditures, comes into consideration in wit, in respect to the hearer. The one of these two conceptions, by taking the hints contained in wit, follows the train of thought through the unconscious, while the other conception remains on the surface and presents the witticism like any wording from the foreconscious which has become conscious. Perhaps it would not be considered an unjustified statement if we should refer the pleasure of the witticism heard to the difference between these two forms of presentation.

Concerning wit, we here repeat our former statement concerning its [802] Janus-like double-facedness, a simile we used when the relation between wit and the comic still appeared to us unsettled. [2]

The character thus put into the foreground becomes indistinct when we deal with humor. To be sure, we feel the humoristic pleasure where an emotional feeling is evaded, which we might have expected

---

[1] If one does not hesitate to do some violence to the conception of expectation, one may ascribe—according to the process of Lipps—a very large sphere of the comic to the comic of expectation; but probably the most original cases of the comic which result through a comparison of a strange expenditure with one's own, will fit least into this conception.

[2] The characteristic of the "double face" naturally did not escape the authors. Mélinaud, from whom I borrowed the above expression, conceives the condition for laughing in the following formula: "Ce qui fait rire, c'est qui est à la fois, d'un côté, absurde et de l'autre, familier" ("Pourquoi rit-on?" *Revue de deux mondes,* February, 1895). This formula fits in better with wit than with the comic, but it really does not altogether cover the former. Bergson (l.c., p. 96) defines the comic situation by the "reciprocal interference of series," and states: "A situation is invariably comic when it belongs simultaneously to two altogether independent series of events and is capable of being interpreted in two entirely different meanings at the same time." According to Lipps the comic is "the greatness and smallness of the same."

as a pleasure usually belonging to the situation; and in so far humor really falls under the broadened conception of the comic of expectation. But in humor it is no longer a question of two different kinds of ideas having the same content. The fact that the situation comes under the domination of a painful emotional feeling which should have been avoided, puts an end to possible comparison with the nature of the comic and of wit. The humoristic displacement is really a case of that different kind of utilization of a freed expenditure, which proved to be so dangerous for the comic effect.

Now, that we have reduced the mechanism of humoristic pleasure to a formula analogous to the formula of comic pleasure and of wit, we are at the end of our task. It has seemed to us that the pleasure of wit originates from an *economy of expenditure in inhibition,* of the comic from an *economy of expenditure in thought,* and of humor from an *economy of expenditure in feeling.* All three modes of activity of our psychic apparatus derive pleasure from economy. All three present methods strive to bring back from the psychic activity a pleasure which has really been lost in the development of this activity. For the euphoria which we are thus striving to obtain is nothing but the state of a bygone time, in which we were wont to defray our psychic work with slight expenditure. It is the state of our childhood in which we did not know the comic, were incapable of wit, and did not need humor to make us happy. [803]

Feeling and Form

◆◆◆   SUSANNE K. LANGER

Susanne K. Langer, from *Feeling and Form* (New York, Charles Scribner's Sons, 1953).

MANKIND HAS its rhythm of animal existence, too—the strain of maintaining a vital balance amid the alien and impartial chances of the world, complicated and heightened by passional desires. The pure sense of life springs from that basic rhythm, and varies from the composed well-being of sleep to the intensity of spasm, rage, or ecstasy. But the process of living is incomparably more complex for human beings than for even the highest animals; man's world is, above all, intricate and puzzling. The powers of language and imagination have set it utterly apart from that of other creatures. In human society an individual is not, like a member of a herd or a hive, exposed only to others that visibly or tangibly surround him, but is consciously bound to people who are absent, perhaps far away, at the moment. Even the dead may still play into his life. His awareness of events is far greater than the scope of his physical perceptions. Symbolic construction has made this vastly involved and extended world: and mental adroitness is his chief asset for exploiting it. The pattern [330] of his vital feeling, therefore, reflects his deep emotional relation to those symbolic structures that are his realities, and his instinctual life modified in almost every way by thought—a brainy opportunism in face of an essentially dreadful universe.

This human life-feeling is the essence of comedy. It is at once religious and ribald, knowing and defiant, social and freakishly individual. The illusion of life which the comic poet creates is the oncoming future fraught with dangers and opportunities, that is, with physical or social events occurring by chance and building up the coincidences with which individuals cope according to their lights. This ineluctable future—ineluctable because its countless factors are beyond human knowledge and control—is Fortune. Destiny in the guise of Fortune is the fabric of comedy; it is developed by comic action, which is the upset and recovery of the protagonist's equilibrium, his contest with

---

the world and his triumph by wit, luck, personal power, or even humorous, or ironical, or philosophical acceptance of mischance. Whatever the theme—serious and lyrical as in *The Tempest,* coarse slapstick as in the *Schwänke* of Hans Sachs, or clever and polite social satire—the immediate sense of life is the underlying feeling of comedy, and dictates its rhythmically structured unity, that is to say its organic form.

Comedy is an art form that arises naturally wherever people are gathered to celebrate life, in spring festivals, triumphs, birthdays, weddings, or initiations. For it expresses the elementary strains and resolutions of animate nature, the animal drives that persist even in human nature, the delight man takes in his special mental gifts that make him the lord of creation; it is an image of human vitality holding its own in the world amid the surprises of unplanned coincidence. The most obvious occasions for the performance of comedies are thanks or challenges to fortune. What justifies the term "Comedy" is not that the ancient ritual procession, the Comus, honoring the god of that name, was the source of this great art form—for comedy has arisen in many parts of the world, where the Greek god with his particular worship was unknown—but that the Comus was a fertility rite, and the god it celebrated a fertility god, a symbol of perpetual rebirth, eternal life. . . . [331]

Marcel Pagnol, who published his theory of laughter in a little book entitled *Notes sur le rire,* remarks that his predecessors—he names particularly Bergson, Fabre, and Mélinand—all sought the source of laughter in funny things or situations, i.e. in nature, whereas it really lies in the subject who laughs. Laughter always—without exception—betokens a sudden sense of superiority. "Laughter is a song of triumph," he says. "It expresses the laugher's sudden discovery of his own momentary superiority over the person he laughs at." This, he maintains, "explains all bursts of laughter in all times and all countries," and lets us dispense with all classifications of laughter by different kinds or causes: "One cannot classify or arrange in categories the radii of a circle." [12]

Yet he proceeds directly to divide laughter into "positive" and "negative" kinds, according to its social or antisocial inspiration. This

[12] *Notes sur le rire,* p. 41. His argument is, unfortunately, not as good as his ideas, and finally leads him to include the song of the nightingale and the rooster's crow as forms of laughter.

indicates that we are still dealing with *ludicrous situations,* though these situations always involve the person to whom they are ludicrous, so it may be said that "the source of the comical is in the laugher." [13] The situation, moreover, is something the subject must discover, that is, laughter requires a conceptual element; on that M. Pagnol agrees with Bergson, Mélinand, and Fabre. Whether, according to Bergson's much-debated view, we see living beings following the law of mechanism, or see absurdity in the midst of plausibility as Mélinand says, or, as Fabre has it, create a [339] confusion only to dispel it suddenly, we feel our own superiority in detecting the irrational element; more particularly, we feel superior to those who perform mechanical actions, introduce absurdities, or make confusions. Therefore M. Pagnol claims that his definition of the laughable applies to all these supposedly typical situations.

It probably does; but it is still too narrow. *What is laughable* does not explain the nature of laughter, any more than what is rational explains the nature of reason. The ultimate source of laughter is physiological, and the various situations in which it arises are simply its normal or abnormal stimuli.

Laughter, or the tendency to laugh (the reaction may stop short of the actual respiratory spasm, and affect only the facial muscles, or even meet with complete inhibition) seems to arise from a surge of vital feeling. This surge may be quite small, just so it be sudden enough to be felt distinctly; but it may also be great, and not particularly swift, and reach a marked climax, at which point we laugh or smile with joy. Laughter is not a simple overt act, as the single word suggests; it is the spectacular end of a complex process. As speech is the culmination of a mental activity, laughter is a culmination of a feeling—the crest of a wave of felt vitality. . . . [340]

The amoral character of the comic protagonist goes through the whole range of what may be called the comedy of laughter. Even the most civilized products of this art—plays that George Meredith would honor with the name of "comedy," because they provoke "thoughtful laughter"—do not present moral distinctions and issues, but only the ways of wisdom and of folly. Aristophanes, Menander, Molière—practically the only authors this most exacting of critics admitted as truly comic poets—are not moralists, yet they do not flaunt or depre-

[13] *Ibid.,* p. 17.

cate morality; they have, literally, "no use" for moral principles—that is, they do not use them. Meredith, like practically all his contemporaries, labored under the belief that poetry must teach society lessons, and that comedy was valuable for what it revealed concerning the social order. [19] He tried hard to hold its exposé of foibles and vindication of common sense to an ethical standard, yet in his very efforts to justify its amoral personages he only admitted their amoral nature, and their simple relish for life, as when he [345] said: "The heroines of comedy are like women of the world, not necessarily heartless from being clear-sighted. . . . [sic] Comedy is an exhibition of their battle with men, and that of men with them. . . ." [sic]

There it is, in a nutshell: the contest of men and women—the most universal contest, humanized, in fact civilized, yet still the primitive joyful challenge, the self-preservation and self-assertion whose progress is the comic rhythm. . . . [346]

Real comedy sets up in the audience a sense of general exhilaration, because it presents the very image of "livingness" and the perception of it is exciting. Whatever the story may be, it takes the form of a temporary triumph over the surrounding world, complicated, and thus stretched out, by an involved succession of coincidences. This illusion of life, the stage-life, has a rhythm of feeling which is not transmitted to us by separate successive stimulations, but rather by our perception of its entire *Gestalt*—a whole world moving into its own future. The "livingness" of the human world is abstracted, composed, and presented to us; with it the high points of the composition that are illuminated by humor. They belong to the life we see, and our laugh belongs to the theatrical exhilaration, which is universally human and impersonal. It is not what the joke happens to mean to us that measures our laughter, but what the joke does in the play.

[19] His well-known little work is called *An Essay on Comedy and the Uses of the Comic Spirit*. These uses are entirely non-artistic. Praising the virtues of "good sense" (which is whatever has survival value in the eyes of society), he says: "The French have a school of stately comedy to which they can fly for renovation whenever they have fallen away from it; and their having such a school is the main reason why, as John Stuart Mill pointed out, they know men and women more accurately than we do." (Pp. 13–14.) And a few pages later: "The *Femmes Savantes* is a capital instance of the uses of comedy in teaching the world to understand what ails it. The French had felt the burden of this new nonsense [the fad of academic learning, new after the fad of excessive nicety and precision in speech, that had marked the *Précieuses*]; but they had to see the comedy several times before they were consoled in their suffering by seeing the cause of it exposed." (Pp. 19–20.)

For this reason we tend to laugh at things in the theater that we might not find funny in actuality. The technique of comedy often has to clear the way for its humor by forestalling any backsliding into "the world of anxious interest and selfish solicitude." It does this by various devices—absurd coincidences, stereotyped expressions of feeling (like the clown's wails of dismay), a quickened pace of action, and other unrealistic effects which serve to emphasize the comic structure. . . .

That "light rhythm of thought" is the rhythm of life; and the reason it is "light" is that all creatures love life, and the symbolization of its impetus and flow makes us really aware of it. The conflict with the world whereby a living being maintains its own complex organic unity is a delightful encounter; the world is as promising and alluring as it is dangerous and opposed. The feeling of comedy is a feeling of heightened [348] vitality, challenged wit and will, engaged in the great game with Chance. The real antagonist is the World. Since the personal antagonist in the play is really that great challenger, he is rarely a complete villain; he is interesting, entertaining, his defeat is a hilarious success but not his destruction. There is no permanent defeat and permanent human triumph except in tragedy; for nature must go on if life goes on, and the world that presents all obstacles also supplies the zest of life. In comedy, therefore, there is a general trivialization of the human battle. Its dangers are not real disasters, but embarrassment and loss of face. That is why comedy is "light" compared to tragedy, which exhibits an exactly opposite tendency to general exaggeration of issues and personalities.

The same impulse that drove people, even in prehistoric times, to enact fertility rites and celebrate all phases of their biological existence, sustains their eternal interest in comedy. It is in the nature of comedy to be erotic, risqué, and sensuous if not sensual, impious, and even wicked. This assures it a spontaneous emotional interest, yet a dangerous one: for it is easy and tempting to command an audience by direct stimulation of feeling and fantasy, not by artistic power. But where the formulation of feeling is really achieved, it probably reflects the whole development of mankind and man's world, for feeling is the intaglio image of reality. The sense of precariousness that is the typical tension of light comedy was undoubtedly developed in the eternal struggle with chance that every farmer knows only too well—with weather, blights, beasts, birds and beetles. The embarrassments, perplexities and mounting panic which characterize that favorite genre, comedy

of manners, may still reflect the toils of ritual and taboo that complicated the caveman's existence. Even the element of aggressiveness in
comic action serves to develop a fundamental trait of the comic rhythm
—the deep cruelty of it, as all life feeds on life. There is no biological
truth that feeling does not reflect, and that good comedy, therefore,
will not be prone to reveal.

But the fact that the rhythm of comedy is the basic rhythm of life
does not mean that biological existence is the "deeper meaning" of all
its themes, and that to understand the play is to interpret all the
characters as symbols and the story as a parable, a disguised rite of
spring or fertility magic, performed four hundred and fifty times on
Broadway. The stock characters are probably symbolic both in origin
and in appeal. [349] There are such independently symbolic factors, or
residues of them, in all the arts, [23] but their value for art lies in the
degree to which their significance can be "swallowed" by the single
symbol, the art work. Not the derivation of personages and situations,
but of the rhythm of "felt life" that the poet puts upon them, seems to
me to be of artistic importance: the essential comic feeling, which is
the sentient aspect of organic unity, growth, and self-preservation. [350]

[23] E.g., the symbolization of the zodiac in some sacred architecture, of our
bodily orientation in the picture plane, or of walking measure, a primitive
measure of actual time, in music. But a study of such non-artistic symbolic
functions would require a monograph.

Anatomy of Criticism

Northrop Frye, from *Anatomy of Criticism* (Princeton, Princeton University Press, 1957).

THERE ARE two ways of developing the form of comedy: one is to throw the main emphasis on the blocking characters; the other is to throw it forward on the scenes of discovery and reconciliation. One is the general tendency of comic irony, satire, realism, and [166] studies of manners; the other is the tendency of Shakespearean and other types of romantic comedy. In the comedy of manners the main ethical interest falls as a rule on the blocking characters. The technical hero and heroine are not often very interesting people: the *adulescentes* of Plautus and Terence are all alike, as hard to tell apart in the dark as Demetrius and Lysander, who may be parodies of them. Generally the hero's character has the neutrality that enables him to represent a wish-fulfilment. It is very different with the miserly or ferocious parent, the boastful or foppish rival, or the other characters who stand in the way of the action. In Molière we have a simple but fully tested formula in which the ethical interest is focussed on a single blocking character, a heavy father, a miser, a misanthrope, a hypocrite, or a hypochondriac. These are the figures that we remember, and the plays are usually named after them, but we can seldom remember all the Valentins and Angeliques who wriggle out of their clutches. In *The Merry Wives* the technical hero, a man named Fenton, has only a bit part, and this play has picked up a hint or two from Plautus's *Casina,* where the hero and heroine are not even brought on the stage at all. Fictional comedy, especially Dickens, often follows the same practice of grouping its interesting characters around a somewhat dullish pair of technical leads. Even Tom Jones, though far more fully realized, is still deliberately associated, as his commonplace name indicates, with the conventional and typical.

Comedy usually moves toward a happy ending, and the normal response of the audience to a happy ending is "this should be," which sounds like a moral judgement. So it is, except that it is not moral in the restricted sense, but social. Its opposite is not the villainous but the absurd, and comedy finds the virtues of Malvolio as absurd as the vices of Angelo. Molière's misanthrope, being committed to sincerity, which is a virtue, is morally in a strong position, but the audience soon realizes that his friend Philinte, who is ready to lie quite cheerfully in order to enable other people to preserve their self-respect, is the more genuinely sincere of the two. It is of course quite possible to have a moral comedy, but the result is often the kind of melodrama that we have described as comedy without humor, and which achieves its happy ending with a self-righteous tone that most comedy avoids. It is hardly possible to imagine a drama without conflict, and it is hardly possible to imagine a conflict without some kind of enmity. But just as love, [167] including sexual love, is a very different thing from lust, so enmity is a very different thing from hatred. In tragedy, of course, enmity almost always includes hatred; comedy is different, and one feels that the social judgement against the absurd is closer to the comic norm than the moral judgement against the wicked.

The question then arises of what makes the blocking character absurd. Ben Jonson explained this by his theory of the "humor," the character dominated by what Pope calls a ruling passion. The humor's dramatic function is to express a state of what might be called ritual bondage. He is obsessed by his humor, and his function in the play is primarily to repeat his obsession. A sick man is not a humor, but a hypochondriac is, because, *qua* hypochondriac, he can never admit to good health, and can never do anything inconsistent with the role that he has prescribed for himself. A miser can do and say nothing that is not connected with the hiding of gold or saving of money. In *The Silent Woman,* Jonson's nearest approach to Molière's type of construction, the whole action recedes from the humor of Morose, whose determination to eliminate noise from his life produces so loquacious a comic action.

The principle of the humor is the principle that unincremental repetition, the literary imitation of ritual bondage, is funny. In a tragedy—*Oedipus Tyrannus* is the stock example—repetition leads logically to catastrophe. Repetition overdone or not going anywhere belongs to comedy, for laughter is partly a reflex, and like other reflexes it can be conditioned by a simple repeated pattern. In Synge's *Riders to the Sea* a mother, after losing her husband and five sons at sea, finally loses her last son, and the result is a very beautiful and moving play. But if it had been a full-length tragedy plodding glumly through the seven drownings one after another, the audience would have been helpless with unsympathetic laughter long before it was over. The principle of repetition as the basis of humor both in Jonson's sense and in ours is well known to the creators of comic strips, in which a character is established as a parasite, a glutton (often confined to one dish), or a shrew, and who begins to be funny after the point has been made every day for several months. Continuous comic radio programs, too, are much more amusing to habitués than to neophytes. The girth of Falstaff and the hallucinations of Quixote are based on much the same comic laws. Mr. E. M. Forster speaks with disdain of Dickens's Mrs. Micawber, who never says anything except that she will never [168] desert Mr. Micawber: a strong contrast is marked here between the refined writer too finicky for popular formulas, and the major one who exploits them ruthlessly.

The humor in comedy is usually someone with a good deal of social prestige and power, who is able to force much of the play's society into line with his obsession. Thus the humor is intimately connected with the theme of the absurd or irrational law that the action of comedy moves toward breaking. It is significant that the central character of our earliest humor comedy, *The Wasps,* is obsessed by law cases: Shylock, too, unites a craving for the law with the humor of revenge. Often the absurd law appears as a whim of a bemused tyrant whose will is law, like Leontes or the humorous Duke Frederick in Shakespeare, who makes some arbitrary decision or rash promise: here law is replaced by "oath," also mentioned in the *Tractatus.* Or it may take the form of a sham Utopia, a society of ritual bondage constructed by an act of humorous or pedantic will, like the academic retreat in *Love's Labor's Lost.* This theme is also as old as Aristophanes, whose parodies of Platonic social schemes in *The Birds* and *Ecclesiazusae* deal with it.

The society emerging at the conclusion of comedy represents, by contrast, a kind of moral norm, or pragmatically free society. Its ideals are seldom defined or formulated: definition and formulation belong to the humors, who want predictable activity. We are simply given to understand that the newly-married couple will live happily ever after, or that at any rate they will get along in a relatively unhumorous and clear-sighted manner. That is one reason why the character of the successful hero is so often left undeveloped: his real life begins at the end of the play, and we have to believe him to be potentially a more interesting character than he appears to be. In Terence's *Adelphoi,* Demea, a harsh father, is contrasted with his brother Micio, who is indulgent. Micio being more liberal, he leads the way to the comic resolution, and converts Demea, but then Demea points out the indolence inspiring a good deal of Micio's liberality, and releases him from a complementary humorous bondage.

Thus the movement from *pistis* to *gnosis,* from a society controlled by habit, ritual bondage, arbitrary law and the older characters to a society controlled by youth and pragmatic freedom is fundamentally, as the Greek words suggest, a movement from illusion to reality. Illusion is whatever is fixed or definable, and reality [169] is best understood as its negation: whatever reality is, it's not *that.* Hence the importance of the theme of creating and dispelling illusion in comedy: the illusions caused by disguise, obsession, hypocrisy, or unknown parentage.

The comic ending is generally manipulated by a twist in the plot. In Roman comedy the heroine, who is usually a slave or courtesan, turns out to be the daughter of somebody respectable, so that the hero can marry her without loss of face. The *cognitio* in comedy, in which the characters find out who their relatives are, and who is left of the opposite sex not a relative, and hence available for marriage, is one of the features of comedy that have never changed much: *The Confidential Clerk* indicates that it still holds the attention of dramatists. There is a brilliant parody of a *cognitio* at the end of *Major Barbara* (the fact that the hero of this play is a professor of Greek perhaps indicates an unusual affinity to the conventions of Euripides and Menander), where Undershaft is enabled to break the rule that he cannot appoint his son-in-law as successor by the fact that the son-in-law's own father married his deceased wife's sister in Australia, so that the son-in-law is his own first cousin as well as himself. It sounds complicated, but the plots of comedy often are complicated because there is something inherently absurd about complications. As the main character interest in comedy is so often focussed on the defeated characters, comedy regularly illustrates a victory of arbitrary plot over consistency of character. Thus, in striking contrast to tragedy, there can hardly be such a thing as inevitable comedy, as far as the action of the individual play is concerned. That is, we may know that the convention of comedy will make some kind of happy ending inevitable, but still for each play the dramatist must produce a distinctive "gimmick" or "weenie," to use two disrespectful Hollywood synonyms for *anagnorisis*. Happy endings do not impress us as true, but as desirable, and they are brought about by manipulation. The watcher of death and tragedy has nothing to do but sit and wait for the inevitable end; but something gets born at the end of comedy, and the watcher of birth is a member of a busy society.

The manipulation of plot does not always involve metamorphosis of character, but there is no violation of comic decorum when it does. Unlikely conversions, miraculous transformations, and providential assistance are inseparable from comedy. Further, whatever emerges is supposed to be there for good: if the [170] curmudgeon becomes lovable, we understand that he will not immediately relapse again into his ritual habit. Civilizations which stress the desirable rather than the real, and the religious as opposed to the scientific perspective, think of drama almost entirely in terms of comedy. In the classical drama of India, we are told, the tragic ending was regarded as bad taste, much as the manipulated endings of comedy are regarded as bad taste by novelists interested in ironic realism. [171]

Verbal Behavior

◆◆◆   B. F. SKINNER

B. F. Skinner, from *Verbal Behavior* * (New York, Appleton-Century-Crofts, Inc., 1957).

MUCH of the time, however, a man acts only indirectly upon the environment from which the ultimate consequences of his behavior emerge. His first effect is upon other men. Instead of going to a drinking fountain, a thirsty man may simply "ask for a glass of water"—that is, may engage in behavior which produces a certain pattern of sounds which in turn induces someone to bring him a glass of water. The sounds themselves are easy to describe in physical terms; but the glass of water reaches the speaker only as a result of a complex series of events including the behavior of a listener. The ultimate consequence, the receipt of water, bears no useful geometrical or mechanical relation to the form of the behavior of "asking for water." Indeed, it is [1] characteristic of such behavior that it is impotent against the physical world. Rarely do we shout down the walls of a Jericho or successfully command the sun to stop or the waves to be still. Names do not break bones. The consequences of such behavior are mediated by a train of events no less physical or inevitable than direct mechanical action, but clearly more difficult to describe. . . .

A definition of verbal behavior as behavior reinforced through the mediation of other persons needs, as we shall see, certain refinements. Moreover, it does not say much about the behavior of the listener, even though there would be little verbal behavior to consider if someone had not already acquired special responses to the patterns of energy generated by the speaker. This omission can be justified, for

* The following general description of "behavior" is quoted from C. B. Ferster and B. F. Skinner, *Schedules of Reinforcement* (New York, Appleton-Century-Crofts, Inc., 1957), p. 1: When an organism acts upon the environment in which it lives, it changes that environment in ways which often affect the organism itself. Some of these changes are what the layman calls rewards, or what are now generally referred to technically as reinforcers: when they follow behavior in this way, they increase the likelihood that the organism will behave in the same way again. Most events which function as reinforcers are related to biological processes important to the survival of the organism.

the behavior of the listener in mediating the consequences of the behavior of the speaker is not necessarily verbal in any special sense. It cannot, in fact, be distinguished from behavior in general, and an adequate account of verbal behavior need cover only as much of the behavior of the listener as is needed to explain the behavior of the speaker. The behaviors of speaker and listener taken together compose what may be called a total speech episode. There is nothing in such an episode which is more than the combined behavior of two or more individuals. Nothing "emerges" in the social unit. The speaker can be studied while assuming a listener, and the listener while assuming a speaker. The separate accounts which result exhaust the episode in which both participate. . . . [2]

A single response may have different effects upon different audiences. A distinguished scholar used to acknowledge complimentary copies of books by writing immediately to the author: *I shall lose no time in reading the book you have so kindly sent me.* With respect to the audience of which the author was a member, this was synonymous with *I am anxious to read your book* or *I am going to read your book as soon as possible.* With respect to another audience, of which the scholar himself was a member, it was synonymous with *I shan't waste my time on such stuff.* Several types of irony exemplify this kind of multiple audience. Socrates encourages an innocent newcomer with a response which has one effect upon the newcomer (synonymous with *We are anxious to hear what you have to say*) but a very different effect upon the group (synonymous with *Show us how poorly informed you are*). In dramatic irony, the dramatist puts into the mouth of a character a remark which has one supposed effect upon the characters on the stage and a very different effect upon the spectators. When Macbeth reassures himself of his invincibility by repeating the prediction that he will be unharmed so long as Birnam Wood does not come to Dunsinane, he has a very different effect upon the audience, to whom the expression is no longer synonymous with the impossible. The artistic achievement in dramatic irony [232] requires that the spectator respond to some extent as a member of both audiences.

In one form of mockery, the speaker's behavior appears to be strongly under the control of one audience but is so extravagant or outrageous to a second audience that the control exerted by the first is seen to be spurious. Let us say that a critic is to review a new play by the wife of the editor of his paper. What he says is in part determined by the play he sees, but its special effect upon his employer is not irrelevant. By resorting to fulsome praise, he may satisfy the latter contingency, yet salvage his reputation as a critic with his colleagues and with part of his public who, detecting the extremity of his review, will draw another conclusion about his reaction to the play.

Fable, satire, and allegory are composed of responses emitted with respect to one audience but effective upon another in a different way. At the time it was written, *Gulliver's Travels* had very different effects upon the young and the socially sophisticated adult reader, though it was not written in a secret language. As a description of, say, a disturbing social condition, a satire may be regarded as extreme metaphorical or metonymical extension. A stricter description would be punished, and the conditions are therefore ripe for metaphorical extension. But satire is not merely metaphorical extension; it takes a form appropriate to another audience. Many details may be appropriate, say, to a story for children and incapable of explanation as metaphorical extension with respect to the first audience. From a practical point of view, the part of the satire directed to the child as an audience acts as an additional guarantee against punishment. But both audiences are important for the satirical effect. The writer would not have written for the second audience alone, and an innocent member of that audience does not "get the point." The reader who "appreciates the satire" must be a member of both audiences.

Allegory commonly refers to two or more audiences of which none is necessarily negative. Bunyan's *Pilgrim's Progress,* as a metaphorical discussion of moral precepts, is directed toward an audience which might not require the allegorical form, but it is also a story of personal adventure and, as such, is directed toward an audience uninterested in moral precepts. The strategy of the allegory is to induce the second audience to respond with behavior appropriate to the first. Readers may vary considerably in the extent to which they are members of the two audiences. A child, reading the story, may be but [233] little affected by the moral precepts; a moralist, reading it as metaphorical extension, may be scarcely touched by the personalities and episodes.

Fable, satire, and allegory resemble the behavior of the speaker who talks to someone "through" a second listener. The energy level and other characteristics of verbal behavior in, say, a crowded waiting room may indicate that the speaker is also talking to those who cannot choose but hear. The technique is useful with respect to potentially negative audiences. It is sometimes possible to speak to a person of real or ceremonial importance, to whom direct speech is forbidden, by speaking to a second audience in his hearing. One may complain of injustice in the presence of, but not speaking directly to, a magistrate. The second audience may be the speaker himself; the complaint may be mumbled to no one in particular. A child who has been punished for teasing may simply say to himself *I wish I had some candy* or *Candy is awfully good.* A doll or pet animal will serve the purpose of a second audience. . . . [234]

Some of the best examples of multiple sources of strength are puns and other forms of wit. The effect upon the listener or reader . . . may be amusing or delightful, particularly in a period in which punning is fashionable, or it may share the sober profundity of dramatic irony. Jesus was presumably not joking when he said *Thou art Peter* (*Tu es Petrus = Thou art a rock*) *and upon this rock I will build my church.* Nor was Shakespeare when he wrote

> Golden lads and girls all must,
> As chimney-sweepers, come to dust.

Sometimes a response is repeated, as if under the control of multiple variables taken one at a time. Thus, Othello says *Put out the light and then put out the light,* responding to separate variables as if he were to say *Snuff the candle and smother Desdemona.*

Nonverbal behavior may, of course, have multiple sources of strength. For example, one may slam a door partly to close the door and partly to make a noise under the influence of emotional variables. If the emotional effect is to be felt by a second person, the sources of strength are both verbal and nonverbal. A verbal but nonvocal pun is made by the executive at his desk who rejects a proposition by turning "thumbs down" in the fashion of a Roman emperor at gladiatorial games and, with the tip of his thumb, pressing a button to have his visitor shown out of his office. Punning is easier in verbal behavior because forms of response are less dependent on the environment. [239]

The pun as a form of humor is currently in disrepute. Its disfavor could be due to the fact that under multiple causation trivial and irrelevant sources make themselves felt. The irrelevant pun is a nuisance. The difference between good and bad puns seems to be just the difference in the relevance of the variables. In a "far-fetched" pun one source of strength would ordinarily have no effect. But if behavior due to multiple sources is specially reinforced—if the speaker is applauded for punning, for example—the feeble source gets its chance. The chimney-sweeper in the quotation from *Cymbeline* is dragged in to give *come to dust* a second source of strength; possibly it was *come to dust* which strengthened *chimney-sweepers*. But both sources of *Put out the light* are relevant. When Dr. Johnson offered to make a pun on any subject and "the King" was suggested, he immediately replied *The King is not a subject*. This is "good" because both sources of strength are relevant. Dr. Johnson was among those who felt that the pun was one of the "smaller excellencies of lively conversation." . . . [240]

The formal preparation of the listener or reader which develops as a poem is heard or read bears upon a problem of long standing in literary criticism. It is generally assumed, in line with traditional conceptions of verbal behavior, that there are only two elements in a literary work—form and meaning. Some works, particularly [284] poems, seem to be enjoyable because of their form: they are nice noises, and they can be enjoyed in this sense by one who does not know the language. Literary works are also enjoyable because of their meanings: they describe things which are pleasant or interesting. But there is obviously something more in good writing—something not far from wit or verbal play. This has been argued to be a subtle connection between form and meaning, but a more likely possibility is that it has to do with how a reader's behavior is prepared and released by a text. A parallel distinction has been made between "melopoeia," or the musical art of literature, "phanopoeia," or the art of images and meanings, and "logopoeia," the artistic use of the reader's disposition to emit words. In logopoeia the writer utilizes strong patterns arising from the reader's verbal history and constructs others on the spur of the moment. Joyce's line *Wring out the clothes, wring in the dew* borrows strength from the latent intraverbal sequence *Ring out the old, ring in the new,* as well as from a current theme of women washing clothes in the open air. The line may or may not be musical, it may or may not evoke emotional or practical responses, but it clearly manipulates verbal strength. It is this verbal play which is reinforcing to the reader and hence indirectly to the writer.

Logopoeia is most obvious in verbal play or wit. The reinforcing effect of a clever style is hard to analyze; we usually simply report our delight and prove it by returning to the same writer for more of the same stimulation. But the laughter generated in verbal play is more objective. Laughs can be counted and even, as in a television audience, measured in decibels. Each of the literary effects already described has a parallel in the field of humor, where the response of the listener or reader may be more closely followed.

There are many reasons why men laugh, and they do not all apply here. Even in the verbal field, some behavior may be laughable merely because it is clumsy, awkward, surprising, or otherwise amusing in character. Stuttering or lisping and marked dialects are stock devices in humorous writing. The tongue-twisting distortions . . . are often laughable. Verbal behavior is also amusing when it describes an amusing episode. . . . The effect of wit as a [285] form of verbal play, however, involves the listener's verbal behavior.

The supplementary evocation of any *feeble* response is usually funny. A trivial feature of a stimulating situation may be responsible for a tenuous metaphorical extension, as in the classical anecdote about the dentist who, in repairing his car, took a firm grip on a sparkplug with a pair of pliers and said *Now this is going to hurt a little*. Farfetched intraverbal sequences, nearly senseless flights of ideas, are usually amusing, and many non-sequiturs are funny. The classical "bull" offers an example. The exchange:

> SOLDIER: I've caught a tartar.
> SERGEANT: Bring him along.
> SOLDIER: I can't.
> SERGEANT: Then come along yourself.
> SOLDIER: He won't let me.

is funny possibly not because it is illogical but because *He won't let me* following upon *I've caught him* is very weak. We describe the condition of the reader by saying he doesn't "expect" the response.

Multiple variables produce funny results not because they are variable but because the supplementation encourages a tenuous source of strength. The newspaper clipping:

> Fertile, Minn., June 27.—Aged 83, Henry L. Gaylord, Fertile attorney, is the father of a bouncing son, his eighteenth child . . . [sic]

is amusing because of a remote thematic supplement. . . . [286]

The devices of poetry are all amusing when the multiple contributions of strength lie within proper bounds. Rhyme is ordinarily not funny, but if it is far-fetched it may be. Polysyllabic rhymes are likely to be far-fetched in this sense, and can scarcely be used in serious poetry.

W. S. Gilbert, following the distinguished precedent of *Ingoldsby Legends,* made the most of this sort of humor:

> I know the Kings of England and I quote the fights historical
> From Marathon to Waterloo in order categorical.
> I'm very well acquainted, too, with matters mathematical,
> I understand equations, both simple and quadratical . . . [sic]

The distortion produced by too strong a rhyme . . . is almost invariably funny. Excessive rhythms and alliteration have become a part of folk-humor: *Peter Piper picked a peck of pickled peppers.* The rhythmic scanning of poetry presents many opportunities to play with the strength of a response. A forced delay in reaching a strong response, as in the unduly prolonged last line of a limerick, is often humorous.

Although supplemental strengthening of weak verbal responses seems to be reinforcing in itself and to explain much wit, as well as the success of witty people, we must not overlook a more serious function. Freud has emphasized the fact that witty responses are often (a) automatically reinforcing to the speaker and (b) punishable by the listener or community. Humor is preoccupied with tabooed [287] subjects, in particular sex, and with having aversive effects upon the listener or others. Freud argued that wit permits the "release" of repressed responses, but the point can be made by saying that the response receiving supplemental support is weak because of punishment. Both interpretations miss an important point. Consider the witty remark of an English woman who had helped Napoleon the Third when he was in exile in England and who was virtually ignored by him after he had returned to the throne. On a chance encounter he casually asked *Restez-vous longtemps à Paris?* and to her reply she added *Et vous, sire?* The aggressive nature of the remark no doubt accounted for much of its strength; the function of the wit was to make an aggressive response unpunishable. But it is not enough to say that the speaker could appeal to the "harmless meaning" in a legalistic extenuation (*I was only adding a rather thoughtless conversational remark*) because the "aggressive meaning" (*You may not be on the throne long* or *You will be in England again soon, asking for my help*) was clear to everyone. Rather we have to appeal to a particular characteristic of the witty verbal community. Just as the literary community tolerates weak determiners of strength, so the witty community exacts a *quid pro quo* for otherwise offensive behavior. It is almost as if the community had agreed: You may be aggressive *provided* you are also amusing. This is now an established practice, but we may search for its origins in the well-known fact that the amusing is generally only a small measure of the annoying and that an event is less annoying if taken with a sense of humor. The witty person can be aggressive or otherwise offensive by inducing the listener to "laugh it off." [288]

Introduction to Joseph Andrews

Maynard Mack, from "Introduction," in Henry Fielding, *Joseph Andrews* (New York, Rinehart & Co., Inc., 1948).

. . . THE TRAGIC EMPHASIS seems to be on the uniqueness and finality of human experience, as man the transient individual moves through his world from a situation which is a datum to a destiny developing from himself. The curve of tragic action, [xiii] in other words, is a curve of self-discovery. On the other hand, the comic curve is one of self-exposure. Here the emphasis is on the permanence and typicality of human experience, as projected in persistent social species whose sufficient destiny is simply to go on revealing themselves to us. For this reason, the great comic characters of literature, whether Shakespeare's, Fielding's, or Dickens's, do not *essentially* change. They are enveloped in events without being involved by them, and they remain immutable like Fielding's lawyer, who has been "alive . . . these four thousand years" and seems good for as many more. Thus at the close of *Joseph Andrews,* Lady Booby, on the one hand, and Parson Adams, on the other, are as self-deceived as they were at the start; they have uncovered others, but they have not discovered themselves. Had they done so—had Fielding allowed them to do so, in any of the senses which matter in art—they would have lost precisely that perpetual possession of being well-deceived in which their comic essence consists. . . . [xiv]

These features of Fielding's plot and character seem to be dictated by the distinctive nature of the comic point of view. If we are usually aware with comic characters that we are looking around them as well as at them, the reason seems to be that comedy presents us with life apprehended in the form of spectacle rather than in the form of experience. In the tragic mode, since the meaning lies in the protagonist's consciousness of the uniqueness of this moment, this choice, this irreversible event for him, our consciousness must be continuous with his, and we are given a point of view inside that consciousness, or at any rate inside the consciousness of some other character who can interpret it for us. But in comedy the case is different because there the consciousness that matters most is ours and is a consciousness of the typicality of *all* moments, choices, and events. Again and again in life-as-spectacle (though only once in life-as-experience), the same moments, choices, and events recur: a Lady Booby lays her hand "accidentally" on a Joseph's and asks if he has ever been in love; or an Adams descants half the night with an acquaintance on contempt of riches while both lack money to pay their bill. For this kind of vision we must be not inside the character but outside him, in a position that compels us to observe discrepancies between the persuasive surfaces of personalities as they see themselves and these personalities as they are. Thus the point of view that ours must be continuous with in comedy is not the character's but the author's. Laughter, Bergson says, implies a complicity with other laughers. This is only another way of saying that the comic artist subordinates the presentation of life as experience, where the relationship between ourselves and the characters experiencing it is the primary one, to the presentation of life as spectacle, where the primary relationship is between himself and us as onlookers. The imposed plot, the static character are among the comic writer's surest means of establishing this rapport, and these are implemented in Fielding's case by devices [xv] of comic irony and mock-heroic, which always imply complicity, by serious essays and reflections, which poise him and us outside the action, and by the formality of his highly articulated prose, whose elegant surface keeps us coolly separated from the violences, grotesqueries, and postures that it mirrors. The result of all this, in novels like *Joseph Andrews* and *Tom Jones,* is the continuous conversion of act into reflection and experience into spectacle, which seems to be the secret of the comic art. Our reactions to reality, we may remind ourselves, depend upon the context. Even a rabbit, were it suddenly to materialize before us without complicity, could be a terrifying event. What makes us laugh is our secure consciousness of the magician and his hat. [xvi]

Some Remarks on Humor

◊◊◊ E. B. WHITE

E. B. White, "Some Remarks on Humor" [1954],* in *The Second Tree from the Corner* (New York, Harper & Brothers, [1954]).

ANALYSTS have had their go at humor, and I have read some of this interpretative literature, but without being greatly instructed. Humor can be dissected, as a frog can, but the thing dies in the process and the innards are discouraging to any but the pure scientific mind.

In a newsreel theatre the other day I saw a picture of a man who had developed the soap bubble to a higher point than it had ever before reached. He had become the ace soap bubble blower of America, had perfected the business of blowing bubbles, refined it, doubled it, squared it, and had even worked himself up into a convenient lather. The effect was not pretty. Some of the bubbles were too big to be beautiful, and the blower was always jumping into them or out of them, or playing some sort of unattractive trick with them. It was, if anything, a rather repulsive sight. Humor is a little like that: it won't stand much blowing up, and it won't stand much poking. It has a certain fragility, an evasiveness, which one had best respect. Essentially, it is a complete mystery. A human frame convulsed with laughter, and the laughter becoming hysterical and uncontrollable, is as far out of balance as one shaken with the hiccoughs or in the throes of a sneezing fit.

One of the things commonly said about humorists is that they are really very sad people—clowns with a breaking heart. There [173] is some truth in it, but it is badly stated. It would be more accurate, I think, to say that there is a deep vein of melancholy running through everyone's life and that the humorist, perhaps more sensible of it than some others, compensates for it actively and positively. Humorists fatten on trouble. They have always made trouble pay. They struggle along with a good will and endure pain cheerfully, knowing how well it will serve them in the sweet by and by. You find them wrestling with foreign languages, fighting folding ironing boards and swollen

* Adapted from the preface to "A Subtreasury of American Humor," Coward-McCann, 1941.

drainpipes, suffering the terrible discomfort of tight boots (or as Josh Billings wittily called them, "tite" boots). They pour out their sorrows profitably, in a form that is not quite fiction nor quite fact either. Beneath the sparkling surface of these dilemmas flows the strong tide of human woe.

Practically everyone is a manic depressive of sorts, with his up moments and his down moments, and you certainly don't have to be a humorist to taste the sadness of situation and mood. But there is often a rather fine line between laughing and crying, and if a humorous piece of writing brings a person to the point where his emotional responses are untrustworthy and seem likely to break over into the opposite realm, it is because humor, like poetry, has an extra content. It plays close to the big hot fire which is Truth, and sometimes the reader feels the heat.

The world likes humor, but it treats it patronizingly. It decorates its serious artists laurel, and its wags with Brussels sprouts. It feels that if a thing is funny it can be presumed to be something less than great, because if it were truly great it would be wholly serious. Writers know this, and those who take their literary selves with great seriousness are at considerable pains never to associate their name with anything funny or flippant or nonsensical or "light." They suspect it would hurt their reputation, and they are right. Many a poet writing today signs his real name [174] to his serious verse and a pseudonym to his comical verse, being unwilling to have the public discover him in any but a pensive and heavy moment. It is a wise precaution. (It is often a bad poet, too.)

When I was reading over some of the parody diaries of Franklin P. Adams, I came across this entry for April 28, 1926:

Read H. Canby's book, *Better Writing,* very excellent. But when he says, "A sense of humour is worth gold to any writer," I disagree with him vehemently. For the writers who amass the greatest gold have, it seems to me, no sense of humour; and I think also that if they had, it would be a terrible thing for them, for it would paralyze them so that they would not write at all. For in writing, emotion is more to be treasured than a sense of humour, and the two are often in conflict.

That is a sound observation. The conflict is fundamental. There constantly exists, for a certain sort of person of high emotional content, at work creatively, the danger of coming to a point where something cracks within himself or within the paragraph under construction—

cracks and turns into a snicker. Here, then, is the very nub of the
conflict: the careful form of art, and the careless shape of life itself.
What a man does with this uninvited snicker (which may closely
resemble a sob, at that) decides his destiny. If he resists it, conceals it,
destroys it, he may keep his architectural scheme intact and save his
building, and the world will never know. If he gives in to it, he becomes a humorist, and the sharp brim of the fool's cap leaves a mark
forever on his brow.

I think the stature of humor must vary some with the times. The
court fool in Shakespeare's day had no social standing and was no
better than a lackey, but he did have some artistic standing and was
listened to with considerable attention, there being a well-founded
belief that he had the truth hidden somewhere [175] about his person.
Artistically he stood probably higher than the humorist of today, who
has gained social position but not the ear of the mighty. (Think of the
trouble the world would save itself if it would pay some attention to
nonsense!) A narrative poet at court, singing of great deeds, enjoyed
a higher standing than the fool and was allowed to wear fine clothes;
yet I suspect that the ballad singer was more often than not a second-
rate stooge, flattering his monarch lyrically, while the fool must often
have been a first-rate character, giving his monarch good advice in bad
puns.

In the British Empire of our time, satirical humor of the Gilbert
and Sullivan sort enjoys a solid position in the realm, and *Punch,*
which is as British as vegetable marrow, is socially acceptable everywhere an Englishman is to be found. The *Punch* editors not only
write the jokes but they help make the laws of England. Here in
America we have an immensely humorous people in a land of milk
and honey and wit, who cherish the ideal of the "sense" of humor and
at the same time are highly suspicious of anything that is nonserious.
Whatever else an American believes or disbelieves about himself, he
is absolutely sure he has a sense of humor.

Frank Moore Colby, one of the most intelligent humorists operat-
ing in this country in the early years of the century, in an essay called
"The Pursuit of Humor" described how the American loves and
guards his most precious treasure:

. . . Now it is the commonest thing in the world to hear people call
the absence of a sense of humor the one fatal defect. No matter how owlish
a man is, he will tell you that. It is a miserable falsehood, and it does in-

calculable harm. A life without humor is like a life without legs. You are haunted by a sense of incompleteness, and you cannot go where your friends go. You are also somewhat of a burden. But the only really fatal thing is the shamming of humor when you have it not. There are people whom nature meant to be solemn from their cradle to their grave. They [176] are under bonds to remain so. In so far as they are true to themselves they are safe company for any one; but outside their proper field they are terrible. Solemnity is relatively a blessing, and the man who was born with it should never be encouraged to wrench himself away.

We have praised humor so much that we have started an insincere cult, and there are many who think they must glorify it when they hate it from the bottom of their hearts. False humor-worship is the deadliest of social sins, and one of the commonest. People without a grain of humor in their composition will eulogize it by the hour. Men will confess to treason, murder, arson, false teeth, or a wig. How many of them will own up to a lack of humor? The courage that could draw this confession from a man would atone for everything.

Relatively few American humorists have become really famous, so that their name is known to everyone in the land in the way that many novelists and other solemn literary characters have become famous. Mark Twain made it. He had, of course, an auspicious start, since he was essentially a story teller and his humor was an added attraction. (It was also very, very good.) In the 1920's and 30's, Ring Lardner was the idol of professional humorists and of plenty of other people, too; but I think I am correct in saying that at the height of his career he was not one of the most widely known literary figures in this country, and the name Lardner was not known to the millions but only to the thousands. He never reached Mr. and Mrs. America and all the ships at sea, to the extent that Mark Twain reached them, and I doubt if he ever will. On the whole, humorists who give pleasure to a wide audience are the ones who create characters and tell tales, the ones who are story tellers at heart. Lardner told stories and gave birth to some characters, but I think he was a realist and a parodist and a satirist first of all, not essentially a writer of fiction. [177] The general public needs something to get a grip on—a Penrod, a Huck Finn, a Br'er Rabbit, or a Father Day. The subtleties of satire and burlesque and nonsense and parody and criticism are not to the general taste; they are for the top (or, if you want, for the bottom) layer of intellect. Clarence Day, for example, was relatively inconspicuous when he was oozing his incomparable "Thoughts without Words," which are his best creations; he became generally known and generally loved only after he had brought Father to life. (Advice to young writers who want to get ahead without any annoying delays: don't write about Man, write about *a* man.)

I was interested, in reading DeVoto's "Mark Twain in Eruption," to come across some caustic remarks of Mr. Clemens's about an anthology of humor which his copyright lawyer had sent him and which Mark described as "a great fat, coarse, offensive volume." He was not amused. "This book is a cemetery," he wrote.

In this mortuary volume [he went on] I find Nasby, Artemus Ward, Yawcob Strauss, Derby, Burdette, Eli Perkins, the Danbury News Man, Orpheus C. Kerr, Smith O'Brien, Josh Billings, and a score of others, maybe two score, whose writings and sayings were once in everybody's mouth but are now heard of no more and are no longer mentioned. Seventy-eight seems an incredible crop of well-known humorists for one forty-year period to have produced, and yet this book has not harvested the entire crop—far from it. It has no mention of Ike Partington, once so welcome and so well known; it has no mention of Doesticks, nor of the Pfaff crowd, nor of Artemus Ward's numerous and perishable imitators, nor of three very popular Southern humorists whose names I am not able to recall, nor of a dozen other sparkling transients whose light shone for a time but has now, years ago, gone out.

Why have they perished? Because they were merely humorists. Humorists of the "mere" sort cannot survive. Humor is only a [178] fragrance, a decoration. Often it is merely an odd trick of speech and of spelling, as in the case of Ward and Billings and Nasby and the "Disbanded Volunteer," and presently the fashion passes and the fame along with it.

Not long ago I plunged back fifty to a hundred years into this school of dialect humor that Mark Twain found perishable. Then was the heyday of the crackerbarrel philosopher, sometimes wise, always wise-seeming, and when read today rather dreary. It seemed to me, in reading the dialect boys, that a certain basic confusion often exists in the use of tricky or quaint or illiterate spelling to achieve a humorous effect. I mean, it is not always clear whether the author intends his character to be writing or speaking—and I, for one, feel that unless I know at least this much about what I am reading, I am off to a bad start. For instance, here are some spellings from the works of Petroleum V. Nasby: he spells "would" *wood,* "of" *uv,* "you" *yoo,* "hence" *hentz,* "office" *offis.*

Now, it happens that I pronounce "office" *offis.* And I pronounce "hence" *hentz,* and I even pronounce "of" *uv.* Therefore, I infer that Nasby's character is supposed not to be speaking but to be writing. Yet in either event, justification for this perversion of the language is lacking; for if the character is speaking, the queer spelling is unnecessary, since the pronunciation is almost indistinguishable from the natural or ordinary pronunciation, and if the character is writing, the spelling is most unlikely. Who ever wrote "uv" for "of"? Nobody. Anyone who knows how to write at all knows how to spell a simple word like "of." If you can't spell "of" you wouldn't be able to spell anything and wouldn't be attempting to set words to paper—much less words like "solissitood." A person who can't spell "of" is an illiterate, and the only time such a person attempts to write anything down is in a great crisis. He doesn't write political essays or diaries or letters or satirical paragraphs. [179]

In the case of Dooley, the Irish dialect is difficult but worth the effort, and it smooths out after the first hundred miles. Finley Peter Dunne was a sharp and gifted humorist, who wrote no second-rate stuff, and he had the sympathetic feeling for his character which is indispensable. This same sympathy is discernible in contemporary Jewish humor—in the work of Milt Gross, Arthur Kober, Leonard Q. Ross. It is sympathy, not contempt or derision, that makes their characters live. Lardner's ballplayer was born because the author had a warm feeling for ballplayers, however boyish or goofy. The spelling in all these cases is not a device for gaining a humorous effect but a necessary tool for working the material, which is inherently humorous.

I suspect that the popularity of all dialect stuff derives in part from flattery of the reader—giving him a pleasant sensation of superiority which he gets from working out the intricacies of misspelling, and the satisfaction of detecting boorishness or illiteracy in someone else. This is not the whole story but it has some bearing in the matter. Incidentally, I am told by an authority on juvenile literature that dialect is tops with children. They like to puzzle out the words. When they catch on to the thing, they must feel that first fine glow of maturity—the ability to exercise higher intellectual powers than those of the character they are looking at.

But to get back to Mark Twain and the "great fat, coarse volume" that offended him so:

There are those [he continued], who say that a novel should be a work of art solely, and you must not preach in it, you must not teach in it. That may be true as regards novels but it is not true as regards humor. Humor must not professedly teach, and it must not professedly preach, but it must do both if it would live forever. By forever I mean thirty years. With all its preaching it is not likely to outlive so long a term as that. The very things it preaches [180] about, and which are novelties when it preaches about them, can cease to be novelties and become commonplaces in thirty years. Then that sermon can thenceforth interest no one.

I have always preached. That is the reason that I have lasted thirty years. If the humor came of its own accord and uninvited, I have allowed it a place in my sermon, but I was not writing the sermon for the sake of humor. I should have written the sermon just the same, whether any humor applied for admission or not. I am saying these vain things in this frank way because I am a dead person speaking from the grave. Even I would be too modest to say them in life. I think we never become really and genuinely our entire and honest selves until we are dead—and not then until we have been dead years and years. People ought to start dead, and then they would be honest so much earlier.

I don't think I agree that humor must preach in order to live; it need only speak the truth—and I notice it usually does. But there is no question at all that people ought to start dead. [181]

Notes on the Comic

◆◆◆   W. H. AUDEN

W. H. Auden, from "Notes on the Comic," in *Thought*, XXVII (Spring, 1952), 57–71.

GENERAL DEFINITION OF THE COMIC

A CONTRADICTION IN THE RELATION of the individual or personal to the universal or impersonal which does not involve the spectator in suffering or pity.

When we consider the history of epic or tragic or lyric art, we see change but no progress; *Paradise Lost* is different from *The Iliad* but no better. When, however, we consider comic art, it seems to us that the progress has been immense. The jokes in ancient literature seem singularly unfunny and there is hardly a line written before the middle of the eighteenth century which, on reading, can make us laugh out loud.

*

A sense of wit and humor develops in a society to the degree that its members are simultaneously conscious of being each a unique individual and of being all in common subjection to unalterable laws.

Among primitive peoples the sense of individuality is weak, and is only aroused by exceptional suffering; they only perceive a contradiction between the individual and the universal when it is a tragic contradiction—(any comic contradiction which they do perceive is of the most obvious kind). [57]

In our own society, those individuals, like gamblers and dabblers in spiritualism, who believe in chance or magic, not in impersonal law, are usually humorless. . . . [58]

SOME TYPES OF COMIC CONTRADICTION

1) The operation of physical laws upon inorganic objects associated with a person in such a way that it is they who appear to be acting from personal volition and he who is or appears to be the helpless thing.

109

EXAMPLES

A man is walking in a storm protected by his umbrella when a sudden gust of wind blows it inside out. This is comic for two reasons:

a) an umbrella is itself a mechanism designed by man to function in a particular manner. Its existence and its effectiveness as a protection depend upon man's understanding of physical laws. An umbrella turning inside out is funnier than a hat blowing off because an umbrella is made to be opened, to change its shape when its owner wills. It now continues to change its shape, in obedience to the same laws, but against his will.

b) The activating agent, the wind, is invisible so that the cause of the umbrella turning inside out appears to lie in the umbrella itself. It is not particularly funny if a tile falls and makes a hole in the umbrella, because the cause is visibly natural.

When a film is run backwards, reversing the historical succession of events, the flow of volition is likewise reversed and proceeds from the object toward the subject. What was originally the action of a man taking off his coat becomes the action of a coat putting itself on its man.

The same contradiction is the basis of most of the comic effects of the clown. In appearance he is the clumsy one whom inanimate objects conspire against to torment; this in itself is funny to watch, but our profounder amusement is derived from our consciousness that it is only an appearance, that, in reality, the accuracy of the objects in tripping him up or hitting him on the head is caused by the clown's own skill.

2) A clash between the laws of the inorganic which have no *telos* and the laws of the organic which do. [59]

EXAMPLE

A man walking down the street, with his mind concentrated on the purpose of his journey, fails to notice a banana skin, slips and falls down. Under the obsession of his goal, he ignores his subjection to the law of gravity.

The goal need not necessarily be a unique and personal one; he may simply be looking for a public lavatory. All that matters is that he should be ignoring the present for the sake of the future.

A child learning to walk, or a grown man picking his way carefully over the icy surface, are not funny if they fall down, because they are conscious of the present.

*

COMIC SITUATIONS IN THE
RELATIONSHIPS BETWEEN SEXES

Sex is a sphere peculiarly rich in comic possibilities precisely because of its sacred nature, its size as a social fact, and the intense personal relationship it involves. A special comic possibility in the sex relation comes from the contradiction between man as a natural creature and man as a historical person.

As a natural creature man is born either male or female and endowed with an impersonal tendency to reproduce his kind by mating with any member of the opposite sex who is neither immature nor senile. ("Male and female created he them. . . . [sic] Be fruitful and multiply.") In this tendency the relation between a given male and a given female is subordinated to its general reproductive function.

As a historical person, every man and woman is a unique individual capable of entering into a unique relation of love with another person. As a person, the relationship takes psychological precedence over any function it may also have ("It is not good for man to be alone").

The ideal of marriage is a relationship in which both these elements are synthesized; husband and wife are simultaneously involved in relations of physical love and the love of personal friendship.

This synthesis might be easier to achieve, if the two elements remained distinct, if the physical, that is, remained as impersonal as it is among animals, and the personal relation was completely unerotic. In fact, however, the physical is always a natural and general principle modified by social and personal history—such as a preference for pretty blond ladies under forty. [60]

Sex on the level of nature is impersonal in that it lacks all consideration for the person who belongs to our type, but personal in that our type is our personal and free taste and election, not a blind need.

This contradiction is fertile ground for self-deception. It allows us to persuade ourselves that we value the person of another, when in fact we only value her or him as a sexual object and it allows us to endow her or him with an imaginary personality which has little or no relation to the real one.

> For each an imagined image brings
> And finds a real image there.
> —W. B. Yeats . . . [61]

THE BANAL

The human person is a unique singular, analogous to all other persons but identical with none. Banality is an illusion of identity, for, when people describe their experiences in clichés, it is impossible to distinguish the experience of one from the experience of another.

The cliché-user is comic because the illusion of being identical with others is created by his personal act. He is the megalomaniac in reverse. Both have fantastic conceptions of themselves but, whereas the megalomaniac thinks of himself as being somebody else—Julius Caesar, Napoleon, Michael Angelo, etc.—the banal man thinks of himself as being everybody else, that is, nobody in particular.

THE COMIC AND THE WITTY CONTRADICTION

The comic is an actual contradiction which is not intentionally [64] created by the person or persons involved in it. The witty contradiction is intentionally created by the wit (the clown is the wit of action) and may be imaginary. Thus one of the most fruitful devices of wit is the imaginary treatment of analogous situations as if they were identical. During a period of riots and social unrest when the mob had set fire to hayricks all over the country, Sidney Smith wrote to his friend Mrs. Meynell:

> What do you think of all these burnings? and have you heard of the new sort of burnings? Ladies' maids have taken to set their mistresses on fire. Two dowagers were burned last week, and large rewards are offered! They are inventing little fire-engines for the toilet table, worked with lavender water.

Metaphor (the relation by analogy) is pushed to the absurd point where it is made to appear as exact concrete description. A similar process is at work in Oscar Wilde's epigram:

Twenty years of romance make a woman look like a ruin; twenty years of marriage make her look like a public building.

The term "ruin" is commonly used metaphorically, the term "public building" only concretely. The juxtaposition removes the metaphorical meanings of "ruin" and restores it to its exact descriptive meaning.

THE SPOONERISM AND THE PUN

Spoonerism.

Your tutor tells me that you have hissed all the mystery lectures and tasted nearly three worms.

or, We will now sing Hymn 366. "Shoving leopard of my sheep."

Pun.

> When I am dead I hope it may be said:
> His sins were scarlet but his books were read.
> —Hilaire Belloc

The origin of the comic effect is the same in both cases, namely that mere chance, a slip of the tongue, an accidental homophone, appears as providence and, instead of resulting in unintelligibility, makes unexpected sense.

In the spoonerism, however, the meaning created is only meaning [65] in a formal syntactical sense; the sentence is made of real words and is grammatically correct, but otherwise nonsense, and it is important for the comic effect that the intended sentence shall not be immediately obvious to the listener, but require thought to discover, while in the pun both meanings of the homophone are simultaneously present and both make equally good sense.

The spoonerism is comic and should at least appear to be involuntary; the pun is witty and should appear to be deliberate. . . . [66]

SATIRE

The Object of Satire

The comic butt of satire is a person who, though in possession of moral faculties, transgresses the moral law beyond the normal call of temptation.

Thus the lunatic cannot be an object for satire because he is not responsible for his actions, nor can the devilish be an object because, while responsible, he lacks the normal faculty of conscience.

Any person who causes serious suffering to the innocent partakes of the devilish and is the object, not of satire, but of prophetic denunciation. For example, a black marketeer in sugar is satirizable because the existence of such a black market depends upon the greed of others and to do without sugar is not a serious suffering; a black marketeer in penicillin is not satirizable because those who need it are innocent and, if they cannot pay his prices, die.

The mere fact of transgressing the moral law is not enough to make a person the object of satire, for all men do so, but the average man's transgression is tempered by various considerations, conscience, prudence, reason, competing desires. Most men, for example, desire wealth and are sometimes unscrupulous in their means of obtaining it, but their desire is tempered by laziness. A miser is satirizable because his desire for money overrides all other desires, such as a desire for physical comfort or love for his family. The commonest object of satire is a monomaniac.

*

The Satirical Strategy

There is not only a moral norm but also a normal way of transgressing it. At the moment of yielding to temptation, the normal human being has to exercise self-deception and rationalization, he requires the illusion of acting with a good conscience; after the immoral act, when desire is satisfied or absent, he realizes the nature [67] of his act and feels guilty. He who feels no guilt after transgressing the moral law is mad, and he who, at the moment he is transgressing it, is completely conscious of what he is doing is demonic.

The two commonest satirical devices, therefore, are as follows:

1) to present the object of satire *as if* he or she were mad, i.e., as unaware of the nature of his act.

> Now Night descending, the proud scene was o'er,
> But liv'd in Settle's numbers, one day more.
>   —POPE

The writing of poetry which, even in the case of the worst poets, is a personal and voluntary act is presented as if it were as impersonal and necessary as the revolution of the earth, and the value of the poems produced which, even in a bad poet, varies, is presented as invariable and therefore subject to a quantitative measurement like dead matter.

The satiric effect presupposes that we know that Settle in real life is not a certifiable lunatic for real lunacy overcomes a man against his will; Settle is, as it were, a self-made lunatic.

2) To present the object of satire *as if* he or she were demonic, i.e., completely conscious.

> Although, dear Lord, I am a sinner,
> I have done no major crime;
> Now I'll come to Evening Service
>   Whensoever I have time.
> So, Lord, reserve for me a crown,
> And do not let my shares go down.
>   —John Betjeman

Again, the satiric effect depends upon our knowing that in real life the lady is not wicked, for if she really were as truthful with herself as she is presented, she could not go into a Christian church but would have to attend the Temple of Mammon, and become a formidable criminal.

Satire flourishes in a homogeneous society with a common conception of the moral law, for satirist and audience must agree as to how normal people can be expected to behave, and in times of [68] relative stability and contentment, for satire cannot deal with serious evil and suffering. In an age like our own it cannot flourish except in private circles as an expression of private feuds; in public life, the serious evils are so importunate that satire seems trivial and the only suitable kind of attack prophetic denunciation. [69]

The Thread of Laughter

◆◆◆ LOUIS KRONENBERGER

Louis Kronenberger, from *The Thread of Laughter* (New York, Alfred A. Knopf, Inc., 1952).

COMEDY IS NOT just a happy as opposed to an unhappy ending, but a way of surveying life so that happy endings must prevail. But it is not to be confused, on that account, with optimism, any more than a happy ending is to be confused with happiness. Comedy is much more reasonably associated with pessimism—with at any rate a belief in the smallness that survives as against the greatness that is scarred or destroyed. In mortal affairs it is tragedy, like forgiveness, that seems divine; and comedy, like error, that is human. . . . [3]

Comedy appeals to the laughter, which is in part at least the malice, in us; for comedy is concerned with human imperfection, with people's failure to measure up either to the world's or to their own conception of excellence. All tragedy is idealistic and says in effect, "The pity of it"—that owing to this fault of circumstance or that flaw of character, a man who is essentially good does evil, a man who is essentially great is toppled from the heights. But all comedy tends to be skeptical and says in effect, "The absurdity of it"—that in spite of his fine talk or noble resolutions, a man is the mere creature of pettiness and vanity and folly. Tragedy is always lamenting the Achilles tendon, the [4] destructive flaw in man; but comedy, in a sense, is always looking for it. Not cheaply, out of malevolence or cynicism; but rather because even at his greatest, man offers some touch of the fatuous and small, just as a murderer, even at his cleverest, usually makes some fatal slip. In tragedy men aspire to more than they can achieve; in comedy, they pretend to more.

The difference, again, between the two is the very question of difference. A great tragic hero—an Oedipus or Lear—strikes us as tremendously far removed from common humanity. But comedy, stripping off the war-paint and the feathers, the college degrees or the military medals, shows how very like at bottom the hero is to everybody else. Tragedy cannot flourish without giving its characters a

116

kind of aura of poetry, or idealism, or doom; comedy scarcely functions till the aura has been dispelled. And as it thrives on a revelation of the true rather than the trumped-up motive, as it is in one way sustained by imposture, so in another it is sustained by incongruity. Here is the celebrated philosopher cursing the universe because he has mislaid a book. Here are all those who, like King Canute, would bid the clock go backward or the waves stand still. Here is not only the cheat, but the victim who but for his own dishonest desires could never be cheated.

Comedy, in brief, is criticism. If through laughing at others we purge ourselves of certain spiteful and ungenerous instincts—as through tragedy we achieve a higher and more publicized catharsis—that is not quite the whole of it. Comedy need not be hostile to idealism; it need only show how far human beings fall short of the ideal. The higher comedy mounts, the airier and more brilliant its forms, the more are we aware of man's capacity for being foolish or self-deluded or complacent; in the very highest comedy, such as the finale of Mozart's *Marriage of Figaro,* we are in a very paradise of self-deceptions and misunderstandings and cross-purposes. At the heart of high comedy there is always a strain of melancholy, as round the edges there is all gaiety and ebullience and glitter; and Schiller was perhaps right in regarding high comedy as the greatest of all literary forms.

Comedy is criticism, then, because it exposes human beings [5] for what they are in contrast to what they profess to be. How much idealism, it asks, shall we find entirely free from self-love? How much beneficence is born of guilt, how much affection is produced by flattery? At its most severe, doubtless, comedy is not just skeptical but cynical; and asks many of the same questions, returning many of the same answers, as that prince—or at any rate duke—of cynics, La Rochefoucauld. "Pride," La Rochefoucauld remarked, "does not wish to owe, and vanity does not wish to pay." Or again: "To establish oneself in the world, one does all one can to seem established there." Of these and many similar maxims, a play or story might easily be written; from each much cold and worldly comedy, or harsh and worldly farce, might be contrived. But comedy need not be so harsh, and seldom is: though it can be harsher still, can be—as in Ben Jonson —gloating and sardonic. But always it is the enemy, not of virtue or idealism, but of hypocrisy and pretense; and what it does in literature is very much, I suppose, what experience does for most of us in life: it knocks the bloom off the peach, the gilt off the gingerbread.

But though the comic spirit is, in Meredith's phrase, "humanely malign," it is also kindly and even companionable, in the sense that it brings men together as fellow-fools and sinners, and is not only criticism but understanding. Comedy is always jarring us with the evidence that we are no better than other people, and always comforting us with the knowledge that most other people are no better than we are. It makes us more critical but it leaves us more tolerant; and to that extent it performs a very notable social function. Its whole character, indeed—quite aside from that point—is rather social than individual.

The social basis rests in the very subject-matter of comedy—in all that has to do with one's life as part of a group; with one's wish to charm or persuade or deceive or dazzle others. Thus no exhibitionist can exist in solitude, no hypocrite or poseur can work without an audience. There are indeed so many social situations that engender comedy that many of them are notably hackneyed. There are all kinds of classic family jokes—the mother-in-law joke preëminently; but equally the rich-uncle [6] theme, or the country cousin, or the visiting relative who forgets to leave, or the one that proffers advice, or the one that prophesies disaster. Right in the home there is the precocious brat or the moping adolescent; there are countless varieties of comic servants; and there is finally the question, though it perhaps belongs in a different category, of who heads the family—the husband or the wife.

The idea of husband and wife more likely belongs with the social aspects of sex, with the War Between the Sexes as it is fought out in the drawing room. As a purely sexual conflict, this war would not be social; but by the same token it would not be comedy. The question whether man really makes the decisions—including the decision to marry—or is merely permitted to think he does, is, whatever the answer, thoroughly social in nature. Or there is the business of how men and women perform in society for one another's benefit: being the fearless protector or the clinging vine, the woman who always understands or the man who is never understood. We have social comedy again when we pit one nationality as well as one sex against another, when the American puritan is ensnared by a continental siren, or when the suitor is German and humorless, and the besought one is

French and amused. There is still another social aspect when we add a third person to the situation, a mistress as well as a wife, or a lover as well as a husband; or—for the situation need not be illicit, it need only be triangular—when the wife's old beau or the husband's old flame reappears on the scene. Or there is the man who does not know which of two sisters, or two heiresses, or two widows to marry; or the girl which of a half dozen suitors.

Comedy, indeed, must gain admittance into any part of the world —including prisons and sickrooms and funerals—where people are thrown together. Any institution involving hierarchies and rivalries— for example, a university—is a perfect hotbed of it. There will be everybody's relation to the President or the President's wife; or the President's relation to the President's wife; or to his trustees; all the struggles for precedence and the problems of protocol; the progressives on the faculty [7] and the die-hards; the wives who can't help looking dowdy, the wives who suppose they look chic. For obviously any institution, whether a college or a department store, an artist colony or a country club, provides a cross-section of social types and traits, and brings us face to face with a hundred things out of which comedy is distilled: ambition and pride, arrogance and obsequiousness; a too-slavish following or a too-emphatic flouting of convention; all the stratagems men use in order to outwit or get their way.

And of course comedy becomes purely social in that best known and perhaps best liked of all its higher forms—the comedy of manners. Here we have hardly less than a picture of society itself; here the men and women are but parts of a general whole, and what survives—if we have it from the past—is likely to be known as the Restoration Scene, or Regency London, or Victorian Family Life. Here the drawing room is not merely the setting of the play or novel, but the subject and even the hero; here enter all the prejudices, the traditions, the taboos, the aspirations, the absurdities, the snobberies, of a group. The group, to constitute itself one, must partake of a common background and accept a similar view of life: though there will usually exist some out-sider, some rebel, some nonconformist who, as the case may be, is ringing the doorbell or shattering the window panes; trying des-perately to get in or desperately to get out; bending the knee or thumb-ing his nose. Or the comedy of manners will contrast one social milieu with another—the urban and the rustic, the capital and the provinces, Philistia and Bohemia, America and Europe. And in the comedy of manners, ignorance of good form has much the same value that, in straight drama, ignorance of some vital fact has.

And with ignorance of one kind or another we begin coming close to the very mainspring of comedy, or at any rate of comedy in action. For most comedy is born of ignorance or false knowledge; is based on misunderstanding. (Obviously not knowing the truth—though here one might add "until it is too late"—applies to much tragedy also.) At the level of ordinary farce or romantic comedy, the lovers are estranged until a quarter of [8] eleven because the young man misunderstood why the young lady was walking with Sir Robert in the garden. At a higher level, it will not be mere circumstance or coincidence, but qualities of character that block the way. Envy proves an obstruction, or arrogance; or a too-great tendency to be suspicious or to take offense. . . . Comedy at its greatest is criticism indeed; is nothing less, in fact, than a form of moral enlightenment. . . . [9]

And this brings up the point that though Comedy has its permanent subject-matter and even its body of laws, it is liable, like everything else, to changes in fashion and taste, to differences of sensibility. One generation's pleasure is the next generation's embarrassment: much that the Victorians shuddered at merely makes us laugh, much that they laughed at might well make us shudder. One always reacts—and quite fortunately—from the vantage-point of one's own age; and it is probably a mistake, and certainly a waste of breath, to be arrogant or snobbish or moral about what amuses or does not amuse one: we may fancy we are less callous than our grandfathers and only be less callous about different things. The cuckold was clearly, in Restoration comedy, a figure to hoot at. Simply for being cuckolded we do not today find a man so comic, or even comic at all: though the moment we add an extra element to his role, such as his elation over cuckolding others, he becomes a comic figure for us. To what extent sex itself is a comic theme must naturally vary with the morality of a particular age: there are times when it seems shocking for a man ever to have a mistress; there are times when it seems even more shocking for a man never to have one. Right in the same age, what is considered virtue by the parson may be termed repression by the psychiatrist; and in such an age, which is usually one of moral transition, we may well find conflicting comedy values. The pendulum-swing of taste always makes it hard for people to know what they really like: if they are in revolt against gentility, they are [10] likely to confuse what is funny with what is merely bold or obscene; if they are converts to gentility, they will be too much outraged by the indecent to inquire whether it is funny. There is nothing at which the Comic Spirit must smile more than our fickle and inconstant notions as to what constitutes comedy. We need not always look back to Shakespeare's drearier clowns as an instance of how tastes change: sometimes we need only attend a revival of what convulsed us ten years before. [11]

Part II

ESSAYS, NARRATIVES, & VERSE

My Financial Career

Stephen Leacock, "My Financial Career" [1910], in *The Leacock Round-about* (New York, Dodd, Mead & Co., 1946).

WHEN I GO into a bank I get rattled. The clerks rattle me; the wickets rattle me; the sight of the money rattles me; everything rattles me.

The moment I cross the threshold of a bank and attempt to transact business there, I become an irresponsible idiot.

I knew this beforehand, but my salary had been raised to fifty dollars a month and I felt that the bank was the only place for it.

So I shambled in and looked timidly round at the clerks. I had an idea that a person about to open an account must needs consult the manager.

I went up to a wicket marked "Accountant." The accountant was a tall, cool devil. The very sight of him rattled me. My voice was sepulchral.

"Can I see the manager?" I said, and added solemnly, "alone." I don't know why I said "alone."

"Certainly," said the accountant, and fetched him.

The manager was a grave, calm man. I held my fifty-six dollars clutched in a crumpled ball in my pocket.

"Are you the manager?" I said. God knows I didn't doubt it.

"Yes," he said.

"Can I see you," I asked, "alone?" I didn't want to say "alone" again, but without it the thing seemed self-evident.

The manager looked at me in some alarm. He felt that I had an awful secret to reveal.

"Come in here," he said, and led the way to a private room. He turned the key in the lock.

"We are safe from interruption here," he said; "sit down."

We both sat down and looked at each other. I found no voice to speak.

"You are one of Pinkerton's men, I presume," he said.

He had gathered from my mysterious manner that I was a detective. [11] I knew what he was thinking, and it made me worse.

"No, not from Pinkerton's," I said, seeming to imply that I came
from a rival agency.

"To tell the truth," I went on, as if I had been prompted to lie
about it, "I am not a detective at all. I have come to open an account.
I intend to keep all my money in this bank."

The manager looked relieved but still serious; he concluded now
that I was a son of Baron Rothschild or a young Gould.

"A large account, I suppose," he said.

"Fairly large," I whispered. "I propose to deposit fifty-six dollars
now and fifty dollars a month regularly."

The manager got up and opened the door. He called to the accountant.

"Mr. Montgomery," he said unkindly loud, "this gentleman is
opening an account, he will deposit fifty-six dollars. Good morning."

I rose.

A big iron door stood open at the side of the room.

"Good morning," I said, and stepped into the safe.

"Come out," said the manager coldly, and showed me the other
way.

I went up to the accountant's wicket and poked the ball of money
at him with a quick convulsive movement as if I were doing a con-
juring trick.

My face was ghastly pale.

"Here," I said, "deposit it." The tone of the words seemed to
mean, "Let us do this painful thing while the fit is on us."

He took the money and gave it to another clerk.

He made me write the sum on a slip and sign my name in a book.
I no longer knew what I was doing. The bank swam before my eyes.

"Is it deposited?" I asked in a hollow, vibrating voice.

"It is," said the accountant.

"Then I want to draw a check."

My idea was to draw out six dollars of it for present use. Someone
gave me a check-book through a wicket and someone else began telling
me how to write it out. The people in the bank had the impression that
I was an invalid millionaire. I wrote something on the check and
thrust it in at the clerk. He looked at it.

"What! are you drawing it all out again?" he asked in surprise. [12]

Then I realized that I had written fifty-six instead of six. I was too far gone to reason now. I had a feeling that it was impossible to explain the thing. All the clerks had stopped writing to look at me.

Reckless with misery, I made a plunge.

"Yes, the whole thing."

"You withdraw your money from the bank?"

"Every cent of it."

"Are you not going to deposit any more?" said the clerk, astonished.

"Never."

An idiot hope struck me that they might think something had insulted me while I was writing the check and that I had changed my mind. I made a wretched attempt to look like a man with a fearfully quick temper.

The clerk prepared to pay the money.

"How will you have it?" he said.

"What?"

"How will you have it?"

"Oh"—I caught his meaning and answered without even trying to think—"in fifties."

He gave me a fifty-dollar bill.

"And the six?" he asked dryly.

"In sixes," I said.

He gave it me and I rushed out.

As the big door swung behind me I caught the echo of a roar of laughter that went up to the ceiling of the bank. Since then I bank no more. I keep my money in cash in my trousers pocket and my savings in silver dollars in a sock. [13]

On Riding

◆◆◆   CORNELIA OTIS SKINNER

Cornelia Otis Skinner, "On Riding," in *Excuse It, Please!* (New York, Dodd, Mead & Co., 1936).

PERHAPS IT'S SPRING and the sap rising in the limbs of trees, as well as in those somewhat passive members of my own, that yearly stirs in me an ambition to become athletic, to find some enjoyable form of sport in which the enjoyment is not purely on the side of those who watch me.

Certain years I decide upon tennis, other seasons swimming; yet one crowded bus trip to the courts on the upper West Side or a single frisk in the chlorine bosom of a New York swimming pool discourages the ambition at burgeoning, until the ensuing year when it again sends forth new shoots. This spring it blossomed in a desire to ride, a desire that might quickly have found satiety in one Sunday's contemplation of the equestrians in the Park had not a Virginia friend informed me that I was the perfect build for a sidesaddle (I, simple soul, took it as a compliment, not a geographical survey). And had [75] not a card arrived from London's most famous bootmakers, to the effect that their Mr. Judkin would be at the Murray Hill Hotel and that unless I permitted him to measure me for a pair of riding boots he would probably have a long crying spell.

I hated to spoil Mr. Judkin's trip; besides, I have always secretly entertained a Winterhalter vision of myself romantically cantering on a horse named "Prince" down wooded avenues with a bright smile for the yokel and a kind word for the poor woodcutter. It seemed a lady's sport and I broached a horsey friend on the possibilities of my learning it.

"Pooh!" he said. "You'll do it as easily as rolling off a log." (His whimsical way of substituting the word log for horse.)

He was, of course, the last person on earth I should have consulted. He lives, talks and breathes horses. He almost eats them (maybe he does, in Paris). His favorite pastime is riding to hounds, and he takes a broken collar bone or a fractured skull as if it were a scene from the Marx Brothers. His ambition is to die on the hunting field. Altogether he is the original "Heigh-ho the fox!" —I suspect slightly pathological. [76]

He so expatiated upon the amenities of the sport with all the charm and lack of accuracy of an old English print that I was all for rushing home to unpack the divided skirt in which at the age of sixteen I rode down the Grand Canyon on a mule named "Carrie Nation." However, my friend, meticulous to the degree that a badly tied stock or an ill-fitting jodhpur causes him to turn a bright Hunter's Pink, failed to respond with any great warmth to the idea of the divided skirt. Accordingly, at the end of ten days I found my bank account emptied and my closet filled with a sidesaddle habit that has as many mysterious parts as a novel by Proust.

The sidesaddle, I'm told, was invented for a crippled woman; and the truth of that statement I am willing to prove, as are the clerks at the corner drug store where I now take most of my standing meals, the sidesaddle being less an effect than a cause. And it looks so pretty, so easy. I, at least, thought so as I waited that first morning in the stable of a riding academy. The walls were gay with French equestrian prints, charming Victorian ladies in flowing skirts and green veils rocking on contented hobby-horses beneath trees of emerald sponge. "*Première* [77] *Leçon d'Equitation*" —it sounded very elegant and, in that most deceiving of languages, as remote from "First Riding Lesson" as "Oo la-la!" is from "Whoopee!" Jauntily I pulled at my gloves, already completely on. I sniffed the rich scent of the stable and, despite a tendency to be ill, told myself it was delicious.

I was to ride Luke. Luke is the Academy's oldest horse and is credited with all the virtues of his apostolic namesake. He is considered as suitable for children and invalids as Bovril and has never been known to step on anyone—an attribute scarcely extraordinary in other domestic animals, but in a horse nothing short of miraculous. While my courage oozed and I stood wondering if I couldn't have my habit made over into a bicycling costume, there appeared a groom with one tooth and Luke. I buried myself in an old copy of "Town & Country," but the groom, with no respect for my study, accosted me with the question did I prefer to mount from the block or the ground. Pride forbade my telling him my preference lay in not mounting at all, so I croakingly indicated the block. The groom implied that his conversation was a mere formality by announcing [78] that Luke wouldn't go up to the block, which simplified things.

Luke was standing in what looked to be a Buddhistic trance that it seemed a pity to disturb. The groom, however, approached him, at the same time clasping his hands in a manner that led one to assume that he and Luke were about to execute a Japanese tumbling act. He told me to give him my foot and to jump when he counted three. I gave him my right foot which he informed me wasn't right. I then gave him the left and jumped when he counted two. We managed to laugh that off and the next time I jumped on the "three" but not on the horse. The spring and the straining groom landed me at the same awkward angle one reaches trying to climb over the side of a swimming pool, when progress in either direction seems impossible.

The groom, staggering, but with British doggedness, pushed and I pulled until I found myself lying on Luke gracefully if perpendicularly in an attitude the equestrian clown Poodles Hanneford would have paid fifty pounds sterling to copy.

At that unfortunate moment one of those hateful little girls of five, who ride sixteen-hand hunters in [79] the Park and race Sunday mornings with Grover Whalen, happened in with a shrill, "Oh, look at the funny lady!" Pretending I had been examining the saddle on the far side, I managed to right myself and to wind my leg about the pommel. The groom, whose wind was slightly broken, asked me how the stirrup was. I replied I trusted it was well, and he led Luke with his precious cargo to the ring where Mr. Benedict took us in tow, literally as well as figuratively; for Luke, inclined still to continue his meditations, had to be persuaded about the ring by a leading strap held by Mr. Benedict.

Mr. Benedict is the riding master and the ring is a square. It is covered in a tanbark that encourages violent hay fever and is bordered with a mirror wherein one can see what one's best friend couldn't tell one. We walked about it for a time with dignity, while Mr. Benedict discoursed on the principles of riding as Socrates might have expounded to Crito the meaning of Good. It sounded simple and rather beautiful. Then he announced that we'd go for a bit of a trot. His horse, a creature that might easily be called a steed, broke into an exquisite prance. Luke, who borders on the nag, followed in an animated [80] Morris Dance. Mr. Benedict placed a steadying hand under my arm.

"Rise!" he shouted. "Rise and breathe! Sit up! Keep your left toe in and your heel down! Put your right shoulder back! Hold your hands down! Lean away from the pommel! Relax! Relax and breathe!"

"Shall I say 'Ah' too?" I gasped.

"No, just breathe!" he replied.

I had never before known such emphasis to be placed on that seemingly ordinary physical process. Mr. Benedict has succeeded in making me horribly self-conscious about it. There are times now when I pause in the midst of the most simple pursuits to wonder if I'm breathing; and my nights are hideous with lying awake, terrified lest in my sleep I forget to continue that essential function.

"Lean to the right! To the right!" Mr. Benedict continued, in the tone of a captain of a sinking vessel.

"I don't dare. I suffer from height phobia!" I screamed. "It makes me want to jump!"

"If you don't lean to the right your saddle will slip around under your horse."

"It has already," I stated. [81]

It had. My weight on the stirrup had pulled the saddle until I was rising at an angle of forty-five degrees from Luke's patient belly. I have seen cowboys in rodeos ride this way as a particularly hazardous stunt, but Mr. Benedict, who lacks a sense of the dramatic, failed to appreciate my act.

Luke, meantime, was continuing his Morris Dance to an accompaniment of sounds such as the Sicilians inform us issue from Etna before an eruption. His ears were twitching and his lips (I presume he has lips), were curled back in a grin of intense pain. Once, twice, thrice, four times round the ring we rode. I kept assuring myself that all things have an end, even a horse, and that, in the words of Voltaire, "*Tout lasse, tout casse, tout passe*"; and wondered if it would be the girth that would *casse*. Mr. Benedict kept ordering me to do everything but pat my head and rub my stomach, and my eyes filled with tears of self-pity at the thought of my limp body being carried home on a shutter.

The half hour finally ended, but not my troubles. Three weeks have passed and I as yet show no signs of becoming the Diana Vernon of the Reservoir. True, I no longer mount as if I were climbing the [82] Rigi. In fact, I now require two grooms for the purpose, one to help me spring and the other to keep me from o'erleaping myself, like vaulting ambition, and falling completely clear of the animal. Nor have I yet fallen off. But that is because Luke, who has an instinct of pity, senses the way I'm going and jumps beneath to catch me. I still list to port until I am parallel with the ground, my right foot still does a wild tattoo on the horse's shoulder, and Mr. Benedict tells me I still don't breathe.

All I have learned about horses is that they are beautiful overrated creatures and are all born quite insane, Luke and Black Beauty notwithstanding. There is no comprehending their psychology because they possess none. They will pass a phalanx of onrushing traffic on the way to the Park with cool unconcern; but, let them espy a discarded Cracker Jack box in the shrubbery, they will go mad with fright and dance about it like an intoxicated coryphee. They will pass their own reflection in the Academy mirror a hundred times, then suddenly notice it and bolt; whether with fright or pleasure is an open question. In the case of Luke and myself this last idiosyncrasy is understandable. Mr. Benedict says I [83] don't co-ordinate.

"But," he adds, "you're getting on, my dear, you're getting on."

And in my brooding heart I wonder if he refers to my riding, or my years. [84]

Showing Off

◆◇◆   ROSE MACAULAY

Rose Macaulay, "Showing Off" [1935], in *Personal Pleasures* (London, Victor Gollancz, Ltd., 1949).

WHAT IS THAT you say you have done? Walked across Jamaica on your hands? That is nothing at all. Besides, it is probably not true. I once rode a dolphin across the Messina straits. And swam from Corsica to Sardinia. I ate seventy plums at one go, stones and all. I lived six days in a tree. I won a prize on the ocean for chalking a pig's head. I won a prize at school for the quarter mile. And for the high jump. I wrote out "The Ride from Ghent to Aix" backwards. What did you say? You have a certificate of *what?* Signed by the Pope. . . . *And* three children. . . . Well, that was just a mistake, wasn't it; you should have told him. . . . You gave ringworm to two archbishops? I really do not see that that is much to boast of. You converted Cherokee Indians when you were six? That is better. And had a tract written about you, called "How Little ———— came to Jesus." That is better still. But I have had my conversion prayed for by a Lama. No, not in Thibet; we met in Syracuse. Yes, I know Sicily well. I understand Sicilian more or less. And modern Greek. Yes, I know Greece. I didn't go there with one of those mass cruises; I went separately; I always think one sees it better that way. I know Greek literature pretty thoroughly. And Greek history, of course. I have done some verse translations of the Anthology that they tell me are not so bad. So bad as what? As most people's, of course. However that may be, I felt thoroughly at home in Greece. How long was I there? Well, I don't quite remember; certainly over a week. I had to go on to Constantinople after that. And then to Russia. I saw something of Stalin in Moscow; he wanted me to write something about my impressions, but the fact was I [333] hadn't any, because I knew no Russian to speak of. You need to know a language really colloquially before you can begin to understand the people, I always say. The way I know Catalan, Mallorquin, and even Basque. Oh, yes, I know quite a lot of Basque words.

* The points of ellipsis in this selection are the author's.—Eds.

Well, where was I? Yes, after Moscow I visited Germany. I saw Goering and Goebbels; the Führer would not see me; he had heard I was coming, and ordered Goering and Goebbels to send for me for an interview; they tried to trap me in conversation into saying something they could have arrested me for, but I wouldn't. Though I let them see my views all right. How they loathed me! They knew I was a writer of more influence in England than . . . well, than most writers, I suppose I might say . . . anyhow, they were scared to death. However, there was nothing they could get on me. I got safely over into France, and had a gay week in Paris; I know so many people there, I'm never at a loss. I had another proposal, too. Then I visited the place in Normandy my ancestors came from in 1066; they tell me one of the angels in the roof has my face, and that it must have been done from one of our family, in the thirteenth century. I must say, I always *feel* Norman, a kind of arrogant feeling, as if the English were under my heel. Not that ancestors matter: one makes one's own way. What do you say? Your ancestors were Saxon thegns? Well, some of mine were British druids. I always feel at home at Stonehenge. And I learnt to talk Welsh and Breton as easily as possible. And, of course, I could learn Erse and Gaelic too, if I cared to. But they don't seem very much use to-day, do they?

Well, I must go; I am going on to Buckingham Palace. No, quite a small party, I believe; no, the Garden Party [334] is quite another thing; everyone is asked there. This one is for Ruth Draper; she is going to give a command performance, to a few special people. I don't know why *I* should be asked . . . oh, you are going, too? How strange. . . .

Well, now they know what I am; now they, left behind in the house, are talking of me, saying it is not often one meets anyone at once so intelligent, cultured, travelled, handsome, modest, witty and gay. I strut down the street, I get into my car, start the engine, trundle along Piccadilly. How well I drive! Traffic to right of me, traffic to left of me, volleys and thunders; I wriggle unscathed through the middle of it. I am thinking still of the lunch party I have left. I am trying to make sense of something someone seemed to be murmuring to someone else as the door shut behind me.

What was she saying? It sounded like "Ho, ho! I am the Toad. . . ." But that does not seem to make sense, so it must have been something else. . . . [335]

Dr. Arbuthnot's Academy

◆◆◆   FRANK SULLIVAN

Frank Sullivan, "Dr. Arbuthnot's Academy," in *The Night the Old Nostalgia Burned Down* (Boston, Little, Brown & Co., 1948).

DR. MAGNUS ARBUTHNOT'S ACADEMY for the proof of puddings has attracted so much attention in educational circles that I paid it a visit recently, and I'm most happy to report that it is really a remarkable experiment in ultramodern, freewheeling cliché-testing.

The academy was a hive of odd activities the day I was there. Dr. Arbuthnot himself I found in his office grappling playfully with a comely young woman, who was laughing uproariously.

"Oh, please, Doctor!" she gasped. "Stop! Oh, ha, ha, ha, ho, ho, ho! Oh, do quit!"

"I beg your pardon," I said, hastily starting to withdraw.

"Hello, there! Come in, come in," said Dr. Arbuthnot cheerily. "I'm teaching Miss Filkins, here, how to tickle people pink. Now, do you get the idea, Miss Filkins? The right forefinger placed firmly between the second and third ribs, and then you apply the pressure. Shall we try once more?"

"I'm afraid I'll be late for court if we do," Miss Filkins said. [115]

"Oh, your court. I forgot. Well, hurry along, and good luck to you."

Miss Filkins hurried along.

"Smart girl," said Dr. Arbuthnot. "An ex-Wac. Coming along famously with her tickling, but she wasn't getting quite the shade of pink I had in mind. She's really majoring in laughing people out of court. You should have seen her in Part Two, Special Sessions, last Thursday. She cleared the chamber, including three judges, in four minutes and twenty-six seconds. I clocked her myself. When she does it in four minutes flat, she'll get her sheepskin."

"I never knew people actually tickled other people pink," I said. "What else do you teach here?"

"It's hard to say," Dr. Arbuthnot said. "The curriculum changes weekly—sometimes daily. That's in order to avoid getting into a rut.

135

My main idea is to fit young people for the actual business of living in these troubled times. I want them to have a healthy skepticism, to challenge everything. For instance, when you say that someone is 'as sober as a judge,' everybody accepts it as gospel that all judges are always sober. Now, that's sloppy thinking. I don't want my students to take the sobriety of the judiciary for granted. By the way, I'm glad to see you looking so well."

"I'm fit as a fiddle, Doctor, thanks."

"Are you really? We'll have our Professor Heifetz check that before you go."

"Gracious sakes, what is that roaring sound?" I asked.

"The elocution class testing the rooftop. They want [116] to find out if rooftops are really the best spots to shout things from. But suppose we take a jaunt about the school and let you see for yourself what we're trying to do. Come along."

The Doctor escorted me into a room where a dozen eager-looking young people were seated in a semi-circle in front of a lady with a pitch pipe.

"Music Department," the Doctor whispered. "Sh-h-h!"

"All right, now," said the instructress. "We'll try that last movement again. I thought I saw one or two lips move that last time. Now, then, no pear-shaped tones, please." She sounded her A, and all twelve scholars started making a kind of low, eerie noise, between a moan and a buzz.

"Learning to impersonate bees?" I ventured.

"No, but you're warm," said Dr. Arbuthnot. "They're learning to keep things humming. Highly important in these bustling times."

"Now, in here," the Doctor said as we entered the next room, "is the gymnasium. Those young men charging at the masonry are learning the futility of butting their heads against a stone wall. We require the course of all freshmen. Those are pillows tied to their heads. Later on, when they get the hang of it, they won't use the pillows. Ah, good work there, Gumbielski!" He was addressing a well-built youth who was doing something very complicated on a trapeze. "He's exercising his prerogative," Dr. Arbuthnot explained. "Those other young fellows over there are practicing effort-bending. I think we have two or three [117] sophomore effort-benders this year who will give Princeton rather a run for her money at the Inter-collegiates. I imagine you can deduce what those boys are doing." He indicated four chaps shoving manfully against a wheel, and continued, "Nothing like putting the shoulder to the wheel for developing initiative, self-reliance, and the neck and shoulder muscles. Those boys fiddling with rocks are learning to leave no stone unturned. By the way, Merrypants" —Dr. Arbuthnot addressed the group's instructor—"please set aside a dozen large stones tomorrow, will you? I want to start the blood-extraction demonstration Monday."

An odd sight now caught my eye. Two massive lads were standing on a wrestling mat. Just as I glanced their way, one made a remark to the other. The second lad looked aghast, and the first then gave him the merest touch with something he held in his hand. At this, the second boy went down in a heap. An assistant manager rushed up with a pail of water and dashed it over the fallen athlete.

Dr. Arbuthnot took charge. "Give him air. Don't crowd around, boys. That was unnecessarily rough, Heffelduffer," said Dr. Arbuthnot, but he held Heffelduffer's arm aloft in token of victory. "You don't know your own strength. Heffelduffer is our feather champion," he said to me.

"You mean he knocked that big boy down with that feather?"

"It's a trick. You catch your opponent off guard, say something shocking to him, and then strike him with the feather while he is still astounded." [118]

"A remarkable accomplishment, Doctor."

"A very useful one. I believe every boy should learn how to defend himself," Dr. Arbuthnot said as we passed on. "Now, in the steam room, here, the boys get their Russian massage after exercise."

"Russian massage? What's that?"

"Rubbing people the wrong way."

In the next chamber I noticed an earnest but perplexed-looking young man who seemed to be wrestling with an irascible but highly decorative animal of a saffron hue picked out with black spots. We paused for a moment to observe the match.

"I don't really know whether Brackett can change that leopard's spots," said Dr. Arbuthnot. "Sometimes I wonder. But he says it can be done, and he insists on trying, so who am I to discourage him? If success should crown his efforts, it will, of course, be quite a feather in the academy's cap."

We came now to a large, spotlessly clean kitchen.

"Home Economics Department," said the Doctor.

"My, what a delicious aroma," I said, sniffing.

"Isn't it?" the Doctor agreed, smiling. "Always makes me hungry to come in here when the hash-settling seminar is on. Those young men sampling things over there are Democrats tasting defeat. The young woman sitting in the kettle on the stove may look uncomfortable—in fact, *is* uncomfortable—but what she is establishing may eventually be of considerable value to you and me and many others."

"What's she doing?"

"Stewing in her own juice." At this point, the [119] Doctor lifted his nose and inhaled deeply. "Smell *that* aroma?" he said.

"Mmm! Good! What is it?"

"The hot-cakes class. Do hot cakes really sell so well? I have often wondered. I am relying on the energetic youngsters in our salesmanship course to find out."

We passed next into a chamber that, to put it mildly, lacked the agreeable aroma of the hash-settling seminar.

"Not so pleasant, is it?" Dr. Arbuthnot commented, noticing my wry expression. "But it's unavoidable. Those vats contain dishwater of varying strengths, for our dullness experiments. We have to use several grades. For instance, you could not test a radio quiz-master in anything but a vintage dishwater. What are you doing, young man?"

"None of your damn business," the young man retorted.

"Oh, it's you, Farquahar. I didn't recognize you. Good! I like your spirit. Don't take any nonsense from the faculty. One of the troubles with modern education is that faculties interfere too much in the education of students."

As we went on, the Doctor explained about Farquahar.

"We're rather proud of the job we've done on Farquahar," he said. "When he came to us, butter wouldn't melt in his mouth. Well, a growing boy needs some fat in his diet. It was telling on him; he looked undernourished. [120] We put him in an impudence seminar, gave him a course on short answers and another on what to call a spade, and so on. That was three months ago. Today, as you just saw, he is simply insufferable. Liquefies butter at twenty paces."

We now came to a room full of commotion. There was a great clatter of adding machines, which were being operated by alarming young men and women who made nasty faces at each other and exchanged surly remarks.

"Accounting Department," said the Doctor. "They're adding

insult to injury. All of them are experienced aspersions-casters. Now, these pleasanter-looking boys and girls totting up figures, here, are different. They're our blessings-counters."

"You have a truly remarkable curriculum, Doctor."

"Oh, you're just seeing the lab work. I wish you could see some of our field work. Dr. Argetsinger's class, for instance, is out on the town this week exploring every avenue."

In contrast to the racket of the Accounting Department was the atmosphere of the next classroom, in which twoscore students dozed in an atmosphere of utter languor.

"One of our busiest research labs," said Dr. Arbuthnot. "That young man snoring on the sofa is hard at work on his thesis, called 'Some Observations on the Extent of Somnolence Among Logs.'"

"Those young ladies with the sad expressions don't look too busy, Doctor." [121]

"But they are. They're the class in day-ruing, one of our most practical courses. Sooner or later, everyone has a day or days he would like to rue, but how few of us really know how to do it. Those girls looking like Whistler's mother, sitting with folded hands, are in the time-biding seminar. That girl over there is minding her 'M's and 'N's."

"'M's and 'N's?"

"Yes, or 'J's and 'K's, or 'E's and 'F's, or 'Y's and 'Z's, if she likes. Why should 'P's and 'Q's get all the coddling?"

We left that room and came across a group of youths who seemed to be rushing about aimlessly.

"These boys are learning to brook no delay," said Dr. Arbuthnot.

"No, we're not," said one of the boys. "We're flouting tradition."

"You *are*? Why, who put that course into the curriculum?" asked the Doctor.

"We did."

"Well, good for you. I like your enterprise. And I want you to be sure and give yourselves good marks in the course." Dr. Arbuthnot turned to me. "You see how beautifully empiric our system is," he said. "I'm the president here, and even I do not know precisely what goes on. That's my idea of the right kind of college."

A gong rang and students poured from the classrooms. Dr. Arbuthnot said he had to leave me. "Hour for my plot-thickening class," he explained. "Haven't decided yet whether it belongs in the Home Economics [122] or the Novel Construction Department. Well, see you in the funny paper."

"Oh, yeah?" I retorted, for I believe that in the field of repartee one should give as good as he gets, if possible. [123]

You Were Perfectly Fine

◆◆◆ DOROTHY PARKER

Dorothy Parker, "You Were Perfectly Fine" [1930], in *Here Lies* (New York, The Viking Press, Inc., 1939).

THE PALE YOUNG MAN eased himself carefully into the low chair, and rolled his head to the side, so that the cool chintz comforted his cheek and temple.

"Oh, dear," he said. "Oh, dear, oh, dear, oh, dear. Oh."

The clear-eyed girl, sitting light and erect on the couch, smiled brightly at him.

"Not feeling so well today?" she said.

"Oh, I'm great," he said. "Corking, I am. Know what time I got up? Four o'clock this afternoon, sharp. I kept trying to make it, and every time I took my head off the pillow, it would roll under the bed. This isn't my head I've got on now. I think this is something that used to belong to Walt Whitman. Oh, dear, oh, dear, oh, dear."

"Do you think maybe a drink would make you feel better?" she said. [341]

"The hair of the mastiff that bit me?" he said. "Oh, no, thank you. Please never speak of anything like that again. I'm through. I'm all, all through. Look at that hand; steady as a humming-bird. Tell me, was I very terrible last night?"

"Oh, goodness," she said, "everybody was feeling pretty high. You were all right."

"Yeah," he said. "I must have been dandy. Is everybody sore at me?"

"Good heavens, no," she said. "Everyone thought you were terribly funny. Of course, Jim Pierson was a little stuffy there, for a minute at dinner. But people sort of held him back in his chair, and got him calmed down. I don't think anybody at the other tables noticed it at all. Hardly anybody."

"He was going to sock me?" he said. "Oh, Lord. What did I do to him?"

"Why, you didn't do a thing," she said. "You were perfectly fine.

But you know how silly Jim gets, when he thinks anybody is making too much fuss over Elinor."

"Was I making a pass at Elinor?" he said. "Did I do that?"

"Of course you didn't," she said. "You were only fooling, that's all. She thought you were awfully amusing. She was having a marvelous time. She only got a [342] little tiny bit annoyed just once, when you poured the clam-juice down her back."

"My God," he said. "Clam-juice down that back. And every vertebra a little Cabot. Dear God. What'll I ever do?"

"Oh, she'll be all right," she said. "Just send her some flowers, or something. Don't worry about it. It isn't anything."

"No, I won't worry," he said. "I haven't got a care in the world. I'm sitting pretty. Oh, dear, oh, dear. Did I do any other fascinating tricks at dinner?"

"You were fine," she said. "Don't be so foolish about it. Everybody was crazy about you. The maître d'hôtel was a little worried because you wouldn't stop singing, but he really didn't mind. All he said was, he was afraid they'd close the place again, if there was so much noise. But he didn't care a bit, himself. I think he loved seeing you have such a good time. Oh, you were just singing away, there, for about an hour. It wasn't so terribly loud, at all."

"So I sang," he said. "That must have been a treat. I sang."

"Don't you remember?" she said. "You just sang one song after another. Everybody in the place was listening. They loved it. Only you kept insisting that you wanted [343] to sing some song about some kind of fusiliers or other, and everybody kept shushing you, and you'd keep trying to start it again. You were wonderful. We were all trying to make you stop singing for a minute, and eat something, but you wouldn't hear of it. My, you were funny."

"Didn't I eat any dinner?" he said.

"Oh, not a thing," she said. "Every time the waiter would offer you something, you'd give it right back to him, because you said that he was your long-lost brother, changed in the cradle by a gypsy band, and that anything you had was his. You had him simply roaring at you."

"I bet I did," he said. "I bet I was comical. Society's Pet, I must have been. And what happened then, after my overwhelming success with the waiter?"

"Why, nothing much," she said. "You took a sort of dislike to some old man with white hair, sitting across the room, because you didn't like his necktie and you wanted to tell him about it. But we got you out, before he got really mad."

"Oh, we got out," he said. "Did I walk?"

"Walk! Of course you did," she said. "You were absolutely all right. There was that nasty stretch of ice on the sidewalk, and you did sit down awfully hard, you poor dear. But good heavens, that might have happened to anybody." [344]

"Oh, sure," he said. "Louisa Alcott or anybody. So I fell down on the sidewalk. That would explain what's the matter with my— Yes. I see. And then what, if you don't mind?"

"Ah, now, Peter!" she said. "You can't sit there and say you don't remember what happened after that! I did think that maybe you were just a little tight at dinner—oh, you were perfectly all right, and all that, but I did know you were feeling pretty gay. But you were so serious, from the time you fell down—I never knew you to be that way. Don't you know, how you told me I had never seen your real self before? Oh, Peter, I just couldn't bear it, if you didn't remember that lovely long ride we took together in the taxi! Please, you do remember that, don't you? I think it would simply kill me, if you didn't."

"Oh, yes," he said. "Riding in the taxi. Oh, yes, sure. Pretty long ride, hmm?"

"Round and round and round the park," she said. "Oh, and the trees were shining so in the moonlight. And you said you never knew before that you really had a soul."

"Yes," he said. "I said that. That was me."

"You said such lovely, lovely things," she said. "And I'd never known, all this time, how you had been feeling about me, and I'd never dared to let you see how I felt [345] about you. And then last night—oh, Peter dear, I think that taxi ride was the most important thing that ever happened to us in our lives."

"Yes," he said. "I guess it must have been."

"And we're going to be so happy," she said. "Oh, I just want to tell everybody! But I don't know—I think maybe it would be sweeter to keep it all to ourselves."

"I think it would be," he said.

"Isn't it lovely?" she said.

"Yes," he said. "Great."

"Lovely!" she said.

"Look here," he said, "do you mind if I have a drink? I mean, just medicinally, you know. I'm off the stuff for life, so help me. But I think I feel a collapse coming on."

"Oh, I think it would do you good," she said. "You poor boy, it's a shame you feel so awful. I'll go make you a whisky and soda."

"Honestly," he said, "I don't see how you could ever want to speak to me again, after I made such a fool of myself, last night. I think I'd better go join a monastery in Tibet."

"You crazy idiot!" she said. "As if I could ever let you go away now! Stop talking like that. You were perfectly fine."

She jumped up from the couch, kissed him quickly on the forehead, and ran out of the room. [346]

The pale young man looked after her and shook his head long and slowly, then dropped it in his damp and trembling hands.

"Oh, dear," he said. "Oh, dear, oh, dear, oh, dear." [347]

The Catbird Seat

◆◆◆   JAMES THURBER

James Thurber, "The Catbird Seat," in *The Thurber Carnival* (New York, Harper & Brothers, 1945).

MR. MARTIN BOUGHT the pack of Camels on Monday night in the most crowded cigar store on Broadway. It was theater time and seven or eight men were buying cigarettes. The clerk didn't even glance at Mr. Martin, who put the pack in his overcoat pocket and went out. If any of the staff at F & S had seen him buy the cigarettes, they would have been astonished, for it was generally known that Mr. Martin did not smoke, and never had. No one saw him.

It was just a week to the day since Mr. Martin had decided to rub out Mrs. Ulgine Barrows. The term "rub out" pleased him because it suggested nothing more than the correction of an error—in this case an error of Mr. Fitweiler. Mr. Martin had spent each night of the past week working out his plan and examining it. As he walked home now he went over it again. For the hundredth time he resented the element of imprecision, the margin of guesswork that entered into the business. The project as he had worked it out was casual and bold, the risks were considerable. Something might go wrong anywhere along the line. And therein lay the cunning of his scheme. No one would ever see in it the cautious, painstaking hand of Erwin Martin, head of the filing department at F & S, of whom Mr. Fitweiler had once said, "Man is fallible but Martin isn't." No one would see his hand, that is, unless it were caught in the act.

Sitting in his apartment, drinking a glass of milk, Mr. Martin reviewed his case against Mrs. Ulgine Barrows, as he had every night for seven nights. He began at the beginning. Her quacking voice and braying laugh had first profaned the halls of F & S on March 7, 1941 (Mr. Martin had a head for dates). Old Roberts, the personnel chief, had introduced her as the newly appointed special adviser to the president of the firm, Mr. Fitweiler. The woman had appalled Mr. Martin instantly, but he hadn't shown it. He had given her his dry hand, a look of studious concentration, and a faint smile. "Well," she had said, looking at the papers on his desk, "are you lifting the oxcart out of the ditch?" As Mr. [9] Martin recalled that moment, over his milk, he squirmed slightly. He must keep his mind on her crimes as a special adviser, not on her peccadillos as a personality. This he found difficult to do, in spite of entering an objection and sustaining it. The faults of the woman as a woman kept chattering on in his mind like an unruly witness. She had, for almost two years now, baited him. In the halls, in the elevator, even in his own office, into which she romped now and then like a circus horse, she was constantly shouting these silly questions at him. "Are you lifting the oxcart out of the ditch? Are you tearing up the pea patch? Are you hollering down the rain barrel? Are you scraping around the bottom of the pickle barrel? Are you sitting in the catbird seat?"

It was Joey Hart, one of Mr. Martin's two assistants, who had explained what the gibberish meant. "She must be a Dodger fan," he had said. "Red Barber announces the Dodger games over the radio and he uses those expressions—picked 'em up down South." Joey had gone on to explain one or two. "Tearing up the pea patch" meant going on a rampage; "sitting in the catbird seat" meant sitting pretty, like a batter with three balls and no strikes on him. Mr. Martin dismissed all this with an effort. It had been annoying, it had driven him near to distraction, but he was too solid a man to be moved to murder by anything so childish. It was fortunate, he reflected as he passed on to the important charges against Mrs. Barrows, that he had stood up under it so well. He had maintained always an outward appearance of polite tolerance. "Why, I even believe you like the woman," Miss Paird, his other assistant, had once said to him. He had simply smiled.

A gavel rapped in Mr. Martin's mind and the case proper was resumed. Mrs. Ulgine Barrows stood charged with willful, blatant, and persistent attempts to destroy the efficiency and system of F & S. It was competent, material, and relevant to review her advent and rise to power. Mr. Martin had got the story from Miss Paird, who seemed always able to find things out. According to her, Mrs. Barrows had met Mr. Fitweiler at a party, where she had rescued him from the embraces of a powerfully built drunken man who had mistaken the president of F & S for a famous retired Middle Western football coach. She had led him to a sofa and somehow worked upon him a monstrous magic. The aging gentleman had jumped to the conclusion there and then that this was a woman of singular attainments, equipped to bring out the best in him and in the firm. A week later he had introduced [10] her into F & S as his special adviser. On that day confusion got its foot in the door. After Miss Tyson, Mr. Brundage, and Mr. Bartlett had been fired and Mr. Munson had taken his hat and stalked out, mailing in his resignation later, old Roberts had been emboldened to speak to Mr. Fitweiler. He mentioned that Mr. Munson's department had been "a little disrupted" and hadn't they perhaps better resume the old system there? Mr. Fitweiler had said certainly not. He had the greatest faith in Mrs. Barrows' ideas. "They require a little seasoning, a little seasoning, is all," he had added. Mr. Roberts had given it up. Mr. Martin reviewed in detail all the changes wrought by Mrs. Barrows. She had begun chipping at the cornices of the firm's edifice and now she was swinging at the foundation stones with a pickaxe.

Mr. Martin came now, in his summing up, to the afternoon of Monday, November 2, 1942—just one week ago. On that day, at 3 P.M., Mrs. Barrows had bounced into his office. "Boo!" she had yelled. "Are you scraping around the bottom of the pickle barrel?" Mr. Martin had looked at her from under his green eyeshade, saying nothing. She had begun to wander about the office, taking it in with her great, popping eyes. "Do you really need *all* these filing cabinets?" she had demanded suddenly. Mr. Martin's heart had jumped. "Each of these files," he had said, keeping his voice even, "plays an indispensable part in the system of F & S." She had brayed at him, "Well, don't tear up the pea patch!" and gone to the door. From there she had bawled, "But you sure have got a lot of fine scrap in here!" Mr. Martin could no longer doubt that the finger was on his beloved department. Her pickaxe was on the upswing, poised for the first blow. It had not come yet; he had received no blue memo from the enchanted Mr. Fitweiler bearing nonsensical instructions deriving from the obscene woman. But there was no doubt in Mr. Martin's mind that one would be forthcoming. He must act quickly. Already a precious week had gone by. Mr. Martin stood up in his living room, still holding his milk glass. "Gentlemen of the jury," he said to himself, "I demand the death penalty for this horrible person."

The next day Mr. Martin followed his routine, as usual. He polished his glasses more often and once sharpened an already sharp pencil, but not even Miss Paird noticed. Only once did he catch sight of his victim; she swept past him in the hall with [11] a patronizing

"Hi!" At five-thirty he walked home, as usual, and had a glass of milk, as usual. He had never drunk anything stronger in his life—unless you could count ginger ale. The late Sam Schlosser, the S of F & S, had praised Mr. Martin at a staff meeting several years before for his temperate habits. "Our most efficient worker neither drinks nor smokes," he had said. "The results speak for themselves." Mr. Fitweiler had sat by, nodding approval.

Mr. Martin was still thinking about that red-letter day as he walked over to the Schrafft's on Fifth Avenue near Forty-sixth Street. He got there, as he always did, at eight o'clock. He finished his dinner and the financial page of the *Sun* at a quarter to nine, as he always did. It was his custom after dinner to take a walk. This time he walked down Fifth Avenue at a casual pace. His gloved hands felt moist and warm, his forehead cold. He transferred the Camels from his overcoat to a jacket pocket. He wondered, as he did so, if they did not represent an unnecessary note of strain. Mrs. Barrows smoked only Luckies. It was his idea to puff a few puffs on a Camel (after the rubbing-out), stub it out in the ashtray holding her lipstick-stained Luckies, and thus drag a small red herring across the trail. Perhaps it was not a good idea. It would take time. He might even choke, too loudly.

Mr. Martin had never seen the house on West Twelfth Street where Mrs. Barrows lived, but he had a clear enough picture of it. Fortunately, she had bragged to everybody about her ducky first-floor apartment in the perfectly darling three-story red-brick. There would be no doorman or other attendants; just the tenants of the second and third floors. As he walked along, Mr. Martin realized that he would get there before nine-thirty. He had considered walking north on Fifth Avenue from Schrafft's to a point from which it would take him until ten o'clock to reach the house. At that hour people were less likely to be coming in or going out. But the procedure would have made an awkward loop in the straight thread of his casualness, and he had abandoned it. It was impossible to figure when people would be entering or leaving the house, anyway. There was a great risk at any hour. If he ran into anybody, he would simply have to place the rubbing-out of Ulgine Barrows in the inactive file forever. The same thing would hold true if there were someone in her apartment. In that case he would just say that he had been passing by, recognized her charming house and thought to drop in. [12]

It was eighteen minutes after nine when Mr. Martin turned into Twelfth Street. A man passed him, and a man and a woman talking. There was no one within fifty paces when he came to the house, half-way down the block. He was up the steps and in the small vestibule in no time, pressing the bell under the card that said "Mrs. Ulgine Barrows." When the clicking in the lock started, he jumped forward against the door. He got inside fast, closing the door behind him. A bulb in a lantern hung from the hall ceiling on a chain seemed to give a monstrously bright light. There was nobody on the stair, which went up ahead of him along the left wall. A door opened down the hall in the wall on the right. He went toward it swiftly, on tiptoe.

"Well, for God's sake, look who's here!" bawled Mrs. Barrows, and her braying laugh rang out like the report of a shotgun. He rushed past her like a football tackle, bumping her. "Hey, quit shoving!" she said, closing the door behind them. They were in her living room, which seemed to Mr. Martin to be lighted by a hundred lamps. "What's after you?" she said. "You're as jumpy as a goat." He found he was unable to speak. His heart was wheezing in his throat. "I—yes," he finally brought out. She was jabbering and laughing as she started to help him off with his coat. "No, no," he said. "I'll put it here." He took it off and put it on a chair near the door. "Your hat and gloves, too," she said. "You're in a lady's house." He put his hat on top of the coat. Mrs. Barrows seemed larger than he had thought. He kept his gloves on. "I was passing by," he said. "I recognized—is there anyone here?" She laughed louder than ever. "No," she said, "we're all alone. You're as white as a sheet, you funny man. Whatever *has* come over you? I'll mix you a toddy." She started toward a door across the room. "Scotch-and-soda be all right? But say, you don't drink, do you?" She turned and gave him her amused look. Mr. Martin pulled himself together. "Scotch-and-soda will be all right," he heard himself say. He could hear her laughing in the kitchen.

Mr. Martin looked quickly around the living room for the weapon. He had counted on finding one there. There were andirons and a poker and something in a corner that looked like an Indian club. None of them would do. It couldn't be that way. He began to pace around. He came to a desk. On it lay a metal paper knife with an ornate handle. Would it be sharp enough? He reached for it and knocked over a small brass jar. Stamps [13] spilled out of it and it fell to the floor with a clatter. "Hey," Mrs. Barrows yelled from the kitchen, "are you tearing up the pea patch?" Mr. Martin gave a strange laugh. Picking up the knife, he tried its point against his left wrist. It was blunt. It wouldn't do.

When Mrs. Barrows reappeared, carrying two highballs, Mr. Martin, standing there with his gloves on, became acutely conscious of the fantasy he had wrought. Cigarettes in his pocket, a drink prepared for him—it was all too grossly improbable. It was more than that; it was impossible. Somewhere in the back of his mind a vague idea stirred, sprouted. "For heaven's sake, take off those gloves," said Mrs. Barrows. "I always wear them in the house," said Mr. Martin. The idea began to bloom, strange and wonderful. She put the glasses on a coffee table in front of a sofa and sat on the sofa. "Come over here, you odd little man," she said. Mr. Martin went over and sat beside her. It was difficult getting a cigarette out of the pack of Camels, but he managed it. She held a match for him, laughing. "Well," she said, handing him his drink, "this is perfectly marvelous. You with a drink and a cigarette."

Mr. Martin puffed, not too awkwardly, and took a gulp of the highball. "I drink and smoke all the time," he said. He clinked his glass against hers. "Here's nuts to that old windbag, Fitweiler," he said, and gulped again. The stuff tasted awful, but he made no grimace. "Really, Mr. Martin," she said, her voice and posture changing, "you are insulting our employer." Mrs. Barrows was now all special adviser to the president. "I am preparing a bomb," said Mr. Martin, "which will blow the old goat higher than hell." He had only had a little of the drink, which was not strong. It couldn't be that. "Do you take dope or something?" Mrs. Barrows asked coldly. "Heroin," said Mr. Martin. "I'll be coked to the gills when I bump that old buzzard off." "Mr. Martin!" she shouted, getting to her feet. "That will be all of that. You must go at once." Mr. Martin took another swallow of his drink. He tapped his cigarette out in the ashtray and put the pack of Camels on the coffee table. Then he got up. She stood glaring at him. He walked over and put on his hat and coat. "Not a word about this," he said, and laid an index finger against his lips. All Mrs. Barrows could bring out was "Really!" Mr. Martin put his hand on the doorknob. "I'm sitting in the catbird seat," he [14] said. He stuck his tongue out at her and left. Nobody saw him go.

Mr. Martin got to his apartment, walking, well before eleven.

No one saw him go in. He had two glasses of milk after brushing his teeth, and he felt elated. It wasn't tipsiness, because he hadn't been tipsy. Anyway, the walk had worn off all effects of the whisky. He got in bed and read a magazine for a while. He was asleep before midnight.

Mr. Martin got to the office at eight-thirty the next morning, as usual. At a quarter to nine, Ulgine Barrows, who had never before arrived at work before ten, swept into his office. "I'm reporting to Mr. Fitweiler now!" she shouted. "If he turns you over to the police, it's no more than you deserve!" Mr. Martin gave her a look of shocked surprise. "I beg your pardon?" he said. Mrs. Barrows snorted and bounced out of the room, leaving Miss Paird and Joey Hart staring after her. "What's the matter with that old devil now?" asked Miss Paird. "I have no idea," said Mr. Martin, resuming his work. The other two looked at him and then at each other. Miss Paird got up and went out. She walked slowly past the closed door of Mr. Fitweiler's office. Mrs. Barrows was yelling inside, but she was not braying. Miss Paird could not hear what the woman was saying. She went back to her desk.

Forty-five minutes later, Mrs. Barrows left the president's office and went into her own, shutting the door. It wasn't until half an hour later that Mr. Fitweiler sent for Mr. Martin. The head of the filing department, neat, quiet, attentive, stood in front of the old man's desk. Mr. Fitweiler was pale and nervous. He took his glasses off and twiddled them. He made a small, bruffing sound in his throat. "Martin," he said, "you have been with us more than twenty years." "Twenty-two, sir," said Mr. Martin. "In that time," pursued the president, "your work and your—uh—manner have been exemplary." "I trust so, sir," said Mr. Martin. "I have understood, Martin," said Mr. Fitweiler, "that you have never taken a drink or smoked." "That is correct, sir," said Mr. Martin. "Ah, yes." Mr. Fitweiler polished his glasses. "You may describe what you did after leaving the office yesterday, Martin," he said. Mr. Martin allowed less than a second for his bewildered pause. "Certainly, sir," he said. "I walked home. Then I went to Schrafft's for dinner. Afterward I walked home again. I went to bed early, sir, and read a magazine for a [15] while. I was asleep before eleven." "Ah, yes," said Mr. Fitweiler again. He was silent for a moment, searching for the proper words to say to the head of the filing department. "Mrs. Barrows," he said finally, "Mrs. Barrows has

worked hard, Martin, very hard. It grieves me to report that she has
suffered a severe breakdown. It has taken the form of a persecution
complex accompanied by distressing hallucinations." "I am very sorry,
sir," said Mr. Martin. "Mrs. Barrows is under the delusion," continued
Mr. Fitweiler, "that you visited her last evening and behaved yourself in an—uh—unseemly manner." He raised his hand to silence Mr.
Martin's little pained outcry. "It is the nature of these psychological
diseases," Mr. Fitweiler said, "to fix upon the least likely and most
innocent party as the—uh—source of persecution. These matters are
not for the lay mind to grasp, Martin. I've just had my psychiatrist,
Dr. Fitch, on the phone. He would not, of course, commit himself, but
he made enough generalizations to substantiate my suspicions. I suggested to Mrs. Barrows when she had completed her—uh—story to me
this morning, that she visit Dr. Fitch, for I suspected a condition at
once. She flew, I regret to say, into a rage, and demanded—uh—requested that I call you on the carpet. You may not know, Martin, but
Mrs. Barrows had planned a reorganization of your department—
subject to my approval, of course, subject to my approval. This brought
you, rather than anyone else, to her mind—but again that is a phenomenon for Dr. Fitch and not for us. So, Martin, I am afraid Mrs
Barrows' usefulness here is at an end." "I am dreadfully sorry, sir,"
said Mr. Martin.

It was at this point that the door to the office blew open with the
suddenness of a gas-main explosion and Mrs. Barrows catapulted
through it. "Is the little rat denying it?" she screamed. "He can't get
away with that!" Mr. Martin got up and moved discreetly to a point
beside Mr. Fitweiler's chair. "You drank and smoked at my apartment," she bawled at Mr. Martin, "and you know it! You called Mr.
Fitweiler an old windbag and said you were going to blow him up
when you got coked to the gills on your heroin!" She stopped yelling
to catch her breath and a new glint came into her popping eyes. "If
you weren't such a drab, ordinary little man," she said, "I'd think
you'd planned it all. Sticking your tongue out, saying you were sitting
in the catbird seat, because you thought no one would believe me
when I told it! My God, it's really too perfect!" She brayed loudly
and [16] hysterically, and the fury was on her again. She glared at Mr.
Fitweiler. "Can't you see how he has tricked us, you old fool? Can't
you see his little game?" But Mr. Fitweiler had been surreptitiously
pressing all the buttons under the top of his desk and employees of

F & S began pouring into the room. "Stockton," said Mr. Fitweiler, "you and Fishbein will take Mrs. Barrows to her home. Mrs. Powell, you will go with them." Stockton, who had played a little football in high school, blocked Mrs. Barrows as she made for Mr. Martin. It took him and Fishbein together to force her out of the door into the hall, crowded with stenographers and office boys. She was still screaming imprecations at Mr. Martin, tangled and contradictory imprecations. The hubbub finally died out down the corridor.

"I regret that this has happened," said Mr. Fitweiler. "I shall ask you to dismiss it from your mind, Martin." "Yes, sir," said Mr. Martin, anticipating his chief's "That will be all" by moving to the door. "I will dismiss it." He went out and shut the door, and his step was light and quick in the hall. When he entered his department he had slowed down to his customary gait, and he walked quietly across the room to the W20 file, wearing a look of studious concentration. [17]

Laura

◆◆◆ SAKI [H. H. MUNRO]

Saki [H. H. Munro], "Laura" [1914], in *The Short Stories of Saki* (New
York, The Viking Press, Inc., 1930).

"YOU ARE NOT really dying, are you?" asked Amanda.

"I have the doctor's permission to live till Tuesday," said Laura.

"But today is Saturday; this is serious!" gasped Amanda. [267]

"I don't know about it being serious; it is certainly Saturday," said
Laura.

"Death is always serious," said Amanda.

"I never said I was going to die. I am presumably going to leave
off being Laura, but I shall go on being something. An animal of some
kind, I suppose. You see, when one hasn't been very good in the life
one has just lived, one reincarnates in some lower organism. And I
haven't been very good, when one comes to think of it. I've been petty
and mean and vindictive and all that sort of thing when circumstances
have seemed to warrant it."

"Circumstances never warrant that sort of thing," said Amanda
hastily.

"If you don't mind my saying so," observed Laura, "Egbert is a
circumstance that would warrant any amount of that sort of thing.
You're married to him—that's different; you've sworn to love, honour,
and endure him: I haven't."

"I don't see what's wrong with Egbert," protested Amanda.

"Oh, I dare say the wrongness has been on my part," admitted
Laura dispassionately; "he has merely been the extenuating circumstance. He made a thin, peevish kind of fuss, for instance, when I took
the collie puppies from the farm out for a run the other day."

"They chased his young broods of speckled Sussex and drove two
sitting hens off their nests, besides running all over the flower beds.
You know how devoted he is to his poultry and garden."

"Anyhow, he needn't have gone on about it for the entire evening
and then have said, 'Let's say no more about it' just when I was
beginning to enjoy the discussion. That's where one of my petty

vindictive revenges came in," added Laura with an unrepentant chuckle; "I turned the entire family of speckled Sussex into his seedling shed the day after the puppy episode."

"How could you?" exclaimed Amanda.

"It came quite easy," said Laura; "two of the hens pretended to be laying at the time, but I was firm."

"And we thought it was an accident!" [268]

"You see," resumed Laura, "I really *have* some grounds for supposing that my next incarnation will be in a lower organism. I shall be an animal of some kind. On the other hand, I haven't been a bad sort in my way, so I think I may count on being a nice animal, something elegant and lively, with a love of fun. An otter, perhaps."

"I can't imagine you as an otter," said Amanda.

"Well, I don't suppose you can imagine me as an angel, if it comes to that," said Laura.

Amanda was silent. She couldn't.

"Personally I think an otter life would be rather enjoyable," continued Laura; "salmon to eat all the year round, and the satisfaction of being able to fetch the trout in their own homes without having to wait for hours till they condescend to rise to the fly you've been dangling before them; and an elegant svelte figure—"

"Think of the otter hounds," interposed Amanda; "how dreadful to be hunted and harried and finally worried to death!"

"Rather fun with half the neighbourhood looking on, and anyhow not worse than this Saturday-to-Tuesday business of dying by inches; and then I should go on into something else. If I had been a moderately good otter I suppose I should get back into human shape of some sort; probably something rather primitive—a little brown, unclothed Nubian boy, I should think."

"I wish you would be serious," sighed Amanda; "you really ought to be if you're only going to live till Tuesday."

As a matter of fact Laura died on Monday.

"So dreadfully upsetting," Amanda complained to her uncle-in-law, Sir Lulworth Quayne. "I've asked quite a lot of people down for golf and fishing, and the rhododendrons are just looking their best."

"Laura always was inconsiderate," said Sir Lulworth; "she was born during Goodwood week, with an Ambassador staying in the house who hated babies."

"She had the maddest kind of ideas," said Amanda; "do you know if there was any insanity in her family?" [269]

"Insanity? No, I never heard of any. Her father lives in West Kensington, but I believe he's sane on all other subjects."

"She had an idea that she was going to be reincarnated as an otter," said Amanda.

"One meets with those ideas of reincarnation so frequently, even in the West," said Sir Lulworth, "that one can hardly set them down as being mad. And Laura was such an unaccountable person in this life that I should not like to lay down definite rules as to what she might be doing in an after state."

"You think she really might have passed into some animal form?" asked Amanda. She was one of those who shape their opinions rather readily from the standpoint of those around them.

Just then Egbert entered the breakfast-room, wearing an air of bereavement that Laura's demise would have been insufficient, in itself, to account for.

"Four of my speckled Sussex have been killed," he exclaimed; "the very four that were to go to the show on Friday. One of them was dragged away and eaten right in the middle of that new carnation bed that I've been to such trouble and expense over. My best flower bed and my best fowls singled out for destruction; it almost seems as if the brute that did the deed had special knowledge how to be as devastating as possible in a short space of time."

"Was it a fox, do you think?" asked Amanda.

"Sounds more like a polecat," said Sir Lulworth.

"No," said Egbert, "there were marks of webbed feet all over the place, and we followed the tracks down to the stream at the bottom of the garden; evidently an otter."

Amanda looked quickly and furtively across at Sir Lulworth.

Egbert was too agitated to eat any breakfast, and went out to superintend the strengthening of the poultry yard defences.

"I think she might at least have waited till the funeral was over," said Amanda in a scandalized voice.

"It's her own funeral, you know," said Sir Lulworth; "it's a nice point in etiquette how far one ought to show respect to one's own mortal remains." [270]

Disregard for mortuary convention was carried to further lengths next day; during the absence of the family at the funeral ceremony the remaining survivors of the speckled Sussex were massacred. The marauder's line of retreat seemed to have embraced most of the flower beds on the lawn, but the strawberry beds in the lower garden had also suffered.

"I shall get the otter hounds to come here at the earliest possible moment," said Egbert savagely.

"On no account! You can't dream of such a thing!" exclaimed Amanda. "I mean, it wouldn't do, so soon after a funeral in the house."

"It's a case of necessity," said Egbert; "once an otter takes to that sort of thing it won't stop."

"Perhaps it will go elsewhere now that there are no more fowls left," suggested Amanda.

"One would think you wanted to shield the beast," said Egbert.

"There's been so little water in the stream lately," objected Amanda; "it seems hardly sporting to hunt an animal when it has so little chance of taking refuge anywhere."

"Good gracious!" fumed Egbert, "I'm not thinking about sport. I want to have the animal killed as soon as possible."

Even Amanda's opposition weakened when, during church time on the following Sunday, the otter made its way into the house, raided half a salmon from the larder and worried it into scaly fragments on the Persian rug in Egbert's studio.

"We shall have it hiding under our beds and biting pieces out of our feet before long," said Egbert, and from what Amanda knew of this particular otter she felt that the possibility was not a remote one.

On the evening preceding the day fixed for the hunt Amanda spent a solitary hour walking by the banks of the stream, making what she imagined to be hound noises. It was charitably supposed by those who overheard her performance, that she was practising for farmyard imitations at the forthcoming village entertainment.

It was her friend and neighbour, Aurora Burret, who brought her news of the day's sport. [271]

"Pity you weren't out; we had quite a good day. We found at once, in the pool just below your garden."

"Did you—kill?" asked Amanda.

"Rather. A fine she-otter. Your husband got rather badly bitten in trying to 'tail it.' Poor beast, I felt quite sorry for it, it had such a human look in its eyes when it was killed. You'll call me silly, but do you know who the look reminded me of? My dear woman, what is the matter?"

When Amanda had recovered to a certain extent from her attack of nervous prostration Egbert took her to the Nile Valley to recuperate. Change of scene speedily brought about the desired recovery of health and mental balance. The escapades of an adventurous otter in search of a variation of diet were viewed in their proper light. Amanda's normally placed temperament reasserted itself. Even a hurricane of shouted curses, coming from her husband's dressing-room, in her husband's voice, but hardly in his usual vocabulary, failed to disturb her serenity as she made a leisurely toilet one evening in a Cairo hotel.

"What is the matter? What has happened?" she asked in amused curiosity.

"The little beast has thrown all my clean shirts into the bath! Wait till I catch you, you little—"

"What little beast?" asked Amanda, suppressing a desire to laugh; Egbert's language was so hopelessly inadequate to express his outraged feelings.

"A little beast of a naked brown Nubian boy," spluttered Egbert.

And now Amanda is seriously ill. [272]

Why I Live at the P.O.

◆◇◆   EUDORA WELTY

Eudora Welty, "Why I Live at the P.O.," in *A Curtain of Green* (New York, Harcourt, Brace and Company, 1941).

I WAS getting along fine with Mama, Papa-Daddy and Uncle Rondo until my sister Stella-Rondo just separated from her husband and came back home again. Mr. Whitaker! Of course I went with Mr. Whitaker first, when he first appeared here in China Grove, taking "Pose Yourself" photos, and Stella-Rondo broke us up. Told him I was one-sided. Bigger on one side than the other, which is a deliberate, calculated falsehood: I'm the same. Stella-Rondo is exactly twelve months to the day younger than I am and for that reason she's spoiled.

She's always had anything in the world she wanted and then she'd throw it away. Papa-Daddy gave her this gorgeous Add-a-Pearl necklace when she was eight years old and she threw it away playing baseball when she was nine, with only two pearls. [89]

So as soon as she got married and moved away from home the first thing she did was separate! From Mr. Whitaker! This photographer with the popeyes she said she trusted. Came home from one of those towns up in Illinois and to our complete surprise brought this child of two.

Mama said she like to make her drop dead for a second. "Here you had this marvelous blonde child and never so much as wrote your mother a word about it," says Mama. "I'm thoroughly ashamed of you." But of course she wasn't.

Stella-Rondo just calmly takes off this *hat,* I wish you could see it. She says, "Why, Mama, Shirley-T.'s adopted, I can prove it."

"How?" says Mama, but all I says was, "H'm!" There I was over the hot stove, trying to stretch two chickens over five people and a completely unexpected child into the bargain, without one moment's notice.

"What do you mean—'H'm!'?" says Stella-Rondo, and Mama says, "I heard that, Sister."

I said that oh, I didn't mean a thing, only that whoever Shirley-T.

159

was, she was the spit-image of Papa-Daddy if he'd cut off his beard, which of course he'd never do in the world. Papa-Daddy's Mama's papa and sulks.

Stella-Rondo got furious! She said, "Sister, I don't need to tell you you got a lot of nerve and always did have and I'll thank you to make no [90] future reference to my adopted child whatsoever."

"Very well," I said. "Very well, very well. Of course I noticed at once she looks like Mr. Whitaker's side too. That frown. She looks like a cross between Mr. Whitaker and Papa-Daddy."

"Well, all I can say is she isn't."

"She looks exactly like Shirley Temple to me," says Mama, but Shirley-T. just ran away from her.

So the first thing Stella-Rondo did at the table was turn Papa-Daddy against me.

"Papa-Daddy," she says. He was trying to cut up his meat. "Papa-Daddy!" I was taken completely by surprise. Papa-Daddy is about a million years old and's got this long-long beard. "Papa-Daddy, Sister says she fails to understand why you don't cut off your beard."

So Papa-Daddy l-a-y-s down his knife and fork! He's real rich. Mama says he is, he says he isn't. So he says, "Have I heard correctly? You don't understand why I don't cut off my beard?"

"Why," I says, "Papa-Daddy, of course I understand, I did not say any such of a thing, the idea!"

He says, "Hussy!"

I says, "Papa-Daddy, you know I wouldn't any more want you to cut off your beard than the man in the moon. It was the farthest thing from [91] my mind! Stella-Rondo sat there and made that up while she was eating breast of chicken."

But he says, "So the postmistress fails to understand why I don't cut off my beard. Which job I got you through my influence with the government. 'Bird's nest'—is that what you call it?"

Not that it isn't the next to smallest P.O. in the entire state of Mississippi.

I says, "Oh, Papa-Daddy," I says, "I didn't say any such of a thing, I never dreamed it was a bird's nest, I have always been grateful though this is the next to smallest P.O. in the state of Mississippi, and I do not enjoy being referred to as a hussy by my own grandfather."

But Stella-Rondo says, "Yes, you did say it too. Anybody in the world could of heard you, that had ears."

"Stop right there," says Mama, looking at *me*.

So I pulled my napkin straight back through the napkin ring and left the table.

As soon as I was out of the room Mama says, "Call her back, or she'll starve to death," but Papa-Daddy says, "This is the beard I started growing on the Coast when I was fifteen years old." He would of gone on till nightfall if Shirley-T. hadn't lost the Milky Way she ate in Cairo.

So Papa-Daddy says, "I am going out and lie in the hammock, and you can all sit here and remember my words: I'll never cut off my beard [92] as long as I live, even one inch, and I don't appreciate it in you at all." Passed right by me in the hall and went straight out and got in the hammock.

It would be a holiday. It wasn't five minutes before Uncle Rondo suddenly appeared in the hall in one of Stella-Rondo's flesh-colored kimonos, all cut on the bias, like something Mr. Whitaker probably thought was gorgeous.

"Uncle Rondo!" I says. "I didn't know who that was! Where are you going?"

"Sister," he says, "get out of my way, I'm poisoned."

"If you're poisoned stay away from Papa-Daddy," I says. "Keep out of the hammock, Papa-Daddy will certainly beat you on the head if you come within forty miles of him. He thinks I deliberately said he ought to cut off his beard after he got me the P.O., and I've told him and told him and told him, and he acts like he just don't hear me. Papa-Daddy must of gone stone deaf."

"He picked a fine day to do it then," says Uncle Rondo, and before you could say "Jack Robinson" flew out in the yard.

What he'd really done, he'd drunk another bottle of that prescription. He does it every single Fourth of July as sure as shooting, and it's horribly expensive. Then he falls over in the hammock and snores. So he insisted on zigzagging [93] right on out to the hammock, looking like a half-wit.

Papa-Daddy woke up with this horrible yell and right there without moving an inch he tried to turn Uncle Rondo against me. I heard every word he said. Oh, he told Uncle Rondo I didn't learn to read till I was eight years old and he didn't see how in the world I ever got the mail put up at the P.O., much less read it all, and he said if Uncle Rondo could only fathom the lengths he had gone to to get me that job! And he said on the other hand he thought Stella-Rondo had a brilliant mind and deserved credit for getting out of town. All the time he was just lying there swinging as pretty as you please and looping out his beard, and poor Uncle Rondo was *pleading* with him to slow down the hammock, it was making him as dizzy as a witch to watch it. But that's what Papa-Daddy likes about a hammock. So Uncle Rondo was too dizzy to get turned against me for the time being. He's Mama's only brother and is a good case of a one-track mind. Ask anybody. A certified pharmacist.

Just then I heard Stella-Rondo raising the upstairs window. While she was married she got this peculiar idea that it's cooler with the windows shut and locked. So she has to raise the window before she can make a soul hear her outdoors.

So she raises the window and says, "*Oh!*" You [94] would have thought she was mortally wounded.

Uncle Rondo and Papa-Daddy didn't even look up, but kept right on with what they were doing. I had to laugh.

I flew up the stairs and threw the door open! I says, "What in the wide world's the matter, Stella-Rondo? You mortally wounded?"

"No," she says, "I'm not mortally wounded but I wish you would do me the favor of looking out that window there and telling me what you see."

So I shade my eyes and look out the window.

"I see the front yard," I says.

"Don't you see any human beings?" she says.

"I see Uncle Rondo trying to run Papa-Daddy out of the hammock," I says. "Nothing more. Naturally, it's so suffocating-hot in the house, with all the windows shut and locked, everybody who cares to stay in their right mind will have to go out and get in the hammock before the Fourth of July is over."

"Don't you notice anything different about Uncle Rondo?" asks Stella-Rondo.

"Why, no, except he's got on some terrible-looking flesh-colored contraption I wouldn't be found dead in, is all I can see," I says.

"Never mind, you won't be found dead in it, because it happens to be part of my trousseau, and Mr. Whitaker took several dozen [95] photographs of me in it," says Stella-Rondo. "What on earth could Uncle Rondo *mean* by wearing part of my trousseau out in the broad open daylight without saying so much as 'Kiss my foot,' *knowing* I only got home this morning after my separation and hung my negligee up on the bathroom door, just as nervous as I could be?"

"I'm sure I don't know, and what do you expect me to do about it?" I says. "Jump out the window?"

"No, I expect nothing of the kind. I simply declare that Uncle Rondo looks like a fool in it, that's all," she says. "It makes me sick to my stomach."

"Well, he looks as good as he can," I says. "As good as anybody in reason could." I stood up for Uncle Rondo, please remember. And I said to Stella-Rondo, "I think I would do well not to criticize so freely if I were you and came home with a two-year-old child I had never said a word about, and no explanation whatever about my separation."

"I asked you the instant I entered this house not to refer one more time to my adopted child, and you gave me your word of honor you would not," was all Stella-Rondo would say, and started pulling out every one of her eyebrows with some cheap Kress tweezers.

So I merely slammed the door behind me and [96] went down and made some green-tomato pickle. Somebody had to do it. Of course Mama had turned both the niggers loose; she always said no earthly power could hold one anyway on the Fourth of July, so she wouldn't even try. It turned out that Jaypan fell in the lake and came within a very narrow limit of drowning.

So Mama trots in. Lifts up the lid and says, "H'm! Not very good for your Uncle Rondo in his precarious condition, I must say. Or poor little adopted Shirley-T. Shame on you!"

That made me tired. I says, "Well, Stella-Rondo had better thank her lucky stars it was her instead of me came trotting in with that very peculiar-looking child. Now if it had been me that trotted in from Illinois and brought a peculiar-looking child of two, I shudder to think of the reception I'd of got, much less controlled the diet of an entire family."

"But you must remember, Sister, that you were never married to Mr. Whitaker in the first place and didn't go up to Illinois to live," says Mama, shaking a spoon in my face. "If you had I would of been just as overjoyed to see you and your little adopted girl as I was to see Stella-Rondo, when you wound up with your separation and came on back home."

"You would not," I says.

"Don't contradict me, I would," says Mama. [97]

But I said she couldn't convince me though she talked till she was blue in the face. Then I said, "Besides, you know as well as I do that that child is not adopted."

"She most certainly is adopted," says Mama, stiff as a poker.

I says, "Why, Mama, Stella-Rondo had her just as sure as anything in this world, and just too stuck up to admit it."

"Why, Sister," said Mama. "Here I thought we were going to have a pleasant Fourth of July, and you start right out not believing a word your own baby sister tells you!"

"Just like Cousin Annie Flo. Went to her grave denying the facts of life," I remind Mama.

"I told you if you ever mentioned Annie Flo's name I'd slap your face," says Mama, and slaps my face.

"All right, you wait and see," I says.

"I," says Mama, "*I* prefer to take my children's word for anything when it's humanly possible." You ought to see Mama, she weighs two hundred pounds and has real tiny feet.

Just then something perfectly horrible occurred to me.

"Mama," I says, "can that child talk?" I simply had to whisper! "Mama, I wonder if that child can be—you know—in any way? Do you realize," I says, "that she hasn't spoken one single, solitary [98] word to a human being up to this minute? This is the way she looks," I says, and I looked like this.

Well, Mama and I just stood there and stared at each other. It was horrible!

"I remember well that Joe Whitaker frequently drank like a fish," says Mama. "I believed to my soul he drank *chemicals*." And without another word she marches to the foot of the stairs and calls Stella-Rondo.

"Stella-Rondo? O-o-o-o-o! Stella-Rondo!"

"What?" says Stella-Rondo from upstairs. Not even the grace to get up off the bed.

"Can that child of yours talk?" asks Mama.

Stella-Rondo says, "Can she what?"

"Talk! Talk!" says Mama. "Burdyburdyburdyburdy!"

So Stella-Rondo yells back, "Who says she can't talk?"

"Sister says so," says Mama.

"You didn't have to tell me, I know whose word of honor don't mean a thing in this house," says Stella-Rondo.

And in a minute the loudest Yankee voice I ever heard in my life yells out, "OE'm Pop-OE the Sailor-r-r Ma-a-an!" and then somebody jumps up and down in the upstairs hall. In another second the house would of fallen down.

"Not only talks, she can tap-dance!" calls [99] Stella-Rondo. "Which is more than some people I won't name can do."

"Why, the little precious darling thing!" Mama says, so surprised. "Just as smart as she can be!" Starts talking baby talk right there. Then she turns on me. "Sister, you ought to be thoroughly ashamed! Run upstairs this instant and apologize to Stella-Rondo and Shirley-T."

"Apologize for what?" I says. "I merely wondered if the child was normal, that's all. Now that she's proved she is, why, I have nothing further to say."

But Mama just turned on her heel and flew out, furious. She ran right upstairs and hugged the baby. She believed it was adopted. Stella-Rondo hadn't done a thing but turn her against me from upstairs while I stood there helpless over the hot stove. So that made Mama, Papa-Daddy and the baby all on Stella-Rondo's side.

Next, Uncle Rondo.

I must say that Uncle Rondo has been marvelous to me at various times in the past and I was completely unprepared to be made to jump out of my skin, the way it turned out. Once Stella-Rondo did something perfectly horrible to him—broke a chain letter from Flanders Field—and he took the radio back he had given her and gave it to me. Stella-Rondo was furious! For six months we all had to call her Stella instead of [100] Stella-Rondo, or she wouldn't answer. I always thought Uncle Rondo had all the brains of the entire family. Another time he sent me to Mammoth Cave, with all expenses paid.

But this would be the day he was drinking that prescription, the Fourth of July.

So at supper Stella-Rondo speaks up and says she thinks Uncle Rondo ought to try to eat a little something. So finally Uncle Rondo said he would try a little cold biscuits and ketchup, but that was all. So *she* brought it to him.

"Do you think it wise to disport with ketchup in Stella-Rondo's flesh-colored kimono?" I says. Trying to be considerate! If Stella-Rondo couldn't watch out for her trousseau, somebody had to.

"Any objections?" asks Uncle Rondo, just about to pour out all the ketchup.

"Don't mind what she says, Uncle Rondo," says Stella-Rondo. "Sister has been devoting this solid afternoon to sneering out my bedroom window at the way you look."

"What's that?" says Uncle Rondo. Uncle Rondo has got the most terrible temper in the world. Anything is liable to make him tear the house down if it comes at the wrong time.

So Stella-Rondo says, "Sister says, 'Uncle Rondo certainly does look like a fool in that pink kimono!'"

Do you remember who it was really said that? [101]

Uncle Rondo spills out all the ketchup and jumps out of his chair and tears off the kimono and throws it down on the dirty floor and puts his foot on it. It had to be sent all the way to Jackson to the cleaners and re-pleated.

"So that's your opinion of your Uncle Rondo, is it?" he says. "I look like a fool, do I? Well, that's the last straw. A whole day in this house with nothing to do, and then to hear you come out with a remark like that behind my back!"

"I didn't say any such of a thing, Uncle Rondo," I says, "and I'm not saying who did, either. Why, I think you look all right. Just try to take care of yourself and not talk and eat at the same time," I says. "I think you better go lie down."

"Lie down my foot," says Uncle Rondo. I ought to of known by that he was fixing to do something perfectly horrible.

So he didn't do anything that night in the precarious state he was in—just played Casino with Mama and Stella-Rondo and Shirley-T. and gave Shirley-T. a nickel with a head on both sides. It tickled her nearly to death, and she called him "Papa." But at 6:30 A.M. the next morning, he threw a whole five-cent package of some unsold one-inch firecrackers from the store as hard as he could into my bedroom and they every one went off. Not one bad one in the string. Anybody else, there'd be one that wouldn't go off. [102]

Well, I'm just terribly susceptible to noise of any kind, the doctor has always told me I was the most sensitive person he had ever seen in his whole life, and I was simply prostrated. I couldn't eat! People tell me they heard it as far as the cemetery, and old Aunt Jep Patterson, that had been holding her own so good, thought it was Judgment Day and she was going to meet her whole family. It's usually so quiet here.

And I'll tell you it didn't take me any longer than a minute to make up my mind what to do. There I was with the whole entire house on Stella-Rondo's side and turned against me. If I have anything at all I have pride.

So I just decided I'd go straight down to the P.O. There's plenty of room there in the back, I says to myself.

Well! I made no bones about letting the family catch on to what I was up to. I didn't try to conceal it.

The first thing they knew, I marched in where they were all playing Old Maid and pulled the electric oscillating fan out by the plug, and everything got real hot. Next I snatched the pillow I'd done the needlepoint on right off the davenport from behind Papa-Daddy. He went "Ugh!" I beat Stella-Rondo up the stairs and finally found my charm bracelet in her bureau drawer under a picture of Nelson Eddy. [103]

"So that's the way the land lies," says Uncle Rondo. There he was, piecing on the ham. "Well, Sister, I'll be glad to donate my army cot if you got any place to set it up, providing you'll leave right this minute and let me get some peace." Uncle Rondo was in France.

"Thank you kindly for the cot and 'peace' is hardly the word I would select if I had to resort to firecrackers at 6:30 A.M. in a young girl's bedroom," I says back to him. "And as to where I intend to go, you seem to forget my position as postmistress of China Grove, Mississippi," I says. "I've always got the P.O."

Well, that made them all sit up and take notice.

I went out front and started digging up some four-o'clocks to plant around the P.O.

"Ah-ah-ah!" says Mama, raising the window. "Those happen to be my four-o'clocks. Everything planted in that star is mine. I've never known you to make anything grow in your life."

"Very well," I says. "But I take the fern. Even you, Mama, can't stand there and deny that I'm the one watered that fern. And I happen to know where I can send in a box top and get a packet of one thousand mixed seeds, no two the same kind, free."

"Oh, where?" Mama wants to know.

But I says, "Too late. You 'tend to your house, and I'll 'tend to mine. You hear things like that [104] all the time if you know how to listen to the radio. Perfectly marvelous offers. Get anything you want free."

So I hope to tell you I marched in and got that radio, and they could of all bit a nail in two, especially Stella-Rondo, that it used to belong to, and she well knew she couldn't get it back, I'd sue for it like a shot. And I very politely took the sewing-machine motor I helped pay the most on to give Mama for Christmas back in 1929, and a good big calendar, with the first-aid remedies on it. The thermometer and the Hawaiian ukulele certainly were rightfully mine, and I stood on the step-ladder and got all my watermelon-rind preserves and every fruit and vegetable I'd put up, every jar. Then I began to pull the tacks out of the bluebird wall vases on the archway to the dining room.

"Who told you you could have those, Miss Priss?" says Mama, fanning as hard as she could.

"I bought 'em and I'll keep track of 'em," I says. "I'll tack 'em up one on each side the post-office window, and you can see 'em when you come to ask me for your mail, if you're so dead to see 'em."

"Not I! I'll never darken the door to that post office again if I live to be a hundred," Mama says. "Ungrateful child! After all the money we spent on you at the Normal." [105]

"Me either," says Stella-Rondo. "You can just let my mail lie there and *rot*, for all I care. I'll never come and relieve you of a single, solitary piece."

"I should worry," I says. "And who you think's going to sit down and write you all those big fat letters and postcards, by the way? Mr. Whitaker? Just because he was the only man ever dropped down in China Grove and you got him—unfairly—is he going to sit down and write you a lengthy correspondence after you come home giving no rhyme nor reason whatsoever for your separation and no explanation for the presence of that child? I may not have your brilliant mind, but I fail to see it."

So Mama says, "Sister, I've told you a thousand times that Stella-Rondo simply got homesick, and this child is far too big to be hers," and she says, "Now, why don't you all just sit down and play Casino?"

Then Shirley-T. sticks out her tongue at me in this perfectly horrible way. She has no more manners than the man in the moon. I told her she was going to cross her eyes like that some day and they'd stick.

"It's too late to stop me now," I says. "You should have tried that yesterday. I'm going to the P.O. and the only way you can possibly see me is to visit me there." [106]

So Papa-Daddy says, "You'll never catch me setting foot in that post office, even if I should take a notion into my head to write a letter some place." He says, "I won't have you reachin' out of that little old window with a pair of shears and cuttin' off any beard of mine. I'm too smart for you!"

"We all are," says Stella-Rondo.

But I said, "If you're so smart, where's Mr. Whitaker?"

So then Uncle Rondo says, "I'll thank you from now on to stop reading all the orders I get on postcards and telling everybody in China Grove what you think is the matter with them," but I says, "I draw my own conclusions and will continue in the future to draw them." I says, "If people want to write their inmost secrets on penny postcards, there's nothing in the wide world you can do about it, Uncle Rondo."

"And if you think we'll ever *write* another postcard you're sadly mistaken," says Mama.

"Cutting off your nose to spite your face then," I says. "But if you're all determined to have no more to do with the U.S. mail, think of this: What will Stella-Rondo do now, if she wants to tell Mr. Whitaker to come after her?"

"Wah!" says Stella-Rondo. I knew she'd cry. She had a conniption fit right there in the kitchen. [107]

"It will be interesting to see how long she holds out," I says. "And now—I am leaving."

"Good-bye," says Uncle Rondo.

"Oh, I declare," says Mama, "to think that a family of mine should quarrel on the Fourth of July, or the day after, over Stella-Rondo leaving old Mr. Whitaker and having the sweetest little adopted child! It looks like we'd all be glad!"

"Wah!" says Stella-Rondo, and has a fresh conniption fit.

"*He* left *her*—you mark my words," I says. "That's Mr. Whitaker. I know Mr. Whitaker. After all, I knew him first. I said from the beginning he'd up and leave her. I foretold every single thing that's happened."

"Where did he go?" asks Mama.

"Probably to the North Pole, if he knows what's good for him," I says.

But Stella-Rondo just bawled and wouldn't say another word. She flew to her room and slammed the door.

"Now look what you've gone and done, Sister," says Mama. "You go apologize."

"I haven't got time, I'm leaving," I says.

"Well, what are you waiting around for?" asks Uncle Rondo.

So I just picked up the kitchen clock and marched off, without saying "Kiss my foot" or [108] anything, and never did tell Stella-Rondo good-bye.

There was a nigger girl going along on a little wagon right in front.

"Nigger girl," I says, "come help me haul these things down the hill, I'm going to live in the post office."

Took her nine trips in her express wagon. Uncle Rondo came out on the porch and threw her a nickle.

And that's the last I've laid eyes on any of my family or my family laid eyes on me for five solid days and nights. Stella-Rondo may be telling the most horrible tales in the world about Mr. Whitaker, but I haven't heard them. As I tell everybody, I draw my own conclusions.

But oh, I like it here. It's ideal, as I've been saying. You see, I've got everything cater-cornered, the way I like it. Hear the radio? All the war news. Radio, sewing machine, book ends, ironing board and that great big piano lamp—peace, that's what I like. Butter-bean vines planted all along the front where the strings are.

Of course, there's not much mail. My family are naturally the main people in China Grove, and if they prefer to vanish from the face of the earth, for all the mail they get or the mail they write, why, I'm not going to open my mouth. [109] Some of the folks here in town are taking up for me and some turned against me. I know which is which. There are always people who will quit buying stamps just to get on the right side of Papa-Daddy.

But here I am, and here I'll stay. I want the world to know I'm happy.

And if Stella-Rondo should come to me this minute, on bended knees, and *attempt* to explain the incidents of her life with Mr. Whitaker, I'd simply put my fingers in both my ears and refuse to listen. [110]

A Reasonable Facsimile

◆◇◆   JEAN STAFFORD

Jean Stafford, "A Reasonable Facsimile," in *The New Yorker*, XXXIII (August 3, 1957), 20–30.

FAR from withering on the vine from apathy and loneliness after his retirement as chairman of the Philosophy Department at Nevilles College, Dr. Bohrmann had a second blooming, and it was observed amongst his colleagues and his idolatrous students that he would age with gusto and live to be a hundred. He looked on the end of his academic career—an impressive one that had earned him an international reputation in scholarly quarters—as simply the end of one phase of his life, and when he began the new one, he did so with fresh accoutrements, for, as he had been fond of saying to his students, "Change is the only stimulus." He took up the study of Japanese (he said with a smile that he would write hokku as tributes to his friends on stormy days); he took up engraving and lettering (designed a new bookplate, designed a gravestone for his dead wife); he began to grow Persian melons under glass; he took up mycology, and mycophagy as well, sending his fidgety housekeeper off into shrill protests as he flirted with death by eating mushrooms gathered in cow pastures and on golf links. He abandoned chess for bridge, and two evenings a week played a cutthroat game with Miss Blossom Duveen, the bursar's blond and bawdy secretary, as his partner and as his opponents Mr. Street, the logician, and Mr. Street's hopelessly scatterbrained wife.

But the radical thing about his new life was the house he had had built for himself in the spring semester of his last year at the college. It was a house of tomorrow—cantilevered, half glass—six miles out on the prairies that confronted the mountain range in whose foothills lay Adams, the town where the college was. The house, though small and narrow, was long, and it looked like a ship, for there was a deck that went all the way around it; from certain points Dr. Bohrmann could see Pikes Peak, a hundred and fifty miles away, and from every point he could watch the multiform weather: there dark rain, here blinding sunshine, yonder a sulphurous dust storm, haze on the summit of one

peak, a pillow of cloud concealing a second, hyaline light on the glacier
of a third. The house amazed that nondescript, stick-in-the-mud
Western town, which, from the day it was founded, had been putting
up the worst eyesores it could think of. Whoever on earth would have
dreamed that the professor, absent-minded and old, riding a bicycle,
wearing oldfangled gaiters and an Old World cape, would make such
an angular nest for himself and drastically paint it bright pink? The
incongruity between the man and his habitat could not possibly have
been greater. He belonged in and had, in fact, spent most of his life in
fusty parlors where stout, permanent furniture (bookcases with glass
fronts, mahogany secretaries with big claw feet, lounges upholstered
in quilted black leather, ottomans, immovable bureaus, round tables
as heavy as lead) bulked larger than life in the dim-orange light of
hanging lamps with fringe. You could see him cleaving through those
portières people used to have that were made of long strands of brown
wooden beads; you could see him hanging his hat on a much ramified
hatrack. Imagine, then, this character, with his silver beard, wearing
a hazel coat-sweater from J. C. Penney, and a mussed green tweed
suit, those gaiters, a stiff-collared shirt, a Tyrolian hat—dressed, in
general, for an altogether different *mise en scène*—sitting in a black
sling chair on the front deck of this gleaming, youthful house, drinking
ginger beer out of an earthenware mug and looking through binocu-
lars at eagles and the weather. Or look at him pottering in his pretty
Oriental garden (it had a steeply arching bridge over a lily pond and
a weeping willow, and a deformed pine tree that he had brought down
from up near the timber line), shading himself with the kind of giant
black bumbershoot one associates with hotel doormen in a pouring
rain. See him in his sleek, slender blond dining room eating a mutton
chop or blood pudding with red cabbage, drinking *dunkles Bier* from
a stein. No matter where you placed him in that house, he simply
would not match. It was the joke of Adams, but a good-natured one,
for Dr. Bohrmann was the pet of the town.

Dr. Bohrmann and his wife, who died two years before his retirement, had arrived in Colorado from Freiburg by way of Montreal,
where, just as he was beginning to make his presence felt at the university, he was halted in his stride by a sudden, astounding hemorrhage
of the lungs. When, after seventeen wan, lengthy months, he was discharged from the sanitarium, not as cured but as arrested, his careful
doctors counselled him to go West, to the Rocky Mountains, under

whose blue, bright skies he could, in time, rout the last bacterium. On their further recommendation, he applied for an appointment at Nevilles College, since Adams was famous for the particular salubrity of its air. And providence was pleased to accommodate him, having a few months earlier created a vacancy on the staff through the death—from tuberculosis—of a young instructor. Adams was high above sea level and its prospect of soaring palisades and pinnacles of rock was magnificent, if, at first, dismaying to European eyes that had been accustomed to grandeur on a smaller scale. Moreover, the faculty of its college was remarkable—was, in part, illustrious—because so many of its members had come here for Dr. Bohrmann's reason; if their distemper had been of a different nature, they would have lectured in much grander but moister groves—in New Haven or Princeton, in Oxford or Bonn. For the most part, they accepted their predicament with grace—it is no myth that the tubercular is by and large a sanguine fellow—and lived urbanely in rented houses, year by year meaning it less and less when they stated their resolve that as soon as their health was completely restored they would go back to the East or to their foreign fatherlands. Although their New York *Times* came four days late, and although perhaps they were not in the thick of things, neither did their minds abide in Shangri-La. Visiting lecturers and vacationing friends were bound to admit that the insular community was remarkably *au courant* and that within it there was an exchange of ideas as brilliant and constant as the Colorado sun.

At first, when the Bohrmanns came, in 1912, they had no intention of lingering any longer [20] than was absolutely necessary. But after little more than a year, neither of them could imagine living anywhere else; the immaculate air was deliciously inebriating and the sun, in those superlative heavens, fed them with the vibrancy of youth. They daily rejoiced in their physical existence, breathed deeply, and slept like children. They liked to walk on the mesas, gathering kinnikinnick in the winter and pasqueflowers in the spring; sometimes they rented sweet-faced burros and rode up to a waterfall of great temperament and beauty. They admired the turbulent colors of the sunsets, the profound snows of winter, the plangent thunderstorms of summer. There was, they said, some sort of spell upon the place that bound them to it; roving the tablelands, whence one could gaze for miles on miles upon the works of God, they paused in silence, their hands upon their quickened, infatuated hearts. And besides the land, they loved the people of it, both the autochthonous Town and the dislocated Gown; students thronged their house at the *gemütlich* coffee hour, and their coevals and their elders came at night to drink hot wine or beer and, endlessly, in witty, learned periods, to talk.

Sometimes Dr. Bohrmann and Hedda spoke of summering in Europe—in spite of their contentment, they were often grievously homesick for Freiburg—and occasionally they went so far as to book passage, but something always prevented them from going. One year, Wolfgang was engaged in writing a monograph on Maimonides for the *Hibbert Journal,* another year Hedda was bedridden for a long while after a miscarriage that doomed them, to their everlasting sorrow, to childlessness. After the Second World War, they no longer even spoke of going back, for the thought of how Freiburg now must look sickened them.

All in all, they had an uncommonly happy life and they so much enjoyed each other that when Hedda died, with no warning at all, of heart disease, Wolfgang's friends were afraid that he, too, might die, of grief. And, indeed, he asked for a semester's leave and spent the whole of it indoors, seldom answering his doorbell and never answering his telephone. But, at the end of that time, he emerged as companionable and as exuberant as ever, as much at home with life.

It was then, upon his return to the mild and miniature hurly-burly of the campus, that he began to lay in his supplies against the lean times when his rank would be emeritus. He started Japanese with Professor Symington, the historian, who, until he had got tuberculosis, had been an Orientalist resident in Kyoto; he read Goren and Culbertson on bridge; he studied every magazine on architecture that was published, and throughout that winter he worked on designs for his new house. In the beginning, when he went to the builders, they dismissed his plans as the work of a visionary—all that expanse of window, they said, was impractical in a cold climate; they said he would rue the day he put a flat roof over his head. If it had been anyone but Dr. Bohrmann, they probably never would have come round, but Dr. Bohrmann had a way about him that could persuade a river to stand still or a builder to build a pavilion at the North Pole. So, in the end, they took on the job, and they admitted, grudgingly but still with fondness, that he had not faltered in his specifications by so much as a fraction of an inch. While the house was going up, he rode out on his bicycle each afternoon at tremendous speed, his romantic mantle billowing, the brim of his hat standing straight up in the wind, to watch the installation of his windows and the progress of his grass; he was like a mother watching, in pride and fascination, the extraordinary daily changes in her first-born.

In June, after his last Commencement, he moved out of the house in which he and Hedda had lived all those years, and he transferred to the new house his vast polylingual library, his busts of Plato and Lucretius and Aesculapius and Kant, his collection of maps and of antique firearms, and Hedda's pure-linen sheets. He sold or gave away the durable, lubberly furniture he and Hedda had accumulated and all those souvenirs of another time—antimacassars, needlepoint cushions, afghans, porcelain umbrella stands, Lalique bud vases. He transplanted his tuberous begonias to the terrace on the west side of the new house and, at the back, he put in mountain-ash trees, a row of eight Lombardy poplars, and an ambitious kitchen garden, bordered with herbs, pinks, primroses, and bachelor's-buttons.

On the morning he moved, after the vans had gone, Dr. Bohrmann got on his bicycle, with his fiddle strapped in its case behind him and his ginger cat in a basket in front of him, and he [21] pedalled out to the plains, singing "Gaudeamus Igitur" in a rich, if untrue, baritone. Street, the logician, saw him wheeling past his house and later said on the telephone to Symington, the historian, "You should have seen *mein Herr Doktor Professor* this morning, with his cat and his fiddle, singing hi-diddle-diddle, ready to hop right over the moon." Symington, with a laugh, rejoined, "When we're pushing up daisies, he'll be learning jujitsu." Blossom Duveen saw him, too; she drove past him in her brash crimson convertible on her way to Denver and a flicker of interest started a flame in her heart; he was really a dear, she thought, and by no means all that old. She wouldn't mind in the least little bit going to live in that snappy, streamlined house.

The moving men, aided by Mrs. Pritchard, the housekeeper who had taken care of Dr. Bohrmann since Hedda's death, and by a crew of students who were staying on for the summer term, had everything in place by midday and had even cleared away the excelsior and the cartons and barrels, and, on the dot of noon, the jocund old professor fired a shot into the sky from a harquebus he himself had restored to working order, the boys gave a cheer, and Dr. Bohrmann opened up a keg of beer. To each of his helpers in turn he genially raised his glass and said "*Prosit.*" Momentarily, as he saluted them, he wished he had bedrooms enough to lodge every one of these warmhearted lads who talked like cow hands but whose minds were critical and tough and appreciative of his own appreciations. He was sorry, so very sorry, that he had no sons. But he erased his useless regret by telling himself that the next best thing to a son was a student and the Lord knew he had a host of those.

When the beer was gone, and the last raffish jalopy had roared away, and Mrs. Pritchard was in the kitchen making his lunch, he went into his new library, handsomely appointed in black wood and saffron upholstery, and, sitting before his windows that commanded a view from the plains to the tundra, he smiled on everything as if he were smiling on a gathering of intimate friends. Then his smile ebbed and his eyes grew grave, for he realized that in a year or two there would be no more of his students to come and match wits with him as they ate apples and pecans and fanned the fire on his hearth with bellows. Once they were out in the world, they seldom came back to Adams, and when they did, they were not the same, for they had outgrown their lucubrations; they were no longer so fervent as they had been, and often their eyes strayed to their wristwatches in the midst of a conversation. Dr. Bohrmann sighed at his sad loss of the young, and he sighed again, sorely missing Hedda; she had laughed so charmingly, he had liked her so extremely well. He thought of her sitting opposite him over a backgammon board, her fingers approaching and then withdrawing from the men, and his heart broke with longing for the sweet look of her perplexity. But then he chided himself for his unphilosophical egocentricity, and reminded himself of the marvels that were to emerge in his gardens and of the quotidian pleasure he was to know in this house with its kingly prospects, and, ashamed that he had brooded even for a minute, he resolutely turned to the morning mail, separating the journals and bulletins from the letters.

For many years, Dr. Bohrmann had kept up a prodigious correspondence with all manner of people all over the world—with a handful of relatives scattered by war and pogroms, with the friends he had known at Freiburg and in Montreal, with his fellow-invalids and the doctors in the tuberculosis sanitarium, with philosophers he had argued with at meetings of learned societies. And besides these, he wrote to a great many people he had never met. His was a nature so benign, so full of generous heart, that whenever he read a book he liked, or a short story or a poem in a magazine, whenever he heard on the radio a piece of music by a contemporary composer, he wrote the author a letter of congratulation—a careful, specific letter that showed he had read or listened with diligence and discrimination. More often than not this ingratiating overture led to a lasting friendship by mail, and, through the years, Dr. Bohrmann grew as conversant with these friends' families and pets and illnesses and sorrows and triumphs as if [22] he had frequently dined at their houses. One time, Rosalind Throop, the greatly gifted young woman novelist in Johannesburg, flatteringly asked him to send a photograph of himself, saying, "Since the shape of your heart is now so clear to me, I am impelled to know the shape of your face as well." He sent a snapshot of himself and Hedda, up to their knees in columbines, a grand reach of snowy peaks behind them, and Mrs. Throop wrote by return mail, "What are these flowers you and the *Frau Professor* wade in? Only last night, before the photograph came, I dreamed I met you in a meadow in the Cots-wolds abloom with Michaelmas daisies, and you said to me, 'We must gather our daisies quickly, for the snows are on their way.' And here in the picture you stand in flowers and at your back there is snow!" Thereafter, in their letters they made allusions to their pastoral en-counter in England, where neither of them had ever been, until it no longer seemed fantasy.

To South Africa and to Japan, to Scotland and France, to Israel and Germany, he sent presents of books and subscriptions to maga-zines and CARE packages; to his friends' children he sent arrowheads and feathered Indian headbands. His correspondents sent him presents in return, and now and then someone dedicated a book to him. When he had been obliged to write of Hedda's death, they mourned sincerely and worried over his solitude, but they took heart once again when he started building his house, of which he sent them photographs.

There was another side to the coin, for often an admiring reader wrote him an appreciation of or an objection to an essay of his that had appeared in the *Journal of the History of Ideas* or in *Revue de Métaphysique et de Morale;* he was a prolific writer and, by his own wry, rueful admission, a prolix one. (Once he had written to Mrs. Throop, "I have read your new novel with the monster's green eye. How you write! If I had but a tittle of talent! I have instead a galloping *cacoëthes scribendi* and you don't go to Heaven on the strength of that! May I be summoned by the Gabriel horn when I'm about a modest business—gathering toadstools, e.g., or making Jap squiggles.") But in spite of the turgid vocabulary and the Germanic, backward syntax of his monographs, Dr. Bohrmann had a wide following, and really nothing in the world pleased him more than a letter from someone who had read him through to the end.

At the time he withdrew from society, after Hedda's death, he acquired a new correspondent, a young man named Henry Medley, who taught English at a college in Florida, and who had come across Dr. Bohrmann's "A Reinquiry into Burke's Aesthetic." This princely lad (Dr. Bohrmann did not stint in his use of laudatory adjectives when he described his partisans) had been inspired to look further into the philosopher's work, and painstakingly he compiled a complete bibliography, which included early studies that Dr. Bohrmann had forgotten altogether and, in some cases, would have preferred to disown. Medley's dossier, gradually revealed in the course of a two-year exchange of letters, was this: he came from the upper regions of New York State and he was in his early twenties; he was the only child of a lawyer father, who had been dead for many years, and of a pedigreed but impecunious mother, who had been reduced to the status of paid companion to "a dragon nearly ninety who hurles her hideous taile about a Hudson-River-Bracketed den. It's here I spend my holidays, keeping a civil tongue in my head." He had worked his way through Harvard by tutoring the rich and retarded, and he had caught swift glimpses of Europe one summer when he had escorted a band of adolescents on a bicycle tour. He wrote Miltonic epics and Elizabethan songs which, someday, when the time and the poems were ripe, he hoped to show Dr. Bohrmann.

Medley had apparently read everything and forgotten nothing, and his immense letters, written on onionskin in a hand so fine that it could only be properly seen through a magnifying glass, were the most learned Dr. Bohrmann had ever got from anyone. When he mentioned that he was taking up Japanese, Medley sent him a list of "musts" to read; when he announced that he was going to build a modern house, Medley wrote at length on Frank Lloyd Wright vs. Miës van der Rohe; he knew about opera, medicine (he could quote from Sydenham, Pliny the Elder, René Théophile Hyacinthe Laënnec), painting, horticulture ("You speak of planting peonies and I presume to warn you, lest you don't know, that they are extremely crotchety. They detest any direct contact with manure and they detest being encroached upon by the roots of trees. And plant shallow!"). He knew movies and jazz and Marx and Freud and Catullus and the Koran, military strategy, iconography, geography, geology, anthropology, theology; he was amused by such cryptosciences as phrenology, alchemy, and astrology; he knew about wines and fish and cheese; he read German, French, Italian, [23] Latin, Greek. He played tennis, swam among coral reefs, and during his Christmas vacations in the North he skied; he repaired the dragon's electrical appliances and designed his mother's clothes. Dr. Bohrmann wrote him once that his name was so apt it could have been taken from the dramatis personae of an allegorical play.

Once in a while, when Medley replied in five close-written pages to something that in Dr. Bohrmann's letter had been virtually no more than a parenthetical musing, Dr. Bohrmann was annoyed and brought him to book for his excess. One time he wrote, "I think you have made a Jungfrau out of the hill of a pygmy mole. My reflections don't *all* deserve such attention, dear boy, and I fear I must have expressed myself more abominably than usual to inspire you to this support of my wisecrack about Euripides. I can't possibly agree with you that he has 'the shabbiest mind in history.' My joke was no good to begin with and I am much ashamed." By return post came an apology so abject that Dr. Bohrmann was further ashamed; nevertheless, he continued to scold Medley whenever he committed that sin he so much deplored —of impassioned, uncritical agreement.

It had been a challenging interchange; the chap was brilliant, though undisciplined and incorrigibly highfalutin. "Don't be so hard on the dumb blondes in your classes," Dr. Bohrmann once wrote him. "What sort of world would it be if we didn't have the Philistines to judge ourselves by? God bless 'em." After that, Medley barely mentioned his trials when he confronted girls in his classrooms who had never heard of Aristotle. But while Medley's voracity was greater than his digestion, Dr. Bohrmann was sure that time would balance his chemistry. No one, these days, was mature at twenty-four. Often, after some especially felicitous letter—for when the boy was at his best and dropped his airs, he was a charmer—Dr. Bohrmann was moved to wish that Henry Medley had been his son. What a delight it would have been to nurture and prune a mind like that! To have a son in whose lineaments he could read dear Hedda's face and his own mind

—ah, *that* would be a harvest for the autumn of an old philosopher's life!

Today, as if to salute him on his first day in his new house, there was a letter from Medley, as thick as ever, and sent, as always, by air-mail. It was posted from the Hudson River town, since his teaching in Florida was over until fall, and he was back with his mother and the dragon, who had got, he wrote, "a barkless dog to match the dummy piano, on which for years she has been playing the Ballades of Chopin. That is, she *says* she is playing Chopin." The first five pages of the letter—there were seven altogether, written in that microscopic hand —gave an account of a few days he had spent in New York on his way up from Florida; he had gone to the museums, and reported his reactions to Matisse and Rembrandt, he had heard some contemporary chamber music, and he had found a set of the eleventh edition of the Encyclopædia Britannica for twenty dollars. He enjoined Dr. Bohrmann to read the article on the alphabet without delay, and from that he went on to say that he had resumed his study of philology and that he found Holthausen's glossary to "Beowulf" far inferior to Klaeber's.

As he read on, Dr. Bohrmann shifted his position from time to time to ease the arthritic pain in his left hip, remembering that in the confusion of moving today, he had forgotten to take his pain-killing pills. He was, on the whole, in remarkably good health for a man of his age, but he was wearing out in the joints and the eyes—not grievously but in a bothersome way. The energy expended on Medley's New York stay made his legs and his heart ache. Page six of the letter began, "Now for the surprise, which I hope you will accept with as much pleasure as I take in the telling of it." We all like surprises and Dr. Bohrmann was no different from the rest of us; hoping for news of the arrival of a box of oranges from Florida [24] perhaps, or something edible that was indigenous to upstate New York, he polished the magnifying glass and read on. He learned that Medley was getting a free automobile ride to the West with some former Harvard classmates who were going out to dig in Arizona, and that he would like to propose himself, "as our English cousins say, for a week or two weeks, or however long you enjoy me as your vis-à-vis. I will come with my own quarters (pup tent), and my own kitchen (portable grill), and hope you will give me houseroom in your back yard, though, should I detract from the aspect, I'll go up to your famous mesa. If my calculations are correct, and if we are not hindered by any act of God, and *if,* etc., I should be on your doorstep, with my camp, my typewriter, a change of shirt, and a sheaf of poems, on the 25th of June." He went on to say that he was anxious to do some mountain climbing and visit a cattle ranch and tour the ghost towns; that he had all sorts of ideas for Dr. Bohrmann's Oriental garden, which he would disclose on his arrival; that he had enough questions to ask, and theories to expound, and half theories to solidify, to last "till two each morning for a lifetime." He added, in a postscript, "Since I'm leaving tomorrow, I'm afraid there will be no way for you to put me off. But the cordiality of your letters, dear sir, gives me confidence in your welcome. I cherish the prospect of your midnight oil."

In all his life, Dr. Bohrmann had never had a house guest (it would, of course, be unthinkably infra dig to let the kid pitch a tent in the yard when there was an unused bedroom), not through any want of hospitality but because it was a matter that had never arisen, and he was so surprised by Medley's precipitous and inexorable assignment to him of the role of host that, while he never drank before five and seldom then drank spirits, he called to Mrs. Pritchard for the whiskey bottle and a glass.

Mrs. Pritchard, who was shaped like a pear and wore a blue mustache under a fleshy and ferocious bill, was punctual to the point of addiction (the professor said that she suffered from "chronic chronomania"), and, moreover, the slightest breach in routine sent her into a flushed and flustered minor nervous breakdown. "Whiskey? In the middle of the day?" she shouted from the kitchen, appalled. "But you've already had your beer, and I'm putting the soufflé in. This nice soufflé with chives in will be a fizzle." But she came bustling into the library anyhow with the whiskey and some ice, and, setting them down beside him, she said, "I declare! Are we going to have meals any which way just because we've moved into a modernistic house?"

"I don't know," said Dr. Bohrmann thoughtfully. "I don't know what our life is going to be from now on, Mrs. Pritchard. We have a guest arriving—a Mr. Henry Medley."

"A guest for lunch? You *might* have told me!"

"No, no. Not a guest for lunch today. On Friday a young man is arriving to spend several days—perhaps weeks. Who knows? He offers to live in a wigwam under the trees. But we'll give him the spare room, Mrs. Pritchard."

Mrs. Pritchard gaped like a landed fish, but all she managed to say was, "He can't come Friday. Friday is your night for bridge, and the Streets and Miss Duveen are coming to dinner. You might have remembered that when you invited him."

"Well, the fact is, I didn't exactly invite him," said Dr. Bohrmann. "He is dropping out of the blue, so to speak. He is springing full grown out of the Hudson River."

"You mean you don't know him? Do you mean to tell me that I am to [25] fetch and carry for a total stranger? A strange *young man?*" Mrs. Pritchard keenly disliked the young, and when students came to call, she was as rude to them as she could possibly be without actually boxing their ears.

Dr. Bohrmann, flinching under his housekeeper's snapping eyes, timorously said, "If we don't like him, we'll turn him out. But I think we're going to like him. I think we're going to find him a man of parts."

"Then why do you have to have whiskey just the selfsame minute I've put my soufflé in the oven?" Mrs. Pritchard, as she often said of herself, was nobody's fool. With this retort, she went back to the kitchen, and the needless bangings and crashes that came from it indicated plainly that she did not mean to take Medley's intrusion lying down.

As the professor drank, he was in a tumult of emotions, a most uncommon condition for him, a placid man. He was a little uneasy at contemplating a change of pace in his life (the remark about the midnight oil alarmed him; he had gone to bed at ten o'clock ever since he could remember), and he was a little scared of Medley's erudition; part of the pleasure, shameful to be sure, of teaching at Nevilles had been that for the most part his students were as green as grass. But, on the other hand, he was touched to think of having a daily companion of such enthusiasm; they could walk together on the mesas and dispute matters pertaining to God and man and, in lighter moods, they could go to the movies. He began to consider how he might influence and temper his young friend's thought; in his imagination Henry Medley became so malleable that Dr. Bohrmann, with tenderness and tact, molded him into one of the most impressive figures on the intellectual scene of the twentieth century. How about adopting him? He could be a sort of monument to Dr. Bohrmann after Dr. Bohrmann's bones were laid to rest, beside Hedda's.

He caught himself up in the midst of his daydream and said to himself, "Come off it, Bohrmann," and turned aside to read a light-hearted scenic postcard from Mrs. Throop, sent from Durban, where she was having a holiday with her children. "I like gathering sea shells beside the Indian Ocean so very much better than writing novels," she wrote in a relaxed and generous hand, "and I do it so much better. These lovely shells! Jon is making a collection of them, to repay you for the arrowheads. You see, you're a daily part of our life."

Darling Mrs. Throop! He wished he could adopt *her*. He wished that all his distant friends were coming to bless his house.

When Henry Medley arrived, at about dusk, he greeted his host in a torrent of epigrammatic and perfect Hanoverian German, refused the offer of the spare bedroom, and then, cajoled, accepted it. And he began to unload his gear from the taxi that had brought him up from the interurban station. (He had parted with his companions in Denver.) Besides the tent and the portable grill and the sleeping bag, he had brought two bulging Gladstones, a typewriter, a tennis racket, a pair of skis, a rifle, a fishing rod and tackle box, a recorder, a green baize bag full of books, extensive photographic equipment, and two large boxes of cuttings of field flowers from the Hudson Valley. At the sight of the skis, Mrs. Pritchard's eyebrows disappeared into her hair; there would be no skiing near Adams for three months. Before Medley went up to his room, he produced two bottles of Bernkasteler Doktor from the depths of one of the Gladstones and asked Mrs. Pritchard, with ineffable sweetness, to make a *Bowle* (for which he gave her the recipe), so that he could toast "the most distinguished scholar in America." Such was his sweetness and such, also, his air of authority that Mrs. Pritchard, that virago and nobody's fool, was disarmed, and trotted obediently to the kitchen and began to cut up fruit.

Before Dr. Bohrmann had got any real impression of the youth at all—beyond the fact that he lived like a gale—he found himself sitting on the western deck, sipping the wine (how had Medley guessed that this was his favorite of all Mosels—the *Bowle* was delicious), and answering Medley's rapid and knowledgeable questions about the differences between ground and push moraines, about glacier flora, about the mining history of this region. The young man listened to the old man's answers as closely as a doctor listening to a heartbeat through a stethoscope, and Dr. Bohrmann had the feeling that he was indelibly recording every fact and every speculation, however irrelevant or tenuous. It is flattering to be so closely attended and so respected, and Dr. Bohrmann glowed as he talked, slaking this burning student's thirst.

Henry Medley wore glasses and a beard, and a beholder, looking at the two from afar, would have said they bore a close resemblance. Nearer at hand, it would have been observed that the frames of the young man's glasses were of thick tortoise shell and that the old man's were gold, that Medley's curly beard was black and Dr. Bohrmann's was straight and frosty. An eavesdropper would have said their German was the same, but an expert would have heard the academy in Medley's inflections and his stilted usages, and would, in Dr. Bohrmann's accent, have heard a southern softening.

At first, dismissing the beard as an amusing coincidence, Dr. Bohrmann's view of the boy was an agreeable one. Henry Medley was small, constructed thriftily and well, and he emanated indestructibility from the soles of his neat little feet, shod in immaculate white sneakers, to the top of his shapely and close-cropped head. His hands were quick and nervous, and darkly stained with nicotine, for he smoked cigarettes ceaselessly, down to nothing; his clever eyes glinted as they swiftly detached themselves from one focus and fixed upon the next. His voice was high and tended to be phrenetic. Despite the voice, despite the crew cut, despite the lissome limbs, Medley gave the impression of having existed on the earth for much more than twenty-four years, and Dr. Bohrmann was sure that at seventy he would not look much different from the way he did now. He was, thought Dr. Bohrmann as the sun began to set, darkening Henry Medley's face and whitening his perfect teeth, like a spruce, good-looking, ageless imp. He was respectful, responsive, articulate, enthusiastic, astoundingly catholic in his information. Dr. Bohrmann, however, was pleased to note that he wasn't perfect: there was somewhere in him a lack—a lack of a quality an imp did not need but a man could not live without. For example, when Dr. Bohrmann inquired about his journey, really wanting to know, Medley was perfunctory. "The Lincoln [26] Highway is as hot as Tophet, and as ugly as sin—the trip was no Odyssey to put into dactylic hexameters," and then asked Dr. Bohrmann how he would evaluate Croce as a historian. Generally people of this age were so self-centered that one was obliged to defend oneself against autobiography with the greatest diplomacy. But Medley was so unselfcentered that Dr. Bohrmann began to wonder if he had a self at all. He would discuss his plans, but not his aspirations; he would talk about his ideas on a subject, but not his feelings on it; he would quote from "Voyage of the 'Beagle,'" but would not say that he longed to go on a voyage himself. It comes from having no father, and only a mother and a dragon and dumb little blondes, said Dr. Bohrmann to himself, and he resolved to rear this orphan imp into a human creature.

That evening, at dinner, Medley was a smashing success. As Mr. Street said afterward, he had never found anyone who had so fully grasped Whitehead and Russell; the ladies were delighted with his droll descriptions of Hudson River Bracketed and his account of a meeting with a manufacturer of embalming supplies. When Medley praised the *coq au vin,* Mrs. Pritchard fell head over heels in love; when he gave a short talk on the viticulture of the Rhine, the Hochheimer in their glasses turned to nectar. After dinner, when the bridge game began, he sat quietly in a distant corner of the library reading the "Diary of William Dunlap" until Blossom Duveen protested and archly told her host that he was rude. Thereafter, at the end of each rubber, someone sat out, and, in the end, as it happened, Medley was always at the table. He played, said the overwhelmed logician Street, like a rattlesnake.

At half past nine, as his elders were yawning, having had enough bridge and having finished the one weak highball they allowed themselves, Medley said, "I don't suppose you'd like me to teach you ombre? I learned it after a close reading of 'The Rape of the Lock.'"

And so, for two more hours, the company spent a stimulating, if puzzling, time with a pack of forty cards, learning—or, rather, failing to learn—such terms as *manille* and *basto,* and being reminded every so often by their teacher that "There is no *ponto* in black trumps, and this is most important to remember."

When the Streets and Miss Duveen departed, they were seen to the door not only by their host but by Medley as well, who warmly shook hands with them all and cordially said he hoped they would meet again soon. Back in the library, he tidied up, emptying ashtrays, putting away the cards, plumping up the cushions. Suddenly, in the midst of his housewifery, his eyes began to water, and then he sneezed explosively and repeatedly; in the lacunae between these detonations, he grimaced painfully and mopped his face and made a sort of moaning sound.

"Poor chap," said Dr. Bohrmann. "I expect it's some pollen or other from the prairie. We've been very dry this year."

"Not pollen," gasped Medley. "That!" And with a quivering fore-finger he pointed at Grimalkin, the ginger cat, who had apparently come into the house through his own entrance, which Dr. Bohrmann had had cut into the kitchen door, and was sitting on the window sill, looking with interest at the shaking and sneezing and wheezing stranger.

What a way for the visit to begin and the evening to end! Breathing with difficulty, Medley told Dr. Bohrmann that from earliest childhood, cats had affected him thus. What was there to do? Plainly Grimalkin, an admirable cat and the lord of the manor, would not dream of changing his habits. And Dr. Bohrmann would not dream of Medley's going up to the mesa with his tent or—for Medley, in his discomfort that was mixed with fear, proposed this—of his returning at once to the dragon and her barkless dog.

"But look here," said Dr. Bohrmann. "My beast has never set foot in the spare room—I assure you it's innocent of his dangerous dander. Come along upstairs and let's see if you don't feel better."

Once in his bedroom, Medley gulped down antihistamines of divers colors and did presently feel better. He said he would stay out of the cat's way, and Dr. Bohrmann, very unhappy over the contre-temps, said that he and Mrs. Pritchard would do what they could to keep Grimalkin out of the house; at this time of year he had a good deal of business outdoors, what with hunting shrews and smelling flowers. Dr. Bohrmann would board up the cat door first thing the next day.

In the morning, as Dr. Bohrmann was going through the upper hall, he found the corpse of a gopher on the floor in front of Medley's door. In spite of himself he smiled, and when he went into the dining room and found Grimalkin in his accustomed chair, opposite his own, he stroked the tom's big manly head and said, "Rotten cat! Wicked cat! How did you get in?" though he knew perfectly well Grimalkin had got in through his own private door. The cat, according to his lifetime habit, had his breakfast of corn flakes, well saturated with heavy cream. His purr, as he ate, was loud and smug.

Mrs. Pritchard had, since Dr. Bohrmann [27] had known her, loved three creatures: Hedda, himself, and Grimalkin. For the cat she bought toys at the five-and-ten, grew catnip in a flowerpot in the kitchen, made special dishes (he was particularly fond of corn pudding); she brushed him, scratched him behind the ears, petted him, talked to him, suffered him to involve himself in her knitting. And when Dr. Bohrmann, strengthening himself with an unwonted third cup of coffee, announced to her that he was going to board up the cat door, and that Grimalkin must henceforth live outside because of Medley's disaffection, she was outraged.

"What next!" she cried. "I've been giving that boy some second thoughts. For all his kowtowing and his mealy mouth and his 'Sublime chicken, Mrs. Pritchard' and his 'After you, Dr. Bohrmann,' there's something about him that tells me he's sneaky. Put Grimalkin out of the house indeed! And what if milord takes a scunner to me? Will my door be boarded up, too?"

"Oh, come, Mrs. Pritchard," said Dr. Bohrmann. "It's summer and Grimalkin has plenty to do outdoors. He won't mind for a few days."

"A few days! Did you see those skis? Whoever heard of skiing here before October? To my way of thinking, Mr. Henry Medley brought his entire worldly goods with him and means to stay till kingdom come."

"Oh, lady, be good!" said Dr. Bohrmann, and he sighed. He was not used to domestic trouble and it embarrassed him. Moreover, he was not entirely sure that Mrs. Pritchard was wrong about Medley and he found himself hoping that the boy slept late; he did not feel like a deep conversation just now.

"Very well," said Mrs. Pritchard. "But we shall see what we shall see." And she closed her mouth firmly, scooped Grimalkin up in her loving arms, and marched to the kitchen.

Henry Medley stayed with Dr. Bohrmann for three weeks and was, during this lengthy time, the most sedulous of apes. He rented a bicycle and he bought a Tyrolean hat; he appropriated Dr. Bohrmann's politics and his taste in music and food; in company, he quoted his host continually but did not acknowledge his source. On the second day of his visit, Dr. Bohrmann began to tire of him; on the third day he began to avoid him; on the fourth, he begged a ride to Denver with Blossom Duveen, where he went to a double-feature Western while she was shopping. But Henry Medley was not aware that he bored his host; on the contrary, he often observed that their meeting of minds was enough almost to make him believe in a magnanimous God. He was very busy. Besides tirelessly picking Dr. Bohrmann's brains, he gardened ferociously, moved the porch furniture about, played his recorder and Dr. Bohrmann's fiddle, read his poems aloud (they were awful and long), took hundreds of photographs. At the end of the first week, Dr. Bohrmann, worn out with company and conversation, suggested that Medley join an organized tour that was going to the ghost towns, but Medley replied that unless Dr. Bohrmann went with him, he would prefer to stay at home. He did not go fishing, because Dr. Bohrmann did not fish; he did not play tennis, because Dr. Bohrmann was too old for the courts. They were invited out as a pair, and when Dr. Bohrmann had guests, Medley did the honors. "We are giving you a Piesporter tonight," he would say, or, "We prevailed upon Mrs. Pritchard to make cold sorrel soup." It was *us* and *our* and *we* until Dr. Bohrmann began to feel that his identity was ebbing away from him. Or that he had attached to his side an unmovable homunculus, who, by the way, now spoke German with a Breisgau accent and who mimicked his every thought and every gesture. The gratification he had felt on that first afternoon when Medley had seemed to listen so wisely and so well never returned.

Mrs. Pritchard would not speak to Medley. Her hatred was murderous; it was evident that she would have liked to put arsenic in his food. And it was Mrs. Pritchard who in the end—guileful, beloved thing that she was—dislodged him. Mrs. Pritchard, ably assisted by Grimalkin. She accomplished this through the simple expedient of taking away the board that had immobilized the swinging cat door. But she was very [28] sly. Later on, she confessed that each night she waited up until the young man had gone to bed and then she would creep down to the kitchen and take away the board; in the morning, long before either of the men got up, she nailed it on again.

One night, Dr. Bohrmann was in a restive sleep, troubled by his arthritis and wakened often by the brightness of the moon. He was distressed, moreover, about Medley, for this was the first time in his long life that he had ever really disliked anyone; he had come to detest that bearded and permanent fixture almost as keenly as Mrs. Pritchard did. And what was the matter with him, a man full of years and of experience, that he could not gracefully remove himself from this dilemma? He dozed, and woke, and dozed again. He dreamed sadly of Hedda. They were cycling, he and Hedda, through the Schwarzwald, toiling up a hill but talking continually, though they had little breath. "Aunt Gertrude will be cross because we're late for tea and I promised to bring the butter," said Hedda. Her worry at last made her weep, then sob tragically, and Wolfgang comforted her in shouts; he tried to lower his voice but he could not, and he woke himself by yelling, "We're not too late, my darling! We have until the sun goes down." Startled by the sound of his own voice, he switched on the light. Medley was standing in the doorway.

"Is the cat in here?" he said.

"Look here, Medley," said Dr. Bohrmann in an amazing burst of courage. "I don't like having people walk into my bedroom in the middle of the night."

"I'm sorry, sir, I wouldn't have, only—" and he was seized with a violent paroxysm of sneezes. His red eyes streamed and his breathing, after the sneezes, was stertorous. Obviously he was in for an asthma attack.

Dr. Bohrmann sat up in bed and he grasped at a straw. "Poor chap," he said kindly. "I'm afraid my old ginger tomcat has outwitted us. That's the way they are, you know—foxy."

Medley, in a choked voice, said, "I have concealed this from you, sir, but every morning for a week now, that cat has brought some unspeakable piece of carrion to my bedroom door. Tonight, though, it went the limit. It got into my room through some diabolical system of its own, and now the room will be dangerous for me for days."

Dr. Bohrmann smiled behind his concealing hand. "I'm sorry for that," he said, and clucked his tongue.

"I don't suppose you would . . . No, I don't suppose you would."

"Would what, Medley?"

"Would—oh, no, sir, I won't propose it."

"Get rid of Grimalkin? Is that what you're trying to say?"

"Well, in a manner of speaking."

"No, I would not. I've had my handsome ginger tomcat for fifteen years, and I'll have him till he dies."

"Then, if he's to have the run of the house," said Medley, "I'd better move out to the yard."

"Well, I'll tell you, Medley," said Dr. Bohrmann, ashamed of his cunning and pleased as punch with it, "if Grimalkin has got your number, and it's plain that he has, moving outdoors won't do a particle of good. He'll get into your tent and plague you there. No, Medley, my boy, I'm afraid Grimalkin has us over a barrel."

A frenzy of sneezes—the intellectual face turned red and blue. When the storm was over, Medley leaned weakly against the door and groaned. When he spoke again, there was a decided testiness in his voice. "If I had known you had a cat," he said, "I wouldn't have made this trip. Isn't there *anything* we can do?"

"I'm afraid not," said Dr. Bohrmann. "I'm just afraid there isn't a thing we can do."

"I could go up to the mesa, I suppose?"

"I wouldn't recommend that," said Dr. Bohrmann. "It's rattle-snake time."

"Then what *shall* I do?" He was plaintive and pathetic, and for a split second Dr. Bohrmann almost weakened, but he remembered in time the sapping tedium of Medley's monologues and interroga-tions, and the feeling he had that Medley had robbed him of his own personality, and he said, "It looks like Hudson River Bracketed and the barkless dog for you."

In the morning, when they met at breakfast, Henry Medley was pale and shaky; obviously he had had a very bad night. Dr. Bohrmann, who had slept excellently after his visitor left his room, tried to start a conversation about Spanish cave drawings. But the wind was out of Medley's sails; he smiled wanly and asked to be excused.

The taxi came an hour later, and Medley piled his mountain of belongings into the back seat. Mrs. Pritchard, beaming, brought him a box lunch. Grimalkin, sitting in a lake of sun under [29] the weeping-willow tree, was cleaning a shoulder blade.

"Now you write to me," said Dr. Bohrmann heartily. "Now *auf Wiedersehen,* Medley."

"Goodbye," said Medley sorrowfully. "To think that a cat . . . I might almost think there was a plan behind it."

"Have a good trip, son," said Dr. Bohrmann, and shuddered at the appellation.

At last, sulkily, Medley got into the taxi, and then he rallied and his old self reappeared. He said, in German with a South German accent, "If Grimalkin ever goes to join his ancestors, perhaps you will invite me again? We haven't scratched the surface of our common interests."

But happily the driver started the motor and went off before Dr.

Bohrmann was obliged to reply. Mrs. Pritchard had gone into the
house and now came out again with a dish of sardines, which, without
a word, she handed to Dr. Bohrmann; he received it without a word
and took it to the heroic tom, who accepted it with an open diapason
of purrs. The old man, squatting on his heels beside the cat, surveyed
his pretty garden with delight and looked at his house with amazement. How beautiful and bountiful was life! How charming it was
of accident to cause contrast: it was good to be cold, so that one could
get warm; it was good to wear out so that one could renew oneself; it
was really a lovely thing that Medley had come and had gone. With
these heart-warming and reasonable thoughts, Dr. Bohrmann watched
his cat finish the last fishtail, and then, fetching his big black umbrella, he began to work in his garden. He uprooted the field flowers
Medley had brought from the Hudson Valley, not in anger but because
they had never really belonged with the rest of the planting, and just
as he threw them into the lily pond, Blossom Duveen drove up.

"Came by to remind you it's bridge night," she called out in her
vulgar, brassy voice. "No goulashes tonight, I hope, I hope."

As he strolled over to talk to her, Dr. Bohrmann listed to himself
some of the other pleasures of life: this dumb dear, for example, after
Medley with his hellbent enlightenment; bridge after ombre; a contented Mrs. Pritchard.

"What gives?" said Miss Duveen. "You look like the cat that
swallowed the canary."

"I am," said Dr. Bohrmann, grinning conspiratorially at Grimalkin who was washing the top of his brainy head. [30]

A Voyage
to the Country of the Houyhnhnms

◆◆◆ JONATHAN SWIFT

Jonathan Swift, "A Voyage to the Country of the Houyhnhnms" [1726], in *Gulliver's Travels* (New York, Random House, 1958).

CHAP. I

The Author sets out as Captain of a Ship. His Men conspire against him, confine him a long Time to his Cabbin, set him on Shore in an unknown Land. He travels up into the Country. The Yahoos, *a strange Sort of Animal, described. The Author meets two* Houyhnhnms.

I CONTINUED at home with my Wife and Children about five Months in a very happy Condition, if I could have learned the Lesson of knowing when I was well. I left my poor Wife big with Child, and accepted an advantageous Offer made me to be Captain of the *Adventure,* a stout Merchant-man of 350 Tuns: For I understood Navigation well, and being grown weary of a Surgeon's Employment at Sea, which however I could exercise upon Occasion, I took a skilful young Man of that Calling, one *Robert Purefoy,* into my Ship. We set sail from *Portsmouth* upon the 7th Day of *September,* 1710; on the 14th we met with Captain *Pocock* of *Bristol,* at *Tenariff,* who was going to the Bay of *Campeachy,* to cut Logwood. On the 16th he was parted from us by a Storm: I heard since my Return, that his Ship foundered, and none escaped, but one Cabbin-Boy. He was an honest Man, and a good Sailor, but a little too positive in his own Opinions, which was the Cause of his Destruction, as it hath been of several others. For if he had followed my Advice, he might at this Time have been safe at home with his Family as well as my self.

I had several Men died in my Ship of Calentures, so that I was forced to get Recruits out of *Barbadoes,* and the *Leeward Islands,* where I touched by the Direction of the Merchants who employed me; which I had soon too much Cause to repent; for I [179] found afterwards that most of them had been Buccaneers. I had fifty Hands on

Board; and my Orders were, that I should trade with the *Indians* in the *South-Sea,* and make what Discoveries I could. These Rogues whom I had picked up, debauched my other Men, and they all formed a Conspiracy to seize the Ship and secure me; which they did one Morning, rushing into my Cabbin, and binding me Hand and Foot, threatening to throw me overboard, if I offered to stir. I told them, I was their Prisoner, and would submit. This they made me swear to do, and then unbound me, only fastening one of my Legs with a Chain near my Bed; and placed a Centry at my Door with his Piece charged, who was commanded to shoot me dead if I attempted my Liberty. They sent me down Victuals and Drink, and took the Government of the Ship to themselves. Their Design was to turn Pirates, and plunder the *Spaniards,* which they could not do, till they got more Men. But first they resolved to sell the Goods in the Ship, and then go to *Madagascar* for Recruits, several among them having died since my Confinement. They sailed many Weeks, and traded with the *Indians;* but I knew not what Course they took, being kept close Prisoner in my Cabbin, and expecting nothing less than to be murdered, as they often threatened me.

Upon the 9th Day of *May,* 1711, one *James Welch* came down to my Cabbin; and said he had Orders from the Captain to set me ashore. I expostulated with him, but in vain; neither would he so much as tell me who their new Captain was. They forced me into the Long-boat, letting me put on my best Suit of Cloaths, which were as good as new, and a small Bundle of Linnen, but no Arms except my Hanger; and they were so civil as not to search my Pockets, into which I conveyed what Money I had, with some other little Necessaries. They rowed about a League; and then set me down on a Strand. I desired them to tell me what Country it was: They all swore, they knew no more than my self, but said, that the Captain (as they called him) was resolved, after they had sold the Lading, to get rid of me in the first Place where they discovered Land. They pushed off immediately, advising me to make haste, for fear of being overtaken by the Tide; and bade me farewell.

In this desolate Condition I advanced forward, and soon got upon firm Ground, where I sat down on a Bank to rest my self, and consider what I had best to do. When I was a little refreshed, I went up into the Country, resolving to deliver my self to the first Savages I should meet; and purchase my Life from them by some Bracelets,

Glass Rings, and other Toys, which Sailors usually [180] provide themselves with in those Voyages, and whereof I had some about me: The Land was divided by long Rows of Trees, not regularly planted, but naturally growing; there was great Plenty of Grass, and several Fields of Oats. I walked very circumspectly for fear of being surprised, or suddenly shot with an Arrow from behind, or on either Side. I fell into a beaten Road, where I saw many Tracks of human Feet, and some of Cows, but most of Horses. At last I beheld several Animals in a Field, and one or two of the same Kind sitting in Trees. Their Shape was very singular, and deformed, which a little discomposed me, so that I lay down behind a Thicket to observe them better. Some of them coming forward near the Place where I lay, gave me an Opportunity of distinctly marking their Form. Their Heads and Breasts were covered with a thick Hair, some frizzled and others lank; they had Beards like Goats, and a Long Ridge of Hair down their Backs, and the fore Parts of their Legs and Feet; but the rest of their Bodies were bare, so that I might see their Skins, which were of a brown Buff Colour. They had no Tails, nor any Hair at all on their Buttocks, except about the *Anus;* which, I presume Nature had placed there to defend them as they sat on the Ground; for this Posture they used, as well as lying down, and often stood on their hind Feet. They climbed high Trees, as nimbly as a Squirrel, for they had strong extended Claws before and behind, terminating on sharp Points, hooked. They would often spring, and bound, and leap with prodigious Agility. The Females were not so large as the Males; they had long lank Hair on their Heads, and only a Sort of Down on the rest of their Bodies, except about the *Anus,* and *Pudenda.* Their Dugs hung between their fore Feet, and often reached almost to the Ground as they walked. The Hair of both Sexes was of several Colours, brown, red, black and yellow. Upon the whole, I never beheld in all my Travels so disagreeable an Animal, or one against which I naturally conceived so strong an Antipathy. So that thinking I had seen enough, full of Contempt and Aversion, I got up and pursued the beaten Road, hoping it might direct me to the Cabbin of some *Indian.* I had not gone far when I met one of these Creatures full in my Way, and coming up directly to me. The ugly Monster, when he saw me, distorted several Ways every Feature of his Visage, and stared as at an Object he had never seen before; then approaching nearer, lifted up his fore Paw, whether out of Curiosity or Mischief, I could not tell: But I drew my Hanger, and

gave him a good Blow with the flat Side of it; for I durst not strike
him with the Edge, fearing [181] the Inhabitants might be provoked
against me, if they should come to know, that I had killed or maimed
any of their Cattle. When the Beast felt the Smart, he drew back, and
roared so loud, that a Herd of at least forty came flocking about me
from the next Field, howling and making odious Faces; but I ran to
the Body of a Tree, and leaning my Back against it, kept them off, by
waving my Hanger. Several of this cursed Brood getting hold of the
Branches behind, leaped up into the Tree, from whence they began
to discharge their Excrements on my Head: However, I escaped pretty
well, by sticking close to the Stem of the Tree, but was almost stifled
with the Filth, which fell about me on every Side.

In the Midst of this Distress, I observed them all to run away on
a sudden as fast as they could; at which I ventured to leave the Tree,
and pursue the Road, wondering what it was that could put them into
this Fright. But looking on my Left-Hand, I saw a Horse walking
softly in the Field; which my Persecutors having sooner discovered,
was the Cause of their Flight. The Horse started a little when he came
near me, but soon recovering himself, looked full in my Face with
manifest Tokens of Wonder: He viewed my Hands and Feet, walking
round me several times. I would have pursued my Journey, but he
placed himself directly in the Way, yet looking with a very mild
Aspect, never offering the least Violence. We stood gazing at each
other for some time; at last I took the Boldness, to reach my Hand
towards his Neck, with a Design to stroak it; using the common Style
and Whistle of Jockies when they are going to handle a strange Horse.
But, this Animal seeming to receive my Civilities with Disdain, shook
his Head, and bent his Brows, softly raising up his Left Fore-Foot to
remove my Hand. Then he neighed three or four times, but in so
different a Cadence, that I almost began to think he was speaking to
himself in some Language of his own.

While He and I were thus employed, another Horse came up;
who applying himself to the first in a very formal Manner, they gently
struck each others Right Hoof before, neighing several times by Turns,
and varying the Sound, which seemed to be almost articulate. They
went some Paces off, as if it were to confer together, walking Side by
Side, backward and forward, like Persons deliberating upon some
Affair of Weight; but often turning their Eyes towards me, as it were
to watch that I might not escape. I was amazed to see such Actions and

Behaviour in Brute Beasts; and concluded with myself, that if the Inhabitants [182] of this Country were endued with a proportionable Degree of Reason, they must needs be the wisest People upon Earth. This Thought gave me so much Comfort, that I resolved to go forward until I could discover some House or Village, or meet with any of the Natives; leaving the two Horses to discourse together as they pleased. But the first, who was a Dapple-Grey, observing me to steal off, neighed after me in so expressive a Tone, that I fancied myself to understand what he meant; whereupon I turned back, and came near him, to expect his farther Commands; but concealing my Fear as much as I could; for I began to be in some Pain, how this Adventure might terminate; and the Reader will easily believe I did not much like my present Situation.

The two Horses came up close to me, looking with great Earnestness upon my Face and Hands. The grey Steed rubbed my Hat all round with his Right Fore-hoof, and discomposed it so much, that I was forced to adjust it better, by taking it off, and settling it again; whereat both he and his Companion (who was a brown Bay) appeared to be much surprized; the latter felt the Lappet of my Coat, and finding it to hang loose about me, they both looked with new Signs of Wonder. He stroaked my Right Hand, seeming to admire the Softness, and Colour; but he squeezed it so hard between his Hoof and his Pastern, that I was forced to roar; after which they both touched me with all possible Tenderness. They were under great Perplexity about my Shoes and Stockings, which they felt very often, neighing to each other, and using various Gestures, not unlike those of a Philosopher, when he would attempt to solve some new and difficult Phænomenon.

Upon the whole, the Behaviour of these Animals was so orderly and rational, so acute and judicious, that I at last concluded, they must needs be Magicians, who had thus metamorphosed themselves upon some Design; and seeing a Stranger in the Way, were resolved to divert themselves with him; or perhaps were really amazed at the Sight of a Man so very different in Habit, Feature and Complexion from those who might probably live in so remote a Climate. Upon the Strength of this Reasoning, I ventured to address them in the following Manner: Gentlemen, if you be Conjurers, as I have good Cause to believe, you can understand any Language; therefore I make bold to let your Worships know, that I am a poor distressed *Englishman,* driven by his Misfortunes upon your Coast; and I entreat one of you, to let me ride upon his Back, as if he were a real Horse, to some House or Village, where I can be relieved. In return of which [183] Favour, I will make you a Present of this Knife and Bracelet, (taking them out of my Pocket.) The two Creatures stood silent while I spoke, seeming to listen with great Attention; and when I had ended, they neighed frequently towards each other, as if they were engaged in serious Conversation. I plainly observed, that their Language expressed the Passions very well, and the Words might with little Pains be resolved into an Alphabet more easily than the *Chinese.*

I could frequently distinguish the Word *Yahoo,* which was repeated by each of them several times; and although it were impossible for me to conjecture what it meant, yet while the two Horses were busy in Conversation, I endeavoured to practice this Word upon my Tongue; and as soon as they were silent, I boldly pronounced *Yahoo* in a loud Voice, imitating, at the same time, as near as I could, the Neighing of a Horse; at which they were both visibly surprized, and the Grey repeated the same Word twice, as if he meant to teach me the right Accent, wherein I spoke after him as well as I could, and found myself perceivably to improve every time, although very far from any Degree of Perfection. Then the Bay tried me with a second Word, much harder to be pronounced; but reducing it to the *English Orthography,* may be spelt thus, *Houyhnhnm.* I did not succeed in this so well as the former, but after two or three farther Trials, I had better Fortune; and they both appeared amazed at my Capacity.

After some farther Discourse, which I then conjectured might relate to me, the two Friends took their Leaves, with the same Compliment of striking each other's Hoof; and the Grey made me Signs that I should walk before him; wherein I thought it prudent to comply, till I could find a better Director. When I offered to slacken my Pace, he would cry *Hhuun, Hhuun;* I guessed his Meaning, and gave him to understand, as well as I could, that I was weary, and not able to walk faster; upon which, he would stand a while to let me rest. [184]

CHAP. II

The Author conducted by a Houyhnhnm *to his House. The House described. The Author's Reception. The Food of the* Houyhnhnms. *The Author in Distress for want of Meat, is at last relieved. His Manner of feeding in that Country.*

Having travelled about three Miles, we came to a long Kind of Building, made up of Timber, stuck in the Ground, and wattled across; the Roof was low, and covered with Straw. I now began to be a little comforted; and took out some Toys, which Travellers usually carry for Presents to the Savage *Indians* of *America* and other Parts, in hopes the People of the House would be thereby encouraged to receive me kindly. The Horse made me a Sign to go in first; it was a large Room with a smooth Clay Floor, and a Rack and Manger extending the whole Length on one Side. There were three Nags, and two Mares, not eating, but some of them sitting down upon their Hams, which I very much wondered at; but wondered more to see the rest employed in domestick Business: The last seemed but ordinary Cattle; however this confirmed my first Opinion, that a People who could so far civilize brute Animals, must needs excel in Wisdom all the Nations of the World. The Grey came in just after, and thereby prevented any ill Treatment, which the others might have given me. He neighed to them several times in a Style of Authority, and received Answers.

Beyond this Room there were three others, reaching the Length of the House, to which you passed through three Doors, opposite to each other, in the Manner of a Vista: We went through the second Room towards the third; here the Grey walked in first, beckoning me to attend: I waited in the second Room, and got ready my Presents, for the Master and Mistress of the House: They were two Knives, three Bracelets of false Pearl, a small Looking Glass and a Bead Necklace. The Horse neighed three or four Times, and I waited to hear some Answers in a human Voice, but I heard no other Returns than in the same Dialect, only one or two a little shriller than his. I began to think that this House must belong to some Person of great Note among them, because there appeared so much ceremony before I could gain Admittance. But, that a Man of Quality should be [185] served all by Horses, was beyond my Comprehension. I feared my Brain was disturbed by my Sufferings and Misfortunes: I roused my self, and looked about me in the Room where I was left alone; this was furnished as the first, only after a more elegant Manner. I rubbed mine Eyes often, but the same Objects still occurred. I pinched my Arms and Sides, to awake my self, hoping I might be in a Dream. I then absolutely concluded, that all these Appearances could be nothing else but Necromancy and Magick. But I had no Time to pursue these Reflections;

for the Grey Horse came to the Door, and made me a Sign to follow him into the third Room; where I saw a very comely Mare, together with a Colt and Fole, sitting on their Haunches, upon Mats of Straw, not unartfully made, and perfectly neat and clean.

The Mare soon after my Entrance, rose from her Mat, and coming up close, after having nicely observed my Hands and Face, gave me a most contemptuous Look; then turning to the Horse, I heard the Word *Yahoo* often repeated betwixt them; the meaning of which Word I could not then comprehend, although it were the first I had learned to pronounce; but I was soon better informed, to my everlasting Mortification: For the Horse beckoning to me with his Head, and repeating the Word *Hhuun, Hhuun,* as he did upon the Road, which I understood was to attend him, led me out into a kind of Court, where was another Building at some Distance from the House. Here we entered, and I saw three of those detestable Creatures, which I first met after my landing, feeding upon Roots, and the Flesh of some Animals, which I afterwards found to be that of Asses and Dogs, and now and then a Cow dead by Accident or Disease. They were all tied by the Neck with strong Wyths, fastened to a Beam; they held their Food between the Claws of their fore Feet, and tore it with their Teeth.

The Master Horse ordered a Sorrel Nag, one of his Servants, to untie the largest of these Animals, and take him into a Yard. The Beast and I were brought close together; and our Countenances diligently compared, both by Master and Servant, who thereupon repeated several Times the Word *Yahoo.* My Horror and Astonishment are not to be described, when I observed, in this abominable Animal, a perfect human Figure; the Face of it indeed was flat and broad, the Nose depressed, the Lips large, and the Mouth wide: But these Differences are common to all savage Nations, where the Lineaments of the Countenance are distorted by the Natives suffering their Infants to lie grovelling on the Earth, or by carrying them on their Backs, nuzzling with [186] their Face against the Mother's Shoulders. The Forefeet of the *Yahoo* differed from my Hands in nothing else, but the Length of the Nails, the Coarseness and Brownness of the Palms, and the Hairiness on the Backs. There was the same Resemblance between our Feet, with the same Differences, which I knew very well, although the Horses did not, because of my Shoes and Stockings; the same in every Part of our Bodies, except as to Hairiness and Colour, which I have already described.

The great Difficulty that seemed to stick with the two Horses, was, to see the rest of my Body so very different from that of a *Yahoo,* for which I was obliged to my Cloaths, whereof they had no Conception: The Sorrel Nag offered me a Root, which he held (after their Manner, as we shall describe in its proper Place) between his Hoof and Pastern; I took it in my Hand, and having smelt it, returned it to him again as civilly as I could. He brought out of the *Yahoo's* Kennel a Piece of Ass's Flesh, but it smelt so offensively that I turned from it with loathing; he then threw it to the *Yahoo,* by whom it was greedily devoured. He afterwards shewed me a Whisp of Hay, and a Fettlock full of Oats; but I shook my Head, to signify, that neither of these were Food for me. And indeed, I now apprehended, that I must absolutely starve, if I did not get to some of my own Species: For as to those filthy *Yahoos,* although there were few greater Lovers of Mankind, at that time, than myself; yet I confess I never saw any sensitive Being so detestable on all Accounts; and the more I came near them, the more hateful they grew, while I stayed in that Country. This the Master Horse observed by my Behaviour, and therefore sent the *Yahoo* back to his Kennel. He then put his Forehoof to his Mouth, at which I was much surprized, although he did it with Ease, and with a Motion that appear'd perfectly natural; and made other Signs to know what I would eat; but I could not return him such an Answer as he was able to apprehend; and if he had understood me, I did not see how it was possible to contrive any way for finding myself Nourishment. While we were thus engaged, I observed a Cow passing by; whereupon I pointed to her, and expressed a Desire to let me go and milk her. This had its Effect; for he led me back into the House, and ordered a Mare-servant to open a Room, where a good Store of Milk lay in Earthen and Wooden Vessels, after a very orderly and cleanly Manner. She gave me a large Bowl full, of which I drank very heartily, and found myself well refreshed.

About Noon I saw coming towards the House a Kind of Vehicle, drawn like a Sledge by four *Yahoos.* There was in it an [187] old Steed, who seemed to be of Quality; he alighted with his Hind-feet forward, having by Accident got a Hurt in his Left Fore-foot. He came to dine with our Horse, who received him with great Civility. They dined in the best Room, and had Oats boiled in Milk for the second Course, which the old Horse eat warm, but the rest cold. Their Mangers were placed circular in the Middle of the Room, and divided into several

Partitions, round which they sat on their Haunches upon Bosses of Straw. In the Middle was a large Rack with Angles answering to every Partition of the Manger. So that each Horse and Mare eat their own Hay, and their own Mash of Oats and Milk, with much Decency and Regularity. The Behaviour of the young Colt and Fole appeared very modest; and that of the Master and Mistress extremely chearful and complaisant to their Guest. The Grey ordered me to stand by him; and much Discourse passed between him and his Friend concerning me, as I found by the Stranger's often looking on me, and the frequent Repetition of the Word *Yahoo*.

I happened to wear my Gloves; which the Master Grey observing, seemed perplexed; discovering Signs of Wonder what I had done to my Fore-feet; he put his Hoof three or four times to them, as if he would signify, that I should reduce them to their former Shape, which I presently did, pulling off both my Gloves, and putting them into my Pocket. This occasioned farther Talk, and I saw the Company was pleased with my Behaviour, whereof I soon found the good Effects. I was ordered to speak the few Words I understood; and while they were at Dinner, the Master taught me the Names for Oats, Milk, Fire, Water, and some others; which I could readily pronounce after him; having from my Youth a great Facility in learning Languages.

When Dinner was done, the Master Horse took me aside, and by Signs and Words made me understand the Concern he was in, that I had nothing to eat. Oats in their Tongue are called *Hlunnh*. This Word I pronounced two or three times; for although I had refused them at first, yet upon second Thoughts, I considered that I could contrive to make of them a Kind of Bread, which might be sufficient with Milk to keep me alive, till I could make my Escape to some other Country, and to Creatures of my own Species. The Horse immediately ordered a white Mare-servant of his Family to bring me a good Quantity of Oats in a Sort of wooden Tray. These I heated before the Fire as well as I could, and rubbed them till the Husks came off, which I made a shift to winnow from the Grain; I ground and beat them between [188] two Stones, then took Water, and made them into a Paste or Cake, which I toasted at the Fire, and eat warm with Milk. It was at first a very insipid Diet, although common enough in many Parts of *Europe,* but grew tolerable by Time; and having been often reduced to hard Fare in my Life, this was not the first Experiment I had made how easily Nature is satisfied. And I cannot but observe, that I never had one Hour's Sickness, while I staid in this Island. It is true, I sometimes made a shift to catch a Rabbet, or Bird, by Springes made of *Yahoos* Hairs; and I often gathered wholesome Herbs, which I boiled, or eat as Salades with my Bread; and now and then, for a Rarity, I made a little Butter, and drank the Whey. I was at first at a great Loss for Salt; but Custom soon reconciled the Want of it; and I am confident that the frequent Use of Salt among us is an Effect of Luxury, and was first introduced only as a Provocative to Drink; except where it is necessary for preserving of Flesh in long Voyages, or in Places remote from great Markets. For we observe no Animal to be fond of it but Man: And as to myself, when I left this Country, it was a great while before I could endure the Taste of it in any thing that I eat.

This is enough to say upon the Subject of my Dyet, wherewith other Travellers fill their Books, as if the Readers were personally concerned, whether we fare well or ill. However, it was necessary to mention this Matter, lest the World should think it impossible that I could find Sustenance for three Years in such a Country, and among such Inhabitants.

When it grew towards Evening, the Master Horse ordered a Place for me to lodge in; it was but Six Yards from the House, and separated from the Stable of the *Yahoos*. Here I got some Straw, and covering myself with my own Cloaths, slept very sound. But I was in a short time better accommodated, as the Reader shall know hereafter, when I come to treat more particularly about my Way of living. [189]

CHAP. III

The Author studious to learn the Language, the Houyhnhnm *his Master assists in teaching him. The Language described. Several* Houyhnhnms *of Quality come out of Curiosity to see the Author. He gives his Master a short Account of his Voyage.*

My principal Endeavour was to learn the Language, which my Master (for so I shall henceforth call him) and his Children, and every Servant of his House were desirous to teach me. For they looked upon it as a Prodigy, that a brute Animal should discover such Marks of a rational Creature. I pointed to every thing, and enquired the Name of it, which I wrote down in my *Journal Book* when I was alone, and corrected my bad Accent, by desiring those of the Family to pronounce it often. In this Employment, a Sorrel Nag, one of the under Servants, was very ready to assist me.

In speaking, they pronounce through the Nose and Throat, and their Language approaches nearest to the *High Dutch* or *German,* of any I know in *Europe;* but is much more graceful and significant. The Emperor *Charles* V. made almost the same Observation when he said, That if he were to speak to his Horse, it should be in *High Dutch*.

The Curiosity and Impatience of my Master were so great, that he spent many Hours of his Leisure to instruct me. He was convinced (as he afterwards told me) that I must be a *Yahoo,* but my Teachableness, Civility and Cleanliness astonished him; which were Qualities altogether so opposite to those Animals. He was most perplexed about my Cloaths, reasoning sometimes with himself, whether they were a Part of my Body; for I never pulled them off till the Family were asleep, and got them on before they waked in the Morning. My Master was eager to learn from whence I came; how I acquired those Appearances of Reason, which I discovered in all my Actions; and to know my Story from my own Mouth, which he hoped he should soon do by the great Proficiency I made in learning and pronouncing their Words and Sentences. To help my Memory, I formed all I learned into the *English* Alphabet, and writ the Words down with the Translations. This last, after some time, I ventured to do in my Master's Presence. It cost me much Trouble to explain to him what I was [190] doing; for the Inhabitants have not the least Idea of Books or Literature.

In about ten Weeks time I was able to understand most of his Questions; and in three Months could give him some tolerable Answers. He was extremely curious to know from what Part of the Country I came, and how I was taught to imitate a rational Creature; because the *Yahoos,* (whom he saw I exactly resembled in my Head, Hands and Face, that were only visible,) with some Appearance of Cunning, and the strongest Disposition to Mischief, were observed to be the most unteachable of all Brutes. I answered; that I came over the Sea, from a far Place, with many others of my own Kind, in a great hollow Vessel made of the Bodies of Trees: That, my Companions forced me to land on this Coast, and then left me to shift for myself. It was with some Difficulty, and by the Help of many Signs, that I brought him to understand me. He replied, That I must needs be mistaken, or that I *said the thing which was not.* (For they have no

Word in their Language to express Lying or Falshood.) He knew it
was impossible that there could be a Country beyond the Sea, or that
a Parcel of Brutes could move a wooden Vessel whither they pleased
upon Water. He was sure no *Houyhnhnm* alive could make such a
Vessel, or would trust *Yahoos* to manage it.

The Word *Houyhnhnm,* in their Tongue, signifies a *Horse;* and
in its Etymology, *the Perfection of Nature.* I told my Master, that I was
at a Loss for Expression, but would improve as fast as I could; and
hoped in a short time I should be able to tell him Wonders: He was
pleased to direct his own Mare, his Colt and Fole, and the Servants
of the Family to take all Opportunities of instructing me; and every
Day for two or three Hours, he was at the same Pains himself: Several
Horses and Mares of Quality in the Neighbourhood came often to our
House, upon the Report spread of a wonderful *Yahoo,* that could speak
like a *Houyhnhnm,* and seemed in his Words and Actions to discover
some Glimmerings of Reason. These delighted to converse with me;
they put many Questions, and received such Answers, as I was able to
return. By all which Advantages, I made so great a Progress, that in
five Months from my Arrival, I understood whatever was spoke, and
could express myself tolerably well.

The *Houyhnhnms* who came to visit my Master, out of a Design
of seeing and talking with me, could hardly believe me to be a right
Yahoo, because my Body had a different Covering from others of my
Kind. They were astonished to observe me without the usual Hair or
Skin, except on my Head, Face and Hands: [191] But I discovered that
Secret to my Master, upon an Accident, which happened about a
Fortnight before.

I have already told the Reader, that every Night when the Family
were gone to Bed, it was my Custom to strip and cover myself with
my Cloaths: It happened one Morning early, that my Master sent for
me, by the Sorrel Nag, who was his Valet; when he came, I was fast
asleep, my Cloaths fallen off on one Side, and my Shirt above my
Waste. I awaked at the Noise he made, and observed him to deliver
his Message in some Disorder; after which he went to my Master, and
in a great Fright gave him a very confused Account of what he had
seen: This I presently discovered; for going as soon as I was dressed,
to pay my Attendance upon his Honour, he asked me the Meaning of
what his Servant had reported; that I was not the same Thing when
I slept as I appeared to be at other times; that his Valet assured him,

some Part of me was white, some yellow, at least not so white, and some brown.

I had hitherto concealed the Secret of my Dress, in order to distinguish myself as much as possible, from that cursed Race of *Yahoos;* but now I found it in vain to do so any longer. Besides, I considered that my Cloaths and Shoes would soon wear out, which already were in a declining Condition, and must be supplied by some Contrivance from the Hides of *Yahoos,* or other Brutes; whereby the whole Secret would be known. I therefore told my Master, that in the Country from whence I came, those of my Kind always covered their Bodies with the Hairs of certain Animals prepared by Art, as well for Decency, as to avoid Inclemencies of Air both hot and cold; of which, as to my own Person I would give him immediate Conviction, if he pleased to command me; only desiring his Excuse, if I did not expose those Parts that Nature taught us to conceal. He said, my Discourse was all very strange, but especially the last Part; for he could not understand why Nature should teach us to conceal what Nature had given. That neither himself nor Family were ashamed of any Parts of their Bodies; but however I might do as I pleased. Whereupon, I first unbuttoned my Coat, and pulled it off. I did the same with my Wastecoat; I drew off my Shoes, Stockings and Breeches. I let my Shirt down to my Waste, and drew up the Bottom, fastening it like a Girdle about my Middle to hide my Nakedness.

My Master observed the whole Performance with great Signs of Curiosity and Admiration. He took up all my Cloaths in his Pastern, one Piece after another, and examined them diligently; [192] he then stroaked my Body very gently, and looked round me several Times; after which he said, it was plain I must be a perfect *Yahoo;* but that I differed very much from the rest of my Species, in the Whiteness, and Smoothness of my Skin, my want of Hair in several Parts of my Body, the Shape and Shortness of my Claws behind and before, and my Affectation of walking continually on my two hinder Feet. He desired to see no more; and gave me leave to put on my Cloaths again, for I was shuddering with Cold.

I expressed my Uneasiness at his giving me so often the Appellation of *Yahoo,* an odious Animal, for which I had so utter an Hatred and Contempt. I begged he would forbear applying that Word to me, and take the same Order in his Family, and among his Friends whom he suffered to see me. I requested likewise, that the Secret of my having a false Covering to my Body might be known to none but himself, at least as long as my present Cloathing should last: For as to what the Sorrel Nag his Valet had observed, his Honour might command him to conceal it.

All this my Master very graciously consented to; and thus the Secret was kept till my Cloaths began to wear out, which I was forced to supply by several Contrivances, that shall hereafter be mentioned. In the mean Time, he desired I would go on with my utmost Diligence to learn their Language, because he was more astonished at my Capacity for Speech and Reason, than at the Figure of my Body, whether it were covered or no; adding, that he waited with some Impatience to hear the Wonders which I promised to tell him.

From thenceforward he doubled the Pains he had been at to instruct me; he brought me into all Company, and made them treat me with Civility, because, as he told them privately, this would put me into good Humour, and make me more diverting.

Every Day when I waited on him, beside the Trouble he was at in teaching, he would ask me several Questions concerning my self, which I answered as well as I could; and by those Means he had already received some general Ideas, although very imperfect. It would be tedious to relate the several Steps, by which I advanced to a more regular Conversation: But the first Account I gave of my self in any Order and Length, was to this Purpose:

That, I came from a very far Country, as I already had attempted to tell him, with about fifty more of my own Species; that we travelled upon the Seas, in a great hollow Vessel made [193] of Wood, and larger than his Honour's House. I described the Ship to him in the best Terms I could; and explained by the Help of my Handkerchief displayed, how it was driven forward by the Wind. That, upon a Quarrel among us, I was set on Shoar on this Coast, where I walked forward without knowing whither, till he delivered me from the Persecution of those execrable *Yahoos*. He asked me, Who made the Ship, and how it was possible that the *Houynhnhnms* of my Country would leave it to the Management of Brutes? My Answer was, that I durst proceed no farther in my Relation, unless he would give me his Word and Honour that he would not be offended; and then I would tell him the Wonders I had so often promised. He agreed; and I went on by assuring him, that the Ship was made by Creatures like myself, who in all the Countries I had travelled, as well as in my own, were the only governing, rational Animals; and that upon my Arrival hither, I was as much astonished to see the *Houyhnhnms* act like rational Beings, as he or his Friends could be in finding some Marks of Reason in a Creature he was pleased to call a *Yahoo;* to which I owned my Resemblance in every Part, but could not account for their degenerate and brutal Nature. I said farther, That if good Fortune ever restored me to my native Country, to relate my Travels hither, as I resolved to do; every Body would believe that I *said the Thing which was not;* that I invented the Story out of my own Head: And with all possible Respect to Himself, his Family, and Friends, and under his Promise of not being offended, our Countrymen would hardly think it probable, that a *Houyhnhnm* should be the presiding Creature of a Nation, and a *Yahoo* the Brute.

CHAP. IV

The Houyhnhnms *Notion of Truth and Falshood. The Author's Discourse disapproved by his Master. The Author gives a more particular Account of himself, and the Accidents of his Voyage.*

My Master heard me with great Appearances of Uneasiness in his Countenance; because *Doubting* or *not believing,* are so little known in this Country, that the Inhabitants cannot tell how to behave themselves under such Circumstances. And I remember in frequent Discourses with my [194] Master concerning the Nature of Manhood, in other Parts of the World; having Occasion to talk of *Lying,* and *false Representation,* it was with much Difficulty that he comprehended what I meant; although he had otherwise a most acute Judgment. For he argued thus; That the Use of Speech was to make us understand one another, and to receive Information of Facts; now if any one *said the Thing which was not,* these Ends were defeated; because I cannot properly be said to understand him; and I am so far from receiving Information, that he leaves me worse than in Ignorance; for I am led to believe a Thing *Black* when it is *White,* and *Short* when it is *Long.* And these were all the Notions he had concerning that Faculty of *Lying,* so perfectly well understood, and so universally practised among human Creatures.

To return from this Digression; when I asserted that the *Yahoos* were the only governing Animals in my Country, which my Master said was altogether past his Conception, he desired to know, whether we had *Houyhnhnms* among us, and what was their Employment: I told him, we had great Numbers; that in Summer they grazed in the Fields, and in Winter were kept in Houses, with Hay and Oats, where *Yahoo*-Servants were employed to rub their Skins smooth, comb their Manes, pick their Feet, serve them with Food, and make their Beds. I understand you well, said my Master; it is now very plain from all you have spoken, that whatever Share of Reason the *Yahoos* pretend to, the *Houyhnhnms* are your Masters; I heartily wish our *Yahoos* would be so tractable. I begged his Honour would please to excuse me from proceeding any farther, because I was very certain that the Account he expected from me would be highly displeasing. But he insisted in commanding me to let him know the best and the worst: I told him he should be obeyed. I owned, that the *Houyhnhnms* among us, whom we called *Horses,* were the most generous and comely Animal we had; that they excelled in Strength and Swiftness; and when they belonged to Persons of Quality, employed in Travelling, Racing, and drawing Chariots, they were treated with much Kindness and Care, till they fell into Diseases, or became foundered in the Feet; but then they were sold, and used to all kind of Drudgery till they died; after which their Skins were stripped and sold for what they were worth, and their Bodies left to be devoured by Dogs and Birds of Prey. But the common Race of Horses had not so good Fortune, being kept by Farmers and Carriers, and other mean People, who put them to greater Labour, and feed them worse. I described as well as I could, our Way of Riding; the Shape and [195] Use of a Bridle, a Saddle, a Spur, and a Whip; of Harness and Wheels. I added, that we fastened Plates of a certain hard Substance called *Iron* at the Bottom of their Feet, to preserve their Hoofs from being broken by the Stony Ways on which we often travelled.

My Master, after some Expressions of great Indignation, wondered how we dared to venture upon a *Houyhnhnm's* Back; for he was sure, that the meanest Servant in his House would be able to shake off the strongest *Yahoo;* or by lying down, and rouling upon his Back, squeeze the Brute to Death. I answered, That our Horses were trained up from three or four Years old to the several Uses we intended them for; That if any of them proved intolerably vicious, they were employed for Carriages; that they were severely beaten while they were young for any mischievous Tricks: That the Males, designed for the common Use of Riding or Draught, were generally *castrated* about two Years after their Birth, to take down their Spirits, and make them more tame and gentle: That they were indeed sensible of Rewards and Punishments; but his Honour would please to consider, that they had not the least Tincture of Reason any more than the *Yahoos* in this Country.

It put me to the Pains of many Circumlocutions to give my Master a right Idea of what I spoke; for their Language doth not abound in Variety of Words, because their Wants and Passions are fewer than among us. But it is impossible to express his noble Resentment at our savage Treatment of the *Houyhnhnm* Race; particularly after I had explained the Manner and Use of *Castrating* Horses among us, to hinder them from propagating their Kind, and to render them more servile. He said, if it were possible there could be any Country where *Yahoos* alone were endued with Reason, they certainly must be the governing Animal, because Reason will in Time always prevail against Brutal Strength. But, considering the Frame of our Bodies, and especially of mine, he thought no Creature of equal Bulk was so ill-contrived, for employing that Reason in the common Offices of Life; whereupon he desired to know whether those among whom I lived, resembled me or the *Yahoos* of his Country. I assured him, that I was as well shaped as most of my Age; but the younger and the Females were much more soft and tender, and the Skins of the latter generally as white as Milk. He said, I differed indeed from other *Yahoos,* being much more cleanly, and not altogether so deformed; but in point of real Advantage, he thought I differed for the worse. That my Nails were of no [196] Use either to my fore or hinder Feet: As to my fore Feet, he could not properly call them by that Name, for he never observed me to walk upon them; that they were too soft to bear the Ground; that I generally went with them uncovered, neither was the Covering I sometimes wore on them, of the same Shape, or so strong as that on my Feet behind. That I could not walk with any Security; for if either of my hinder Feet slipped, I must inevitably fall. He then began to find fault with other Parts of my Body; the Flatness of my Face, the Prominence of my Nose, mine Eyes placed directly in Front, so that I could not look on either Side without turning my Head: That I was not able to feed my self, without lifting one of my fore Feet to my Mouth: And therefore Nature had placed those Joints to answer that Necessity. He knew not what could be the Use of those several Clefts and Divisions in my Feet behind; that these were too soft to

bear the Hardness and Sharpness of Stones without a Covering made
from the Skin of some other Brute; that my whole Body wanted a
Fence against Heat and Cold, which I was forced to put on and off
every Day with Tediousness and Trouble. And lastly, that he observed
every Animal in this Country naturally to abhor the *Yahoos,* whom
the Weaker avoided, and the Stronger drove from them. So that supposing us to have the Gift of Reason, he could not see how it were
possible to cure that natural Antipathy which every Creature discovered against us; nor consequently, how we could tame and render
them serviceable. However, he would (as he said) debate the Matter
no farther, because he was more desirous to know my own Story, the
Country, where I was born, and the several Actions and Events of my
Life before I came hither.

I assured him, how extreamly desirous I was that he should be
satisfied in every Point; but I doubted much, whether it would be possible for me to explain my self on several Subjects whereof his Honour
could have no Conception, because I saw nothing in his Country to
which I could resemble them. That however, I would do my best, and
strive to express my self by Similitudes, humbly desiring his Assistance
when I wanted proper Words; which he was pleased to promise me.

I said, my Birth was of honest Parents, in an Island called *England,* which was remote from this Country, as many Days Journey as
the strongest of his Honour's Servants could travel in the Annual
Course of the Sun. That I was bred a Surgeon, whose Trade is to cure
Wounds and Hurts in the Body, got by Accident or Violence. That
my Country was governed by a [197] Female Man, whom we called
Queen. That I left it to get Riches, whereby I might maintain my self
and Family when I should return. That in my last Voyage, I was
Commander of the Ship and had about fifty *Yahoos* under me, many
of which died at Sea, and I was forced to supply them by others picked
out from several Nations. That our Ship was twice in Danger of
being sunk; the first Time by a great Storm, and the second, by striking against a Rock. Here my Master interposed, by asking me, How
I could persuade Strangers out of different Countries to venture with
me, after the Losses I had sustained, and the Hazards I had run. I said,
they were Fellows of desperate Fortunes, forced to fly from the Places
of their Birth, on Account of their Poverty or their Crimes. Some were
undone by Law-suits; others spent all they had in Drinking, Whoring
and Gaming; others fled for Treason; many for Murder, Theft, Poy-

soning, Robbery, Perjury, Forgery, Coining false Money; for committing Rapes or Sodomy; for flying from their Colours, or deserting to the Enemy; and most of them had broken Prison. None of these durst return to their native Countries for fear of being hanged, or of starving in a Jail; and therefore were under a Necessity of seeking a Livelihood in other Places.

During this Discourse, my Master was pleased often to interrupt me. I had made Use of many Circumlocutions in describing to him the Nature of the several Crimes, for which most of our Crew had been forced to fly their Country. This Labour took up several Days Conversation before he was able to comprehend me. He was wholly at a Loss to know what could be the Use or Necessity of practising those Vices. To clear up which I endeavoured to give him some Ideas of the Desire of Power and Riches; of the terrible Effects of Lust, Intemperance, Malice, and Envy. All this I was forced to define and describe by putting of Cases, and making Suppositions. After which, like one whose Imagination was struck with something never seen or heard of before, he would lift up his Eyes with Amazement and Indignation. Power, Government, War, Law, Punishment, and a Thousand other Things had no Terms, wherein that Language could express them; which made the Difficulty almost insuperable to give my Master any Conception of what I meant: But being of an excellent Understanding, much improved by Contemplation and Converse, he at last arrived at a competent Knowledge of what human Nature in our Parts of the World is capable to perform; and desired I would give him some particular Account of that Land, which we call *Europe,* especially, of my own Country. [198]

CHAP. V

The Author at his Master's Commands informs him of the State of England. *The Causes of War among the Princes of* Europe. *The Author begins to explain the* English Constitution.

The Reader may please to observe, that the following Extract of many Conversations I had with my Master, contains a Summary of the most material Points, which were discoursed at several times for above two Years; his Honour often desiring fuller Satisfaction as I farther improved in the *Houyhnhnm* Tongue. I laid before him, as well as I could, the whole State of *Europe;* I discoursed of Trade and Manufactures, of Arts and Sciences; and the Answers I gave to all the Questions he made, as they arose upon several Subjects, were a Fund of Conversation not to be exhausted. But I shall here only set down the Substance of what passed between us concerning my own Country, reducing it into Order as well as I can, without any Regard to Time or other Circumstances, while I strictly adhere to Truth. My only Concern is, that I shall hardly be able to do Justice to my Master's Arguments and Expressions, which must needs suffer by my Want of Capacity, as well as by a Translation into our barbarous *English*.

In Obedience therefore to his Honour's Commands, I related to him the *Revolution* under the Prince of *Orange;* the long War with *France* entered into by the said Prince, and renewed by his Successor the present Queen; wherein the greatest Powers of *Christendom* were engaged, and which still continued: I computed at his Request, that about a Million of *Yahoos* might have been killed in the whole Progress of it; and perhaps a Hundred or more Cities taken, and five times as many Ships burnt or sunk.

He asked me what were the usual Causes or Motives that made one Country go to War with another. I answered, they were innumerable; but I should only mention a few of the chief. Sometimes the Ambition of Princes, who never think they have Land or People enough to govern: Sometimes the Corruption of Ministers, who engage their Master in a War in order to stifle or divert the Clamour of the Subjects against their evil Administration. Difference in Opinions hath cost many Millions of Lives: For Instance, whether *Flesh* be *Bread*, or *Bread* be *Flesh:* [199] Whether the Juice of a certain *Berry* be *Blood* or *Wine:* Whether *Whistling* be a Vice or a Virtue: Whether it be better to *kiss a Post*, or throw it into the Fire: What is the best Colour for a *Coat*, whether *Black, White, Red* or *Grey;* and whether it should be *long* or *short, narrow* or *wide, dirty* or *clean;* with many more. Neither are any Wars so furious and bloody, or of so long Continuance, as those occasioned by Difference in Opinion, especially if it be in things indifferent.

Sometimes the Quarrel between two Princes is to decide which of them shall dispossess a Third of his Dominions, where neither of them pretend to any Right. Sometimes one Prince quarrelleth with another, for fear the other should quarrel with him. Sometimes a War is entered upon, because the Enemy is too *strong,* and sometimes because he is too *weak*. Sometimes our Neighbours *want* the *Things* which we *have,* or *have* the Things which we want; and we both fight, till they take ours or give us theirs. It is a very justifiable Cause of War to invade a Country after the People have been wasted by Famine, destroyed by Pestilence, or embroiled by Factions amongst themselves. It is justifiable to enter into a War against our nearest Ally, when one of his Towns lies convenient for us, or a Territory of Land, that would render our Dominions round and compact. If a Prince send Forces into a Nation, where the People are poor and ignorant, he may lawfully put half of them to Death, and make Slaves of the rest, in order to civilize and reduce them from their barbarous Way of Living. It is a very kingly, honourable, and frequent Practice, when one Prince desires the Assistance of another to secure him against an Invasion, that the Assistant, when he hath driven out the Invader, should seize on the Dominions himself, and kill, imprison or banish the Prince he came to relieve. Allyance by Blood or Marriage, is a sufficient Cause of War between Princes; and the nearer the Kindred is, the greater is their Disposition to quarrel: *Poor* Nations are *hungry,* and *rich* Nations are *proud;* and Pride and Hunger will ever be at Variance. For these Reasons, the Trade of a *Soldier* is held the most honourable of all others: Because a *Soldier* is a *Yahoo* hired to kill in cold Blood as many of his own Species, who have never offended him, as possibly he can.

There is likewise a Kind of beggarly Princes in *Europe,* not able to make War by themselves, who hire out their Troops to richer Nations for so much a Day to each Man; of which they keep three Fourths to themselves, and it is the best Part of their Maintenance; such are those in many *Northern* Parts of *Europe.* [200]

What you have told me, (said my Master) upon the Subject of War, doth indeed discover most admirably the Effects of that Reason you pretend to: However, it is happy that the *Shame* is greater than the *Danger;* and that Nature hath left you utterly uncapable of doing much Mischief: For your Mouths lying flat with your Faces, you can hardly bite each other to any Purpose, unless by Consent. Then, as to the Claws upon your Feet before and behind, they are so short and tender, that one of our *Yahoos* would drive a Dozen of yours before him. And therefore in recounting the Numbers of those who have been killed in Battle, I cannot but think that you have *said the Thing which is not.*

I could not forbear shaking my Head and smiling a little at his

Ignorance. And, being no Stranger to the Art of War, I gave him a
Description of Cannons, Culverins, Muskets, Carabines, Pistols, Bul-
lets, Powder, Swords, Bayonets, Sieges, Retreats, Attacks, Undermines,
Countermines, Bombardments, Sea-fights; Ships sunk with a Thou-
sand Men; twenty Thousand killed on each Side; dying Groans,
Limbs flying in the Air: Smoak, Noise, Confusion, trampling to Death
under Horses Feet: Flight, Pursuit, Victory; Fields strewed with
Carcases left for Food to Dogs, and Wolves, and Birds of Prey;
Plundering, Stripping, Ravishing, Burning and Destroying. And, to
set forth the Valour of my own dear Countrymen, I assured him, that
I had seen them blow up a Hundred Enemies at once in a Siege, and
as many in a Ship; and beheld the dead Bodies drop down in Pieces
from the Clouds, to the great Diversion of all the Spectators.

I was going on to more Particulars, when my Master commanded
me Silence. He said, whoever understood the Nature of *Yahoos* might
easily believe it possible for so vile an Animal, to be capable of every
Action I had named, if their Strength and Cunning equalled their
Malice. But, as my Discourse had increased his Abhorrence of the
whole Species, so he found it gave him a Disturbance in his Mind, to
which he was wholly a Stranger before. He thought his Ears being
used to such abominable Words, might by Degrees admit them with
less Detestation. That, although he hated the *Yahoos* of this Country,
yet he no more blamed them for their odious Qualities, than he did a
Gnnayh (a Bird of Prey) for its Cruelty, or a sharp Stone for cutting
his Hoof. But, when a Creature pretending to Reason, could be capable
of such Enormities, he dreaded lest the Corruption of that Faculty
might be worse than Brutality itself. He seemed therefore confident,
that instead of Reason, we were only possessed of some Quality fitted
to increase our natural Vices; as the [201] Reflection from a troubled
Stream returns the Image of an ill-shapen Body, not only *larger,* but
more *distorted.*

He added, That he had heard too much upon the Subject of War,
both in this, and some former Discourses. There was another Point
which a little perplexed him at present. I had said, that some of our
Crew left their Country on Account of being ruined by *Law:* That I
had already explained the Meaning of the Word; but he was at a Loss
how it should come to pass, that the *Law* which was intended for
every Man's Preservation, should be any Man's Ruin. Therefore he

desired to be farther satisfied what I meant by *Law*, and the Dispensers thereof, according to the present Practice in my own Country: Because he thought, Nature and Reason were sufficient Guides for a reasonable Animal, as we pretended to be, in shewing us what we ought to do, and what to avoid.

I assured his Honour, that *Law* was a Science wherein I had not much conversed, further than by employing Advocates, in vain, upon some Injustices that had been done me. However, I would give him all the Satisfaction I was able.

I said there was a Society of Men among us, bred up from their Youth in the Art of proving by Words multiplied for the Purpose, that *White* is *Black*, and *Black* is *White*, according as they are paid. To this Society all the rest of the People are Slaves.

For example. If my Neighbour hath a mind to my *Cow*, he hires a Lawyer to prove that he ought to have my *Cow* from me. I must then hire another to defend my Right; it being against all Rules of *Law* that any Man should be allowed to speak for himself. Now in this Case, I who am the true Owner lie under two great Disadvantages. First, my Lawyer being practiced almost from his Cradle in defending Falshood; is quite out of his Element when he would be an Advocate for Justice, which as an Office unnatural, he always attempts with great Awkwardness, if not with Ill-will. The second Disadvantage is, that my Lawyer must proceed with great Caution: Or else he will be reprimanded by the Judges, and abhorred by his Brethren, as one who would lessen the Practice of the Law. And therefore I have but two Methods to preserve my *Cow*. The first is, to gain over my Adversary's Lawyer with a double Fee; who will then betray his Client, by insinuating that he hath Justice on his Side. The second Way is for my Lawyer to make my Cause appear as unjust as he can; by allowing the *Cow* to belong to my Adversary; and this if it be skilfully done, will certainly bespeak the Favour of the Bench. [202]

Now, your Honour is to know, that these Judges are Persons appointed to decide all Controversies of Property, as well as for the Tryal of Criminals; and picked out from the most dextrous Lawyers who are grown old or lazy: And having been byassed all their Lives against Truth and Equity, lie under such a fatal Necessity of favouring Fraud, Perjury and Oppression; that I have known some of them to have refused a large Bribe from the Side where Justice lay, rather than injure the *Faculty,* by doing any thing unbecoming their Nature or their Office.

It is a Maxim among these Lawyers, that whatever hath been done before, may legally be done again: And therefore they take special Care to record all the Decisions formerly made against common Justice and the general Reason of Mankind. These, under the Name of *Precedents,* they produce as Authorities to justify the most iniquitous Opinions; and the Judges never fail of directing accordingly.

In pleading, they studiously avoid entering into the *Merits* of the Cause; but are loud, violent and tedious in dwelling upon all *Circumstances* which are not to the Purpose. For Instance, in the Case already mentioned: They never desire to know what Claim or Title my Adversary hath to my *Cow;* but whether the said *Cow* were Red or Black; her Horns long or short; whether the Field I graze her in be round or square; whether she were milked at home or abroad; what Diseases she is subject to, and the like. After which they consult *Precedents,* adjourn the Cause, from Time to Time, and in Ten, Twenty, or Thirty Years come to an Issue.

It is likewise to be observed, that this Society hath a peculiar Cant and Jargon of their own, that no other Mortal can understand, and wherein all their Laws are written, which they take special Care to multiply; whereby they have wholly confounded the very Essence of Truth and Falshood, of Right and Wrong; so that it will take Thirty Years to decide whether the Field, left me by my Ancestors for six Generations, belong to me, or to a Stranger three Hundred Miles off.

In the Tryal of Persons accused for Crimes against the State, the Method is much more short and commendable: The Judge first sends to sound the Disposition of those in Power; after which he can easily hang or save the Criminal, strictly preserving all the Forms of Law.

Here my Master interposing, said it was a Pity, that Creatures endowed with such prodigious Abilities of Mind as these Lawyers, by the Description I gave of them must certainly be, [203] were not rather encouraged to be Instructors of others in Wisdom and Knowledge. In Answer to which, I assured his Honour, that in all Points out of their own Trade, they were usually the most ignorant and stupid Generation among us, the most despicable in common Conversation, avowed Enemies to all Knowledge and Learning; and equally disposed to pervert the general Reason of Mankind, in every other Subject of Discourse, as in that of their own Profession.

CHAP. VI

A Continuation of the State of England, *under Queen* Anne. *The Character of a first Minister in the Courts of* Europe.

My Master was yet wholly at a loss to understand what Motives could incite this Race of Lawyers to perplex, disquiet, and weary themselves by engaging in a Confederacy of Injustice, merely for the Sake of injuring their Fellow-Animals; neither could he comprehend what I meant in saying they did it for *Hire.* Whereupon I was at much Pains to describe to him the Use of *Money,* the Materials it was made of, and the Value of the Metals: That when a *Yahoo* had got a great Store of this precious Substance, he was able to purchase whatever he had a mind to; the finest Cloathing, the noblest Houses, great Tracts of Land, the most costly Meats and Drinks; and have his Choice of the most beautiful Females. Therefore since *Money* alone, was able to perform all these Feats, our *Yahoos* thought, they could never have enough of it to spend or to save, as they found themselves inclined from their natural Bent either to Profusion or Avarice. That, the rich Man enjoyed the Fruit of the poor Man's Labour, and the latter were a Thousand to One in Proportion to the former. That the Bulk of our People was forced to live miserably, by labouring every Day for small Wages to make a few live plentifully. I enlarged myself much on these and many other Particulars to the same Purpose: But his Honour was still to seek: For he went upon a Supposition that all Animals had a Title to their Share in the Productions of the Earth; and especially those who presided over the rest. Therefore he desired I would let him know, what these costly Meats were, and how any of us happened to want them. Whereupon I enumerated as many Sorts as came into my Head, with the various [204] Methods of dressing them, which could not be done without sending Vessels by Sea to every Part of the World, as well for Liquors to drink, as for Sauces, and innumerable other Conveniences. I assured him, that this whole Globe of Earth must be at least three Times gone round, before one of our better Female *Yahoos* could get her Breakfast, or a Cup to put it in. He said, That must needs be a miserable Country which cannot furnish Food for its own Inhabitants. But what he chiefly wondered at, was how such vast Tracts of Ground as I described, should be wholly without *Fresh water,* and the People put to the Necessity of sending over the Sea for

Drink. I replied, that *England* (the dear Place of my Nativity) was computed to produce three Times the Quantity of Food, more than its Inhabitants are able to consume, as well as Liquors extracted from Grain, or pressed out of the Fruit of certain Trees, which made excellent Drink; and the same Proportion in every other Convenience of Life. But, in order to feed the Luxury and Intemperance of the Males, and the Vanity of the Females, we sent away the greatest Part of our necessary Things to other Countries, from whence in Return we brought the Materials of Diseases, Folly, and Vice, to spend among ourselves. Hence it follows of Necessity, that vast Numbers of our People are compelled to seek their Livelihood by Begging, Robbing, Stealing, Cheating, Pimping, Forswearing, Flattering, Suborning, Forging, Gaming, Lying, Fawning, Hectoring, Voting, Scribling, Stargazing, Poysoning, Whoring, Canting, Libelling, Free-thinking, and the like Occupations: Every one of which Terms, I was at much Pains to make him understand.

That, *Wine* was not imported among us from foreign Countries, to supply the Want of Water or other Drinks, but because it was a Sort of Liquid which made us merry, by putting us out of our Senses; diverted all melancholy Thoughts, begat wild extravagant Imaginations in the Brain, raised our Hopes, and banished our Fears; suspended every Office of Reason for a Time, and deprived us of the Use of our Limbs, untill we fell into a profound Sleep; although it must be confessed, that we always awaked sick and dispirited; and that the Use of this Liquor filled us with Diseases, which made our Lives uncomfortable and short.

But beside all this, the Bulk of our People supported themselves by furnishing the Necessities or Conveniences of Life to the Rich, and to each other. For Instance, when I am at home and dressed as I ought to be, I carry on my Body the Workmanship [205] of an Hundred Tradesmen; the Building and Furniture of my House employ as many more; and five Times the Number to adorn my Wife.

I was going on to tell him of another Sort of People, who get their Livelihood by attending the Sick; having upon some Occasions informed his Honour that many of my Crew had died of Diseases. But here it was with the utmost Difficulty, that I brought him to apprehend what I meant. He could easily conceive, that a *Houyhnhnm* grew weak and heavy a few Days before his Death; or by some Accident might hurt a Limb. But that Nature, who worketh all things to Perfection, should suffer any Pains to breed in our Bodies, he thought impossible; and desired to know the Reason of so unaccountable an Evil. I told him, we fed on a Thousand Things which operated contrary to each other; that we eat when we were not hungry, and drank without the Provocation of Thirst: That we sat whole Nights drinking strong Liquors without eating a Bit; which disposed us to Sloth, enflamed our Bodies, and precipitated or prevented Digestion. That, prostitute Female *Yahoos* acquired a certain Malady, which bred Rottenness in the Bones of those, who fell into their Embraces: That this and many other Diseases, were propagated from Father to Son; so that great Numbers come into the World with complicated Maladies upon them: That, it would be endless to give him a Catalogue of all Diseases incident to human Bodies; for they could not be fewer than five or six Hundred, spread over every Limb, and Joynt: In short, every Part, external and intestine, having Diseases appropriated to each. To remedy which, there was a Sort of People bred up among us, in the Profession or Pretence of curing the Sick. And because I had some Skill in the Faculty, I would in Gratitude to his Honour, let him know the whole Mystery and Method by which they proceed.

Their Fundamental is, that all Diseases arise from *Repletion;* from whence they conclude, that a great *Evacuation* of the Body is necessary, either through the natural Passage, or upwards at the Mouth. Their next Business is, from Herbs, Minerals, Gums, Oyls, Shells, Salts, Juices, Sea-weed, Excrements, Barks of Trees, Serpents, Toads, Frogs, Spiders, dead Mens Flesh and Bones, Beasts and Fishes, to form a Composition for Smell and Taste the most abominable, nauseous and detestable, that they can possibly contrive, which the Stomach immediately rejects with Loathing: And this they call a *Vomit*. Or else from the same Store-house, with some other poysonous Additions, they command [206] us to take in at the Orifice *above* or *below,* (just as the Physician then happens to be disposed) a Medicine equally annoying and disgustful to the Bowels; which relaxing the Belly, drives down all before it: And this they call a *Purge,* or a *Clyster*. For Nature (as the Physicians alledge) having intended the superior anterior Orifice only for the *Intromission* of Solids and Liquids, and the inferior Posterior for Ejection; these Artists ingeniously considering that in all Diseases Nature is forced out of her Seat; therefore to replace her in it, the Body must be treated in a Manner directly contrary, by interchanging the Use of each Orifice; forcing Solids and Liquids in at the *Anus,* and making Evacuations at the Mouth.

But, besides real Diseases, we are subject to many that are only imaginary, for which the Physicians have invented imaginary Cures; these have their several Names, and so have the Drugs that are proper for them; and with these our Female *Yahoos* are always infested.

One great Excellency in this Tribe is their Skill at *Prognosticks,* wherein they seldom fail; their Predictions in real Diseases, when they rise to any Degree of Malignity, generally portending *Death,* which is always in their Power, when Recovery is not: And therefore, upon any unexpected Signs of Amendment, after they have pronounced their Sentence, rather than be accused as false Prophets, they know how to approve their Sagacity to the World by a seasonable Dose.

They are likewise of special Use to Husbands and Wives, who are grown weary of their Mates; to eldest Sons, to great Ministers of State, and often to Princes.

I had formerly upon Occasion discoursed with my Master upon the Nature of *Government* in general, and particularly of our own *excellent Constitution,* deservedly the Wonder and Envy of the whole World. But having here accidentally mentioned a *Minister of State;* he commanded me some Time after to inform him, what Species of *Yahoo* I particularly meant by that Appellation.

I told him, that a *First* or *Chief Minister of State,* whom I intended to describe, was a Creature wholly exempt from Joy and Grief, Love and Hatred, Pity and Anger; at least makes use of no other Passions but a violent Desire of Wealth, Power, and Titles: That he applies his Words to all Uses, except to the Indication of his Mind; That he never tells a *Truth,* but with an Intent that you should take it for a *Lye;* nor a *Lye,* but with a Design that you should take it for a *Truth;* That those he speaks worst of [207] behind their Backs, are in the surest way to Preferment; and whenever he begins to praise you to others or to your self, you are from that Day forlorn. The worst Mark you can receive is a *Promise,* especially when it is confirmed with an Oath; after which every wise Man retires, and gives over all Hopes.

There are three Methods by which a Man may rise to be Chief Minister: The first is, by knowing how with Prudence to dispose of a Wife, a Daughter, or a Sister: The second, by betraying or undermining his Predecessor: And the third is, by a *furious Zeal* in publick Assemblies against the Corruptions of the Court. But a wise Prince would rather chuse to employ those who practise the last of these Methods; because such Zealots prove always the most obsequious and subservient to the Will and Passions of their Master. That, these *Ministers* having all Employments at their Disposal, preserve themselves in Power by bribing the Majority of a Senate or great Council; and at last by an Expedient called an *Act of Indemnity* (whereof I described the Nature to him) they secure themselves from Afterreckonings, and retire from the Publick, laden with the Spoils of the Nation.

The Palace of a *Chief Minister,* is a Seminary to breed up others in his own Trade: The Pages, Lacquies, and Porter, by imitating their Master, become *Ministers of State* in their several Districts, and learn to excel in the three principal *Ingredients,* of *Insolence, Lying,* and *Bribery.* Accordingly, they have a *Subaltern* Court paid to them by Persons of the best Rank; and sometimes by the Force of Dexterity and Impudence, arrive through several Gradations to be Successors to their Lord.

He is usually governed by a decayed Wench, or favourite Footman, who are the Tunnels through which all Graces are conveyed, and may properly be called, *in the last Resort,* the Governors of the Kingdom.

One Day, my Master, having heard me mention the *Nobility* of my Country, was pleased to make me a Compliment which I could not pretend to deserve: That, he was sure, I must have been born of some Noble Family, because I far exceeded in Shape, Colour, and Cleanliness, all the *Yahoos* of his Nation, although I seemed to fail in Strength, and Agility, which must be imputed to my different Way of Living from those other Brutes; and besides, I was not only endowed with the Faculty of Speech, but likewise with some Rudiments of Reason, to a Degree, that with all his Acquaintance I passed for a Prodigy. [208]

He made me observe, that among the *Houyhnhnms,* the *White,* the *Sorrel,* and the *Iron-grey,* were not so exactly shaped as the *Bay,* the *Dapple-grey,* and the *Black;* nor born with equal Talents of Mind, or a Capacity to improve them; and therefore continued always in the Conditions of Servants, without ever aspiring to match out of their own Race, which in that Country would be reckoned monstrous and unnatural.

I made his Honour my most humble Acknowledgements for the

good Opinion he was pleased to conceive of me; but assured him at the same Time, that my Birth was of the lower Sort, having been born of plain, honest Parents, who were just able to give me a tolerable Education: That, *Nobility* among us was altogether a different Thing from the Idea he had of it; That, our young *Noblemen* are bred from their Childhood in Idleness and Luxury; that, as soon as Years will permit, they consume their Vigour, and contract odious Diseases among lewd Females; and when their Fortunes are almost ruined, they marry some Woman of mean Birth, disagreeable Person, and unsound Constitution, merely for the sake of Money, whom they hate and despise. That, the Productions of such Marriages are generally scrophulous, rickety or deformed Children; by which Means the Family seldom continues above three Generations, unless the Wife take Care to provide a healthy Father among her Neighbours, or Domesticks, in order to improve and continue the Breed. That, a weak diseased Body, a meager Countenance, and sallow Complexion, are the true Marks of *noble Blood;* and a healthy robust Appearance is so disgraceful in a Man of Quality, that the World concludes his real Father to have been a Groom or a Coachman. The Imperfections of his Mind run parallel with those of his Body; being a Composition of Spleen, Dulness, Ignorance, Caprice, Sensuality and Pride.

Without the Consent of this illustrious Body, no Law can be enacted, repealed, or altered: And these Nobles have likewise the Decision of all our Possessions without Appeal. [209]

CHAP. VII

The Author's great Love of his Native Country. His Master's Observations upon the Constitution and Administration of England, *as described by the Author, with parallel Cases and Comparisons. His Master's Observations upon human Nature.*

The Reader may be disposed to wonder how I could prevail on my self to give so free a Representation of my own Species, among a Race of Mortals who were already too apt to conceive the vilest Opinion of Human Kind, from that entire Congruity betwixt me and their *Yahoos.* But I must freely confess, that the many Virtues of those excellent *Quadrupeds* placed in opposite View to human Corruptions, had so far opened mine Eyes, and enlarged my Understanding, that I began to view the Actions and Passions of Man in a very different

Light; and to think the Honour of my own Kind not worth man-
aging; which, besides, it was impossible for me to do before a Person
of so acute a Judgment as my Master, who daily convinced me of a
thousand Faults in my self, whereof I had not the least Perception
before, and which with us would never be numbered even among
human Infirmities. I had likewise learned from his Example an utter
Detestation of all Falsehood or Disguise; and *Truth* appeared so
amiable to me, that I determined upon sacrificing every thing to it.

Let me deal so candidly with the Reader, as to confess, that there
was yet a much stronger Motive for the Freedom I took in my Representation of Things. I had not been a Year in this Country, before I
contracted such a Love and Veneration for the Inhabitants, that I
entered on a firm Resolution never to return to human Kind, but to
pass the rest of my Life among these admirable *Houyhnhnms* in the
Contemplation and Practice of every Virtue; where I could have no
Example or Incitement to Vice. But it was decreed by Fortune, my
perpetual Enemy, that so great a Felicity should not fall to my Share.
However, it is now some Comfort to reflect, that in what I said of my
Countrymen, I *extenuated* their Faults as much as I durst before so
strict an Examiner; and upon every Article, gave as *favourable* a Turn
as the Matter would bear. For, indeed, who is there alive that [210] will
not be swayed by his Byass and Partiality to the Place of his Birth?

I have related the Substance of several Conversations I had with
my Master, during the greatest Part of the Time I had the Honour to
be in his Service; but have indeed for Brevity sake omitted much more
than is here set down.

When I had answered all his Questions, and his Curiosity seemed
to be fully satisfied; he sent for me one Morning early, and commanding me to sit down at some Distance, (an Honour which he had never
before conferred upon me) He said, he had been very seriously considering my whole Story, as far as it related both to my self and my
Country: That, he looked upon us as a Sort of Animals to whose Share,
by what Accident he could not conjecture, some small Pittance of
Reason had fallen, whereof we made no other Use than by its Assistance to aggravate our *natural* Corruptions, and to acquire new ones
which Nature had not given us. That, we disarmed our selves of the
few Abilities she had bestowed; had been very successful in multiply-
ing our original Wants, and seemed to spend our whole Lives in vain
Endeavours to supply them by our own Inventions. That, as to my

self, it was manifest I had neither the Strength or Agility of a common *Yahoo;* that I walked infirmly on my hinder Feet; had found out a Contrivance to make my Claws of no Use or Defence, and to remove the Hair from my Chin, which was intended as a Shelter from the Sun and the Weather. Lastly, That I could neither run with Speed, nor climb Trees like my *Brethren* (as he called them) the *Yahoos* in this Country.

That, our Institutions of *Government* and *Law* were plainly owing to our gross Defects in *Reason,* and by consequence, in *Virtue;* because *Reason* alone is sufficient to govern a *Rational* Creature; which was therefore a Character we had no Pretence to challenge, even from the Account I had given of my own People; although he manifestly perceived, that in order to favour them, I had concealed many Particulars, and often *said the Thing which was not.*

He was the more confirmed in this Opinion, because he observed, that as I agreed in every Feature of my Body with other *Yahoos,* except where it was to my real Disadvantage in point of Strength, Speed and Activity, the Shortness of my Claws, and some other Particulars where Nature had no Part; so, from the Representation I had given him of our Lives, our Manners, and our Actions, he found as near a Resemblance in the Disposition of our Minds. He said, the *Yahoos* were known to hate one another [211] more than they did any different Species of Animals; and the Reason usually assigned, was, the Odiousness of their own Shapes, which all could see in the rest, but not in themselves. He had therefore begun to think it not unwise in us to *cover* our Bodies, and by that Invention, conceal many of our Deformities from each other, which would else be hardly supportable. But, he now found he had been mistaken; and that the Dissentions of those Brutes in his Country were owing to the same Cause with ours, as I had described them. For, if (said he) you throw among five *Yahoos* as much Food as would be sufficient for fifty, they will, instead of eating peaceably, fall together by the Ears, each single one impatient to *have all to it self;* and therefore a Servant was usually employed to stand by while they were feeding abroad, and those kept at home were tied at a Distance from each other. That, if a Cow died of Age or Accident, before a *Houynhnhnm* could secure it for his own *Yahoos,* those in the Neighbourhood would come in Herds to seize it, and then would ensue such a Battle as I had described, with terrible Wounds made by their Claws on both Sides, although they seldom were able to kill one another, for want of such convenient Instruments of Death as we had invented. At other Times the like Battles have been fought between the *Yahoos* of several Neighbourhoods without any visible Cause: Those of one District watching all Opportunities to surprise the next before they are prepared. But if they find their Project hath miscarried, they return home, and for want of Enemies, engage in what I call a *Civil War* among themselves.

That, in some Fields of his Country, there are certain *shining Stones* of several Colours, whereof the *Yahoos* are violently fond; and when Part of these *Stones* are fixed in the Earth, as it sometimes happeneth, they will dig with their Claws for whole Days to get them out, and carry them away, and hide them by Heaps in their Kennels; but still looking round with great Caution, for fear their Comrades should find out their Treasure. My Master said, he could never discover the Reason of this unnatural Appetite, or how these *Stones* could be of any Use to a *Yahoo;* but now he believed it might proceed from the same Principle of *Avarice,* which I had ascribed to Mankind. That he had once, by way of Experiment, privately removed a Heap of these *Stones* from the Place where one of his *Yahoos* had buried it: Whereupon, the sordid Animal missing his Treasure, by his loud lamenting brought the whole Herd to the Place, there miserably howled, then fell to biting and tearing the rest; began to pine [212] away, would neither eat nor sleep, nor work, till he ordered a Servant privately to convey the *Stones* into the same Hole, and hide them as before; which when his *Yahoo* had found, he presently recovered his Spirits and good Humour; but took Care to remove them to a better hiding Place; and hath ever since been a very serviceable Brute.

My Master farther assured me, which I also observed my self; That in the Fields where these *shining Stones* abound, the fiercest and most frequent Battles are fought, occasioned by perpetual Inroads of the neighbouring *Yahoos.*

He said, it was common when two *Yahoos* discovered such a *Stone* in a Field, and were contending which of them should be the Proprietor, a third would take the Advantage, and carry it away from them both; which my Master would needs contend to have some Resemblance with our *Suits at Law;* wherein I thought it for our Credit not to undeceive him; since the Decision he mentioned was much more equitable than many Decrees among us: Because the Plaintiff and Defendant there lost nothing beside the *Stone* they contended for;

whereas our *Courts of Equity,* would never have dismissed the Cause while either of them had any thing left.

My Master continuing his Discourse, said, There was nothing that rendered the *Yahoos* more odious, than their undistinguishing Appetite to devour every thing that came in their Way, whether Herbs, Roots, Berries, corrupted Flesh of Animals, or all mingled together: And it was peculiar in their Temper, that they were fonder of what they could get by Rapine or Stealth at a greater Distance, than much better Food provided for them at home. If their Prey held out, they would eat till they were ready to burst, after which Nature had pointed out to them a certain *Root* that gave them a general Evacuation.

There was also another Kind of *Root* very *juicy,* but something rare and difficult to be found, which the *Yahoos* sought for with much Eagerness, and would suck it with great Delight: It produced the same Effects that Wine hath upon us. It would make them sometimes hug, and sometimes tear one another; they would howl and grin, and chatter, and roul, and tumble, and then fall asleep in the Mud.

I did indeed observe, that the *Yahoos* were the only Animals in this Country subject to any Diseases; which however, were much fewer than Horses have among us, and contracted not by any ill Treatment they meet with, but by the Nastiness and Greediness of that sordid Brute. Neither has their Language any [213] more than a general Appellation for those Maladies; which is borrowed from the Name of the Beast, and called *Hnea Yahoo,* or the *Yahoo's-Evil;* and the Cure prescribed is a Mixture of *their own Dung* and *Urine,* forcibly put down the *Yahoo's* Throat. This I have since often known to have been taken with Success: And do here freely recommend it to my Countrymen, for the publick Good, as an admirable Specifick against all Diseases produced by Repletion.

As to Learning, Government, Arts, Manufactures, and the like; my Master confessed he could find little or no Resemblance between the *Yahoos* of that Country and those in ours. For, he only meant to observe what Parity there was in our Natures. He had heard indeed some curious *Houyhnhnms* observe, that in most Herds there was a Sort of ruling *Yahoo,* (as among us there is generally some leading or principal Stag in a Park) who was always more *deformed* in Body, and *mischievous in Disposition,* than any of the rest. That, this *Leader* had usually a Favourite as *like himself* as he could get, whose Employment was to *lick his Master's Feet and Posteriors, and drive the Female*

Yahoos *to his Kennel;* for which he was now and then rewarded with a Piece of Ass's Flesh. This *Favourite* is hated by the whole Herd; and therefore to protect himself, keeps always *near the Person of his Leader.* He usually continues in Office till a worse can be found; but the very Moment he is discarded, his Successor, at the Head of all the *Yahoos* in that District, Young and Old, Male and Female, come in a Body, and discharge their Excrements upon him from Head to Foot. But how far this might be applicable to our *Courts* and *Favourites,* and *Ministers of State,* my Master said I could best determine.

I durst make no Return to this malicious Insinuation, which debased human Understanding below the Sagacity of a common *Hound,* who hath Judgment enough to distinguish and follow the Cry of the *ablest Dog in the Pack,* without being ever mistaken.

My Master told me, there were some Qualities remarkable in the *Yahoos,* which he had not observed me to mention, or at least very slightly, in the Accounts I had given him of human Kind. He said, those Animals, like other Brutes, had their Females in common; but in this they differed, that the She-*Yahoo* would admit the Male, while she was pregnant; and that the Hees would quarrel and fight with the Females as fiercely as with each other. Both which Practices were such Degrees of infamous Brutality, that no other sensitive Creature ever arrived at. [214]

Another Thing he wondered at in the *Yahoos,* was their strange Disposition to Nastiness and Dirt; whereas there appears to be a natural Love of Cleanliness in all other Animals. As to the two former Accusations, I was glad to let them pass without any Reply, because I had not a Word to offer upon them in Defence of my Species, which otherwise I certainly had done from my own Inclinations. But I could have easily vindicated human Kind from the Imputation of Singularity upon the last Article, if there had been any *Swine* in that Country, (as unluckily for me there were not) which although it may be a *sweeter Quadruped* than a *Yahoo,* cannot I humbly conceive in Justice pretend to more Cleanliness; and so his Honour himself must have owned, if he had seen their filthy Way of feeding, and their Custom of wallowing and sleeping in the Mud.

My Master likewise mentioned another Quality, which his Servants had discovered in several *Yahoos,* and to him was wholly unaccountable. He said, a Fancy would sometimes take a *Yahoo,* to retire into a Corner, to lie down and howl, and groan, and spurn away all that came near him, although he were young and fat, and wanted neither Food nor Water; nor did the Servants imagine what could possibly ail him. And the only Remedy they found was to set him to hard Work, after which he would infallibly come to himself. To this I was silent out of Partiality to my own Kind; yet here I could plainly discover the true Seeds of *Spleen,* which only seizeth on the *Lazy,* the *Luxurous,* and the *Rich;* who, if they were forced to undergo the *same Regimen,* I would undertake for the Cure.

His Honour had farther observed, that a Female *Yahoo* would often stand behind a Bank or a Bush, to gaze on the young Males passing by, and then appear, and hide, using many antick Gestures and Grimaces; at which time it was observed, that she had a most *offensive Smell;* and when any of the Males advanced, would slowly retire, looking often back, and with a counterfeit Shew of Fear, run off into some convenient Place where she knew the Male would follow her.

At other times, if a Female Stranger came among them, three or four of her own Sex would get about her, and stare and chatter, and grin, and smell her all over; and then turn off with Gestures that seemed to express Contempt and Disdain.

Perhaps my Master might refine a little in these Speculations, which he had drawn from what he observed himself, or had been told him by others: However, I could not reflect without some Amazement, and much Sorrow, that the Rudiments of [215] *Lewdness, Coquetry, Censure,* and *Scandal,* should have Place by Instinct in Womankind.

I expected every Moment, that my Master would accuse the *Yahoos* of those unnatural Appetites in both Sexes, so common among us. But Nature it seems hath not been so expert a Schoolmistress; and these politer Pleasures are entirely the Productions of Art and Reason, on our Side of the Globe.

CHAP. VIII

The Author relateth several Particulars of the Yahoos. *The great Virtues of the* Houyhnhnms. *The Education and Exercise of their Youth. Their general Assembly.*

As I ought to have understood human Nature much better than I suppose it possible for my Master to do, so it was easy to apply the Character he gave of the *Yahoos* to myself and my Countrymen; and

I believed I could yet make farther Discoveries from my own Observation. I therefore often begged his Honour to let me go among the Herds of *Yahoos* in the Neighbourhood; to which he always very graciously consented, being perfectly convinced that the Hatred I bore those Brutes would never suffer me to be corrupted by them; and his Honour ordered one of his Servants, a strong Sorrel Nag, very honest and good-natured, to be my Guard; without whose Protection I durst not undertake such Adventures. For I have already told the Reader how much I was pestered by those odious Animals upon my first Arrival. I afterwards failed very narrowly three or four times of falling into their Clutches, when I happened to stray at any Distance without my Hanger. And I have Reason to believe, they had some Imagination that I was of their own Species, which I often assisted myself, by stripping up my Sleeves, and shewing my naked Arms and Breast in their Sight, when my Protector was with me: At which times they would approach as near as they durst, and imitate my Actions after the Manner of Monkeys, but ever with great Signs of Hatred; as a tame *Jack Daw* with Cap and Stockings, is always persecuted by the wild ones, when he happens to be got among them.

They are prodigiously nimble from their Infancy; however, I once caught a young Male of three Years old, and endeavoured [216] by all Marks of Tenderness to make it quiet; but the little Imp fell a squalling, and scratching, and biting with such Violence, that I was forced to let it go; and it was high time, for a whole Troop of old ones came about us at the Noise; but finding the Cub was safe, (for away it ran) and my Sorrel Nag being by, they durst not venture near us. I observed the young Animal's Flesh to smell very rank, and the Stink was somewhat between a *Weasel* and a *Fox,* but much more disagreeable. I forgot another Circumstance, (and perhaps I might have the Reader's Pardon, if it were wholly omitted) that while I held the odious Vermin in my Hands, it voided its filthy Excrements of a yellow liquid Substance, all over my Cloaths; but by good Fortune there was a small Brook hard by, where I washed myself as clean as I could; although I durst not come into my Master's Presence, until I were sufficiently aired.

By what I could discover, the *Yahoos* appear to be the most unteachable of all Animals, their Capacities never reaching higher than to draw or carry Burthens. Yet I am of Opinion, this Defect ariseth chiefly from a perverse, restive Disposition. For they are cunning, malicious, treacherous and revengeful. They are strong and hardy, but of a cowardly Spirit, and by Consequence insolent, abject, and cruel. It is observed, that the *Red-haired* of both Sexes are more libidinous and mischievous than the rest, whom yet they much exceed in Strength and Activity.

The *Houyhnhnms* keep the *Yahoos* for present Use in Huts not far from the House; but the rest are sent abroad to certain Fields, where they dig up Roots, eat several Kinds of Herbs, and search about for Carrion, or sometimes *Weasels* and *Luhimuhs* (a Sort of *wild Rat*) which they greedily devour. Nature hath taught them to dig deep Holes with their Nails on the Side of a rising Ground, wherein they lie by themselves; only the Kennels of the Females are larger, sufficient to hold two or three Cubs.

They swim from their Infancy like Frogs, and are able to continue long under Water, where they often take Fish, which the Females carry home to their Young. And upon this Occasion, I hope the Reader will pardon my relating an odd Adventure.

Being one Day abroad with my Protector the Sorrel Nag, and the Weather exceeding hot, I entreated him to let me bathe in a River that was near. He consented, and I immediately stripped myself stark naked, and went down softly into the Stream. It happened that a young Female *Yahoo* standing behind a Bank, saw the whole Proceeding; and inflamed by Desire, as the Nag [217] and I conjectured, came running with all Speed, and leaped into the Water within five Yards of the Place where I bathed. I was never in my Life so terribly frighted; the Nag was grazing at some Distance, not suspecting any Harm: She embraced me after a most fulsome Manner; I roared as loud as I could, and the Nag came galloping towards me, whereupon she quitted her Grasp, with the utmost Reluctancy, and leaped upon the opposite Bank, where she stood gazing and howling all the time I was putting on my Cloaths.

This was Matter of Diversion to my Master and his Family, as well as of Mortification to my self. For now I could no longer deny, that I was a real *Yahoo*, in every Limb and Feature, since the Females had a natural Propensity to me as one of their own Species: Neither was the Hair of this Brute of a Red Colour, (which might have been some Excuse for an Appetite a little irregular) but black as a Sloe, and her Countenance did not make an Appearance altogether so hideous as the rest of the Kind; for, I think, she could not be above Eleven Years old.

Having already lived three Years in this Country, the Reader I suppose will expect, that I should, like other Travellers, give him some Account of the Manners and Customs of its Inhabitants, which it was indeed my principal Study to learn.

As these noble *Houyhnhnms* are endowed by Nature with a general Disposition to all Virtues, and have no Conceptions or Ideas of what is evil in a rational Creature; so their grand Maxim is, to cultivate *Reason,* and to be wholly governed by it. Neither is *Reason* among them a Point problematical as with us, where Men can argue with Plausibility on both Sides of a Question; but strikes you with immediate Conviction; as it must needs do where it is not mingled, obscured, or discoloured by Passion and Interest. I remember it was with extreme Difficulty that I could bring my Master to understand the Meaning of the Word *Opinion,* or how a Point could be disputable; because *Reason* taught us to affirm or deny only where we are certain; and beyond our Knowledge we cannot do either. So that Controversies, Wranglings, Disputes, and Positiveness in false or dubious Propositions, are Evils unknown among the *Houyhnhnms.* In the like Manner when I used to explain to him our several Systems of *Natural Philosophy,* he would laugh that a Creature pretending to *Reason,* should value itself upon the Knowledge of other Peoples Conjectures, and in Things, where that Knowledge, if it were certain, could be of no Use. Wherein he agreed entirely with the Sentiments of *Socrates,* as *Plato* delivers them; which I mention as [218] the highest Honour I can do that Prince of Philosophers. I have often since reflected what Destruction such a Doctrine would make in the Libraries of *Europe;* and how many Paths to Fame would be then shut up in the Learned World.

Friendship and *Benevolence* are the two principal Virtues among the *Houyhnhnms;* and these not confined to particular Objects, but universal to the whole Race. For, a Stranger from the remotest Part, is equally treated with the nearest Neighbour, and where-ever he goes, looks upon himself as at home. They preserve *Decency* and *Civility* in the highest Degrees, but are altogether ignorant of *Ceremony.* They have no Fondness for their Colts or Foles; but the Care they take in educating them proceedeth entirely from the Dictates of *Reason.* And, I observed my Master to shew the same Affection to his Neighbour's

Issue that he had for his own. They will have it that *Nature* teaches them to love the whole Species, and it is *Reason* only that maketh a Distinction of Persons, where there is a superior Degree of Virtue.

When the Matron *Houyhnhnms* have produced one of each Sex, they no longer accompany with their Consorts, except they lose one of their Issue by some Casualty, which very seldom happens: But in such a Case they meet again; or when the like Accident befalls a Person, whose Wife is past bearing, some other Couple bestows on him one of their own Colts, and then go together a second Time, until the Mother be pregnant. This Caution is necessary to prevent the Country from being overburthened with Numbers. But the Race of inferior *Houyhnhnms* bred up to be Servants is not so strictly limited upon this Article; these are allowed to produce three of each Sex, to be Domesticks in the Noble Families.

In their Marriages they are exactly careful to chuse such Colours as will not make any disagreeable Mixture in the Breed. *Strength* is chiefly valued in the Male, and *Comeliness* in the Female; not upon the Account of *Love,* but to preserve the Race from degenerating: For, where a Female happens to excel in *Strength,* a Consort is chosen with regard to *Comeliness.* Courtship, Love, Presents, Joyntures, Settlements, have no Place in their Thoughts; or Terms whereby to express them in their Language. The young Couple meet and are joined, merely because it is the Determination of their Parents and Friends: It is what they see done every Day; and they look upon it as one of the necessary Actions in a reasonable Being. But the Violation of Marriage, or any other Unchastity, was never heard of: And the [219] married Pair pass their Lives with the same Friendship, and mutual Benevolence that they bear to all others of the same Species, who come in their Way; without Jealousy, Fondness, Quarrelling, or Discontent.

In educating the Youth of both Sexes, their Method is admirable, and highly deserveth our Imitation. These are not suffered to taste a Grain of *Oats,* except upon certain Days, till Eighteen Years old; nor *Milk,* but very rarely; and in Summer they graze two Hours in the Morning, and as many in the Evening, which their Parents likewise observe; but the Servants are not allowed above half that Time; and a great Part of the Grass is brought home, which they eat at the most convenient Hours, when they can be best spared from Work.

Temperance, *Industry, Exercise* and *Cleanliness,* are the Lessons equally enjoyned to the young ones of both Sexes: And my Master thought it monstrous in us to give the Females a different Kind of Education from the Males, except in some Articles of Domestick Management; whereby, as he truly observed, one Half of our Natives were good for nothing but bringing Children into the World: And to trust the Care of their Children to such useless Animals, he said was yet a greater Instance of Brutality.

But the *Houyhnhnms* train up their Youth to Strength, Speed, and Hardiness, by exercising them in running Races up and down steep Hills, or over hard stony Grounds; and when they are all in a Sweat, they are ordered to leap over Head and Ears into a Pond or a River. Four times a Year the Youth of certain Districts meet to shew the Proficiency in Running, and Leaping, and other Feats of Strength or Agility; where the Victor is rewarded with a Song made in his or her Praise. On this Festival the Servants drive a Heard of *Yahoos* into the Field, laden with Hay, and Oats, and Milk for a Repast to the *Houyhnhnms;* after which, these Brutes are immediately driven back again, for fear of being noisome to the Assembly.

Every fourth Year, at the *Vernal Equinox,* there is a Representative Council of the whole Nation, which meets in a Plain about twenty Miles from our House, and continueth about five or six Days. Here they inquire into the State and Condition of the several Districts; whether they abound or be deficient in Hay or Oats, or Cows or *Yahoos?* and wherever there is any Want (which is but seldom) it is immediately supplied by unanimous Consent and Contribution. Here likewise the Regulation of Children is settled: As for instance, if a *Houyhnhnm* hath two Males, he changeth one of them with another who had two Females: [220] And when a Child hath been lost by any Casualty, where the Mother is past Breeding, it is determined what Family shall breed another to supply the Loss.

CHAP. IX

A grand Debate at the General Assembly of the Houyhnhnms; *and how it was determined. The Learning of the* Houyhnhnms. *Their Buildings. Their Manner of Burials. The Defectiveness of their Language.*

One of these Grand Assemblies was held in my time, about three Months before my Departure, whither my Master went as the Representative of our District. In this Council was resumed their old Debate, and indeed, the only Debate that ever happened in their Country;

whereof my Master after his Return gave me a very particular Account.

The Question to be debated was, Whether the *Yahoos* should be exterminated from the Face of the Earth. One of the *Members* for the Affirmative offered several Arguments of great Strength and Weight; alledging, That, as the *Yahoos* were the most filthy, noisome, and deformed Animal which Nature ever produced, so they were the most restive and indocible, mischievous and malicious: They would privately suck the Teats of the *Houyhnhnms* Cows; kill and devour their Cats, trample down their Oats and Grass, if they were not continually watched; and commit a Thousand other Extravagancies. He took Notice of a general Tradition, that *Yahoos* had not been always in their Country: But, that many Ages ago, two of these Brutes appeared together upon a Mountain; whether produced by the Heat of the Sun upon corrupted Mud and Slime, or from the Ooze and Froth of the Sea, was never known. That these *Yahoos* engendered, and their Brood in a short time grew so numerous as to over-run and infest the whole Nation. That the *Houyhnhnms* to get rid of this Evil, made a general Hunting, and at last inclosed the whole Herd; and destroying the Older, every *Houyhnhnm* kept two young Ones in a Kennel, and brought them to such a Degree of Tameness, as an Animal so savage by Nature can be capable of acquiring; using them for Draught and Carriage. That, there seemed to be much Truth in this Tradition, and that those Creatures could not be *Ylnhniamshy* (or *Aborigines* of the Land) because [221] of the violent Hatred the *Houyhnhnms* as well as all other Animals, bore them; which although their evil Disposition sufficiently deserved, could never have arrived at so high a Degree, if they had been *Aborigines,* or else they would have long since been rooted out. That, the Inhabitants taking a Fancy to use the Service of the *Yahoos,* had very imprudently neglected to cultivate the Breed of *Asses,* which were a comely Animal, easily kept, more tame and orderly, without any offensive Smell, strong enough for Labour, although they yield to the other in Agility of Body; and if their Braying be no agreeable Sound, it is far preferable to the horrible Howlings of the *Yahoos.*

Several others declared their Sentiments to the same Purpose; when my Master proposed an Expedient to the Assembly, whereof he had indeed borrowed the Hint from me. He approved of the Tradition, mentioned by the *Honourable Member,* who spoke before;

and affirmed, that the two *Yahoos* said to be first seen among them, had been driven thither over the Sea; that coming to Land, and being forsaken by their Companions, they retired to the Mountains, and degenerating by Degrees, became in Process of Time, much more savage than those of their own Species in the Country from whence these two Originals came. The Reason of his Assertion was, that he had now in his Possession, a certain wonderful *Yahoo,* (meaning myself) which most of them had heard of, and many of them had seen. He then related to them, how he first found me; that, my Body was all covered with an artificial Composure of the Skins and Hairs of other Animals: That, I spoke in a Language of my own, and had thoroughly learned theirs: That, I had related to him the Accidents which brought me thither: That, when he saw me without my Covering, I was an exact *Yahoo* in every Part, only of a whiter Colour, less hairy, and with shorter Claws. He added, how I had endeavoured to persuade him, that in my own and other Countries the *Yahoos* acted as the governing, rational Animal, and held the *Houyhnhnms* in Servitude: That, he observed in me all the Qualities of a *Yahoo,* only a little more civilized by some Tincture of Reason; which however was in a Degree as far inferior to the *Houyhnhnm* Race, as the *Yahoos* of their Country were to me: That, among other things, I mentioned a Custom we had of *castrating Houyhnhnms* when they were young, in order to render them tame; that the Operation was easy and safe; that it was no Shame to learn Wisdom from Brutes, as Industry is taught by the Ant, and Building by the Swallow. (For so I translate the Word *Lyhannh,* although it be a much larger Fowl) That, [222] this Invention might be practiced upon the younger *Yahoos* here, which, besides rendering them tractable and fitter for Use, would in an Age put an End to the whole Species without destroying Life. That, in the mean time the *Houyhnhnms* should be *exhorted* to cultivate the Breed of Asses, which, as they are in all respects more valuable Brutes; so they have this Advantage, to be fit for Service at five Years old, which the others are not till Twelve.

This was all my Master thought fit to tell me at that Time, of what passed in the Grand Council. But he was pleased to conceal one Particular, which related personally to myself, whereof I soon felt the unhappy Effect, as the Reader will know in its proper Place, and from whence I date all the succeeding Misfortunes of my Life.

The *Houyhnhnms* have no Letters, and consequently, their

Knowledge is all traditional. But there happening few Events of any Moment among a People so well united, naturally disposed to every Virtue, wholly governed by Reason, and cut off from all Commerce with other Nations; the historical Part is easily preserved without burthening their Memories. I have already observed, that they are subject to no Diseases, and therefore can have no Need of Physicians. However, they have excellent Medicines composed of Herbs, to cure accidental Bruises and Cuts in the Pastern or Frog of the Foot by sharp Stones, as well as other Maims and Hurts in the several Parts of the Body.

They calculate the Year by the Revolution of the Sun and the Moon, but use no Subdivisions into Weeks. They are well enough acquainted with the Motions of those two Luminaries, and understand the Nature of *Eclipses;* and this is the utmost Progress of their *Astronomy.*

In *Poetry* they must be allowed to excel all other Mortals; wherein the Justness of their Similes, and the Minuteness, as well as Exactness of their Descriptions, are indeed inimitable. Their Verses abound very much in both of these; and usually contain either some exalted Notions of Friendship and Benevolence, or the Praises of those who were Victors in Races, and other bodily Exercises. Their Buildings, although very rude and simple, are not inconvenient, but well contrived to defend them from all Injuries of Cold and Heat. They have a Kind of Tree, which at Forty Years old loosens in the Root, and falls with the first Storm; it grows very strait, and being pointed like Stakes with a sharp Stone, (for the *Houyhnhnms* know not the Use of Iron) they stick them erect in the Ground about ten Inches asunder, and then weave in Oat-straw, or sometimes Wattles betwixt [223] them. The Roof is made after the same Manner, and so are the Doors.

The *Houyhnhnms* use the hollow Part between the Pastern and the Hoof of their Fore-feet, as we do our Hands, and this with greater Dexterity, than I could at first imagine. I have seen a white Mare of our Family thread a Needle (which I lent her on Purpose) with that Joynt. They milk their Cows, reap their Oats, and do all the Work which requires Hands, in the same Manner. They have a Kind of hard Flints, which by grinding against other Stones, they form into Instruments, that serve instead of Wedges, Axes, and Hammers. With Tools made of these Flints, they likewise cut their Hay, and reap their Oats, which there groweth naturally in several

Fields: The *Yahoos* draw home the Sheaves in Carriages, and the Servants tread them in certain covered Hutts, to get out the Grain, which is kept in Stores. They make a rude Kind of earthen and wooden Vessels, and bake the former in the Sun.

If they can avoid Casualties, they die only of old Age, and are buried in the obscurest Places that can be found, their Friends and Relations expressing neither Joy nor Grief at their Departure; nor does the dying Person discover the least Regret that he is leaving the World, any more than if he were upon returning home from a Visit to one of his Neighbours: I remember, my Master having once made an Appointment with a Friend and his Family to come to his House upon some Affair of Importance; on the Day fixed, the Mistress and her two Children came very late; she made two Excuses, first for her Husband, who, as she said, happened that very Morning to *Lhnuwnh*. The Word is strongly expressive in their Language, but not easily rendered into *English;* it signifies, *to retire to his first Mother*. Her Excuse for not coming sooner, was, that her Husband dying late in the Morning, she was a good while consulting her Servants about a convenient Place where his Body should be laid; and I observed she behaved herself at our House, as chearfully as the rest: She died about three Months after.

They live generally to Seventy or Seventy-five Years, very seldom to Fourscore: Some Weeks before their Death they feel a gradual Decay, but without Pain. During this time they are much visited by their Friends, because they cannot go abroad with their usual Ease and Satisfaction. However, about ten Days before their Death, which they seldom fail in computing, they return the Visits that have been made them by those who are nearest in the Neighbourhood, being carried in a convenient [224] Sledge drawn by *Yahoos;* which Vehicle they use, not only upon this Occasion, but when they grow old, upon long Journeys, or when they are lamed by any Accident. And therefore when the dying *Houyhnhnms* return those Visits, they take a solemn Leave of their Friends, as if they were going to some remote Part of the Country, where they designed to pass the rest of their Lives.

I know not whether it may be worth observing, that the *Houyhnhnms* have no Word in their Language to express any thing that is *evil*, except what they borrow from the Deformities or ill Qualities of the *Yahoos*. Thus they denote the Folly of a Servant, an Omission of a Child, a Stone that cuts their Feet, a Continuance of foul or unseasonable Weather, and the like, by adding to each the Epithet of *Yahoo.* For Instance, *Hhnm Yahoo, Whnaholm Yahoo, Ynlhmnawihlma Yahoo,* and an ill contrived House, *Ynholmhnmrohlnw Yahoo.*

I could with great Pleasure enlarge farther upon the Manners and Virtues of this excellent People; but intending in a short time to publish a Volume by itself expressly upon that Subject, I refer the Reader thither. And in the mean time, proceed to relate my own sad Catastrophe.

CHAP. X

The Author's Oeconomy and happy Life among the Houyhnhnms. *His great Improvement in Virtue, by conversing with them. Their Conversations. The Author hath Notice given him by his Master that he must depart from the Country. He falls into a Swoon for Grief, but submits. He contrives and finishes a Canoo, by the Help of a Fellow-Servant, and puts to Sea at a Venture.*

I had settled my little Oeconomy to my own Heart's Content. My Master had ordered a Room to be made for me after their Manner, about six Yards from the House; the Sides and Floors of which I plaistered with Clay, and covered with Rush-mats of my own contriving: I had beaten Hemp, which there grows wild, and made of it a Sort of Ticking: This I filled with the Feathers of several Birds I had taken with Springes made of *Yahoos* Hairs; and were excellent Food. I had worked two Chairs with my Knife, the Sorrel Nag helping me in the grosser and more laborious Part. When my Cloaths were [225] worn to Rags, I made my self others with the Skins of Rabbets, and of a certain beautiful Animal about the same Size, called *Nnuhnoh,* the Skin of which is covered with a fine Down. Of these I likewise made very tolerable Stockings. I soaled my Shoes with Wood which I cut from a Tree, and fitted to the upper Leather, and when this was worn out, I supplied it with the Skins of *Yahoos,* dried in the Sun. I often got Honey out of hollow Trees, which I mingled with Water, or eat it with my Bread. No Man could more verify the Truth of these two Maxims, *That, Nature is very easily satisfied;* and, *That, Necessity is the Mother of Invention.* I enjoyed perfect Health of Body, and Tranquility of Mind; I did not feel the Treachery or Inconstancy of a Friend, nor the Injuries of a secret or open Enemy. I had no Occasion of bribing, flattering or pimping, to procure the

Favour of any great Man, or his Minion. I wanted no Fence against Fraud or Oppression: Here was neither Physician to destroy my Body, nor Lawyer to ruin my Fortune: No Informer to watch my Words and Actions, or forge Accusations against me for Hire: Here were no Gibers, Censurers, Backbiters, Pickpockets, Highwaymen, House-breakers, Attorneys, Bawds, Buffoons, Gamesters, Politicians, Wits, Spleneticks, tedious Talkers, Controvertists, Ravishers, Murderers, Robbers, Virtuoso's; no Leaders or Followers of Party and Faction; no Encouragers to Vice, by Seducement or Examples: No Dungeon, Axes, Gibbets, Whipping-posts, or Pillories; No cheating Shopkeepers or Mechanicks: No Pride, Vanity or Affectation: No Fops, Bullies, Drunkards, strolling Whores, or Poxes: No ranting, lewd, expensive Wives: No stupid, proud Pedants: No importunate, overbearing, quarrelsome, noisy, roaring, empty, conceited, swearing Companions: No Scoundrels raised from the Dust upon the Merit of their Vices; or Nobility thrown into it on account of their Virtues: No Lords, Fidlers, Judges or Dancing-masters.

I had the Favour of being admitted to several *Houyhnhnms,* who came to visit or dine with my Master; where his Honour graciously suffered me to wait in the Room, and listen to their Discourse. Both he and his Company would often descend to ask me Questions, and receive my Answers. I had also sometimes the Honour of attending my Master in his Visits to others. I never presumed to speak, except in answer to a Question; and then I did it with inward Regret, because it was a Loss of so much Time for improving my self: But I was infinitely delighted with the Station of an humble Auditor in such Conversations, where nothing passed but what was useful, expressed in the fewest and [226] most significant Words: Where (as I have already said) the greatest *Decency* was observed, without the least Degree of Ceremony; where no Person spoke without being pleased himself, and pleasing his Companions: Where there was no Inter-ruption, Tediousness, Heat, or Difference of Sentiments. They have a Notion, That when People are met together, a short Silence doth much improve Conversation: This I found to be true; for during those little Intermissions of Talk, new Ideas would arise in their Minds, which very much enlivened the Discourse. Their Subjects are generally on Friendship and Benevolence; on Order and Oeconomy; sometimes upon the visible Operations of Nature, or ancient Tradi-tions; upon the Bounds and Limits of Virtue; upon the unerring

Rules of Reason; or upon some Determinations, to be taken at the next great Assembly; and often upon the various Excellencies of *Poetry.* I may add, without Vanity, that my Presence often gave them sufficient Matter for Discourse, because it afforded my Master an Occasion of letting his Friends into the History of me and my Country, upon which they were all pleased to discant in a Manner not very advantageous to human Kind; and for that Reason I shall not repeat what they said: Only I may be allowed to observe, That his Honour, to my great Admiration, appeared to understand the Nature of *Yahoos* much better than my self. He went through all our Vices and Follies, and discovered many which I had never mentioned to him; by only supposing what Qualities a *Yahoo* of their Country, with a small Proportion of Reason, might be capable of exerting: And concluded, with too much Probability, how vile as well as miserable such a Creature must be.

I freely confess, that all the little Knowledge I have of any Value, was acquired by the Lectures I received from my Master, and from hearing the Discourses of him and his Friends; to which I should be prouder to listen, than to dictate to the greatest and wisest Assembly in *Europe.* I admired the Strength, Comeliness and Speed of the Inhabitants; and such a Constellation of Virtues in such amiable Persons produced in me the highest Veneration. At first, indeed, I did not feel that natural Awe which the *Yahoos* and all other Animals bear towards them; but it grew upon me by Degrees, much sooner than I imagined, and was mingled with a respectful Love and Gratitude, that they would condescend to distinguish me from the rest of my Species.

When I thought of my Family, my Friends, my Countrymen, or human Race in general, I considered them as they really were, *Yahoos* in Shape and Disposition, perhaps a little more civilized, [227] and qualified with the Gift of Speech; but making no other Use of Reason, than to improve and multiply those Vices, whereof their Brethren in this Country had only the Share that Nature allotted them. When I happened to behold the Reflection of my own Form in a Lake or Fountain, I turned away my Face in Horror and detestation of my self; and could better endure the Sight of a common *Yahoo,* than of my own Person. By conversing with the *Houyhnhnms,* and looking upon them with Delight, I fell to imitate their Gait and Gesture, which is now grown into a Habit; and my Friends often tell me in a blunt

Way, that I *trot like a Horse;* which, however, I take for a great
Compliment: Neither shall I disown, that in speaking I am apt to fall
into the Voice and manner of the *Houyhnhnms,* and hear my self
ridiculed on that Account without the least Mortification.

In the Midst of this Happiness, when I looked upon my self to be
fully settled for Life, my Master sent for me one Morning a little
earlier than his usual Hour. I observed by his Countenance that he
was in some Perplexity, and at a Loss how to begin what he had to
speak. After a short Silence, he told me, he did not know how I would
take what he was going to say: That, in the last general Assembly,
when the Affair of the *Yahoos* was entered upon, the Representatives
had taken Offence at his keeping a *Yahoo* (meaning my self) in his
Family more like a *Houyhnhnm* than a Brute Animal. That, he was
known frequently to converse with me, as if he could receive some
Advantage or Pleasure in my Company: That, such a Practice was not
agreeable to Reason or Nature, or a thing ever heard of before among
them. The Assembly did therefore *exhort* him, either to employ me
like the rest of my Species, or command me to swim back to the
Place from whence I came. That, the first of these Expedients was
utterly rejected by all the *Houyhnhnms,* who had ever seen me at
his House or their own: For, they alledged, That because I had some
Rudiments of Reason, added to the natural Pravity of those Animals,
it was to be feared, I might be able to seduce them into the woody
and mountainous Parts of the Country, and bring them in Troops by
Night to destroy the *Houyhnhnms* Cattle, as being naturally of the
ravenous Kind, and averse from Labour.

My Master added, That he was daily pressed by the *Houyhnhnms*
of the Neighbourhood to have the Assembly's *Exhortation* executed,
which he could not put off much longer. He doubted, it would be
impossible for me to swim to another Country; and therefore wished
I would contrive some Sort of Vehicle resembling [228] those I had
described to him, that might carry me on the Sea; in which Work I
should have the Assistance of his own Servants, as well as those of his
Neighbours. He concluded, that for his own Part he could have been
content to keep me in his Service as long as I lived; because he found
I had cured myself of some bad Habits and Dispositions, by endeavouring, as far as my inferior Nature was capable, to imitate the
Houyhnhnms.

I should here observe to the Reader, that a Decree of the general

Assembly in this Country, is expressed by the Word *Hnhloayn,* which signifies an *Exhortation;* as near as I can render it: For they have no Conception how a rational Creature can be *compelled,* but only advised, or *exhorted;* because no Person can disobey Reason, without giving up his Claim to be a rational Creature.

I was struck with the utmost Grief and Despair at my Master's Discourse; and being unable to support the Agonies I was under, I fell into a Swoon at his Feet: When I came to myself, he told me, that he concluded I had been dead. (For these People are subject to no such Imbecillities of Nature) I answered, in a faint Voice, that Death would have been too great an Happiness; that although I could not blame the Assembly's *Exhortation,* or the Urgency of his Friends; yet in my weak and corrupt Judgment, I thought it might consist with Reason to have been less rigorous. That, I could not swim a League, and probably the nearest Land to theirs might be distant about an Hundred: That, many Materials, necessary for making a small Vessel to carry me off, were wholly wanting in this Country, which however, I would attempt in Obedience and Gratitude to his Honour, although I concluded the thing to be impossible, and therefore looked on my self as already devoted to Destruction. That, the certain Prospect of an unnatural Death, was the least of my Evils: For, supposing I should escape with Life by some strange Adventure, how could I think with Temper, of passing my Days among *Yahoos,* and relapsing into my old Corruptions, for want of Examples to lead and keep me within the Paths of Virtue. That, I knew too well upon what solid Reasons all the Determinations of the wise *Houyhnhnms* were founded, not to be shaken by Arguments of mine, a miserable *Yahoo;* and therefore after presenting him with my humble Thanks for the Offer of his Servants Assistance in making a Vessel, and desiring a reasonable Time for so difficult a Work, I told him, I would endeavour to preserve a wretched Being; and, if ever I returned [229] to *England,* was not without Hopes of being useful to my own Species, by celebrating the Praises of the renowned *Houyhnhnms,* and proposing their Virtues to the Imitation of Mankind.

My Master in a few Words made me a very gracious Reply, allowed me the Space of two *Months* to finish my Boat; and ordered the Sorrel Nag, my Fellow-Servant, (for so at this Distance I may presume to call him) to follow my Instructions, because I told my

Master, that his Help would be sufficient, and I knew he had a Tenderness for me.

In his Company my first Business was to go to that Part of the Coast, where my rebellious Crew had ordered me to be set on Shore. I got upon a Height, and looking on every Side into the Sea, fancied I saw a small Island, towards the *North-East:* I took out my Pocket-glass, and could then clearly distinguish it about five Leagues off, as I computed; but it appeared to the Sorrel Nag to be only a blue Cloud: For, as he had no Conception of any Country beside his own, so he could not be as expert in distinguishing remote Objects at Sea, as we who so much converse in that Element.

After I had discovered this Island, I considered no farther; but resolved, it should, if possible, be the first Place of my Banishment, leaving the Consequence to Fortune.

I returned home, and consulting with the Sorrel Nag, we went into a Copse at some Distance, where I with my Knife, and he with a sharp Flint fastened very artificially, after their Manner, to a wooden Handle, cut down several Oak Wattles about the Thickness of a Walking-staff, and some larger Pieces. But I shall not trouble the Reader with a particular Description of my own Mechanicks: Let it suffice to say, that in six Weeks time, with the Help of the Sorrel Nag, who performed the Parts that required most Labour, I finished a Sort of *Indian* Canoo, but much larger, covering it with the Skins of *Yahoos,* well stitched together, with hempen Threads of my own making. My Sail was likewise composed of the Skins of the same Animal; but I made use of the youngest I could get, the older being too tough and thick; and I likewise provided myself with four Paddles. I laid in a Stock of boiled Flesh, of Rabbets and Fowls; and took with me two Vessels, one filled with Milk, and the other with Water.

I tried my Canoo in a large Pond near my Master's House, and then corrected in it what was amiss; stopping all the Chinks with *Yahoos* Tallow, till I found it stanch, and able to bear me, and my Freight. And when it was as compleat as I could possibly make it, I had it drawn on a Carriage very gently by *Yahoos,* to [230] the Sea-side, under the Conduct of the Sorrel Nag, and another Servant.

When all was ready, and the Day came for my Departure, I took Leave of my Master and Lady, and the whole Family, mine Eyes flowing with Tears, and my Heart quite sunk with Grief. But his Honour, out of Curiosity, and perhaps (if I may speak it without

Vanity) partly out of Kindness, was determined to see me in my
Canoo; and got several of his neighbouring Friends to accompany
him. I was forced to wait above an Hour for the Tide, and then
observing the Wind very fortunately bearing towards the Island, to
which I intended to steer my Course, I took a second Leave of my
Master: But as I was going to prostrate myself to kiss his Hoof, he did
me the Honour to raise it gently to my Mouth. I am not ignorant how
much I have been censured for mentioning this last Particular.
Detractors are pleased to think it improbable, that so illustrious a
Person should descend to give so great a Mark of Distinction to a
Creature so inferior as I. Neither have I forgot, how apt some Travel-
lers are to boast of extraordinary Favours they have received. But, if
these Censurers were better acquainted with the noble and courteous
Disposition of the *Houyhnhnms,* they would soon change their
Opinion.

I paid my Respects to the rest of the *Houyhnhnms* in his Honour's
Company; then getting into my Canoo, I pushed off from Shore.

CHAP. XI

The Author's dangerous Voyage. He arrives at New-Holland, *hoping to
settle there. Is wounded with an Arrow by one of the Natives. Is seized
and carried by Force into a* Portugueze *Ship. The great Civilities of the
Captain. The Author arrives at* England.

I began this desperate Voyage on *February* 15, 1714-15, at 9 o'Clock
in the Morning. The Wind was very favourable; however, I made
use at first only of my Paddles; but considering I should soon be
weary, and that the Wind might probably chop about, I ventured
to set up my little Sail; and thus, with the Help of the Tide, I went at
the Rate of a League and a [231] Half an Hour, as near as I could
guess. My Master and his Friends continued on the Shoar, till I was
almost out of Sight; and I often heard the Sorrel Nag (who always
loved me) crying out, *Hnuy illa nyha maiah Yahoo,* Take Care of thy
self, gentle *Yahoo.*

My Design was, if possible, to discover some small Island unin-
habited, yet sufficient by my Labour to furnish me with Necessaries
of Life, which I would have thought a greater Happiness than to be
first Minister in the politest Court of *Europe;* so horrible was the
Idea I conceived of returning to live in the Society and under the

Government of *Yahoos*. For in such a Solitude as I desired, I could at least enjoy my own Thoughts, and reflect with Delight on the Virtues of those inimitable *Houyhnhnms*, without any Opportunity of degenerating into the Vices and Corruptions of my own Species.

The Reader may remember what I related when my Crew conspired against me, and confined me to my Cabbin. How I continued there several Weeks, without knowing what Course we took; and when I was put ashore in the Long-boat, how the Sailors told me with Oaths, whether true or false, that they knew not in what Part of the World we were. However, I did then believe us to be about ten Degrees *Southward* of the *Cape of Good Hope,* or about 45 Degrees *Southern* Latitude, as I gathered from some general Words I overheard among them, being I supposed to the *South-East* in their intended Voyage to *Madagascar*. And although this were but little better than Conjecture, yet I resolved to steer my Course *Eastward,* hoping to reach the *South-West* Coast of *New-Holland,* and perhaps some such Island as I desired, lying *Westward* of it. The Wind was full *West,* and by six in the Evening I computed I had gone *Eastward* at least eighteen Leagues; when I spied a very small Island about half a League off, which I soon reached. It was nothing but a Rock with one Creek, naturally arched by the Force of Tempests. Here I put in my Canoo, and climbing a Part of the Rock, I could plainly discover Land to the *East,* extending from *South* to *North*. I lay all Night in my Canoo; and repeating my Voyage early in the Morning, I arrived in seven Hours to the *South-East* Point of *New-Holland*. This confirmed me in the Opinion I have long entertained, that the *Maps* and *Charts* place this Country at least three Degrees more to the *East* than it really is; which Thought I communicated many Years ago to my worthy Friend Mr. *Herman Moll,* and gave him my Reasons for it, although he hath rather chosen to follow other Authors. [232]

I saw no Inhabitants in the Place where I landed; and being unarmed, I was afraid of venturing far into the Country. I found some Shell-Fish on the Shore, and eat them raw, not daring to kindle a Fire, for fear of being discovered by the Natives. I continued three Days feeding on Oysters and Limpits, to save my own Provisions; and I fortunately found a Brook of excellent Water, which gave me great Relief.

On the fourth Day, venturing out early a little too far, I saw twenty or thirty Natives upon a Height, not above five hundred Yards from me. They were stark naked, Men, Women and Children round a Fire, as I could discover by the Smoke. One of them spied me, and gave Notice to the rest; five of them advanced towards me, leaving the Women and Children at the Fire. I made what haste I could to the Shore, and getting into my Canoo, shoved off: The Savages observing me retreat, ran after me; and before I could get far enough into the Sea, discharged an Arrow, which wounded me deeply on the Inside of my left Knee (I shall carry the Mark to my Grave.) I apprehended the Arrow might be poisoned; and paddling out of the Reach of their Darts (being a calm Day) I made a shift to suck the Wound, and dress it as well as I could.

I was at a Loss what to do, for I durst not return to the same Landing-place, but stood to the *North,* and was forced to paddle; for the Wind, although very gentle, was against me, blowing *North-West.* As I was looking about for a secure Landing-place, I saw a Sail to the *North North-East,* which appearing every Minute more visible, I was in some Doubt, whether I should wait for them or no; but at last my Detestation of the *Yahoo* Race prevailed; and turning my Canoo, I sailed and paddled together to the *South,* and got into the same Creek from whence I set out in the Morning; choosing rather to trust my self among these *Barbarians,* than live with *European Yahoos.* I drew up my Canoo as close as I could to the Shore, and hid my self behind a Stone by the little Brook, which, as I have already said, was excellent Water.

The Ship came within half a League of this Creek, and sent out her Long-Boat with Vessels to take in fresh Water (for the Place it seems was very well known) but I did not observe it until the Boat was almost on Shore; and it was too late to seek another Hiding-Place. The Seamen at their landing observed my Canoo, and rummaging it all over, easily conjectured that the Owner could not be far off. Four of them well armed searched every Cranny and Lurking-hole, till at last they found me flat on [233] my Face behind the Stone. They gazed a while in Admiration at my strange uncouth Dress; my Coat made of Skins, my wooden-soaled Shoes, and my furred Stockings; from whence, however, they concluded I was not a Native of the Place, who all go naked. One of the Seamen in *Portugueze* bid me rise, and asked who I was. I understood that Language very well, and getting upon my Feet, said, I was a poor *Yahoo,* banished from the *Houyhnhnms,* and desired they would please to let me depart. They admired to hear me answer them in their own Tongue, and saw by my Complection I must be an *European;* but were at a Loss to know what I meant by *Yahoos* and *Houyhnhnms,* and at the same Time fell a laughing at my strange Tone in speaking, which resembled the Neighing of a Horse. I trembled all the while betwixt Fear and Hatred: I again desired Leave to depart, and was gently moving to my Canoo; but they laid hold on me, desiring to know what Country I was of? whence I came? with many other Questions. I told them, I was born in *England,* from whence I came about five Years ago, and then their Country and ours were at Peace. I therefore hoped they would not treat me as an Enemy, since I meant them no Harm, but was a poor *Yahoo,* seeking some desolate Place where to pass the Remainder of his unfortunate Life.

When they began to talk, I thought I never heard or saw any thing so unnatural; for it appeared to me as monstrous as if a Dog or a Cow should speak in *England,* or a *Yahoo* in *Houyhnhnm-Land.* The honest *Portuguese* were equally amazed at my strange Dress, and the odd Manner of delivering my Words, which however they understood very well. They spoke to me with great Humanity, and said they were sure their Captain would carry me *gratis* to *Lisbon,* from whence I might return to my own Country; that two of the Seamen would go back to the Ship, to inform the Captain of what they had seen, and receive his Orders; in the mean Time, unless I would give my solemn Oath not to fly, they would secure me by Force. I thought it best to comply with their Proposal. They were very curious to know my Story, but I gave them very little Satisfaction; and they all conjectured, that my Misfortunes had impaired my Reason. In two Hours the Boat, which went loaden with Vessels of Water, returned with the Captain's Commands to fetch me on Board. I fell on my Knees to preserve my Liberty; but all was in vain, and the Men having tied me with Cords, heaved me into the Boat, from whence I was taken into the Ship, and from thence into the Captain's Cabbin. [234]

His Name was *Pedro de Mendez;* he was a very courteous and generous Person; he entreated me to give some Account of my self, and desired to know what I would eat or drink; said, I should be used as well as himself, and spoke so many obliging Things, that I wondered to find such Civilities from a *Yahoo.* However, I remained silent and sullen; I was ready to faint at the very Smell of him and his Men. At last I desired something to eat out of my own Canoo; but he ordered me a Chicken and some excellent Wine, and then directed that I should be put to Bed in a very clean Cabbin. I would not undress my self, but lay on the Bed-cloaths; and in half an Hour stole out, when I thought the Crew was at Dinner; and getting to the Side of the Ship, was going to leap into the Sea, and swim for my Life, rather than continue among *Yahoos*. But one of the Seamen prevented me, and having informed the Captain, I was chained to my Cabbin.

After Dinner *Don Pedro* came to me, and desired to know my Reason for so desperate an Attempt; assured me he only meant to do me all the Service he was able; and spoke so very movingly, that at last I descended to treat him like an Animal which had some little Portion of Reason. I gave him a very short Relation of my Voyage; of the Conspiracy against me by my own Men; of the Country where they set me on Shore, and of my five Years Residence there. All which he looked upon as if it were a Dream or a Vision; whereat I took great Offence: For I had quite forgot the Faculty of Lying, so peculiar to *Yahoos* in all Countries where they preside, and consequently the Disposition of suspecting Truth in others of their own Species. I asked him, Whether it were the Custom of his Country to *say the Thing that was not?* I assured him I had almost forgot what he meant by Falshood; and if I had lived a thousand Years in *Houyhnhnm-land,* I should never have heard a Lie from the meanest Servant. That I was altogether indifferent whether he believed me or no; but however, in return for his Favours, I would give so much Allowance to the Corruption of his Nature, as to answer any Objection he would please to make; and he might easily discover the Truth.

The Captain, a wise Man, after many Endeavors to catch me tripping in some Part of my Story, at last began to have a better Opinion of my Veracity. But he added, that since I professed so inviolable an Attachment to Truth, I must give him my Word of Honour to bear him Company in this Voyage without attempting any thing against my Life; or else he would continue me a Prisoner till we arrived at *Lisbon.* I gave him the Promise [235] he required; but at the same time protested that I would suffer the greatest Hardships rather than return to live among *Yahoos*.

Our Voyage passed without any considerable Accident. In Gratitude to the Captain I sometimes sate with him at his earnest Request, and strove to conceal my Antipathy against human Kind, although it often broke out; which he suffered to pass without Observation.

But the greatest Part of the Day, I confined myself to my Cabbin, to avoid seeing any of the Crew. The Captain had often intreated me to strip myself of my savage Dress, and offered to lend me the best Suit of Cloaths he had. This I would not be prevailed on to accept, abhorring to cover myself with any thing that had been on the Back of a *Yahoo.* I only desired he would lend me two clean Shirts, which having been washed since he wore them, I believed would not so much defile me. These I changed every second Day, and washed them my self.

We arrived at *Lisbon, Nov.* 5, 1715. At our landing, the Captain forced me to cover myself with his Cloak, to prevent the Rabble from crouding about me. I was conveyed to his own House; and at my earnest Request, he led me up to the highest Room backwards. I conjured him to conceal from all Persons what I had told him of the *Houyhnhnms;* because the least Hint of a Story would not only draw Numbers of People to see me, but probably put me in Danger of being imprisoned, or burnt by the *Inquisition.* The Captain persuaded me to accept a Suit of Cloaths newly made; but I would not suffer the Taylor to take my Measure; however, Don *Pedro* being almost of my Size, they fitted me well enough. He accoutred me with other Necessaries all new, which I aired for Twenty-four Hours before I would use them.

The Captain had no Wife, nor above three Servants, none of which were suffered to attend at Meals; and his whole Deportment was so obliging, added to very good *human* Understanding, that I really began to tolerate his Company. He gained so far upon me, that I ventured to look out of the back Window. By Degrees I was brought into another Room, from whence I peeped into the Street, but drew my Head back in a Fright. In a Week's Time he seduced me down to the Door. I found my Terror gradually lessened, but my Hatred and Contempt seemed to increase. I was at last bold enough to walk the Street in his Company, but kept my Nose well stopped with Rue, or sometimes with Tobacco.

In ten Days, Don *Pedro,* to whom I had given some Account of my domestick Affairs, put it upon me as a Point of Honour [236] and Conscience, that I ought to return to my native Country, and live at home with my Wife and Children. He told me, there was an *English* Ship in the Port just ready to sail, and he would furnish me with all things necessary. It would be tedious to repeat his Arguments, and my

Contradictions. He said, it was altogether impossible to find such a solitary Island as I had desired to live in; but I might command in my own House, and pass my time in a Manner as recluse as I pleased.

I complied at last, finding I could not do better. I left *Lisbon* the 24th Day of *November,* in an *English* Merchant-man, but who was the Master I never inquired. Don *Pedro* accompanied me to the Ship, and lent me Twenty Pounds. He took kind Leave of me, and embraced me at parting; which I bore as well as I could. During this last Voyage I had no Commerce with the Master, or any of his Men; but pretending I was sick kept close in my Cabbin. On the Fifth of *December,* 1715, we cast Anchor in the *Downs* about Nine in the Morning, and at Three in the Afternoon I got safe to my House at *Redriff.*

My Wife and Family received me with great Surprize and Joy, because they concluded me certainly dead; but I must freely confess, the Sight of them filled me only with Hatred, Disgust and Contempt; and the more, by reflecting on the near Alliance I had to them. For, although since my unfortunate Exile from the *Houyhnhnm* Country, I had compelled myself to tolerate the Sight of *Yahoos,* and to converse with Don *Pedro de Mendez;* yet my Memory and Imaginations were perpetually filled with the Virtues and Ideas of those exalted *Houyhnhnms.* And when I began to consider, that by copulating with one of the *Yahoo*-Species, I had become a Parent of more; it struck me with the utmost Shame, Confusion and Horror.

As soon as I entered the House, my Wife took me in her Arms, and kissed me; at which, having not been used to the Touch of that odious Animal for so many Years, I fell in a Swoon for almost an Hour. At the Time I am writing, it is five Years since my last Return to *England:* During the first Year I could not endure my Wife or Children in my Presence, the very Smell of them was intolerable; much less could I suffer them to eat in the same Room. To this Hour they dare not presume to touch my Bread, or drink out of the same Cup; neither was I ever able to let one of them take me by the Hand. The first Money I laid out was to buy two young Stone-Horses, which I keep in a good Stable, and next to them the Groom is my greatest Favourite; for I feel my Spirits revived by the Smell he contracts in the [237] Stable. My Horses understand me tolerably well; I converse with them at least four Hours every Day. They are Strangers to Bridle or Saddle; they live in great Amity with me, and Friendship to each other.

CHAP. XII

The Author's Veracity. His Design in publishing this Work. His Censure of those Travellers who swerve from the Truth. The Author clears himself from any sinister Ends in writing. An Objection answered. The Method of planting Colonies. His Native Country commended. The Right of the Crown to those Countries described by the Author, is justified. The Difficulty of conquering them. The Author takes his last Leave of the Reader; proposeth his Manner of Living for the future; gives good Advice, and concludeth.

Thus, gentle Reader, I have given thee a faithful History of my Travels for Sixteen Years, and above Seven Months; wherein I have not been so studious of Ornament as of Truth. I could perhaps like others have astonished thee with strange improbable Tales; but I rather chose to relate plain Matter of Fact in the simplest Manner and Style; because my principal Design was to inform, and not to amuse thee.

It is easy for us who travel into remote Countries, which are seldom visited by *Englishmen* or other *Europeans,* to form Descriptions of wonderful Animals both at Sea and Land. Whereas, a Traveller's chief Aim should be to make Men wiser and better, and to improve their Minds by the bad, as well as good Example of what they deliver concerning foreign Places.

I could heartily wish a Law were enacted, that every Traveller, before he were permitted to publish his Voyages, should be obliged to make Oath before the *Lord High Chancellor,* that all he intended to print was absolutely true to the best of his Knowledge; for then the World would no longer be deceived as it usually is, while some Writers, to make their Works pass the better upon the Publick, impose the grossest Falsities on the unwary Reader. I have perused several Books of Travels with great Delight in my younger Days; but, having since gone over most Parts of the Globe, and been able to contradict many fabulous Accounts from my own Observation; it hath given me a great [238] Disgust against this Part of Reading, and some Indignation to see the Credulity of Mankind so impudently abused. Therefore since my Acquaintance were pleased to think my poor Endeavours might not be unacceptable to my Country; I imposed on my self as a Maxim, never to be swerved from, that I would *strictly adhere to Truth;* neither indeed can I be ever under the least Temptation to vary from it, while I retain in my Mind the Lectures and Examples of my noble Master, and the other illustrious *Houyhnhnms,* of whom I had so long the Honour to be an humble Hearer.

———*Nec si miserum Fortuna Sinonem*
Finxit, vanum etiam, mendacemque improba finget.

I know very well, how little Reputation is to be got by Writings which require neither Genius nor Learning, nor indeed any other Talent, except a good Memory, or an exact *Journal.* I know likewise, that Writers of Travels, like *Dictionary*-Makers, are sunk into Oblivion by the Weight and Bulk of those who come last, and therefore lie uppermost. And it is highly probable, that such Travellers who shall hereafter visit the Countries described in this Work of mine, may by detecting my Errors, (if there be any) and adding many new Discoveries of their own, jostle me out of Vogue, and stand in my Place; making the World forget that ever I was an Author. This indeed would be too great a Mortification if I wrote for Fame: But, as my sole Intention was the PUBLICK GOOD, I cannot be altogether disappointed. For, who can read of the Virtues I have mentioned in the glorious *Houyhnhnms,* without being ashamed of his own Vices, when he considers himself as the reasoning, governing Animal of his Country? I shall say nothing of those remote Nations where *Yahoos* preside; amongst which the least corrupted are the *Brobdingnagians,* whose wise Maxims in Morality and Government, it would be our Happiness to observe. But I forbear descanting further, and rather leave the judicious Reader to his own Remarks and Applications.

I am not a little pleased that this Work of mine can possibly meet with no Censurers: For what Objections can be made against a Writer who relates only plain Facts that happened in such distant Countries, where we have not the least Interest with respect either to Trade or Negotiations? I have carefully avoided every Fault with which common Writers of Travels are often too justly charged. Besides, I meddle not the least with any *Party,* but write without Passion, Prejudice, or Ill-will against [239] any Man or Number of Men whatsoever. I write for the noblest End, to inform and instruct Mankind, over whom I may, without Breach of Modesty, pretend to some Superiority, from the Advantages I received by conversing so long among the most accomplished *Houyhnhnms.* I write without any View towards Profit or Praise. I never suffer a Word to pass that may look like Reflection, or possibly give the least Offence even to those who are most ready to take it. So that, I hope, I may with Justice pronounce myself an Author perfectly blameless; against whom the Tribes of Answerers, Considerers, Observers, Reflectors, Detecters, Remarkers, will never be able to find Matter for exercising their Talents.

I confess, it was whispered to me, that I was bound in Duty as a Subject of *England,* to have given in a Memorial to a Secretary of State, at my first coming over; because, whatever Lands are discovered by a Subject, belong to the Crown. But I doubt, whether our Conquests in the Countries I treat of, would be as easy as those of *Ferdinando Cortez* over the naked *Americans.* The *Lilliputians* I think, are hardly worth the Charge of a Fleet and Army to reduce them; and I question whether it might be prudent or safe to attempt the *Brobdingnagians:* Or, whether an *English* Army would be much at their Ease with the Flying Island over their Heads. The *Houyhnhnms,* indeed, appear not to be so well prepared for War, a Science to which they are perfect Strangers, and especially against missive Weapons. However, supposing myself to be a Minister of State, I could never give my Advice for invading them. Their Prudence, Unanimity, Unacquaintedness with Fear, and their Love of their Country would amply supply all Defects in the military Art. Imagine twenty Thousand of them breaking into the Midst of an *European* Army, confounding the Ranks, overturning the Carriages, battering the Warriors Faces into Mummy, by terrible Yerks from their hinder Hoofs: For they would well deserve the Character given to *Augustus; Recalcitrat undique tutus.* But instead of Proposals for conquering that magnanimous Nation, I rather wish they were in a Capacity or Disposition to send a sufficient Number of their Inhabitants for civilizing *Europe;* by teaching us the first Principles of Honour, Justice, Truth, Temperance, publick Spirit, Fortitude, Chastity, Friendship, Benevolence, and Fidelity. The *Names* of all which Virtues are still retained among us in most Languages, and are to be met with in modern as well as ancient Authors; which I am able to assert from my own small Reading. [240]

But, I had another Reason which made me less forward to enlarge his Majesty's Dominions by my Discoveries: To say the Truth, I had conceived a few Scruples with relation to the distributive Justice of Princes upon those Occasions. For Instance, A Crew of Pyrates are driven by a Storm they know not whither; at length a Boy discovers Land from the Top-mast; they go on Shore to rob and plunder; they see an harmless People, are entertained with Kindness, they give the Country a new Name, they take formal Possession of it for the King, they set up a rotten Plank or a Stone for a Memorial, they murder two or three Dozen of the Natives, bring away a Couple more by Force for a Sample, return home, and get their Pardon. Here commences a new Dominion acquired with a Title by *Divine Right*. Ships are sent with the first Opportunity; the Natives driven out or destroyed, their Princes tortured to discover their Gold; a free Licence given to all Acts of Inhumanity and Lust; the Earth reeking with the Blood of its Inhabitants: And this execrable Crew of Butchers employed in so pious an Expedition, is a *modern Colony* sent to convert and civilize an idolatrous and barbarous People.

But this Description, I confess, doth by no means affect the *British* Nation, who may be an Example to the whole World for their Wisdom, Care, and Justice in planting Colonies; their liberal Endowments for the Advancement of Religion and Learning; their Choice of devout and able Pastors to propagate *Christianity;* their Caution in stocking their Provinces with People of sober Lives and Conversations from this the Mother Kingdom; their strict Regard to the Distribution of Justice, in supplying the Civil Administration through all their Colonies with Officers of the greatest Abilities, utter Strangers to Corruption: And to crown all, by sending the most vigilant and virtuous Governors, who have no other Views than the Happiness of the People over whom they preside, and the Honour of the King their Master.

But, as those Countries which I have described do not appear to have a Desire of being conquered, and enslaved, murdered or driven out by Colonies; nor abound either in Gold, Silver, Sugar or Tobacco; I did humbly conceive they were by no Means proper Objects of our Zeal, our Valour, or our Interest. However, if those whom it may concern, think fit to be of another Opinion, I am ready to depose, when I shall be lawfully called, That no *European* did ever visit these Countries before me. I mean, if the Inhabitants ought to be believed. [241]

But, as to the Formality of taking Possession in my Sovereign's Name, it never came once into my Thoughts; and if it had, yet as my Affairs then stood, I should perhaps in point of Prudence and Self-Preservation, have put it off to a better Opportunity.

Having thus answered the *only* objection that can be raised against me as a Traveller; I here take a final Leave of my Courteous

Readers, and return to enjoy my own Speculations in my little Garden at *Redriff;* to apply those excellent Lessons of Virtue which I learned among the *Houyhnhnms;* to instruct the *Yahoos* of my own Family as far as I shall find them docible Animals; to behold my Figure often in a Glass, and thus if possible habituate my self by Time to tolerate the Sight of a human Creature: To lament the Brutality of *Houyhnhnms* in my own Country, but always treat their Persons with Respect, for the Sake of my noble Master, his Family, his Friends, and the whole *Houyhnhnm* Race, whom these of ours have the Honour to resemble in all their Lineaments, however their Intellectuals came to degenerate.

I began last Week to permit my Wife to sit at Dinner with me, at the farthest End of a long Table; and to answer (but with the utmost Brevity) the few Questions I asked her. Yet the Smell of a *Yahoo* continuing very offensive, I always keep my Nose well stopt with Rue, Lavender, or Tobacco-Leaves. And although it be hard for a Man late in Life to remove old Habits; I am not altogether out of Hopes in some Time to suffer a Neighbour *Yahoo* in my Company, without the Apprehensions I am yet under of his Teeth or his Claws.

My Reconcilement to the *Yahoo*-kind in general might not be so difficult, if they would be content with those Vices and Follies only which Nature hath entitled them to. I am not in the least provoked at the Sight of a Lawyer, a Pick-pocket, a Colonel, a Fool, a Lord, a Gamester, a Politician, a Whoremunger, a Physician, an Evidence, a Suborner, an Attorney, a Traytor, or the like: This is all according to the due Course of Things: But, when I behold a Lump of Deformity, and Diseases both in Body and Mind, smitten with *Pride,* it immediately breaks all the Measures of my Patience; neither shall I be ever able to comprehend how such an Animal and such a Vice could tally together. The wise and virtuous *Houyhnhnms,* who abound in all Excellencies that can adorn a rational Creature, have no Name for this Vice in their Language, which hath no Terms to express any thing that is evil, except those whereby they describe the detestable [242] Qualities of their *Yahoos;* among which they were not able to distinguish this of Pride, for want of thoroughly understanding Human Nature, as it sheweth it self in other Countries, where that Animal presides. But I, who had more Experience, could plainly observe some Rudiments of it among the wild *Yahoos.*

But the *Houyhnhnms,* who live under the Government of Reason, are no more proud of the good Qualities they possess, than I should be for not wanting a Leg or an Arm, which no Man in his Wits would boast of, although he must be miserable without them. I dwell the longer upon this Subject from the Desire I have to make the Society of an *English Yahoo* by any Means not insupportable; and therefore I here intreat those who have any Tincture of this absurd Vice, that they will not presume to appear in my Sight.

FINIS. [243]

The Rape of the Lock

◆◇◆ ALEXANDER POPE

Alexander Pope, "The Rape of the Lock" [1712–1714], in *The Poetry of Pope,* ed. M. H. Abrams (New York, Appleton-Century-Crofts, Inc., 1954).

CANTO I

WHAT DIRE OFFENSE from amorous causes springs,
What mighty contests rise from trivial things,
I sing—This verse to CARYLL, Muse! is due:
This, even Belinda may vouchsafe to view:
Slight is the subject, but not so the praise,
If she inspire, and he approve my lays.
  Say what strange motive, goddess! could compel
A well-bred lord t'assault a gentle belle?
O say what stranger cause, yet unexplored,
Could make a gentle belle reject a lord?   10
In tasks so bold, can little men engage,
And in soft bosoms dwells such mighty rage?
  Sol through white curtains shot a timorous ray,
And oped those eyes that must eclipse the day:
Now lap-dogs give themselves the rousing shake,
And sleepless lovers, just at twelve, awake:
Thrice rung the bell, the slipper knocked the ground,
And the pressed watch returned a silver sound.
Belinda still her downy pillow pressed,
Her guardian sylph prolonged the balmy rest: 20
'Twas he had summoned to her silent bed
The morning dream that hovered o'er her head;
A youth more glittering than a birth-night beau,
(That even in slumber caused her cheek to glow)
Seemed to her ear his winning lips to lay,
And thus in whispers said, or seemed to say.
  "Fairest of mortals, thou distinguished care

257

Of thousand bright inhabitants of air! [28]
If e'er one vision touched thy infant thought,
Of all the nurse and all the priest have taught;   30
Of airy elves by moonlight shadows seen,
The silver token, and the circled green,
Or virgins visited by angel powers,
With golden crowns and wreaths of heavenly flowers;
Hear and believe! thy own importance know,
Nor bound thy narrow views to things below.
Some secret truths, from learnèd pride concealed,
To maids alone and children are revealed:
What though no credit doubting wits may give?
The fair and innocent shall still believe.   40
Know, then, unnumbered spirits round thee fly,
The light militia of the lower sky:
These, though unseen, are ever on the wing,
Hang o'er the box, and hover round the ring.
Think what an equipage thou hast in air.
And view with scorn two pages and a chair.
As now your own, our beings were of old,
And once enclosed in woman's beauteous mold;
Thence, by a soft transition, we repair
From earthly vehicles to these of air,   50
Think not, when woman's transient breath is fled,
That all her vanities at once are dead;
Succeeding vanities she still regards,
And though she plays no more, o'erlooks the cards.
Her joy in gilded chariots, when alive,
And love of omber, after death survive.
For when the fair in all their pride expire,
To their first elements their souls retire:
The sprites of fiery termagants in flame
Mount up, and take a salamander's name.   60
Soft yielding minds to water glide away,
And sip, with nymphs, their elemental tea.
The graver prude sinks downward to a gnome,
In search of mischief still on earth to roam.
The light coquettes in sylphs aloft repair,
And sport and flutter in the fields of air.

"Know farther yet; whoever fair and chaste
Rejects mankind, is by some sylph embraced:
For spirits, freed from mortal laws, with ease
Assume what sexes and what shapes they please. 70
What guards the purity of melting maids,
In courtly balls, and midnight masquerades,
Safe from the treacherous friend, the daring spark, [29]
The glance by day, the whisper in the dark,
When kind occasion prompts their warm desires,
When music softens, and when dancing fires?
'Tis but their sylph, the wise celestials know,
Though honor is the word with men below.
      "Some nymphs there are, too conscious of their face,
For life predestined to the gnomes' embrace. 80
These swell their prospects and exalt their pride,
When offers are disdained, and love denied:
Then gay ideas crowd the vacant brain,
While peers, and dukes, and all their sweeping train,
And garters, stars, and coronets appear,
And in soft sounds, 'Your Grace' salutes their ear.
'Tis these that early taint the female soul,
Instruct the eyes of young coquettes to roll,
Teach infant cheeks a bidden blush to know,
And little hearts to flutter at a beau. 90
      "Oft, when the world imagine women stray,
The sylphs through mystic mazes guide their way,
Through all the giddy circle they pursue,
And old impertinence expel by new.
What tender maid but must a victim fall
To one man's treat, but for another's ball?
When Florio speaks, what virgin could withstand,
If gentle Damon did not squeeze her hand?
With varying vanities, from every part,
They shift the moving toyshop of their heart; 100
Where wigs with wigs, with sword-knots sword-knots strive,
Beaux banish beaux, and coaches coaches drive.
This erring mortals levity may call,
Oh blind to truth! the sylphs contrive it all.
      "Of these am I, who thy protection claim,

A watchful sprite, and Ariel is my name.
Late, as I ranged the crystal wilds of air,
In the clear mirror of thy ruling star
I saw, alas! some dread event impend,
Ere to the main this morning sun descend,   110
But heaven reveals not what, or how, or where:
Warned by the sylph, oh pious maid, beware!
This to disclose is all thy guardian can:
Beware of all, but most beware of man!"
  He said; when Shock, who thought she slept too long,
Leaped up, and waked his mistress with his tongue.
'Twas then, Belinda, if report say true, [30]
Thy eyes first opened on a billet-doux;
Wounds, charms, and ardors were no sooner read,
But all the vision vanished from thy head.   120
  And now, unveiled, the toilet stands displayed,
Each silver vase in mystic order laid.
First, robed in white, the nymph intent adores,
With head uncovered, the cosmetic powers.
A heavenly image in the glass appears,
To that she bends, to that her eyes she rears;
Th' inferior priestess, at her altar's side,
Trembling, begins the sacred rites of pride.
Unnumbered treasures ope at once, and here
The various offerings of the world appear;   130
From each she nicely culls with curious toil,
And decks the goddess with the glittering spoil.
This casket India's glowing gems unlocks,
And all Arabia breathes from yonder box.
The tortoise here and elephant unite,
Transformed to combs, the speckled, and the white.
Here files of pins extend their shining rows,
Puffs, powders, patches, Bibles, billets-doux.
Now awful beauty puts on all its arms;
The fair each moment rises in her charms,   140
Repairs her smiles, awakens every grace,
And calls forth all the wonders of her face;
Sees by degrees a purer blush arise,
And keener lightnings quicken in her eyes.

The busy sylphs surround their darling care,
These set the head, and those divide the hair,
Some fold the sleeve, while others plait the gown;
And Betty's praised for labors not her own.

CANTO II

Not with more glories, in th' ethereal plain,
The sun first rises o'er the purpled main,
Than, issuing forth, the rival of his beams
Launched on the bosom of the silver Thames.
Fair nymphs, and well-dressed youths around her shone,
But every eye was fixed on her alone.
On her white breast a sparkling cross she wore,
Which Jews might kiss, and infidels adore.
Her lively looks a sprightly mind disclose,
Quick as her eyes, and as unfixed as those: 10
Favors to none, to all she smiles extends;
Oft she rejects, but never once offends. [31]
Bright as the sun, her eyes the gazers strike,
And, like the sun, they shine on all alike.
Yet graceful ease, and sweetness void of pride,
Might hide her faults, if belles had faults to hide:
If to her share some female errors fall,
Look on her face, and you'll forget 'em all.
    This nymph, to the destruction of mankind,
Nourished two locks, which graceful hung behind   20
In equal curls, and well conspired to deck
With shining ringlets the smooth ivory neck.
Love in these labyrinths his slaves detains,
And mighty hearts are held in slender chains.
With hairy springes we the birds betray,
Slight lines of hair surprise the finny prey,
Fair tresses man's imperial race ensnare,
And beauty draws us with a single hair.
    Th' adventurous Baron the bright locks admired;
He saw, he wished, and to the prize aspired.   30
Resolved to win, he meditates the way,
By force to ravish, or by fraud betray;

For when success a lover's toil attends,
Few ask, if fraud or force attained his ends.
    For this, ere Phoebus rose, he had implored
Propitious Heaven, and every power adored,
But chiefly Love—to Love an altar built,
Of twelve vast French romances, neatly gilt.
There lay three garters, half a pair of gloves;
And all the trophies of his former loves;   40
With tender billets-doux he lights the pyre,
And breathes three amorous sighs to raise the fire.
Then prostrate falls, and begs with ardent eyes
Soon to obtain, and long possess the prize:
The powers gave ear, and granted half his prayer,
The rest, the winds dispersed in empty air.
    But now secure the painted vessel glides,
The sunbeams trembling on the floating tides:
While melting music steals upon the sky,
And softened sounds along the waters die;   50
Smooth flow the waves, the zephyrs gently play,
Belinda smiled, and all the world was gay.
All but the sylph—with careful thoughts oppressed,
Th' impending woe sat heavy on his breast.
He summons strait his denizens of air;
The lucid squadrons round the sails repair: [32]
Soft o'er the shrouds aërial whispers breathe,
That seemed but zephyrs to the train beneath.
Some to the sun their insect-wings unfold,
Waft on the breeze, or sink in clouds of gold;   60
Transparent forms, too fine for mortal sight,
Their fluid bodies half dissolved in light.
Loose to the wind their airy garments flew,
Thin glittering textures of the filmy dew,
Dipped in the richest tincture of the skies,
Where light disports in ever-mingling dyes,
While every beam new transient colors flings,
Colors that change whene'er they wave their wings.
Amid the circle, on the gilded mast,
Superior by the head, was Ariel placed;   70
His purple pinions opening to the sun,

He raised his azure wand, and thus begun.
　　"Ye sylphs and sylphids, to your chief give ear!
Fays, fairies, genii, elves, and daemons, hear!
Ye know the spheres and various tasks assigned
By laws eternal to th' aërial kind.
Some in the fields of purest ether play,
And bask and whiten in the blaze of day.
Some guide the course of wandering orbs on high,
Or roll the planets through the boundless sky.　　　　80
Some less refined, beneath the moon's pale light,
Pursue the stars that shoot athwart the night,
Or suck the mists in grosser air below,
Or dip their pinions in the painted bow,
Or brew fierce tempests on the wintry main,
Or o'er the glebe distill the kindly rain.
Others on earth o'er human race preside,
Watch all their ways, and all their actions guide:
Of these the chief the care of nations own,
And guard with arms divine the British throne.　　　　90
　　"Our humbler province is to tend the fair,
Not a less pleasing, though less glorious care;
To save the powder from too rude a gale,
Nor let the imprisoned essences exhale;
To draw fresh colors from the vernal flowers;
To steal from rainbows e'er they drop in showers
A brighter wash; to curl their waving hairs,
Assist their blushes, and inspire their airs;
Nay oft, in dreams, invention we bestow,
To change a flounce, or add a furbelow. [33]　　　　100
　　"This day, black omens threat the brightest fair
That e'er deserved a watchful spirit's care;
Some dire disaster, or by force, or slight;
But what, or where, the fates have wrapped in night.
Whether the nymph shall break Diana's law,
Or some frail china jar receive a flaw;
Or stain her honor, or her new brocade;
Forget her prayers, or miss a masquerade;
Or lose her heart, or necklace, at a ball;
Or whether Heaven has doomed that Shock must fall.　　　　110

Haste, then, ye spirits! to your charge repair:
The fluttering fan be Zephyretta's care;
The drops to thee, Brillante, we consign;
And, Momentilla, let the watch be thine;
Do thou, Crispissa, tend her favorite lock;
Ariel himself shall be the guard of Shock.

"To fifty chosen sylphs, of special note,
We trust th' important charge, the petticoat:
Oft have we known that sevenfold fence to fail,
Though stiff with hoops, and armed with ribs of whale.   120
Form a strong line about the silver bound,
And guard the wide circumference around.

"Whatever spirit, careless of his charge,
His post neglects, or leaves the fair at large,
Shall feel sharp vengeance soon o'ertake his sins,
Be stopped in vials, or transfixed with pins;
Or plunged in lakes of bitter washes lie,
Or wedged whole ages in a bodkin's eye:
Gums and pomatums shall his flight restrain,
While clogged he beats his silken wings in vain;   130
Or alum styptics with contracting power
Shrink his thin essence like a riveled flower:
Or, as Ixion fixed, the wretch shall feel
The giddy motion of the whirling mill,
In fumes of burning chocolate shall glow,
And tremble at the sea that froths below!"

He spoke; the spirits from the sails descend;
Some, orb in orb, around the nymph extend;
Some thrid the mazy ringlets of her hair;
Some hang upon the pendants of her ear;   140
With beating hearts the dire event they wait,
Anxious, and trembling for the birth of Fate. [34]

CANTO III

Close by those meads, for ever crowned with flowers,
Where Thames with pride surveys his rising towers,
There stands a structure of majestic frame,
Which from the neighboring Hampton takes its name.

Here Britain's statesmen oft the fall foredoom
Of foreign tyrants, and of nymphs at home;
Here thou, great ANNA! whom three realms obey,
Dost sometimes counsel take—and sometimes tea.
    Hither the heroes and the nymphs resort,
To taste awhile the pleasures of a court;   10
In various talk th' instructive hours they passed,
Who gave the ball, or paid the visit last;
One speaks the glory of the British Queen,
And one describes a charming Indian screen;
A third interprets motions, looks, and eyes;
At every word a reputation dies.
Snuff, or the fan, supply each pause of chat,
With singing, laughing, ogling, and all that.
    Meanwhile, declining from the noon of day,
The sun obliquely shoots his burning ray;   20
The hungry judges soon the sentence sign,
And wretches hang that jurymen may dine;
The merchant from th' exchange returns in peace,
And the long labors of the toilet cease.
Belinda now, whom thirst of fame invites,
Burns to encounter two adventurous knights,
At omber singly to decide their doom;
And swells her breast with conquests yet to come.
Straight the three bands prepare in arms to join,
Each band the number of the sacred nine.   30
Soon as she spreads her hand, th' aërial guard
Descend, and sit on each important card:
First Ariel perched upon a Matadore,
Then each, according to the rank they bore;
For sylphs, yet mindful of their ancient race,
Are, as when women, wondrous fond of place.
    Behold, four Kings in majesty revered,
With hoary whiskers and a forky beard;
And four fair Queens whose hands sustain a flower, [35]
Th' expressive emblem of their softer power;   40
Four Knaves in garbs succinct, a trusty band,
Caps on their heads, and halberds in their hand;
And particolored troops, a shining train,

Draw forth to combat on the velvet plain.
   The skillful nymph reviews her force with care:
"Let Spades be trumps!" she said, and trumps they were.
   Now move to war her sable Matadores,
In show like leaders of the swarthy Moors.
Spadillio first, unconquerable lord!
Led off two captive trumps, and swept the board.   50
As many more Manillio forced to yield,
And marched a victor from the verdant field.
Him Basto followed, but his fate more hard
Gained but one trump and one plebeian card.
With his broad saber next, a chief in years,
The hoary Majesty of Spades appears,
Puts forth one manly leg, to sight revealed,
The rest, his many-colored robe concealed.
The rebel Knave, who dares his prince engage,
Proves the just victim of his royal rage.   60
Even mighty Pam, that kings and queens o'erthrew
And mowed down armies in the fights of Lu,
Sad chance of war! now destitute of aid,
Falls undistinguished by the victor Spade!
   Thus far both armies to Belinda yield;
Now to the baron fate inclines the field.
His warlike Amazon her host invades,
Th' imperial consort of the crown of Spades.
The Club's black tyrant first her victim died,
Spite of his haughty mien, and barbarous pride: 70
What boots the regal circle on his head,
His giant limbs, in state unwieldy spread;
That long behind he trails his pompous robe,
And, of all monarchs, only grasps the globe?
   The baron now his Diamonds pours apace;
Th' embroidered King who shows but half his face,
And his refulgent Queen, with powers combined,
Of broken troops an easy conquest find.
Clubs, Diamonds, Hearts, in wild disorder seen,
With throngs promiscuous strow the level green.   80
Thus when dispersed a routed army runs,
Of Asia's troops, and Afric's sable sons, [36]

With like confusion different nations fly,
Of various habit, and of various dye,
The pierced battalions disunited fall,
In heaps on heaps; one fate o'erwhelms them all.
    The Knave of Diamonds tries his wily arts,
And wins (oh shameful chance!) the Queen of Hearts.
At this, the blood the virgin's cheek forsook,
A livid paleness spreads o'er all her look;   90
She sees, and trembles at th' approaching ill,
Just in the jaws of ruin, and codille.
And now (as oft in some distempered state)
On one nice trick depends the general fate.
An Ace of Hearts steps forth: The King unseen
Lurked in her hand, and mourned his captive Queen:
He springs to vengeance with an eager pace,
And falls like thunder on the prostrate Ace.
The nymph exulting fills with shouts the sky;
The walls, the woods, and long canals reply.   100
    Oh thoughtless mortals! ever blind to fate,
Too soon dejected, and too soon elate.
Sudden, these honors shall be snatched away,
And cursed for ever this victorious day.
    For lo! the board with cups and spoons is crowned,
The berries crackle, and the mill turns round;
On shining altars of Japan they raise
The silver lamp; the fiery spirits blaze:
From silver spouts the grateful liquors glide,
While China's earth receives the smoking tide: 110
At once they gratify their scent and taste,
And frequent cups prolong the rich repast.
Straight hover round the fair her airy band;
Some, as she sipped, the fuming liquor fanned,
Some o'er her lap their careful plumes displayed,
Trembling, and conscious of the rich brocade.
Coffee (which makes the politician wise,
And see through all things with his half-shut eyes)
Sent up in vapors to the baron's brain
New stratagems, the radiant lock to gain.   120
Ah cease, rash youth! desist ere 'tis too late,

Fear the just gods, and think of Scylla's fate!
Changed to a bird, and sent to flit in air, [37]
She dearly pays for Nisus' injured hair!
　　But when to mischief mortals bend their will,
How soon they find fit instruments of ill!
Just then, Clarissa drew with tempting grace
A two-edged weapon from her shining case:
So ladies in romance assist their knight,
Present the spear, and arm him for the fight.   130
He takes the gift with reverence and extends
The little engine on his fingers' ends;
This just behind Belinda's neck he spread,
As o'er the fragrant steams she bends her head.
Swift to the lock a thousand sprites repair,
A thousand wings, by turns, blow back the hair;
And thrice they twitched the diamond in her ear;
Thrice she looked back, and thrice the foe drew near.
Just in that instant, anxious Ariel sought
The close recesses of the virgin's thought;   140
As on the nosegay in her breast reclined,
He watched th' ideas rising in her mind,
Sudden he viewed, in spite of all her art,
An earthly lover lurking at her heart.
Amazed, confused, he found his power expired,
Resigned to fate, and with a sigh retired.
　　The peer now spreads the glittering forfex wide,
T' enclose the lock; now joins it, to divide.
Even then, before the fatal engine closed,
A wretched sylph too fondly interposed;   150
Fate urged the shears, and cut the sylph in twain,
(But airy substance soon unites again)
The meeting points the sacred hair dissever
From the fair head, for ever, and for ever!
　　Then flashed the living lightning from her eyes,
And screams of horror rend th' affrighted skies.
Not louder shrieks to pitying Heaven are cast,
When husbands, or when lap-dogs breathe their last;
Or when rich China vessels fallen from high,
In glittering dust, and painted fragments lie!   160

"Let wreaths of triumph now my temples twine,"
(The victor cried) "the glorious prize is mine!
While fish in streams, or birds delight in air,
Or in a coach and six the British fair,
As long as *Atalantis* shall be read,
Or the small pillow grace a lady's bed, [38]
While visits shall be paid on solemn days,
When numerous wax lights in bright order blaze,
While nymphs take treats, or assignations give,
So long my honor, name, and praise shall live!   170
What time would spare, from steel receives its date,
And monuments, like men, submit to fate!
Steel could the labor of the gods destroy,
And strike to dust th' imperial towers of Troy;
Steel could the works of mortal pride confound,
And hew triumphal arches to the ground.
What wonder then, fair nymph! thy hairs should feel
The conquering force of unresisted steel?"

CANTO IV

But anxious cares the pensive nymph oppressed,
And secret passions labored in her breast.
Not youthful kings in battle seized alive,
Not scornful virgins who their charms survive,
Not ardent lovers robbed of all their bliss,
Not ancient ladies when refused a kiss,
Not tyrants fierce that unrepenting die,
Not Cynthia when her manteau's pinned awry,
E'er felt such rage, resentment, and despair,
As thou, sad virgin! for thy ravished hair.   10
    For, that sad moment, when the sylphs withdrew,
And Ariel weeping from Belinda flew,
Umbriel, a dusky, melancholy sprite,
As ever sullied the fair face of light,
Down to the central earth, his proper scene,
Repaired to search the gloomy Cave of Spleen.
    Swift on his sooty pinions flits the gnome,
And in a vapor reached the dismal dome.

No cheerful breeze this sullen region knows,
The dreaded east is all the wind that blows.   20
Here in a grotto, sheltered close from air,
And screened in shades from day's detested glare,
She sighs for ever on her pensive bed,
Pain at her side, and Megrim at her head.

    Two handmaids wait the throne: alike in place,
But differing far in figure and in face.
Here stood Ill-nature like an ancient maid,
Her wrinkled form in black and white arrayed;
With store of prayers, for mornings, nights, and noons, [39]
Her hand is filled; her bosom with lampoons.   30

    There Affectation, with a sickly mien,
Shows in her cheek the roses of eighteen,
Practiced to lisp, and hang the head aside,
Faints into airs, and languishes with pride,
On the rich quilt sinks with becoming woe,
Wrapped in a gown, for sickness, and for show.
The fair ones feel such maladies as these,
When each new nightdress gives a new disease.

    A constant vapor o'er the palace flies;
Strange phantoms rising as the mists arise;   40
Dreadful, as hermit's dreams in haunted shades,
Or bright, as visions of expiring maids.
Now glaring fiends, and snakes on rolling spires,
Pale specters, gaping tombs, and purple fires:
Now lakes of liquid gold, Elysian scenes,
And crystal domes, and angels in machines.

    Unnumbered throngs on every side are seen
Of bodies changed to various forms by Spleen.
Here living teapots stand, one arm held out,
One bent; the handle this, and that the spout: 50
A pipkin there, like Homer's tripod walks;
Here sighs a jar, and there a goose pie talks;
Men prove with child, as powerful fancy works,
And maids turned bottles, call aloud for corks.

    Safe passed the gnome through this fantastic band,
A branch of healing spleenwort in his hand.
Then thus addressed the power: "Hail, wayward Queen!

Who rule the sex to fifty from fifteen:
Parent of vapors and of female wit,
Who give th' hysteric or poetic fit,   60
On various tempers act by various ways,
Make some take physic, others scribble plays;
Who cause the proud their visits to delay,
And send the godly in a pet to pray.
A nymph there is, that all thy power disdains,
And thousands more in equal mirth maintains.
But oh! if e'er thy gnome could spoil a grace,
Or raise a pimple on a beauteous face,
Like citron waters matrons' cheeks inflame,
Or change complexions at a losing game;   70
If e'er with airy horns I planted heads,
Or rumpled petticoats, or tumbled beds,
Or caused suspicion when no soul was rude,
Or discomposed the headdress of a prude, [40]
Or e'er to costive lap dog gave disease,
Which not the tears of brightest eyes could ease:
Hear me, and touch Belinda with chagrin;
That single act gives half the world the spleen."
    The Goddess with a discontented air
Seems to reject him, though she grants his prayer.   80
A wondrous bag with both her hands she binds,
Like that where once Ulysses held the winds;
There she collects the force of female lungs,
Sighs, sobs, and passions, and the war of tongues.
A vial next she fills with fainting fears,
Soft sorrows, melting griefs, and flowing tears.
The gnome rejoicing bears her gifts away,
Spreads his black wings, and slowly mounts to day.
    Sunk in Thalestris' arms the nymph he found,
Her eyes dejected and her hair unbound.   90
Full o'er their heads the swelling bag he rent,
And all the furies issued at the vent.
Belinda burns with more than mortal ire,
And fierce Thalestris fans the rising fire.
"O wretched maid!" she spread her hands, and cried,
(While Hampton's echoes, "Wretched maid!" replied)

"Was it for this you took such constant care
The bodkin, comb, and essence to prepare?
For this your locks in paper durance bound,
For this with torturing irons wreathed around?   100
For this with fillets strained your tender head,
And bravely bore the double loads of lead?
Gods! shall the ravisher display your hair,
While the fops envy and the ladies stare!
Honor forbid! at whose unrivaled shrine
Ease, pleasure, virtue, all our sex resign.
Methinks already I your tears survey,
Already hear the horrid things they say,
Already see you a degraded toast,
And all your honor in a whisper lost!   110
How shall I, then, your helpless fame defend?
'Twill then be infamy to seem your friend!
And shall this prize, th' inestimable prize,
Exposed through crystal to the gazing eyes,
And heightened by the diamond's circling rays,
On that rapacious hand for ever blaze?
Sooner shall grass in Hyde Park Circus grow, [41]
And wits take lodgings in the sound of Bow;
Sooner let earth, air, sea, to chaos fall,
Men, monkeys, lap dogs, parrots, perish all!"   120
      She said; then raging to Sir Plume repairs,
And bids her beau demand the precious hairs:
(Sir Plume of amber snuffbox justly vain,
And the nice conduct of a clouded cane)
With earnest eyes, and round unthinking face,
He first the snuffbox opened, then the case,
And thus broke out—"My Lord, why, what the devil?
Z——ds! damn the lock! 'fore Gad, you must be civil!
Plague on't! 'tis past a jest—nay prithee, pox!
Give her the hair"—he spoke, and rapped his box.   130
"It grieves me much" (replied the peer again)
"Who speaks so well should ever speak in vain,
But by this lock, this sacred lock I swear,
(Which never more shall join its parted hair;
Which never more its honors shall renew,

Clipped from the lovely head where late it grew)
That while my nostrils draw the vital air,
This hand, which won it, shall for ever wear."
He spoke, and speaking, in proud triumph spread
The long-contended honors of her head.   140
     But Umbriel, hateful gnome! forbears not so;
He breaks the vial whence the sorrows flow.
Then see! the nymph in beauteous grief appears,
Her eyes half languishing, half drowned in tears;
On her heaved bosom hung her drooping head,
Which, with a sigh, she raised; and thus she said:
     "For ever cursed be this detested day,
Which snatched my best, my favorite curl away!
Happy! ah ten times happy had I been,
If Hampton Court these eyes had never seen!   150
Yet am I not the first mistaken maid,
By love of courts to numerous ills betrayed.
Oh had I rather unadmired remained
In some lone isle, or distant northern land;
Where the gilt chariot never marks the way,
Where none learn omber, none e'er taste bohea!
There kept my charms concealed from mortal eye, [42]
Like roses that in deserts bloom and die.
What moved my mind with youthful lords to roam?
Oh had I stayed, and said my prayers at home!   160
'Twas this, the morning omens seemed to tell:
Thrice from my trembling hand the patchbox fell;
The tottering china shook without a wind,
Nay, Poll sat mute, and Shock was most unkind!
A sylph too warned me of the threats of fate,
In mystic visions, now believed too late!
See the poor remnants of these slighted hairs!
My hands shall rend what even thy rapine spares:
These in two sable ringlets taught to break,
Once gave new beauties to the snowy neck;   170
The sister lock now sits uncouth, alone,
And in its fellow's fate foresees its own;
Uncurled it hangs, the fatal shears demands,
And tempts, once more, thy sacrilegious hands.

Oh hadst thou, cruel! been content to seize
Hairs less in sight, or any hairs but these!"

CANTO V

She said: the pitying audience melt in tears.
But fate and love had stopped the baron's ears.
In vain Thalestris with reproach assails,
For who can move when fair Belinda fails?
Not half so fixed the Trojan could remain,
While Anna begged and Dido raged in vain.
Then grave Clarissa graceful waved her fan;
Silence ensued, and thus the nymph began.
   "Say why are beauties praised and honored most,
The wise man's passion, and the vain man's toast?   10
Why decked with all that land and sea afford,
Why angels called, and angel-like adored?
Why round our coaches crowd the white-gloved beaux,
Why bows the side-box from its inmost rows?
How vain are all these glories, all our pains,
Unless good sense preserve what beauty gains:
That men may say, when we the front-box grace,
'Behold the first in virtue as in face!'
Oh! if to dance all night, and dress all day,
Charmed the smallpox, or chased old age away;   20
Who would not scorn what housewife's cares produce,
Or who would learn one earthly thing of use?
To patch, nay ogle, might become a saint, [43]
Nor could it sure be such a sin to paint.
But since, alas! frail beauty must decay,
Curled or uncurled, since locks will turn to gray;
Since painted, or not painted, all shall fade,
And she who scorns a man, must die a maid;
What then remains, but well our power to use,
And keep good-humor still whate'er we lose?   30
And trust me, dear! good-humor can prevail,
When airs, and flights, and screams, and scolding fail.
Beauties in vain their pretty eyes may roll;
Charms strike the sight, but merit wins the soul."

So spoke the dame, but no applause ensued;
Belinda frowned, Thalestris called her prude.
"To arms, to arms!" the fierce virago cries,
And swift as lightning to the combat flies.
All side in parties, and begin th' attack;
Fans clap, silks rustle, and tough whalebones crack;   40
Heroes' and heroines' shouts confusedly rise,
And bass, and treble voices strike the skies.
No common weapons in their hands are found,
Like gods they fight, nor dread a mortal wound.
    So when bold Homer makes the gods engage,
And heavenly breasts with human passions rage;
'Gainst Pallas, Mars; Latona, Hermes arms;
And all Olympus rings with loud alarms:
Jove's thunder roars, Heaven trembles all around,
Blue Neptune storms, the bellowing deeps resound: 50
Earth shakes her nodding towers, the ground gives way,
And the pale ghosts start at the flash of day!
    Triumphant Umbriel on a sconce's height
Clapped his glad wings, and sate to view the fight:
Propped on their bodkin spears, the sprites survey
The growing combat, or assist the fray.
    While through the press enraged Thalestris flies,
And scatters death around from both her eyes,
A beau and witling perished in the throng,
One died in metaphor, and one in song.   60
"O cruel nymph! a living death I bear,"
Cried Dapperwit, and sunk beside his chair.
A mournful glance Sir Fopling upwards cast,
"Those eyes are made so killing"—was his last.
Thus on Maeander's flowery margin lies
Th' expiring swan, and as he sings he dies.
    When bold Sir Plume had drawn Clarissa down,
Chloe stepped in, and killed him with a frown; [44]
She smiled to see the doughty hero slain,
But, at her smile, the beau revived again.   70
    Now Jove suspends his golden scales in air,
Weighs the men's wits against the lady's hair;
The doubtful beam long nods from side to side;

At length the wits mount up, the hairs subside.
    See fierce Belinda on the baron flies,
With more than usual lightning in her eyes:
Nor feared the chief th' unequal fight to try,
Who sought no more than on his foe to die.
But this bold lord with manly strength endued,
She with one finger and a thumb subdued: 80
Just where the breath of life his nostrils drew,
A charge of snuff the wily virgin threw;
The gnomes direct, to every atom just,
The pungent grains of titillating dust.
Sudden with starting tears each eye o'erflows,
And the high dome re-echoes to his nose.
    "Now meet thy fate," incensed Belinda cried,
And drew a deadly bodkin from her side.
(The same, his ancient personage to deck,
Her great-great-grandsire wore about his neck,   90
In three seal rings; which after, melted down,
Formed a vast buckle for his widow's gown:
Her infant grandame's whistle next it grew,
The bells she jingled, and the whistle blew;
Then in a bodkin graced her mother's hairs,
Which long she wore, and now Belinda wears.)
    "Boast not my fall" (he cried) "insulting foe!
Thou by some other shalt be laid as low.
Nor think, to die dejects my lofty mind:
All that I dread is leaving you behind!   100
Rather than so, ah let me still survive,
And burn in Cupid's flames—but burn alive."
    "Restore the lock!" she cries; and all around
"Restore the lock!" the vaulted roofs rebound.
Not fierce Othello in so loud a strain
Roared for the handkerchief that caused his pain.
But see how oft ambitious aims are crossed,
And chiefs contend till all the prize is lost!
The lock, obtained with guilt, and kept with pain,
In every place is sought, but sought in vain: 110
With such a prize no mortal must be blessed,
So Heaven decrees! with Heaven who can contest?

Some thought it mounted to the lunar sphere, [45]
Since all things lost on earth are treasured there.
There heroes' wits are kept in ponderous vases,
And beaux' in snuff-boxes and tweezer-cases.
There broken vows, and deathbed alms are found,
And lovers' hearts with ends of riband bound,
The courtier's promises, and sick man's prayers,
The smiles of harlots, and the tears of heirs,   120
Cages for gnats, and chains to yoke a flea,
Dried butterflies, and tomes of casuistry.
    But trust the Muse—she saw it upward rise,
Though marked by none but quick, poetic eyes:
(So Rome's great founder to the heavens withdrew,
To Proculus alone confessed in view)
A sudden star, it shot through liquid air,
And drew behind a radiant trail of hair.
Not Berenice's locks first rose so bright,
The heavens bespangling with disheveled light.   130
The sylphs behold it kindling as it flies,
And pleased pursue its progress through the skies.
    This the beau monde shall from the Mall survey,
And hail with music its propitious ray.
This the blest lover shall for Venus take,
And send up vows from Rosamonda's lake.
This Partridge soon shall view in cloudless skies,
When next he looks through Galileo's eyes;
And hence th' egregious wizard shall foredoom
The fate of Louis, and the fall of Rome.   140
    Then cease, bright nymph! to mourn thy ravished hair,
Which adds new glory to the shining sphere!
Not all the tresses that fair head can boast,
Shall draw such envy as the lock you lost.
For, after all the murders of your eye,
When, after millions slain, yourself shall die;
When those fair suns shall set, as set they must,
And all those tresses shall be laid in dust; [46]
This lock, the Muse shall consecrate to fame,
And 'midst the stars inscribe Belinda's name. [47]   150

The Cock and the Fox
or, The Tale of the Nun's Priest

◆◆◆ GEOFFREY CHAUCER

Geoffrey Chaucer, "The Cock and the Fox; or, The Tale of the Nun's Priest" [c. 1395; tr. John Dryden, 1700], in *The Works of John Dryden,* ed. Sir Walter Scott; rev. and corr. George Saintsbury (Edinburgh, William Paterson, 1885), 18 vols.

THERE LIVED, as authors tell, in days of yore,
A widow, somewhat old, and very poor;
Deep in a cell her cottage lonely stood,
Well thatched, and under covert of a wood.
　　This dowager, on whom my tale I found,　　　　5
Since last she laid her husband in the ground,
A simple sober life in patience led,
And had but just enough to buy her bread;
But housewifing the little heaven had lent,
She duly paid a groat for quarter rent;　　　　10
And pinched her belly, with her daughters two,
To bring the year about with much ado.
　　The cattle in her homestead were three sows,
An ewe called Mally, and three brinded cows. [XI, 339]
Her parlour-window stuck with herbs around,　　　　15
Of savoury smell, and rushes strewed the ground.
A maple dresser in her hall she had,
On which full many a slender meal she made:
For no delicious morsel passed her throat;
According to her cloth she cut her coat.　　　　20
No poignant sauce she knew, no costly treat,
Her hunger gave a relish to her meat.
A sparing diet did her health assure;
Or sick, a pepper posset was her cure.
Before the day was done, her work she sped,　　　　25
And never went by candle-light to bed.

With exercise she sweat ill humours out;
Her dancing was not hindered by the gout.
Her poverty was glad, her heart content,
Nor knew she what the spleen or vapours meant.   30
Of wine she never tasted through the year,
But white and black was all her homely cheer;
Brown bread and milk, (but first she skimmed her bowls,)
And rashers of singed bacon on the coals;
On holidays an egg, or two at most;   35
But her ambition never reached to roast.
    A yard she had, with pales inclosed about,
Some high, some low, and a dry ditch without.
Within this homestead lived, without a peer,
For crowing loud, the noble Chanticleer;   40
So hight her cock, whose singing did surpass
The merry notes of organs at the mass.
More certain was the crowing of a cock
To number hours, than is an abbey-clock;
And sooner than the matin-bell was rung,   45
He clapped his wings upon his roost, and sung; [XI, 340]
For when degrees fifteen ascended right,
By sure instinct he knew 'twas one at night.
High was his comb, and coral-red withal,
In dents embattled like a castle wall;   50
His bill was raven-black, and shone like jet;
Blue were his legs, and orient were his feet;
White were his nails, like silver to behold,
His body glittering like the burnished gold.
    This gentle cock, for solace of his life,   55
Six misses had, beside his lawful wife;
Scandal, that spares no king, though ne'er so good,
Says, they were all of his own flesh and blood;
His sisters, both by sire and mother's side,
And sure their likeness showed them near allied.   60
But make the worst, the monarch did no more,
Than all the Ptolemys had done before:
When incest is for interest of a nation,
'Tis made no sin by holy dispensation.
Some lines have been maintained by this alone,   65

Which by their common ugliness are known.
    But passing this as from our tale apart,
Dame Partlet was the sovereign of his heart:
Ardent in love, outrageous in his play,
He feathered her a hundred times a day;   70
And she, that was not only passing fair,
But was withal discreet, and debonair, [XI, 341]
Resolved the passive doctrine to fulfil,
Though loath, and let him work his wicked will:
At board and bed was affable and kind,   75
According as their marriage-vow did bind,
And as the Church's precept had enjoined.
Even since she was a se'nnight old, they say,
Was chaste and humble to her dying day,
Nor chick nor hen was known to disobey.   80
    By this her husband's heart she did obtain;
What cannot beauty, joined with virtue, gain?
She was his only joy, and he her pride,
She, when he walked, went pecking by his side;
If, spurning up the ground, he sprung a corn,   85
The tribute in his bill to her was borne.
But oh! what joy it was to hear him sing
In summer, when the day began to spring,
Stretching his neck, and warbling in his throat,
Solus cum sola, then was all his note.   90
For in the days of yore, the birds of parts
Were bred to speak, and sing, and learn the liberal arts.
    It happ'd that perching on the parlour-beam,
Amidst his wives, he had a deadly dream,
Just at the dawn; and sighed, and groaned so fast,   95
As every breath he drew would be his last.
Dame Partlet, ever nearest to his side,
Heard all his piteous moan, and how he cried
For help from gods and men; and sore aghast
She pecked and pulled, and wakened him at last.   100
"Dear heart," said she, "for love of heaven declare
Your pain, and make me partner of your care.
You groan, sir, ever since the morning light,
As something had disturbed your noble sprite." [XI, 342]

"And, madam, well I might," said Chanticleer, 105
Never was shrovetide-cock in such a fear.
Even still I run all over in a sweat,
My princely senses not recovered yet.
For such a dream I had of dire portent,
That much I fear my body will be shent: 110
It bodes I shall have wars and woful strife,
Or in a loathsome dungeon end my life.
Know, dame, I dreamt within my troubled breast,
That in our yard I saw a murderous beast,
That on my body would have made arrest. 115
With waking eyes I ne'er beheld his fellow;
His colour was betwixt a red and yellow:
Tipped was his tail, and both his pricking ears,
With black, and much unlike his other hairs;
The rest, in shape a beagle's whelp throughout, 120
With broader forehead, and a sharper snout:
Deep in his front were sunk his glowing eyes,
That yet, methinks, I see him with surprise.
Reach out your hand, I drop with clammy sweat,
And lay it to my heart, and feel it beat." 125
"Now fie for shame!" quoth she; "by heaven above,
Thou hast for ever lost thy lady's love.
No woman can endure a recreant knight;
He must be bold by day, and free by night:
Our sex desires a husband or a friend, 130
Who can our honour and his own defend;
Wise, hardy, secret, liberal of his purse;
A fool is nauseous, but a coward worse:
No bragging coxcomb, yet no baffled knight,
How dar'st thou talk of love, and dar'st not fight? [XI, 343] 135
How dar'st thou tell thy dame thou art affeared?
Hast thou no manly heart, and hast a beard?
    "If aught from fearful dreams may be divined,
They signify a cock of dunghill kind.
All dreams, as in old Galen I have read, 140
Are from repletion and complexion bred;
From rising fumes of indigested food,
And noxious humours that infect the blood:

And sure, my lord, if I can read aright,
These foolish fancies, you have had to-night,   145
Are certain symptoms (in the canting style)
Of boiling choler, and abounding bile;
This yellow gall, that in your stomach floats,
Engenders all these visionary thoughts.
When choler overflows, then dreams are bred   150
Of flames, and all the family of red;
Red dragons, and red beasts, in sleep we view,
For humours are distinguished by their hue.
From hence we dream of wars and warlike things,
And wasps and hornets with their double wings.   155
    "Choler adust congeals our blood with fear,
Then black bulls toss us, and black devils tear.
In sanguine airy dreams aloft we bound;
With rheums oppressed, we sink in rivers drowned.
    "More I could say, but thus conclude my theme,   160
The dominating humour makes the dream.
Cato was in his time accounted wise,
And he condemns them all for empty lies.
Take my advice, and when we fly to ground,
With laxatives preserve your body sound,   165
And purge the peccant humours that abound. [XI, 344]
I should be loath to lay you on a bier;
And though there lives no 'pothecary near,
I dare for once prescribe for your disease,
And save long bills, and a damned doctor's fees.   170
    "Two sovereign herbs, which I by practice know,
And both at hand, (for in our yard they grow,)
On peril of my soul shall rid you wholly
Of yellow choler, and of melancholy:
You must both purge and vomit; but obey,   175
And for the love of heaven make no delay.
Since hot and dry in your complexion join,
Beware the sun when in a vernal sign;
For when he mounts exalted in the Ram,
If then he finds your body in a flame,   180
Replete with choler, I dare lay a groat,
A tertian ague is at least your lot.

Perhaps a fever (which the gods forefend)
May bring your youth to some untimely end:
And therefore, sir, as you desire to live,   185
A day or two before your laxative,
Take just three worms, nor under nor above,
Because the gods unequal numbers love.
These digestives prepare you for your purge;
Of fumetery, centaury, and spurge,   190
And of ground-ivy add a leaf, or two,
All which within our yard or garden grow.
Eat these, and be, my lord, of better cheer;
Your father's son was never born to fear."
          "Madam," quoth he, "gramercy for your care,   195
But Cato, whom you quoted, you may spare.
'Tis true, a wise and worthy man he seems,
And (as you say) gave no belief to dreams; [XI, 345]
But other men of more authority,
And, by the immortal powers, as wise as he,   200
Maintain, with sounder sense, that dreams forbode;
For Homer plainly says they come from God.
Nor Cato said it; but some modern fool
Imposed in Cato's name on boys at school.
          "Believe me, madam, morning dreams foreshow   205
The events of things, and future weal or woe:
Some truths are not by reason to be tried,
But we have sure experience for our guide.
An ancient author, equal with the best,
Relates this tale of dreams among the rest:—   210
          "Two friends or brothers, with devout intent,
On some far pilgrimage together went.
It happened so, that, when the sun was down,
They just arrived by twilight at a town;
That day had been the baiting of a bull,   215
'Twas at a feast, and every inn so full,
That no void room in chamber, or on ground,
And but one sorry bed was to be found;
And that so little it would hold but one,
Though till this hour they never lay alone.   220
          "So were they forced to part; one stayed behind,

His fellow sought what lodging he could find:
At last he found a stall where oxen stood,
And that he rather chose than lie abroad.
'Twas in a further yard without a door;   225
But, for his ease, well littered was the floor.
    "His fellow, who the narrow bed had kept,
Was weary, and without a rocker slept:
Supine he snored; but in the dead of night,
He dreamt his friend appeared before his sight, [XI, 346]   230
Who, with a ghastly look and doleful cry,
Said, 'Help me, brother, or this night I die:
Arise, and help, before all help be vain,
Or in an ox's stall I shall be slain.'
    "Roused from his rest, he wakened in a start,   235
Shivering with horror, and with aching heart;
At length to cure himself by reason tries;
'Twas but a dream, and what are dreams but lies?
So thinking changed his side, and closed his eyes.
His dream returns: his friend appears again: 240
'The murderers come, now help, or I am slain:'
'Twas but a vision still, and visions are but vain.
    "He dreamt the third; but now his friend appeared
Pale, naked, pierced with wounds, with blood besmeared:
'Thrice warned, awake,' said he; 'relief is late,   245
The deed is done; but thou revenge my fate:
Tardy of aid, unseal thy heavy eyes,
Awake, and with the dawning day arise:
Take to the western gate thy ready way,
For by that passage they my corpse convey: 250
My corpse is in a tumbrel laid, among
The filth, and ordure, and inclosed with dung.
That cart arrest, and raise a common cry;
For sacred hunger of my gold I die:'
Then showed his grisly wounds; and last he drew   255
A piteous sigh, and took a long adieu.
    "The frightened friend arose by break of day,
And found the stall where late his fellow lay.
Then of his impious host inquiring more,
Was answered that his guest was gone before: [XI, 347]   260

"Muttering he went," said he, "by morning light,
And much complained of his ill rest by night."
This raised suspicion in the pilgrim's mind;
Because all hosts are of an evil kind,
And oft to share the spoil with robbers joined.   265
        "His dream confirmed his thought; with troubled look
Straight to the western gate his way he took;
There, as his dream foretold, a cart he found,
That carried compost forth to dung the ground.
This when the pilgrim saw, he stretched his throat,   270
And cried out murder with a yelling note.
'My murdered fellow in this cart lies dead;
Vengeance and justice on the villain's head!
You, magistrates, who sacred laws dispense,
On you I call to punish this offence.'   275
        "The word thus given, within a little space,
The mob came roaring out, and thronged the place.
All in a trice they cast the cart to ground,
And in the dung the murdered body found;
Though breathless, warm, and reeking from the wound.   280
Good heaven, whose darling attribute we find
Is boundless grace, and mercy to mankind,
Abhors the cruel; and the deeds of night
By wondrous ways reveals in open light:
Murder may pass unpunished for a time,   285
But tardy justice will o'ertake the crime.
And oft a speedier pain the guilty feels,
The hue and cry of heaven pursues him at the heels,
Fresh from the fact, as in the present case:
The criminals are seized upon the place;   290
Carter and horse confronted face to face. [XI, 348]
Stiff in denial, as the law appoints,
On engines they distend their tortured joints;
So was confession forced, the offence was known,
And public justice on the offenders done.   295
        "Here may you see that visions are to dread;
And in the page that follows this, I read
Of two young merchants, whom the hope of gain
Induced in partnership to cross the main;

Waiting till willing winds their sails supplied,   300
Within a trading-town they long abide,
Full fairly situate on a haven's side.
    "One evening it befell, that, looking out,
The wind they long had wished was come about;
Well pleased they went to rest; and if the gale   305
Till morn continued, both resolved to sail.
But as together in a bed they lay,
The younger had a dream at break of day.
A man, he thought, stood frowning at his side,
Who warned him for his safety to provide,   310
Nor put to sea, but safe on shore abide.
'I come, thy genius, to command thy stay;
Trust not the winds, for fatal is the day,
And death unhoped attends the wat'ry way.'
    "The vision said, and vanished from his sight.   315
The dreamer wakened in a mortal fright; [XI, 349]
Then pulled his drowsy neighbour, and declared,
What in his slumber he had seen and heard.
His friend smiled scornful, and, with proud contempt,
Rejects as idle what his fellow dreamt.   320
'Stay, who will stay; for me no fears restrain,
Who follow Mercury, the god of gain;
Let each man do as to his fancy seems,
I wait not, I, till you have better dreams.
Dreams are but interludes, which fancy makes;   325
When monarch reason sleeps, this mimic wakes;
Compounds a medley of disjointed things,
A mob of cobblers, and a court of kings:
Light fumes are merry, grosser fumes are sad;
Both are the reasonable soul run mad;   330
And many monstrous forms in sleep we see,
That neither were, nor are, nor e'er can be.
Sometimes, forgotten things long cast behind
Rush forward in the brain, and come to mind.
The nurse's legends are for truths received,   335
And the man dreams but what the boy believed.
    " 'Sometimes we but rehearse a former play,
The night restores our actions done by day,

As hounds in sleep will open for their prey.
In short, the farce of dreams is of a piece, 340
Chimeras all; and more absurd, or less.
You, who believe in tales, abide alone;
Whate'er I get this voyage is my own.'
 "Thus while he spoke, he heard the shouting crew
That called aboard, and took his last adieu. [XI, 350] 345
The vessel went before a merry gale,
And for quick passage put on every sail;
But when least feared, and even in open day,
The mischief overtook her in the way:
Whether she sprung a leak, I cannot find, 350
Or whether she was overset with wind,
Or that some rock below her bottom rent,
But down at once with all the crew she went.
Her fellow-ships from far her loss descried;
But only she was sunk, and all were safe beside. 355
 "By this example you are taught again,
That dreams and visions are not always vain;
But if, dear Partlet, you are yet in doubt,
Another tale shall make the former out.
 "Kenelm, the son of Kenulph, Mercia's king, 360
Whose holy life the legends loudly sing,
Warned in a dream, his murder did foretell,
From point to point as after it befell:
All circumstances to his nurse he told,
(A wonder from a child of seven years old;) 365
The dream with horror heard, the good old wife
From treason counselled him to guard his life;
But close to keep the secret in his mind,
For a boy's vision small belief would find.
The pious child, by promise bound, obeyed, 370
Nor was the fatal murder long delayed;
By Quenda slain, he fell before his time,
Made a young martyr by his sister's crime.
The tale is told by venerable Bede,
Which, at your better leisure, you may read. 375
 "Macrobius too relates the vision sent
To the great Scipio, with the famed event; [XI, 351]

Objections makes, but after makes replies,
And adds, that dreams are often prophecies.
    "Of Daniel you may read in holy writ,   380
Who, when the king his vision did forget,
Could word for word the wondrous dream repeat.
Nor less of patriarch Joseph understand,
Who by a dream enslaved the Egyptian land,
The years of plenty and of dearth foretold,   385
When, for their bread, their liberty they sold.
Nor must the exalted butler be forgot,
Nor he whose dream presaged his hanging lot.
    "And did not Croesus the same death foresee,
Raised in his vision on a lofty tree?   390
The wife of Hector, in his utmost pride,
Dreamt of his death the night before he died:
Well was he warned from battle to refrain,
But men to death decreed are warned in vain;
He dared the dream, and by his fatal foe was slain.   395
    "Much more I know, which I forbear to speak,
For see the ruddy day begins to break:
Let this suffice, that plainly I foresee
My dream was bad, and bodes adversity;
But neither pills nor laxatives I like,   400
They only serve to make a well-man sick;
Of these his gain the sharp physician makes,
And often gives a purge, but seldom takes;
They not correct, but poison all the blood,
And ne'er did any but the doctors good.   405
Their tribe, trade, trinkets, I defy them all,
With every work of 'pothecary's hall.
    "These melancholy matters I forbear;
But let me tell thee, Partlet mine, and swear, [XI, 352]
That when I view the beauties of thy face,   410
I fear not death, nor dangers, nor disgrace;
So may my soul have bliss, as when I spy
The scarlet red about thy partridge eye,
While thou art constant to thy own true knight,
While thou art mine, and I am thy delight,   415
All sorrows at thy presence take their flight.

For true it is, as *in principio,*
Mulier est hominis confusio.
Madam, the meaning of this Latin is,
That woman is to man his sovereign bliss.   420
For when by night I feel your tender side,
Though for the narrow perch I cannot ride,
Yet I have such a solace in my mind,
That all my boding cares are cast behind,
And even already I forget my dream."   425
He said, and downward flew from off the beam,
For daylight now began apace to spring,
The thrush to whistle, and the lark to sing.
Then crowing, clapped his wings, the appointed call,
To chuck his wives together in the hall.   430
    By this the widow had unbarred the door,
And Chanticleer went strutting out before,
With royal courage, and with heart so light,
As showed he scorned the visions of the night.
Now roaming in the yard, he spurned the ground,   435
And gave to Partlet the first grain he found. [XI, 353]
Then often feathered her with wanton play,
And trod her twenty times ere prime of day;
And took by turns and gave so much delight,
Her sisters pined with envy at the sight.   440
He chucked again, when other corns he found,
And scarcely deigned to set a foot to ground;
But swaggered like a lord about his hall,
And his seven wives came running at his call.
    'Twas now the month in which the world began,   445
(If March beheld the first created man;)
And since the vernal equinox, the sun
In Aries twelve degrees, or more, had run;
When casting up his eyes against the light,
Both month, and day, and hour, he measured right,   450
And told more truly than the Ephemeris;
For art may err, but nature cannot miss.
    Thus numbering times and seasons in his breast,
His second crowing the third hour confessed.
Then turning, said to Partlet,—"See, my dear,   455

How lavish nature has adorned the year;
How the pale primrose and blue violet spring,
And birds essay their throats disused to sing:
All these are ours; and I with pleasure see,
Man strutting on two legs, and aping me;   460
An unfledged creature, of a lumpish frame,
Endued with fewer particles of flame:
Our dame sits cowering o'er a kitchen fire,
I draw fresh air, and nature's works admire;
And even this day in more delight abound,   465
Than, since I was an egg, I ever found."
    The time shall come, when Chanticleer shall wish
His words unsaid, and hate his boasted bliss; [XI, 354]
The crested bird shall by experience know,
Jove made not him his masterpiece below,   470
And learn the latter end of joy is woe.
The vessel of his bliss to dregs is run,
And Heaven will have him taste his other tun.
    Ye wise! draw near and hearken to my tale,
Which proves that oft the proud by flattery fall;   475
The legend is as true I undertake
As Tristram is, and Launcelot of the lake;
Which all our ladies in such reverence hold,
As if in Book of Martyrs it were told.
    A Fox, full-fraught with seeming sanctity,   480
That feared an oath, but, like the devil, would lie;
Who looked like Lent, and had the holy leer,
And durst not sin before he said his prayer;
This pious cheat, that never sucked the blood,
Nor chawed the flesh of lambs, but when he could,   485
Had passed three summers in the neighbouring wood;
And musing long, whom next to circumvent,
On Chanticleer his wicked fancy bent;
And in his high imagination cast,
By stratagem to gratify his taste.   490
    The plot contrived, before the break of day,
Saint Reynard through the hedge had made his way;
The pale was next, but proudly, with a bound,
He leapt the fence of the forbidden ground;

Yet fearing to be seen, within a bed   495
Of coleworts he concealed his wily head;
There skulked till afternoon, and watched his time,
(As murderers use,) to perpetrate his crime. [XI, 355]
    O hypocrite, ingenious to destroy!
O traitor, worse than Sinon was to Troy!   500
O vile subverter of the Gallic reign,
More false than Gano was to Charlemaign!
O Chanticleer, in an unhappy hour
Didst thou forsake the safety of thy bower;
Better for thee thou hadst believed thy dream,   505
And not that day descended from the beam!
    But here the doctors eagerly dispute;
Some hold predestination absolute;
Some clerks maintain, that Heaven at first foresees,
And in the virtue of foresight decrees.   510
If this be so, then prescience binds the will,
And mortals are not free to good or ill;
For what he first foresaw, he must ordain,
Or its eternal prescience may be vain;
As bad for us as prescience had not been;   515
For first, or last, he's author of the sin.
And who says that, let the blaspheming man
Say worse even of the devil, if he can.
For how can that Eternal Power be just
To punish man, who sins because he must?   520
Or, how can he reward a virtuous deed,
Which is not done by us, but first decreed?
    I cannot bolt this matter to the bran,
As Bradwardin and holy Austin can: [XI, 356]
If prescience can determine actions so,   525
That we must do, because he did foreknow,
Or that foreknowing, yet our choice is free,
Not forced to sin by strict necessity;
This strict necessity they simple call,
Another sort there is conditional.   530
The first so binds the will, that things foreknown
By spontaneity, not choice, are done.
Thus galley-slaves tug willing at their oar,

Consent to work, in prospect of the shore;
But would not work at all, if not constrained before.   535
That other does not liberty constrain,
But man may either act, or may refrain.
Heaven made us agents free to good or ill,
And forced it not, though he foresaw the will.
Freedom was first bestowed on human race,   540
And prescience only held the second place.
      If he could make such agents wholly free,
I not dispute; the point's too high for me:
For heaven's unfathomed power what man can sound,
Or put to his omnipotence a bound?   545
He made us to his image, all agree;
That image is the soul, and that must be,
Or not the Maker's image, or be free.
But whether it were better man had been
By nature bound to good, not free to sin,   550
I wave, for fear of splitting on a rock;
The tale I tell is only of a cock;
Who had not run the hazard of his life,
Had he believed his dream, and not his wife:
For women, with a mischief to their kind,   555
Pervert, with bad advice, our better mind.
A woman's counsel brought us first to woe,
And made her man his paradise forego, [XI, 357]
Where at heart's ease he lived; and might have been
As free from sorrow as he was from sin.   560
For what the devil had their sex to do,
That, born to folly, they presumed to know,
And could not see the serpent in the grass?
But I myself presume, and let it pass.
      Silence in times of suffering is the best,   565
'Tis dangerous to disturb a hornet's nest.
In other authors you may find enough,
But all they say of dames is idle stuff.
Legends of lying wits together bound,
The wife of Bath would throw them to the ground: 570
These are the words of Chanticleer, not mine,
I honour dames, and think their sex divine.

Now to continue what my tale begun.
Lay madam Partlet basking in the sun,
Breast-high in sand; her sisters in a row, 575
Enjoyed the beams above, the warmth below.
The cock, that of his flesh was ever free,
Sung merrier than the mermaid in the sea;
And so befell, that as he cast his eye,
Among the coleworts, on a butterfly, 580
He saw false Reynard where he lay full low;
I need not swear he had no list to crow;
But cried, *Cock, cock,* and gave a sudden start,
As sore dismayed and frighted at his heart.
For birds and beasts, informed by nature, know 585
Kinds opposite to theirs, and fly their foe.
So Chanticleer, who never saw a fox,
Yet shunned him, as a sailor shuns the rocks.
    But the false loon, who could not work his will
By open force, employed his flattering skill: 590
"I hope, my lord," said he, "I not offend;
Are you afraid of me, that am your friend? [XI, 358]
I were a beast indeed to do you wrong,
I, who have loved and honoured you so long:
Stay, gentle sir, nor take a false alarm, 595
For, on my soul, I never meant you harm!
I come no spy, nor as a traitor press,
To learn the secrets of your soft recess:
Far be from Reynard so profane a thought,
But by the sweetness of your voice was brought: 600
For, as I bid my beads, by chance I heard
The song as of an angel in the yard;
A song that would have charmed the infernal gods,
And banished horror from the dark abodes:
Had Orpheus sung it in the nether sphere, 605
So much the hymn had pleased the tyrant's ear,
The wife had been detained, to keep the husband there.
    "My lord, your sire familiarly I knew,
A peer deserving such a son as you:
He, with your lady-mother, (whom heaven rest!) 610
Has often graced my house, and been my guest:

To view his living features does me good,
For I am your poor neighbour in the wood;
And in my cottage should be proud to see
The worthy heir of my friend's family. 615
    "But since I speak of singing, let me say,
As with an upright heart I safely may,
That, save yourself, there breathes not on the ground
One like your father for a silver sound.
So sweetly would he wake the winter-day, 620
That matrons to the church mistook their way,
And thought they heard the merry organ play.
And he to raise his voice with artful care,
(What will not beaux attempt to please the fair?) [XI, 359]
On tiptoe stood to sing with greater strength, 625
And stretched his comely neck at all the length:
And while he pained his voice to pierce the skies,
As saints in raptures use, would shut his eyes,
That the sound striving through the narrow throat,
His winking might avail to mend the note. 630
By this, in song, he never had his peer,
From sweet Cecilia down to Chanticleer;
Not Maro's muse, who sung the mighty man,
Nor Pindar's heavenly lyre, nor Horace when a swan.
Your ancestors proceed from race divine: 635
From Brennus and Belinus is your line;
Who gave to sovereign Rome such loud alarms,
That even the priests were not excused from arms.
    "Besides, a famous monk of modern times
Has left of cocks recorded in his rhymes, 640
That of a parish priest the son and heir,
(When sons of priests were from the proverb clear,)
Affronted once a cock of noble kind,
And either lamed his legs, or struck him blind; [XI, 360]
For which the clerk his father was disgraced, 645
And in his benefice another placed.
Now sing, my lord, if not for love of me,
Yet for the sake of sweet saint charity;
Make hills and dales, and earth and heaven, rejoice,
And emulate your father's angel-voice." 650

The cock was pleased to hear him speak so fair,
And proud beside, as solar people are;
Nor could the treason from the truth descry,
So was he ravished with this flattery:
So much the more, as from a little elf,   655
He had a high opinion of himself;
Though sickly, slender, and not large of limb,
Concluding all the world was made for him.
    Ye princes, raised by poets to the gods,
And Alexandered up in lying odes,   660
Believe not every flattering knave's report,
There's many a Reynard lurking in the court;
And he shall be received with more regard,
And listened to, than modest truth is heard.
    This Chanticleer, of whom the story sings,   665
Stood high upon his toes, and clapped his wings;
Then stretched his neck, and winked with both his eyes,
Ambitious, as he sought the Olympic prize.
But while he pained himself to raise his note,
False Reynard rushed, and caught him by the throat.   670
Then on his back he laid the precious load,
And sought his wonted shelter of the wood;
Swiftly he made his way, the mischief done,
Of all unheeded, and pursued by none.
    Alas! what stay is there in human state,   675
Or who can shun inevitable fate?
The doom was written, the decree was past,
Ere the foundations of the world were cast! [XI, 361]
In Aries though the sun exalted stood,
His patron-planet to procure his good;   680
Yet Saturn was his mortal foe, and he,
In Libra raised, opposed the same degree:
The rays both good and bad, of equal power,
Each thwarting other, made a mingled hour.
    On Friday-morn he dreamt this direful dream,   685
Cross to the worthy native, in his scheme.
Ah, blissful Venus! goddess of delight!
How couldst thou suffer thy devoted knight,
On thy own day, to fall by foe oppressed,

The wight of all the world who served thee best?   690
Who, true to love, was all for recreation,
And minded not the work of propagation?
Ganfride, who couldst so well in rhyme complain
The death of Richard with an arrow slain,
Why had not I thy muse, or thou my heart,   695
To sing this heavy dirge with equal art!
That I like thee on Friday might complain;
For on that day was Coeur de Lion slain."
    Not louder cries, when Ilium was in flames,
Were sent to heaven by woful Trojan dames,   700
When Pyrrhus tossed on high his burnished blade,
And offered Priam to his father's shade,
Than for the cock the widowed poultry made. [XI, 362]
Fair Partlet first, when he was borne from sight,
With sovereign shrieks bewailed her captive knight;   705
Far louder than the Carthaginian wife,
When Asdrubal her husband lost his life,
When she beheld the smould'ring flames ascend,
And all the Punic glories at an end:
Willing into the fires she plunged her head,   710
With greater ease than others seek their bed.
Not more aghast the matrons of renown,
When tyrant Nero burned the imperial town,
Shrieked for the downfall in a doleful cry,
For which their guiltless lords were doomed to die.   715
    Now to my story I return again:
The trembling widow, and her daughters twain,
This woful cackling cry with horror heard,
Of those distracted damsels in the yard;
And starting up, beheld the heavy sight,   720
How Reynard to the forest took his flight,
And cross his back, as in triumphant scorn,
The hope and pillar of the house was borne.
    "The Fox, the wicked Fox," was all the cry;
Out from his house ran every neighbour nigh: 725
The vicar first, and after him the crew,
With forks and staves the felon to pursue.
Ran Coll our dog, and Talbot with the band,

And Malkin, with her distaff in her hand:
Ran cow and calf, and family of hogs, 730
In panic horror of pursuing dogs;
With many a deadly grunt and doleful squeak,
Poor swine, as if their pretty hearts would break. [XI, 363]
The shouts of men, the women in dismay,
With shrieks augment the terror of the day. 735
The ducks, that heard the proclamation cried,
And feared a persecution might betide,
Full twenty miles from town their voyage take,
Obscure in rushes of the liquid lake.
The geese fly o'er the barn; the bees, in arms, 740
Drive headlong from their waxen cells in swarms.
Jack Straw at London-stone, with all his rout,
Struck not the city with so loud a shout;
Not when with English hate they did pursue
A Frenchman, or an unbelieving Jew; 745
Not when the welkin rung with *One and all,*
And echoes bounded back from Fox's hall;
Earth seemed to sink beneath, and heaven above to fall.
With might and main they chased the murd'rous fox,
With brazen trumpets, and inflated box, 750
To kindle Mars with military sounds,
Nor wanted horns to inspire sagacious hounds.
⠀⠀⠀But see how fortune can confound the wise,
And when they least expect it, turn the dice.
The captive-cock, who scarce could draw his breath, 755
And lay within the very jaws of death; [XI, 364]
Yet in this agony his fancy wrought,
And fear supplied him with this happy thought:
"Yours is the prize, victorious prince," said he,
"The vicar my defeat, and all the village see. 760
Enjoy your friendly fortune while you may,
And bid the churls that envy you the prey
Call back their mongrel curs, and cease their cry:
See fools, the shelter of the wood is nigh,
And Chanticleer in your despite shall die; 765
He shall be plucked and eaten to the bone."
⠀⠀⠀" 'Tis well advised, in faith it shall be done;"

This Reynard said: but as the word he spoke,
The prisoner with a spring from prison broke;
Then stretched his feathered fans with all his might,   770
And to the neighbouring maple winged his flight.

　　Whom, when the traitor safe on tree beheld,
He cursed the gods, with shame and sorrow filled:
Shame for his folly; sorrow out of time,
For plotting an unprofitable crime: 775
Yet, mastering both, the artificer of lies,
Renews the assault, and his last battery tries.

　　"Though I," said he, "did ne'er in thought offend,
How justly may my lord suspect his friend?
The appearance is against me, I confess,   780
Who seemingly have put you in distress.
You, if your goodness does not plead my cause,
May think I broke all hospitable laws,
To bear you from your palace-yard by might,
And put your noble person in a fright. [XI, 365]   785
This, since you take it ill, I must repent,
Though heaven can witness, with no bad intent
I practised it, to make you taste your cheer
With double pleasure, first prepared by fear.
So loyal subjects often seize their prince,   790
Forced (for his good) to seeming violence,
Yet mean his sacred person not the least offence.
Descend; so help me, Jove, as you shall find,
That Reynard comes of no dissembling kind."

　　"Nay," quoth the cock; "but I beshrew us both,   795
If I believe a saint upon his oath:
An honest man may take a knave's advice,
But idiots only will be cozened twice:
Once warned is well bewared; no flattering lies
Shall soothe me more to sing with winking eyes,   800
And open mouth, for fear of catching flies.
Who blindfold walks upon a river's brim,
When he should see, has he deserved to swim?"

　　"Better, Sir Cock, let all contention cease;
Come down," said Reynard, "let us treat of peace."   805
　　"A peace with all my soul," said Chanticleer;

"But, with your favour, I will treat it here:
And lest the truce with treason should be mixt,
'Tis my concern to have the tree betwixt." [XI, 366]

THE MORAL

    In this plain fable you the effect may see   810
Of negligence, and fond credulity:
And learn besides of flatterers to beware,
Then most pernicious when they speak too fair.
The cock and fox, the fool and knave imply;
The truth is moral, though the tale a lie.   815
Who spoke in parables, I dare not say;
But sure he knew it was a pleasing way,
Sound sense, by plain example, to convey.
And in a heathen author we may find,
That pleasure with instruction should be joined;   820
So take the corn, and leave the chaff behind. [XI, 367]

The Frogs Asked for a King

◆◆◆   JEAN DE LA FONTAINE

Jean de La Fontaine, "The Frogs Asked for a King" [1668], in *The Fables of La Fontaine,* tr. Marianne Moore (New York, The Viking Press, Inc., 1954).

Although democratic then,
   The frogs begged a royal yoke,
   Croaking again and again
Till Jupiter sent a king to calm the constant croak.
He sent one who fell from the sky and never spoke
Though the noise of his fall was itself a source of pain
   Since amphibians in those bogs
   Were shallow-brained timorous frogs
   So perturbed when they heard a thud,
   They'd sprung among reeds in the mud,
   Into holes where cattails stood—
Not even looking at the king they'd hoped would be good,
Some of them supposing that he must be a giant frog,
   Whereas he was a forest log
That had hurtled from the sky and filled them with fear.
   Curiosity counseled, Begin:
   A brave one dared to reappear,
   Though with throat skin going out and in.
Another hopped up upon the monarch's skin—
   Millions of them and then more,
As where ants swarm from hills on land one tries to clear—
   Till all were hopping up on King Log
Who had not made a sound or even threatened a frog.
But again the malcontents were making Jupiter ill,
And said, "Grant us a king who will not lie so still."
The king of the gods sent a crane with a long bill,
   Who crushed, pained them at will,
   Devouring anything there—
   Gulped large and small till all complained
And Jove replied, "Give ear! You'd dare direct your arbiter?

You'd have divinity constrained!
You should have managed to get on
With the government of your own;
But no. Your first king was one whom any frog could bear— [61]
Benign, gracious, in every way desirable.
Accept this one as suitable
Or endure a harsher with whom he can't compare." [62]

Ode on the Death of a Favourite Cat, Drowned in a Tub of Gold Fishes

◆◆◆ THOMAS GRAY

Thomas Gray, "Ode on the Death of a Favourite Cat, Drowned in a Tub of Gold Fishes" [1748], in *Works of Thomas Gray,* ed. Edmund Gosse (London, Macmillan & Co., 1884), 4 vols.

'TWAS on a lofty vase's side,
Where China's gayest art had dy'd
    The azure flowers, that blow;
Demurest of the tabby kind,
The pensive Selima reclin'd,
    Gazed on the lake below.

Her conscious tail her joy declar'd;
The fair round face, the snowy beard,
    The velvet of her paws,
Her coat, that with the tortoise vies,
Her ears of jet, and emerald eyes,
    She saw; and purr'd applause. [I, 11]

Still had she gaz'd; but 'midst the tide
Two angel forms were seen to glide,
    The Genii of the stream:
Their scaly armour's Tyrian hue
Thro' richest purple to the view
    Betray'd a golden gleam.

The hapless Nymph with wonder saw:
A whisker first and then a claw,
    With many an ardent wish,
She stretch'd in vain to reach the prize.

What female heart can gold despise?
    What Cat's averse to fish?

Presumptuous Maid! with looks intent
Again she stretch'd, again she bent,
    Nor knew the gulf between.
(Malignant Fate sat by, and smil'd)
The slipp'ry verge her feet beguil'd,
    She tumbled headlong in.

Eight times emerging from the flood
She mew'd to ev'ry wat'ry God,
    Some speedy aid to send.
No Dolphin came, no Nereid stirr'd: [I, 12]
Nor cruel *Tom,* nor *Susan* heard.
    A Fav'rite has no friend!

From hence, ye Beauties, undeceiv'd,
Know, one false step is ne'er retriev'd,
    And be with caution bold.
Not all that tempts your wand'ring eyes
And heedless hearts, is lawful prize,
    Nor all, that glisters, gold. [I, 13]

The Lemmings: A philosophical poem

◆◆◆   DONALD A. STAUFFER

Donald A. Stauffer, "The Lemmings: A philosophical poem," in *The War Poets,* ed. Oscar Williams (New York, The John Day Co., 1945).

LET READERS SAY (description or abuse),
"Pure were his morals, though his verse was loose."
The technical end I blame on Robert Frost,
On Butler, Skelton, and others whose names I've lost,
And, though this debt isn't very hard to find,
I blame it on W. H. Auden—he won't mind—
On Catullus, and Robert Bridges, I am afraid,
And really a host of others whose names I've mislaid:
For just as a Cavalier lyric shows good breeding
A reflective poem must demonstrate wide reading. [244]
In such verse, too, a poet is at a loss if he
Doesn't remind the reader he knows philosophy.
Provided only they see that this poem is deep,
I don't care how many people it puts to sleep.
The special subject is lemmings, the pity of lemmings.
(Whenever I use that word I shall skip the rhyme,
And I think I'll have to use it time after time.)
If I knew what a lemming was, it would help a lot,
For I certainly can't list all things which it is NOT.
But sympathy shall make up for lack of science,
And ignorance be replaced by self-reliance.
After all, this is less like a monograph than a chat:
It is only a poem—philosophical, at that.
It will not be so long as Lucretius' *De Rerum Natura,*
And barely as long as Juvenal's smallest *satura.*
Though briefness seem unphilosophical to some,
I think that's the way philosophy ought to come.
I shall view the result with something akin to pride
If I make you *feel* the lemmings from the inside.

This is the end of the proem
And the beginning of the poem.

. . . . . [sic]
At a sharp, mysterious call, as though in a dream,
The lemmings move, and down to the ocean they stream.
From the Urals and the Carpathians, and the plains
Of Prussia, or Lapland, on they come in trains.
Or secretly, through the silent forests, the hordes
Rush to the sea in the tallest of Norway's fjords.
For them, the whole world beckons and is on fire,
So add what geographical names you desire:
To say the Ganges, Peru, the Cape of Good Hope,
Though it blur our accuracy, increases our scope.
And here I shall use T. S. Eliot's famed device
Of allusion to gain intensity—it's nice!
Read over Browning's *Piper of Hamelin,* please,
Read it slowly, with care, and at your ease,
And wherever he talks about either rats or mice
Just substitute lemmings. Isn't *that* a device?
You will then have sizes and colors of all sorts [245]
And grotesque detail that fascinates as it distorts,
And all of the lemmings streaming in grave glee—
Not after the Piper, mind, but toward the sea.

We've now saved a hundred lines by referring to Browning
And have got to the crucial part where the lemmings start drowning.
Each one making his certain and positive lunge,
Into the black and freezing waters they plunge.
And from their noses, the ripples in endless V's
Complicate webs and woofs on the flux of the seas.
Like flocks of starlings, or minnows in lucent shoals,
Infinite atoms move toward communal goals.
The northern night is above, and the water beneath,
(How far off now is the nest on the rock-strewn heath!)
And all are swimming together in regular tread
As the strokes of their feet keep pulsing their noses ahead.
Beyond, and straight, and sure, and together they swim.
Where they are when the sun looks over the ocean's rim
Nobody knows. I would like to say, if I dare,

That the point of this poem is: *Nobody ought to care.*
So far I could have prettied this up a lot
If this had been a descriptive poem. It's not.
Or I might have given you facts that were terrific,
Provided my aim were solely scientific.
As it is, unless I hear some better suggestions,
We will open this poem to philosophical questions.

But one thing first: I admit I admire the lemmings.
Together plunging far out to sea by night—
How express and admirable! how lemming! how right!
That one act only I know in the lemmings' history;
And although its end may always remain a mystery,
The lemmings fill me with gratitude and cheer
For acting one act that is so sure and clear.
There must be a thousand species of rodents and stoats,
Fieldmice, moles, muskrats, hedgehogs, mink, dwarf goats,
That live the humdrum life of the seasons through:
Gray dawns, gray fear, gray sleep, and little to do.
Even Noah forgot them, above or under the ground.
But we remember the lemmings, because they drowned.
A species famous abroad for a single act [246]
Wins glory that less energetic fauna have lacked.
How various beasts are bigger, stronger, older,
More popular, quicker on trigger, longer, bolder;
But in praise of the lemmings, by all beasts this is allowed:
No other landlubbers swim out to sea in a crowd.
Here let us cease this unreasoning panegyric
And back to our deep and philosophical lyric.

If the lemmings unite to swim out to sea and die,
The inevitable and perplexing question is *Why?*
We might as well face it squarely and on the spot
Without a flippant or cynical asking *Why not?*
(a) Perhaps the lemming race is by nature joyous
And cannot conceive of the ocean flood as noyous.
(b) Their cosmic outlook, perhaps, is far from wide
So that they know of waves, but ignore the tide,
And do not believe that it's leagues from this side to that side.

(c) Some people think that the race as a whole is feckless
And kills itself off for the pleasure of being reckless.
(d) Still more maintain that the lemming brain is blighted;
(e) While some physiologists hold that the creature's nearsighted.
(f) Surroundings and habit, say others, have made them fools:
The lemmings come from countries of lakes and of pools;
They cannot adapt to new places, they are so fond,
And jump in the ocean as if it could be but a pond.
(g) One theory runs that deep in the past of the race
On Atlantis the lemmings were happy all over the place,
And, when that continent sank at some black touch of magic,
The end of the lemmings was comprehensively tragic.
Ancestral mourning now leads them shorewards to weep
And they find the golden age thousand fathoms deep.
This theory, though, I shan't even bother to mention,
For it bears in itself the marks of a febrile invention.
And blaming one's gloom on the dead—on a lot of dead, too—
Is one of the things that a gentleman doesn't do.
(h) A further hypothesis leads to many confusions
Because it supposes the lemmings are conscious Malthusians,
And if these wee beasts have practised his laws for so long
Then Malthus and countless lemmings can't be wrong.
It holds that lemmings, viewed in their breeding habits,
Are as sanguine, redundant, prolific, and careless as rabbits, [247]
And knowing that population outstrips supply,
A certain proportion resolves, quite wisely, to die.
This sort of thing should appeal to G. B. Shaw:
Good sense, you see, no fuss, and community law.
The unemployed, unwanted, unloved, and unwed,
Swim out to ocean, and never a tear is shed;
Or if a tear falls, it mixes quick with the brine
And loses all personal sense of yours and mine.
The Greek youth shipped for the Minotaur's delectation
Is a more romantic means of saving a nation;
But I much prefer this classical lemming way
(As Vigny might put it) of "Nages, et meurs sans parler."
It avoids the melodramatically pathetic
And isn't, like Jude the Obscure's hanged children, frenetic;
Yet Hardy's words fit, for the lemmings, as well as any,

And perhaps the last thought of each lemming is "WE WAS TOO
    MANY."

All these explanations that don't explain
You may, with my kindest permission, throw down the drain.
They cannot illumine, or mar, in the least degree
The simple fact of the lemmings and the sea.
I sometimes think we'd be further out of the wood
If we didn't believe our brains were so frightfully good.
The last infirmity of the noble mind
Is its faith that the noble mind leaves all else behind.
To believe anything which is not the product of reason
Is, to the human race in its latest development, treason.
And thanks to the Russells, the Huxleys, the Deweys and Shaws,
We'll all soon be rescued from Superstition's jaws.
Those ultimate secrets of mystery and sorrow
That we don't grasp today, will be clear as crystal tomorrow.
The fear and the ecstasies that our grandfathers share
Come from another world that isn't there.
Let us endure, our new wise men say, for a season,
For all will be clarified soon in the light of pure reason.

But the lemmings' acts may be past reach of our brain,
Perhaps we had better accept what we can't explain.
Instincts within us are fixed so central and certain
That our tampering minds cannot pull aside the curtain. [248]
And still, though we prove that it should or it shouldn't be,
The lemmings continue their progress out to sea.
I know this amounts almost to accepting God
And know also today such belief is most certainly odd.
Yet I would prefer, when we look at human behavior,
If we must be saved, to have God—not man—for a savior.
Give us a bit less pride and a little more trust:
We but guess we are terribly clever; we know we are dust.
Grace is a ware which should be on the front of our shelves,
And we have most grace when we don't try to make it ourselves.
After all, reflective verse shouldn't give the answers.
It should merely set the questions moving like dancers,
And should leave us, where we began, with the excellent notion
Of the lemmings moving in unison toward the ocean. [249]

Departmental
or, The End of My Ant Jerry

◆◆◆ ROBERT FROST

Robert Frost, "Departmental or, The End of My Ant Jerry" [1936], in
Complete Poems of Robert Frost (New York, Henry Holt & Co.,
1949).

AN ANT on the tablecloth
Ran into a dormant moth
Of many times his size.
He showed not the least surprise.
His business wasn't with such.
He gave it scarcely a touch,
And was off on his duty run.
Yet if he encountered one
Of the hive's enquiry squad
Whose work is to find out God
And the nature of time and space,
He would put him onto the case.
Ants are a curious race;
One crossing with hurried tread
The body of one of their dead
Isn't given a moment's arrest—
Seems not even impressed.
But he no doubt reports to any
With whom he crosses antennae,
And they no doubt report
To the higher up at court.
Then word goes forth in Formic:
"Death's come to Jerry McCormic,
Our selfless forager Jerry.
Will the special Janizary
Whose office it is to bury
The dead of the commissary

Go bring him home to his people.
Lay him in state on a sepal.
Wrap him for shroud in a petal.
Embalm him with ichor of nettle. [372]
This is the word of your Queen."
And presently on the scene
Appears a solemn mortician;
And taking formal position
With feelers calmly atwiddle,
Seizes the dead by the middle,
And heaving him high in air,
Carries him out of there.
No one stands round to stare.
It is nobody else's affair.

It couldn't be called ungentle.
But how thoroughly departmental. [373]

mehitabel dances with boreas

◆◆◆ DON MARQUIS

Don Marquis, "mehitabel dances with boreas" [1927], in *the lives and times of archy & mehitabel* (Garden City, N.Y., Doubleday & Co., Inc., 1950).

[*This poem belongs to a series composed by Archy, a cockroach, who writes in a deserted newspaper office at night by jumping head downward onto the keys of a typewriter. Unable to operate the shift key, he writes in lower case and in a brand of free verse by default. One of his favorite subjects is his friend Mehitabel, a Bohemian alley cat.—Eds.*]

well boss, i saw mehitabel
last evening
she was out in the alley
dancing on the cold cobbles
while the wild december wind
blew through her frozen whiskers
and as she danced
she wailed and sang to herself
uttering the fragments
that rattled in her cold brain
in part as follows [126]

whirl mehitabel whirl
spin mehitabel spin
thank god you re a lady still
if you have got a frozen skin

blow wind out of the north
to hell with being a pet
my left front foot is brittle
but there s life in the old dame yet

dance mehitabel dance
caper and shake a leg
what little blood is left
will fizz like wine in a keg

wind come out of the north
and pierce to the guts within
but some day mehitabel s guts
will string a violin

moon you re as cold as a frozen
skin of yellow banan
that sticks in the frost and ice
on top of a garbage can

and you throw a shadow so chilly
that it can scarcely leap
dance shadow dance
you ve got no place to sleep

whistle a tune north wind
on my hollow marrow bones
i ll dance the time with three good feet
here on the alley stones

freeze you bloody december
i never could stay a pet
but i am a lady in spite of hell
and there s life in the old dame yet [127]

whirl mehitabel whirl
flirt your tail and spin
dance to the tune your guts will cry
when they string a violin

eight of my lives are gone
it s years since my fur was slicked
but blow north wind blow
i m damned if i am licked

girls we was all of us ladies
we was o what the hell
and once a lady always game
by crikey blood will tell

i might be somebody s pet
asleep by the fire on a rug

but me i was always romantic
i had the adventurous bug

caper mehitabel caper
leap shadow leap
you gotta dance till the sun comes up
for you got no place to sleep

i might have been many a tom cat s wife
but i got no regret
i lived my life as i liked my life
and there s pep in the old dame yet

blow wind out of the north
you cut like a piece of tin
slice my guts into fiddle strings
and we ll have a violin

spin mehitabel spin
you had a romantic past
and you re gonna cash in dancing
when you are croaked at last [128]

i will not eat tomorrow
and i did not eat today
but wotthehell i ask you
the word is toujours gai

whirl mehitabel whirl
i once was a maltese pet
till i went and got abducted
and cripes i m a lady yet

whirl mehitabel whirl
and show your shadow how
tonight it s dance with the bloody moon
tomorrow the garbage scow

whirl mehitabel whirl
spin shadow spin
the wind will pipe on your marrow bones
your slats are a mandolin

by cripes i have danced the shimmy
in rooms as warm as a dream
and gone to sleep on a cushion
with a bellyfull of cream

it s one day up and the next day down
i led a romantic life
it was being abducted so many times
as spoiled me for a wife

dance mehitabel dance
till your old bones fly apart
i ain t got any regrets
for i gave my life to my art

whirl mehitabel whirl
caper my girl and grin
and pick at your guts with your frosty feet
they re the strings of a violin [129]

girls we was all of us ladies
until we went and fell
and oncet a thoroughbred always game
i ask you wotthehell

it s last week up and this week down
and always the devil to pay
but cripes i was always the lady
and the word is toujours gai

be a tabby tame if you want
somebody s pussy and pet
the life i led was the life i liked
and there s pep in the old dame yet

whirl mehitabel whirl
leap shadow leap
you gotta dance till the sun comes up
for you got no place to sleep
                                        archy [130]

Macavity: The Mystery Cat

T. S. ELIOT

T. S. Eliot, "Macavity: the Mystery Cat," in *Old Possum's Book of Practical Cats* (New York, Harcourt, Brace & Co., 1939).

MACAVITY'S a Mystery Cat: he's called the Hidden Paw—
For he's the master criminal who can defy the Law.
He's the bafflement of Scotland Yard, the Flying Squad's despair:
For when they reach the scene of crime—*Macavity's not there!*

Macavity, Macavity, there's no one like Macavity,
He's broken every human law, he breaks the law of gravity.
His powers of levitation would make a fakir stare,
And when you reach the scene of crime—*Macavity's not there!*
You may seek him in the basement, you may look up in the air—
But I tell you once and once again, *Macavity's not there!*

Macavity's a ginger cat, he's very tall and thin;
You would know him if you saw him, for his eyes are sunken in.
His brow is deeply lined with thought, his head is highly domed;
His coat is dusty from neglect, his whiskers are uncombed.
He sways his head from side to side, with movements like a snake;
And when you think he's half asleep, he's always wide awake. [32]

Macavity, Macavity, there's no one like Macavity,
For he's a fiend in feline shape, a monster of depravity.
You may meet him in a by-street, you may see him in the square—
But when a crime's discovered, then *Macavity's not there!*

He's outwardly respectable. (They say he cheats at cards.)
And his footprints are not found in any file of Scotland Yard's.
And when the larder's looted, or the jewel-case is rifled,
Or when the milk is missing, or another Peke's been stifled,
Or the greenhouse glass is broken, and the trellis past repair—
Ay, there's the wonder of the thing! *Macavity's not there!*

And when the Foreign Office find a Treaty's gone astray,
Or the Admiralty lose some plans and drawings by the way,
There may be a scrap of paper in the hall or on the stair—
But it's useless to investigate—*Macavity's not there!*
And when the loss has been disclosed, the Secret Service say:
"It *must* have been Macavity!"—but he's a mile away.
You'll be sure to find him resting, or a-licking of his thumbs,
Or engaged in doing complicated long division sums.

Macavity, Macavity, there's no one like Macavity,
There never was a Cat of such deceitfulness and suavity. [33]
He always has an alibi, and one or two to spare:
At whatever time the deed took place—MACAVITY WASN'T
     THERE!

And they say that all the Cats whose wicked deeds are widely known
(I might mention Mungojerrie, I might mention Griddlebone)
Are nothing more than agents for the Cat who all the time
Just controls their operations: the Napoleon of Crime! [34]

A Wooden Darning Egg

◆◆◆ JOHN UPDIKE

John Updike, "A Wooden Darning Egg," in *The Carpentered Hen* (New York, Harper & Brothers, 1958).

THE carpentered hen
unhinges her wings,
abandons her nest
of splinters, and sings.

> The egg she has laid
> is maple and hard
> as a tenpenny nail
> and smooth as a board.

The grain of the wood
embraces the shape
as brown feathers do
the rooster's round nape.

> Pressured by pride,
> her sandpapered throat
> unwarps when she cries
> *Cross-cut! ka-ross-cut!*

Beginning to brood
she tests with a level
the angle, sits down,
and coos *Bevel bevel*. [41]

The Mad Gardener's Song

◆◆◆ LEWIS CARROLL

Lewis Carroll [Charles Lutwidge Dodgson], "The Mad Gardener's Song" [1889], in *The Collected Verse of Lewis Carroll* (New York, The Macmillan Co., 1933).

HE THOUGHT he saw an Elephant,
　That practised on a fife:
He looked again, and found it was
　A letter from his wife.
"At length I realise," he said,
　"The bitterness of Life!" [348]

He thought he saw a Buffalo
　Upon the chimney-piece:
He looked again, and found it was
　His Sister's Husband's Niece.
"Unless you leave this house," he said,
　"I'll send for the Police!"

He thought he saw a Rattlesnake
　That questioned him in Greek:
He looked again, and found it was
　The Middle of Next Week.
"The one thing I regret," he said,
　"Is that it cannot speak!" [349]

He thought he saw a Banker's Clerk
　Descending from the bus:
He looked again, and found it was
　A Hippopotamus:
"If this should stay to dine," he said,
　"There won't be much for us!" [350]

He thought he saw a Kangaroo
　That worked a coffee-mill:

318

He looked again, and found it was
  A Vegetable-Pill.
"Were I to swallow this," he said,
  "I should be very ill!" [351]

He thought he saw a Coach-and-Four
  That stood beside his bed:
He looked again, and found it was
  A Bear without a Head.
"Poor thing," he said, "poor silly thing!
  It's waiting to be fed!" [352]

He thought he saw an Albatross
  That fluttered round the lamp:
He looked again, and found it was
  A Penny-Postage-Stamp.
"You'd best be getting home," he said:
  "The nights are very damp!"

He thought he saw a Garden-Door
  That opened with a key:
He looked again, and found it was
  A Double Rule of Three: [353]
"And all its mystery," he said,
  "Is clear as day to me!"

He thought he saw an Argument
  That proved he was the Pope:
He looked again, and found it was
  A Bar of Mottled Soap.
"A fact so dread," he faintly said,
  "Extinguishes all hope!" [354]

The Flea

◆◆◆ JOHN DONNE

John Donne, "The Flea" [1633], in *The Poems of John Donne*, ed. James
Russell Lowell (New York, The Grolier Club, 1895), 2 vols.

MARK but this flea, and mark in this,
How little that which thou deniest me is;
It sucked me first, and now sucks thee,
And in this flea our two bloods mingled be;
Thou know'st that this cannot be said
A sin, nor shame, nor loss of maidenhead,
    Yet this enjoys before it woo,
    And pampered swells with one blood made of two,
    And this, alas! is more than we would do.

Oh stay, three lives in one flea spare,
Where we almost, yea, more than married are.
This flea is you and I, and this
Our marriage-bed and marriage-temple is;
Though parents grudge, and you, we 're met
And cloistered in these living walls of jet.
    Though use make you apt to kill me,
    Let not, to that, self-murder added be,
    And sacrilege, three sins in killing three. [I, 3]

Cruel and sudden, hast thou since
Purpled thy nail in blood of innocence?
Wherein could this flea guilty be,
Except in that drop which it sucked from thee?
Yet thou triúmph'st and say'st that thou
Find'st not thyself nor me the weaker now;
    'T is true; then learn how false fears be:
    Just so much honour, when thou yield'st to me,
    Will waste, as this flea's death took life from thee. [I, 4]

Under Which Lyre

◆◆◆   W. H. AUDEN

W. H. Auden, "Under Which Lyre, A Reactionary Tract for the Times, [PHI BETA KAPPA POEM. HARVARD. 1946]," in *Nones* (New York, Random House, 1951).

ARES AT LAST has quit the field,
The bloodstains on the bushes yield
    To seeping showers,
And in their convalescent state
The fractured towns associate
    With summer flowers.

Encamped upon the college plain
Raw veterans already train
    As freshman forces;
Instructors with sarcastic tongue
Shepherd the battle-weary young
    Through basic courses.

Among bewildering appliances
For mastering the arts and sciences
    They stroll or run,
And nerves that never flinched at slaughter
Are shot to pieces by the shorter
    Poems of Donne.

Professors back from secret missions
Resume their proper eruditions,
    Though some regret it;
They liked their dictaphones a lot,
They met some big wheels, and do not
    Let you forget it. [64]

But Zeus' inscrutable decree
Permits the will-to-disagree

321

To be pandemic,
Ordains that vaudeville shall preach
And every commencement speech
    Be a polemic.

Let Ares doze, that other war
Is instantly declared once more
    'Twixt those who follow
Precocious Hermes all the way
And those who without qualms obey
    Pompous Apollo.

Brutal like all Olympic games,
Though fought with smiles and Christian names
    And less dramatic,
This dialectic strife between
The civil gods is just as mean,
    And more fanatic.

What high immortals do in mirth
Is life and death on Middle Earth;
    Their a-historic
Antipathy forever gripes
All ages and somatic types,
    The sophomoric

Who face the future's darkest hints
With giggles or with prairie squints
    As stout as Cortez,
And those who like myself turn pale [65]
As we approach with ragged sail
    The fattening forties.

The sons of Hermes love to play,
And only do their best when they
    Are told they oughtn't;
Apollo's children never shrink
From boring jobs but have to think
    Their work important.

Related by antithesis,
A compromise between us is
 Impossible;
Respect perhaps but friendship never:
Falstaff the fool confronts forever
 The prig Prince Hal.

If he would leave the self alone,
Apollo's welcome to the throne,
 Fasces and falcons;
He loves to rule, has always done it;
The earth would soon, did Hermes run it,
 Be like the Balkans.

But jealous of our god of dreams,
His common-sense in secret schemes
 To rule the heart;
Unable to invent the lyre,
Creates with simulated fire
 Official art. [66]

And when he occupies a college,
Truth is replaced by Useful Knowledge;
 He pays particular
Attention to Commercial Thought,
Public Relations, Hygiene, Sport,
 In his curricula.

Athletic, extrovert and crude,
For him, to work in solitude
 Is the offence,
The goal a populous Nirvana:
His shield bears this device: *Mens sana*
 Qui mal y pense.

Today his arms, we must confess,
From Right to Left have met success,
 His banners wave
From Yale to Princeton, and the news

From Broadway to the Book Reviews
    Is very grave.

His radio Homers all day long
In over-Whitmanated song
    That does not scan,
With adjectives laid end to end,
Extol the doughnut and commend
    The Common Man.

His, too, each homely lyric thing
On sport or spousal love or spring
    Or dogs or dusters, [67]
Invented by some court-house bard
For recitation by the yard
    In filibusters.

To him ascend the prize orations
And sets of fugal variations
    On some folk-ballad,
While dietitians sacrifice
A glass of prune-juice or a nice
    Marsh-mallow salad.

Charged with his compound of sensational
Sex plus some undenominational
    Religious matter,
Enormous novels by co-eds
Rain down on our defenceless heads
    Till our teeth chatter.

In fake Hermetic uniforms
Behind our battle-line, in swarms
    That keep alighting,
His existentialists declare
That they are in complete despair,
    Yet go on writing.

No matter; He shall be defied;
White Aphrodite is on our side:

What though his threat
To organize us grow more critical?
Zeus willing, we, the unpolitical,
    Shall beat him yet. [68]

Lone scholars, sniping from the walls
Of learned periodicals,
    Our facts defend,
Our intellectual marines,
Landing in little magazines
    Capture a trend.

By night our student Underground
At cocktail parties whisper round
    From ear to ear;
Fat figures in the public eye
Collapse next morning, ambushed by
    Some witty sneer.

In our morale must lie our strength:
So that we may behold at length
    Routed Apollo's
Battalions melt away like fog,
Keep well the Hermetic Decalogue,
    Which runs as follows:—

Thou shalt not do as the dean pleases,
Thou shalt not write thy doctor's thesis
    On education,
Thou shalt not worship projects nor
Shalt thou or thine bow down before
    Administration.

Thou shalt not answer questionnaires
Or quizzes upon World-Affairs,
    Nor with compliance [69]
Take any test. Thou shalt not sit
With statisticians nor commit
    A social science.

Thou shalt not be on friendly terms
With guys in advertising firms,
        Nor speak with such
As read the Bible for its prose,
Nor, above all, make love to those
        Who wash too much.

Thou shalt not live within thy means
Nor on plain water and raw greens.
        If thou must choose
Between the chances, choose the odd;
Read *The New Yorker,* trust in God;
        And take short views. [70]

Part III

FOR DISCUSSION & THEMES

◆◆◆

SPECIFIC QUESTIONS

The questions in this section, arranged alphabetically by author under each category, lend themselves well either to informal classroom discussions or to shorter papers.

On Theory

1. In what ways do **Aristotle** and Susanne K. Langer touch upon the same topics in their theories on comedy?

2. From the selections in Part II compile a list of illustrations of the various verbal devices which **W. H. Auden** lists in "Notes on the Comic."

3. In what respects does W. H. Auden's "Notes on the Comic" agree with Bergson's discussion of laughter?

4. What other theorists touch upon **Baudelaire's** concept of the grotesque? How valid does this elevation of one aspect of comedy seem?

5. How does **Beerbohm's** assertion, "To have good reason for not laughing is one of the surest aids. Laughter rejoices in bonds," explain the amusement caused by pomposity? What further hints does he provide for distinguishing between the mirth of those within and those without establishments which pretend to dignity?

6. How effectively does **Bergson** substantiate his claim that comedy appeals chiefly to the intellect? What weakness is inherent in this assertion?

7. To what degree does Bergson's view of comedy depend on a somewhat free and changing society? In what ways would it fail to describe equally well countries ruled by a dictator? Compare Shaw's remarks.

8. What elements in Bergson's essay justify his contention, "The comic effect is always obtainable by transposing the natural expression of an idea into another key"? Elaborate upon this statement; provide some illustrations from the selections in Part II.

9. In what ways does **Darwin's** physiological approach to laughter ignore the artistic implications of the comic?

10. What presuppositions underlie **Fielding's** assertions that the function of comedy is ridicule?

11. Compare the analogies that **Freud** draws between dreams and wit with those that Bergson suggests. What connections do these two theorists make between childhood and wit? Contrast what they have to say about imitation as a source of wit and laughter.

12. What importance does **Northrop Frye** assign the happy ending in comedies and what qualifications does he place on it?

13. Select one of the stories in Part II and analyze the role of a figure who fits Northrop Frye's definition of a "blocking character."

14. After explaining the bases on which **Goldsmith** distinguishes laughing comedy from sentimental, list some modern examples of both. What qualities determine their assignment to either category?

15. In what ways do some of the prose sketches and stories transcend **Hazlitt's** "different kinds and degrees of the laughable?"

16. What other justifications come to mind for Hazlitt's claim that ridicule tests truth? Give some examples.

17. Apply Hazlitt's remarks on wit and Louis Kronenberger's about social comedy to an analysis of "The Rape of the Lock."

18. Why does **Johnson** criticize earlier authors for limiting themselves to the "rules" and "means by which the comic writers attain their end?"

19. Give examples of **Louis Kronenberger's** view that "any institution involving hierarchies and rivalries—for example, a university—is a perfect hotbed of [comedy]."

20. How does Louis Kronenberger reconcile the enduring and the transitory aspects of comedy?

21. What characteristics of comedy does **Susanne K. Langer** emphasize in order to show comedy as the triumph of life rather than the criticism of a society?

22. What effects sustain those stories and sketches which seem not to rely on Susanne K. Langer's claim that "the feeling of comedy is a feeling of heightened vitality"?

23. Elaborate upon **Maynard Mack's** definition of the distinctive nature of the comic point of view, particularly as a technique for fiction.

24. What restrictions are put upon comedy by **Meredith's** opinion that "some degree of social equality of the sexes" is necessary for it?

25. How justifiable do Susanne K. Langer's or Bernard Shaw's criticisms of Meredith appear? Do these critics attribute the same function to comedy?

26. Take one story or longer poem and analyze it to illustrate **Schiller's** contention that the subject, as such, has slight importance for comedy.

27. On the basis of **Shaw's** essay discuss his beliefs about the function of comedy.

28. From the prose and poetry in Part II make a catalogue of some of the verbal techniques which **B. F. Skinner** analyzes.

29. Apply B. F. Skinner's observations on rhyme to several of the poems in Part II.

30. Drawing upon both Freud and B. F. Skinner, consider the importance of a "double" audience for comic effects.

31. Summarize **E. B. White's** opinions about American humor and add other examples.

32. Explain the last two sentences in E. B. White's essay. Do they accurately sum up his attitudes toward comedy?

On Essays

1. How does the brevity of **Leacock's** "My Financial Career" contribute to its effectiveness, particularly in view of its title?

2. On what level of society does **Rose Macaulay's** "Showing Off" depend? How does it comment on both the speaker and her milieu?

3. How much of the comic effect in "Showing Off" relies upon exaggeration?

4. Compare **Cornelia Otis Skinner's** attitude toward horses with Gulliver's.

5. By what comic means does Cornelia Otis Skinner create first one personality for herself and then another?

6. Look at Bergson on transposing the natural expression of an idea and at W. H. Auden on clichés. Then analyze **Frank Sullivan's** essay on Dr. Arbuthnot's Academy.

7. Draw up your own list of possible courses for Dr. Arbuthnot's Academy.

On Narratives

1. How does a second reading of **Dorothy Parker's** "You were Perfectly Fine" change your understanding of the girl's innuendoes?

2. Analyze "You Were Perfectly Fine" as an instance of Bergson's "snowball" effect.

3. By what devices does **Saki,** in "Laura," make comic a situation and a subject often considered somber?

4. How would the comic tone of "Laura" differ if Saki explicitly committed himself to belief in reincarnation?

5. How does Laura represent the triumph of vitality?

6. In **Jean Stafford's** "A Reasonable Facsimile" what do the many details about Dr. Bohrmann's way of life contribute to the later action?

7. What social traits do Dr. Bohrmann and Henry Medley embody? How are these traits related to the general comic struggle as defined by several theorists?

8. What aspects of Medley's intellectual prowess make him a fit target for satire? Consider Martin in "The Catbird Seat" and Swift's Houyhnhnms as other examples of superior intellectual achievement.

9. What pleasant aspects of society emerge in "A Reasonable Facsimile" which are almost unique among the short stories in Part II?

10. According to definitions suggested in Part I, is **Swift's** "A Voyage to the Country of the Houyhnhnms" more properly called comedy or satire?

11. Do you find Gulliver's conclusions sound or exaggerated? In either case, what is the significance for the comic effect of this kind of first-person narrative?

12. What qualifications does Gulliver's account place on the attractiveness of the Houyhnhnms' reason? Do the Yahoos have any redeeming traits?

13. Would any other animals serve as well as horses for Swift's purposes? What special effects do the horses contribute?

14. Describe Swift's style. Why would a more extreme one nearly destroy his meaning?

15. In "The Catbird Seat" how does **James Thurber** play one mechanized character against another? How then does the story fit any theory of comedy? Consider Meredith, Bergson, Louis Kronenberger.

16. Analyze Mrs. Barrows in "The Catbird Seat" as a user of clichés.

17. What additional comedy does "The Catbird Seat" gain by reversing the usual traits (cf. Hazlitt) attributed to the sexes? Compare Saki's story, "Laura."

18. Analyze the comic effects of **Eudora Welty's** "Why I Live at the P.O." in terms of (a) the particular regional background, (b) the obtuseness of the narrator, and (c) the "snowballing" of alienations.

19. Consider the episodes in "Why I Live at the P.O." from the point of view of another character. What effects in the story are changed? Does an altered point of view reveal inherent pathos in the narrator's delusions?

On Verse

1. Compare **W. H. Auden's** use of classical deities in "Under Which Lyre" with Pope's in "The Rape of the Lock." Upon what differing views of society do the two rely?

2. In what ways does W. H. Auden's devision of people into two groups sum up many theories and examples of comedy in this book?

3. What sort of universe does **Carroll's** Mad Gardener create? How do animals function in it? To what kind of comedy does this poem belong? Compare "The Rape of the Lock" (Canto IV, lines 39 through 54).

4. To what extent does the action in **Chaucer's** "The Cock and the Fox" prepare for and justify the moral? How does any discrepancy heighten the comic tone?

5. Do Chanticleer and Partlet show the reliance on authority and the skepticism suitable to their sexes? How does their being fowls intensify their individual traits?

6. Compare and contrast the general poetic effects which Pope and Dryden are trying to project.

7. Compare the functions of authorities for dreams in "The Cock and the Fox" with those of the sylphs in "The Rape of the Lock."

8. How do **Donne's** allusions to the flea differ from other uses of animals in these poems?

9. In what ways is the tone of "The Flea" more intense than that of the other animal poems, and what added scope does the conflict of the sexes consequently assume?

10. How does **T. S. Eliot** arouse a certain sympathy for the nearly criminal element in "Macavity: the Mystery Cat" without praising that element? What differences set off Don Marquis's Mehitabel from Macavity?

11. What faults of community efficiency does **Robert Frost** see in the organization man of the anthill? How do these views describe modern society? Contrast Frost's outlook here with Swift's as expressed in the Houyhnhnms.

12. How can the fate of **Gray's** Selima be compared with that of

Pope's Belinda? Does this comparison imply similar social structures behind the two poems? How serious or how frivolous is Gray's moral in the poem?

13. Compare the society of the frogs in **La Fontaine's** "The Frogs Asked for a King" with that of the ants in Robert Frost's "Departmental." What kind of government does La Fontaine's poem seem to recommend and how seriously?

14. How does Mehitabel's song in the poem by **Don Marquis** represent comedy as vitality in the face of superhuman troubles?

15. Compare the human traits embodied by Selima in Gray's "Ode on the Death of a Favourite Cat" and those embodied by Mehitabel. What wit arises from showing a nonconformist Bohemian in the guise of an alley cat?

16. Discuss "The Rape of the Lock" by **Pope** as a series of extended examples of the War between the Sexes and as a comedy of manners.

17. By what devices does Pope present Belinda as somewhat, but not entirely, foolish? Were she only vain how would the comedy differ? Compare, for example, the portrait of Sir Plume as a Bergsonian caricature.

18. What attitudes contrasting with others in "The Rape of the Lock" does Clarissa voice?

19. How do Pope's various epic devices heighten the satire without destroying the comedy?

20. Compare the tone, diction, and verse form of **Donald A. Stauffer's** "The Lemmings" with those of Dryden and Pope.

21. At what points in "The Lemmings" does the tone seem to turn away from comedy? How does it shift back?

22. In "A Wooden Darning Egg" how does **John Updike** reverse the view which the other poems have taken of animals, and in what way does he achieve his comic effects?

GENERAL QUESTIONS

The ensuing questions are designed particularly for more elaborate classroom discussions and term papers.

On Theory

1. What qualities distinguish the outlook in pieces by critics—e.g., Aristotle, Hazlitt, Bergson, Freud, Maynard Mack, and Susanne K.

Langer—from those in works by practicing poets, dramatists, and novelists—e.g., Fielding, Goldsmith, Schiller, Baudelaire, Meredith, Shaw, E. B. White, Max Beerbohm, and W. H. Auden?

2. In their own terms, what other critics agree with Bergson that mechanization is the basis of laughter? In what significant ways do they depart from his theory?

3. What reasons do those who hold that nothing can explain comedy advance for their views, and by what logic do they then proceed to analyze it?

4. Some critics posit that comedy needs simplicity and directness, others that it requires complications and surprises: do any similarities join these two positions, or do they refer to separate aspects of the matter?

5. A frequently repeated assertion holds that comedy has declined in quality and inventiveness since the end of the Second World War. Do any essays suggest conditions in the nature of comedy which make the present antithetical to it?

6. Theorists who allude to happenings for their illustrations include Hazlitt, Baudelaire, Bergson, Shaw, Freud, W. H. Auden, B. F. Skinner, and Susanne K. Langer. Select one or two of these writers and from recent accounts in newspapers or elsewhere compile a list of your own comparable examples.

7. Drawing upon factors from implied attitudes to outright statements, compose an essay based upon the theorists' views about the suitability of comedy as a topic for sober speculation.

8. Differentiate between the pieces published in the twentieth century and those from earlier periods in terms of thoroughness, presuppositions, scope, and simplicity.

On Practice

1. Select some of the places in which someone tells of his own experiences, (e.g., any of the prose sketches or "Why I Live at the P.O."). In which of these does he sound superior to the events in which he participates? In which does he reveal more about himself than he seems to intend? Does any one device result in more effective comedy?

2. How many of the stories have a "happy ending?" In which of them does some condition qualify the rejoicing? How important, therefore, does the outcome appear to comedy?

3. A number of the poems are written in couplets. Compare the different kinds and their varying effects. Why does each style seem appropriate? (Anyone able to read Chaucerian English should include the original "Nun's Priest's Tale" for contrast with Dryden's version.)

4. Select the pieces in which the author deliberately exaggerates and those in which he seems to resort to understatement. Contrast the appeal of the resulting comedy. How do the two aspects differ?

5. What sort of descriptive details frequently give rise to comic touches? From the essays, stories, or poems compile a catalogue of the various types and analyze what they contribute.

6. In the poems taking animals for their subjects, which authors treat animals as people thinly disguised, which concentrate largely upon the animals themselves, and which use them as a point of departure for a fantasy? What differences in the comic tone ensue? Does any one category favor the adding of an obvious moral at the conclusion?

7. What counterparts do the two opposing groups in "Under Which Lyre" have in "Dr. Arbuthnot's Academy" and "A Reasonable Facsimile?" How does this theme of the conflict between official authority and individual freedom (Apollo and Hermes respectively) help explain the poems by Chaucer, La Fontaine, Robert Frost, Don Marquis, and Donald A. Stauffer?

8. Compare the function of the animals in some of the prose pieces (e.g., those by Cornelia Otis Skinner, Saki, Jean Stafford, and Swift) with the purposes which they serve in the poems.

On Theory & Practice

1. Compose a general definition of laughter by considering these points: (a) what is it? (b) does its cause reside predominantly in an outer situation (objective), or does it reveal an individual's psychological traits (subjective)? (c) assuming its source objective, what produces it: something incongruous, surprising, stereotyped, or mechanical? (d) assuming it a manifestation of an inner state, what feelings accompany it: triumph, detachment, sympathy, or relief.

2. Analyze the relationship of laughter to the comic. When can they exist independently?

3. Does comedy treat most effectively any single class of society, e.g., upper, middle, lower? Can comedy successfully view man nearly

in isolation from any given social frame or must it depict him in relation to an economic or cultural group? Defend your answers fully.

4. Using all relevant material, differentiate wit, humor, and satire.

5. What risks are there in employing dialect for comic effects? What ranges in language and idiom does comedy encompass?

6. Does comedy seem to appeal more to people at a certain age? How do views on the laughable change with growing older?

7. Does any general agreement exist about the moral function of comedy? Does any common ground connect those who claim it is primarily disinterested amusement and those who assign it a more practical goal?

8. Does comedy rely more heavily on plot or characters? What importance have "types" for both kinds? From the examples consider the dilemma of the inept individual in an efficiently ordered world. Which emerges superior? What significance has the nonconforming man in comedy, and how does he triumph over the organization?

9. Using any method you think to the point—e.g., the timing or volume of laughter—analyze, in accordance with B. F. Skinner's principles, an audience's response to a performance on the stage or television or the motion picture screen. Then evaluate the importance of your own findings by discussing how valid or how misleading you feel an analysis which omits aesthetic judgments to be.

FURTHER READING

These lists give only a sampling of titles. Translations of comedy pose special problems, and consequently few titles, other than those originally written in English, appear: where such is not the case, particular translations have, in almost every instance, been recommended.

1. Discussions of comedy from a point of view not prominently featured among the theorists in this anthology occur in these works:

Max Eastman, *The Enjoyment of Laughter*
Martin Grotjahn, *Beyond Laughter*
Johan Huizinga, *Homo Ludens*
Arthur Koestler, *Insight and Outlook*
Constance Rourke, *American Humor*

2. Among the books cited in Part II of the text, those by the following authors contain pieces predominantly comic:

Max Beerbohm	La Fontaine
Lewis Carroll	John Updike
T. S. Eliot	Saki
Stephen Leacock	Cornelia Otis Skinner
Rose Macaulay	Frank Sullivan
Don Marquis	Jonathan Swift
Dorothy Parker	James Thurber

3. These four theoretical books may prove valuable for a fuller analysis of stage comedy:

C. L. Barber, *Shakespeare's Festive Comedy*
Eric Bentley, Introduction to *Let's Get a Divorce! and Other Plays*
L. J. Potts, *Comedy*
W. K. Wimsatt, ed., *English Stage Comedy,* English Institute Essays, 1954

Consult also the complete chapters or books by these authors cited in Part I: Bergson, Northrop Frye, Hazlitt, Louis Kronenberger, Susanne K. Langer.

In connection with the studies listed above analyze several of the following plays:

William Shakespeare, *Love's Labors Lost, A Midsummer Night's Dream, Henry IV, Twelfth Night, The Tempest*
Ben Jonson, *Volpone, Epicoene*
Molière, *The Misanthrope* (tr. Richard Wilbur)
William Wycherley, *The Country Wife*
William Congreve, *The Way of the World*
Oliver Goldsmith, *She Stoops to Conquer*
Richard Brinsley Sheridan, *The School for Scandal*
W. S. Gilbert, *The Mikado*
Oscar Wilde, *The Importance of Being Earnest*
Bernard Shaw, *You Never Can Tell, Man and Superman, Misalliance, Pygmalion, Heartbreak House*
Noel Coward, *Private Lives*
W. H. Auden and Christopher Isherwood, *The Dog beneath the Skin*
Jean Giraudoux, *Amphitryon 38* (tr. S. N. Behrman)
Thornton Wilder, *The Skin of Our Teeth*
Jean Anouilh, *Ring Round the Moon* (tr. Christopher Fry)
T. S. Eliot, *The Cocktail Party*
Christopher Fry, *The Lady's Not for Burning*

4. Many novels have employed comic reflections on manners and customs. This short list should lend itself well to studies and analyses of fictional satire:

Henry Fielding, *Tom Jones*
Jane Austen, *Pride and Prejudice, Emma*
Charles Dickens, *Pickwick Papers*
George Meredith, *The Egoist*
Henry James, *The Bostonians*
E. M. Forster, *A Room with a View*
Norman Douglas, *South Wind*
Aldous Huxley, *Antic Hay*
Evelyn Waugh, *Vile Bodies, The Loved One*
Christopher Isherwood, *Mr. Norris Changes Trains*
J. P. Marquand, *The Late George Apley*
Aubrey Menen, *The Prevalence of Witches*
Henry Green, *Nothing*

5. In connection with the use of animals for satire, further possibilities appear in:

Aristophanes, *The Birds* (tr. Peter D. Arnott)
Anatole France, *Penguin Island*
Bernard Shaw, *Androcles and the Lion*
Clarence Day, *This Simian World*
George Orwell, *Animal Farm*
E. B. White, *Charlotte's Web*

6. Additional books which consider comically the matter of education range through many areas; some of the more provocative titles, in different genres, include:

Voltaire, *Candide*
Byron, *Don Juan*
Max Beerbohm, *Zuleika Dobson*
Booth Tarkington, *Seventeen*
Richard Hughes, *A High Wind in Jamaica*
J. D. Salinger, *The Catcher in the Rye*
Mary McCarthy, *The Groves of Academe*
Randall Jarrell, *Pictures from an Institution*
Kingsley Amis, *Lucky Jim*

7. In the difficult matter of fantasy and the unlikely, certain celebrated titles might be of interest:

Rabelais, *Gargantua and Pantagruel*
Cervantes, *Don Quixote* (tr. Samuel Putnam)
Alexander Pope, *The Dunciad*
Laurence Sterne, *Tristram Shandy*
Lewis Carroll, *Alice's Adventures in Wonderland, Through the Looking-Glass*
Edward Lear, *The Complete Nonsense of Edward Lear*
Samuel Butler, *Erewhon*
Ronald Firbank, *Valmouth*
Virginia Woolf, *Orlando*
John Collier, *Fancies and Goodnights*
Saul Bellow, *The Adventures of Augie March*

8. Books illustrating some of the particular varieties of American humor:

Mark Twain, *Huckleberry Finn*
Ambrose Bierce, *The Devil's Dictionary*
Finley Peter Dunne, *Mr. Dooley's Philosophy*
Ring Lardner, *Round Up*
Sinclair Lewis, *Babbitt*
Kenneth S. Lynn (ed.), *The Comic Tradition in America*